GOD'S SAMURAI

GOD'S SAMURAI

Lead Pilot at Pearl Harbor

GORDON W. PRANGE

with

Donald M. Goldstein

and

Katherine V. Dillon

BRASSEY'S (US), INC.

Maxwell Macmillan Pergamon Publishing Corp.

Washington • New York • London • Oxford • Beijing
Frankfurt • São Paulo • Sydney • Tokyo • Toronto

Brassey's (US), Inc.

Editorial Offices
Brassey's (US), Inc.
8000 Westpark Drive, 1st Floor
McLean, VA 22102

Order Department
Macmillan Publishing Co.
Front and Brown Streets
Riverside, NJ 08075

Library of Congress Cataloging-in-Publication Data

Prange, Gordon William, 1910–
    God's samurai : lead pilot at Pearl Harbor / Gordon W. Prange ; in collaboration with Donald M. Goldstein and Katherine V. Dillon.
        p. cm.
    "An AFA book."
    Includes bibliographical references.
    ISBN 0-08-037440-9.
    1. Fuchida, Mitsuo, 1902–   . 2. Pearl Harbor (Hawaii), Attack on, 1941. 3. World War, 1939–1945—Aerial operations, Japanese.
4. World War, 1939–1945—Campaigns—Pacific Ocean. 5. Fighter pilots—Japan—Biography. 6. Japan. Kaigun. Kōkūtai—Biography.
I. Goldstein, Donald M. II. Dillon, Katherine V. III. Title.
D767.92.P7216   1991
940.54′26—dc20   90-31717   CIP

British Library Cataloguing in Publication Data
Prange, Gordon W. (Gordon William), *1910–1980*
    God's samurai : lead pilot at Pearl Harbor.
    1. World War 2. Air operations by Japan. Nihon Rikugun
    Kokubuta. Shimbu Tokubetsu Kogekitai. Biographies
    I. Title II. Goldstein, Donald M. III. Dillon, Katherine
    V.
    940.5449052092
    ISBN 0-08-037440-9

Published in the United States of America
10 9 8 7 6 5 4 3 2 1

CONTENTS

FOREWORD

This is the sixth of the manuscripts that Gordon W. Prange, professor of history at the University of Maryland, had prepared but not published at the time of his death in 1980. For many years, Prange hoped to write a biography of his friend Mitsuo Fuchida, but for a number of reasons Prange was unable to finish the project to his satisfaction, although he reworked the manuscript several times.

The undersigned, both former pupils of Prange's, undertook to prepare this work, as well as his other manuscripts, for publication. Our principal task in connection with *God's Samurai* was to prune and consolidate. Using material from the Prange files, we added most of the descriptions of the political actions going on in Japan near and after the end of World War II to place the Fuchida story in historical context. In addition, the Foreword and Introduction are ours, as are the bibliography and list of key personnel.

Originally, Prange intended that this study be prepared without notes for greater readability. We have added a few brief footnotes for historical credibility, and in the endnotes, we have tried to strike the proverbial happy medium between no notes and overly pedantic documentation. The Fuchida interviews that are the foundation of this narrative often ran to ten or more typewritten pages, and one interview might be used for an entire chapter. To spare the reader a shower of *ibid.*'s, we have not documented every single paragraph or quotation. Instead, we have noted where a break appears in the thought.

In the late 1940s, when Prange was an official of the historical section of MacArthur's Far East Command, he became acquainted with Fuchida. At that time he was beginning his research into the Pearl Harbor operation, and Fuchida's firsthand knowledge was invaluable. They kept in touch over the years, and whenever Fuchida was in the Washington, D.C., area he visited Prange or stayed with him.

Prange admired Fuchida's wartime courage, dedication, and leadership, and appreciated his patriotism, friendliness, and sense of humor. The Prange files show nonetheless that friction sometimes arose between the two. Both were strong personalities and did not always understand one another. Prange's discovery of Fuchida's long-standing affair with the woman given the pseudonym "Kimi Matsumoto" disturbed him, and their friendship was never quite the same after Prange realized that Fuchida had not been candid with Prange about such an important aspect of his life. Contacts between the two men were sporadic after 1967, though they did correspond until Fuchida's death in 1976. Despite their differences, Prange fundamentally liked Fuchida, respected the ideals he espoused, and believed that his story should be told some day.

Because this book is the story of one man, Prange relied principally on the Fuchida interviews. Fuchida kept no diary and at times his memory was at fault, especially with dates; therefore, it was necessary to consult other works on the Pacific war. The unpublished diary of Vice Admiral Matome Ugaki was particularly useful in checking Fuchida's memory and placing incidents in context. Other sources listed in the bibliography provided valuable insights and background. All of the interviews were conducted by Prange.

The questionnaires cited in the endnotes and bibliography were exhaustive lists of queries Prange submitted to certain individuals. In addition to the questionnaire Fuchida himself filled out, those answered by his son Joe and his daughter Miyako were especially helpful.

Prange did not use tape recorders in his interviews. In his day these devices were rather cumbersome. The usual procedure was for Prange and Fuchida to sit together and talk, often for hours at a stretch, with Prange taking notes. They went over the same ground several times so that Fuchida could correct any errors or misunderstandings and examine Prange's drafts.

Fuchida could speak English well enough to get across his meaning, but he was not fluent. In some instances his telegraphic style was exactly right, and in those cases we left it alone. Mostly, however, we have cast Fuchida's words in standard English. Nowhere have we attributed sentiments to Fuchida that he did not express. Throughout the text we have used such phrases as "Fuchida thought" or "Fuchida said to himself." In every such case, Fuchida informed Prange in one or more of their interviews that such were indeed his thoughts, and the typed interviews in the Prange files reflect this.

In no sense is the first part of this book intended to be a dispassionate history of the Pacific war. It is the biography of a man, and part of his life was played out in the Pacific war, most notably at Pearl Harbor. In some ways the second part of his life was more difficult to present than his wartime career; we faced the task of portraying an evangelist without making him appear a prig, a bore, or irritatingly self-righteous.

To understand and evaluate Fuchida's spiritual activities, it is important to keep in mind the role and function of an evangelist. The evangelist is not primarily a theologian, a priest, a pastor, a teacher, or an orator, although he or she may be any of those things in addition. The word *evangelist* has its roots in the Roman custom in Asia Minor of sending out heralds to proclaim an *evangel*, or "good news." The evangelist has no function but to bring good tidings. In the words of Billy Graham, the most famous evangelist of our day,

> The work of an evangelist is very specialized: He is a specialist in winning other people to a commitment to Jesus Christ. And he has *one* message: That Christ died for our sins; that Christ loves you; that He has a plan for your life and that if you will respond to that message in the affirmative, He can bring you peace and joy and happiness and save your soul for eternity.*

That is what Fuchida preached many times a week for almost thirty years. He did not feel called upon to stimulate his listeners intellectually or to entertain or to amuse.

We wish to express our thanks to Goldstein's wife, Mariann, and his children for their patient cooperation over the years. We also wish to express appreciation to Goldstein's research assistant Gregory Alston for his help, and to Frank Margiotta, Don McKeon, Vicki Chamlee, and their colleagues at Brassey's (US), Inc.

We are sure that Prange and Fuchida would wish this book dedicated to Fuchida's devoted wife Haruko; to Fuchida's and Haruko's son Joe and his wife Marie; to their daughter Miyako and her husband Jim Overturf;

---

*Myrna Blyth, "Ideas for Living No. 6: An Interview with Billy Graham," *Family Circle* (April 1972): 152.

and to their grandchildren, in whom flows the blood of Japan and the United States.

DONALD M. GOLDSTEIN, PH.D.
Associate Professor of Public and
    International Affairs
University of Pittsburgh
Pittsburgh, Pennsylvania

KATHERINE V. DILLON
CWO, USAF (Ret.)
Arlington, Virginia

INTRODUCTION

In major conflicts such as World War II many competent and dedicated officers of company and field grade make commendable contributions to their nation's cause. They may enjoy a fleeting moment in the public eye, but on the whole they must find their reward in the personal satisfaction of work well done and in the respect of their colleagues.

Such a man was Mitsuo Fuchida. He enjoyed a measure of fame—or notoriety, depending upon one's viewpoint—as the leader of the air attack on Pearl Harbor. Few Westerners realize that his career spanned the entire course of World War II in the Pacific. In those initial six months when the Japanese navy fulfilled Admiral Isoroku Yamamoto's promise to "run wild,"[1] Fuchida either led or directed a number of air strikes. After recovering from wounds sustained at Midway, he participated in succeeding campaigns as a staff officer. And he, who opened the Pacific war, was present aboard the U.S.S. *Missouri* when Japan formally surrendered to the Allies.

Here, through Fuchida's eyes, one sees most of the major engagements of the naval war in the Pacific. Naturally, his viewpoint was that of an intensely patriotic Japanese, but he spoke of his experiences with understanding toward both Japanese and Americans. His view is a valuable one, coming from the middle ranks. The war experience of the enlisted individual or junior officer is of necessity limited, while that of the flag or general officer is broad. Fuchida served at what is usually termed field grade—first at the level where tactics are hammered into operations, later, at the level where strategy is implemented by tactics.

He was the general flight leader of the First Air Fleet from Pearl Harbor until just before Midway, and would have served in that capacity at Midway had he not been operated on for appendicitis a few days before that crucial battle. As a result, he had the unique opportunity of watching the action aboard and around the carrier *Akagi* without participating in it. Thus he was able to observe and report on the battle as only an experienced naval aviator could.

After recovery, Fuchida served briefly in a teaching capacity at Yokosuka Air Corps and the Naval Staff College, then as air staff officer of the new land-based First Air Fleet. His career culminated in the prestigious position of air officer of the Combined Fleet.

With Japan's surrender, Fuchida's beloved Combined Fleet disbanded. Following brief service with the navy's historical group on war documentation, he returned to his home town of Kashiwara and became a small farmer. During that period he made a surprisingly good adjustment from war hero to obscure citizen. He grew close to the soil and to his fellow man. Through the example of Ms. Peggy Covell, recounted to him by a Japanese prisoner of war, and of Jacob DeShazer, who had participated in the Doolittle Raid and later became a missionary to Japan, Fuchida took his first steps toward spiritual awakening.

Anyone interested in human psychology cannot help but wonder what lay behind Fuchida's conversion. He was a lifelong if not particularly devout Shintoist who had always thought of Christianity with mild dislike and distrust. He did not seek out and read the New Testament consciously searching for Jesus or even for a system of ethics beyond Shinto. Still less was he concerned with perfecting his character. Had his motives been moralistic, he could have found a lofty code in the Buddhist temple and spared himself an almost traumatic break with his Japanese heritage. He had gone to the Gospel in an impersonal spirit of research.

Yet he was ripe for Christianity. The end of the war had left a tremendous void in his life. To a man of his outgoing disposition, nurtured by a life of service, the daily round of scratching for a living with no purpose beyond his own existence and that of his immediate family seemed meaningless and hollow. Subconsciously he hungered for a cause larger than himself into which he could pour his bottled-up reserves of devotion and leadership. For some of his former friends, communism filled this need, but Fuchida's contempt for the Soviet Union kept him from that path.

Along with service, he felt the need for an inspirational leader. He had always served his best under a commander to whom he could give his affection as well as his loyalty. The leaders for the first half of his life, such as Admirals Yamamoto and Kakuta, had passed from the scene. Like an unattached samurai he wanted a liege lord to receive his ardent allegiance, a leader who would bring meaning and direction to his life.

His path to Christianity was a lonely one. He had no Christian friends to show him the way. Nor did he accept Christianity intellectually, for, while he was intelligent and clever, his driving power was his heart, not his mind. So he responded overwhelmingly to Jesus as a person. Once convinced that Christ had died for him and for all mankind, Fuchida's heart went out to Him in gratitude. Now once more Fuchida had a banner worthy of his sword.

Ms. Covell, her martyred parents, and Jacob DeShazer played their important roles. Yet Fuchida must have been ready for their message, hence receptive to their example. A number of Japanese prisoners had known Ms. Covell and had been the direct recipients of her compassion, but while they loved and admired her they had not probed her motives or accepted her religion. In general, DeShazer's story touched Japanese hearts without inspiring them to receive Jesus.

A clipping in Fuchida's files offers an interesting suggestion. A Japanese living in Florida remarked that Fuchida's "conversion from warrior to missionary is not surprising in view of the age-old samurai code. The code, dating back to the days of the ancient warlords of Japan, calls for the loser of a duel to enter a religious order."[2]

The Reverend Ichijiro Saito, son of Fuchida's pastor and a good friend, thought that mystical forces were at work in his conversion. He explained to Prange that Fuchida's home territory—Nara Prefecture and especially Kashiwara—had been a spiritual center for hundreds, perhaps thousands, of years. "The land itself has a spirit," he said poetically, "and when Fuchida came back from the war, the spirit was there ready to call him. . . . Fuchida is a man connected with a heavenly plan. He was ready to accept Christ. It was so ordained."[3]

In his early years Fuchida was no saint. In the prewar days he saw no reason why Japan should not seize any territory or resources it had the desire or strength to take. Nor had he any qualms about Pearl Harbor. In his view, the forces on Oahu should have been on the alert; if they were not, he felt they deserved everything they got.

Fuchida was a man of sharp but by no means deep or broad intellect. His self-confidence was a basic part of his nature. He was very much a product of his rearing as a Japanese male of his generation. For this and other reasons his story requires an objective approach, and objectivity was foreign to Fuchida.

Take, for example, his hostility toward MacArthur's steps to demilitarize Japan. Fuchida didn't realize the force of the tidal wave of hatred the Japanese left in their wake through the war years. MacArthur couldn't have been more lenient even had he wished to be. As it was, a considerable faction of Allied public opinion criticized him for being soft on the Japanese. In brief, Japan was suffering the usual fate of the conquered and liking it as little as any conquered country has ever liked it.

Some of Fuchida's opinions and attitudes may grate on Western sensibilities. He had three objects of animosity: MacArthur's occupation, communism, and the Catholic church. Fuchida's observations on the occupation were those of a shrewd individual who read and pondered these matters but who was on the defensive and naturally prejudiced in favor of his countrymen. In view of Fuchida's war record and background, this is hardly surprising, although in contrast he entertained warm professional and personal regard for Admirals Nimitz and Spruance. Perhaps this sentiment wouldn't have lingered had either of those admirals, rather than MacArthur, headed the occupation forces.

Fuchida's hatred of communism was implacable. This stemmed from the Soviet Union's entering the Pacific war at the last minute, when Japan was already defeated, and from communism's disregard for human rights. His later travels in Europe confirmed him in his belief that this totalitarian system was the enemy of God and man.

More difficult to accept is Fuchida's anti-Catholic bias. There is no evidence that he objected to Catholicism on doctrinal grounds; his attitude sprang from his innate dislike of pomp and circumstance, which he believed drew attention away from the clear vision of Jesus.

The Reverend Saito believed Fuchida's anti-Catholicism was narrow and intolerant. He thought this arose from ignorance of church history and believed more education could have broadened Fuchida's views. "Fuchida has the faith, belief and determination of ten ministers," Saito said. "What he now needs is more knowledge and understanding."[4]

Following the war, Fuchida entered into an extramarital relationship that continued after he began evangelizing. Not until his baptism did he break it off. All of which lends point to his conversion, for the Christian community is not a harbor for stainless knights.

After his conversion and initial testifying in Japan Fuchida came to the United States, where he spent much time and which he came to consider his second home. He never ceased to be grateful for the American people's having received him, the Pearl Harbor raider, in a spirit of understanding and forgiveness. One of the first American friends he made was Billy Graham, for whom he felt unstinting affection and admiration.

Fuchida's horizon later extended to Europe, where he testified with his usual fire and conviction in West Germany, Scandinavia, France, Holland, and England. Wherever he went, the same zeal he had expended for the

Greater East Asia Co-Prosperity Sphere he now channeled into winning souls for Christ. The loving devotion he had given his navy idol, Yamamoto, became in intensified, spiritualized form the loving devotion he gave to Jesus. He continued to serve Him until his death on 30 May 1976.

Here, then, was a man who could be heroic and weak, likable and exasperating, a man of loves and hates, of prejudices and compassion—in short, a human being, although painted in bolder outlines than most. This is his story.

"To Be a Flier"

1

T o be born a boy in Japan at the turn of the century was to be one of the earth's fortunate ones. Few families were so poor, few houses so small, that a son did not receive a joyous welcome. Whatever hardships his infancy and childhood might bring, they also brought the security that comes only from being loved and valued.

This was true of the boy born to Yazo and Shika Fuchida on 3 December 1902. The parents were solid, respected citizens of Nagao, a village in the agricultural countryside of Nara Prefecture. Two sons, Yoshimi and Takeo, had preceded the new baby, so he was named Mitsuo (number-three boy). Over the next eight years two daughters, Shizuko and Chiyoko, were born, rounding out the family circle.[1]

In his youth, Yazo's ambitions soared beyond the bounds of Nara's farms. Fuchida's father prepared to enter the military academy at Ichigaya, Japan's West Point. Just before enrolling, however, he lost sight in his left eye during a baseball game, and with it the chance for a career as an army officer. He went into teaching and exhibited a natural aptitude for it. In time he was appointed principal of the Kammaki Grammar School, a position of some consequence. If he ever felt bitterness over the accident that changed his life, he concealed it. He seemed to be—and probably was—a happy man, content with his place in the imperial realm.[2]

His wife Shika's life had been one of pure romance. She was born Shika Takegami, daughter of Suetsugu Kamaemon Takegami, a famous samurai of Nara Prefecture. He belonged to the Takatori clan, staunch devotees of the

Tokugawa shogunate. In the civil war preceding the Meiji Restoration, he held Takatori castle against the assaults of the imperial henchmen, the Tenchugumi, virtually annihilating them. Eventually the forces of the great Emperor Meiji prevailed, and Takegami went into hiding as a war criminal, leaving behind his small daughter.

A prominent lumber merchant adopted her and gave her the family name, Yoshimura. The Yoshimuras never forgot that she was their chieftain's daughter. They reared her in the traditions of the samurai class, with particular emphasis on ceremonial courtesies. When she reached marriageable age her foster parents wed her to Yazo, son of the chief farmer of the shogun's nearby territory.[3]

Their son Mitsuo had scarcely reached his second month when tragedy struck: his brother, five-year-old Yoshimi, died. However devastating this was to the parents, they did not allow their grief to shadow the lives of their other children. They had enough love remaining to worry over Mitsuo, a puny child.[4]

One wonders if Yazo or Shika took encouragement from the fact that this son had been born in a year of the tiger. Many Japanese believed this presaged good luck, for the animal symbolized leadership and the protection of human life. According to oriental tradition, tiger people were sensitive, affectionate, and courageous. But they could be stubborn, quick to anger, and prone to conflict with their superiors. Sometimes they might delay a decision until it was too late to make the right one. The spring and winter of life would be easy, but midlife would bring difficulties.[5] Anyone who knew Mitsuo Fuchida the man would have to concede that his life fit the thumbnail sketch of a son born in the year of the tiger.

His boyhood flowed gently, with few rocks to ruffle its advance. His mother was unfailingly affectionate and kind, but true to her blood and training, she tolerated no discourtesy. "She always scolded me if I was rude," recalled Fuchida.

His father was the dominant figure of his childhood. Realizing that Mitsuo "was little religious," Yazo wished to guide his son along a spiritual path. So, in flowing Chinese characters, Yazo brushed out a copy of the Buddhist scriptures *Okyo* for the boy to memorize. Although too young to understand the passages, Mitsuo learned them by rote. Yazo's copy was a minor work of art; Mitsuo cherished it all his life.[6]

Yazo saw to it that even as a toddler Mitsuo attended all national holiday ceremonies. And he insisted that the boy memorize the *Kyoiku Chokugo*, the fundamental education catechism endorsed by Emperor Meiji. After the boy had done so, Yazo carefully explained its meanings. But although Yazo took "a severe Spartan" attitude toward Mitsuo's education and training, father and son spent much free time together working in the garden and tramped off to fish and hunt.[7]

From Nagao Primary School, of which Mitsuo later remembered little or nothing, he went to Unebi Middle School. There he especially enjoyed mathematics, history, and soccer. He was so bashful that when the teacher called on him he blushed bright scarlet. His classmates nicknamed him *Tako* (octopus), because that mollusk turns red when boiled.[8]

Yet this thin, shy schoolboy had something that kings might envy, no money could buy, and no education inculcate. His lucky tiger had given him that most unpredictable of qualities, leadership. He discovered this quite early. "I always loved to be out of doors with the neighborhood children, especially boys," he remembered. "They always chose me as their chief when they staged mock battles, or in winter when they hunted hares."[9]

Mitsuo, who was only two years old when the Russo-Japanese War broke out, did not consciously remember those stirring events.[10] But the martial spirit of the day seeped into him. He didn't know the difference between the army and the navy, but he longed to join one or the other. His father encouraged him because a military career carried great prestige. As the years rolled by Yazo reluctantly abandoned his hope for Mitsuo. "I was still so pale, skinny, and shy that no one—not my parents, relatives, or classmates—believed that I could ever become a military man," Fuchida said.[11]

But he had his heart set on it, and he had a goodly measure of that "tiger year" attribute, stubbornness. Predictably, his first choice was to go to the military academy. When he was fifteen years old,* however, in the summer of his fourth year at middle school, he visited the Ise Peninsula. There for the first time he looked upon the ocean. His initial impression was of an awesome natural force, grander than the mountains that had surrounded him all his life. Japan is truly a nation of the sea, he thought. Thus began a lifelong romance. "I loved the sea even when it became stormy and rough," he wrote years later. "The sea was the native place of my heart, and still today many wonderful memories linger."[12]

That summer at the peninsula he attended swimming class. By the end of the course he passed a stiff long-distance examination, to the amazement of his teachers, who never thought such a small boy had it in him. The swimming was excellent for Mitsuo. It built up his self-confidence as well as his body. His class happened to include two cadets from the naval academy at Eta Jima, the Japanese equivalent of Annapolis. In their smart uniforms, these young men so impressed the boy that he made up his mind to follow their example.[13] He knew it wouldn't be easy to get into the academy. In fact,

---

*Sixteen in Japan, where one's age includes the year before birth.

he tried almost every other service academy, as if hesitant to reach for the real prize.

The following year he graduated from middle school, and in January 1918 went to Osaka to qualify for the military academy there. In spite of his prowess as a swimmer, he didn't pass the physical; he was underweight. In March, refusing to wallow in self-pity, he took and passed the examinations for the merchant marine school at Kobe.

In May he returned to Osaka to take the tests that really mattered—the navy examinations. This time he passed the physical but flunked the academic portion. The blow was all the more brutal for being unexpected. Mitsuo had a quick and logical intelligence, and being a diligent student, he had made good marks. The possibility of failing the scholastic portion had never occurred to him.

His parents were not sorry. By this time they wanted him to follow a civilian career. If he absolutely had to get into uniform, they preferred the army to the navy. Perhaps Yazo still entertained a secret hope of seeing Mitsuo fulfill his own youthful dreams of a military career.

Mitsuo knew what he wanted. A year after his failure he took the naval examinations again, and this time passed.[14]

On 27 August 1921 he entered the naval academy at Eta Jima, a small island in the Inland Sea facing Kure Naval Base. His heart was "pounding with great joy," and the sight of the beautiful installation fired his ambition to become an admiral like the great Heihachiro Togo, conqueror of the Russians. He also had a less lofty, more immediate ambition: "I wanted to go back home during winter leave and show everyone who called me 'Tako' what a man I had become!"[15]

Among the three hundred or so other plebes was Eijiro Suzuki. He and Mitsuo, called Fuchida now that he was a man, would frequently be "shipmates" in the days to come. All the plebes eyed one another curiously and hopefully. By tradition, Eta Jima classmates would be more than professional associates; they would make their most enduring personal friends from the ranks of their academy class. In token of this close relationship, classmates used the intimate form of address with one another.[16]

To one classmate Fuchida could never be close. A subject wasn't allowed to befriend the student His Imperial Highness Prince Takamatsu, brother of Crown Prince (later Emperor) Hirohito.[17] Fuchida respected him from a distance. Their paths would cross under dramatic circumstances later in life.

The cadets concentrated on scientific subjects, of which Fuchida liked mathematics best. Offered the choice of English, French, or German, he selected the first. This seemed logical to him, because the U.S. Navy was already regarded as Japan's potential number-one enemy. Fuchida's attitude was entirely political and theoretical. He felt neither hatred nor enmity toward the American people.[18]

Academy life was no breeze. The teachers rapped out their courses vigorously, allowing no pauses for laggards. If a cadet couldn't maintain the pace, he didn't belong at the academy. Fuchida managed to stay within the top twenty-five of his class. Along with the academic curriculum, Eta Jima had a rigorous athletic program. Fuchida became a champion swimmer and played goal in soccer.

During his first year Fuchida was neither favored nor shunned by his fellows. He held himself somewhat aloof. But in time he made a few close friends, chief among whom, in addition to Suzuki, were Eiji Hasegawa, Taketora Uyeda, and Terujiro Urata. These young men were less distinguished for academic standing than for their idealism and keen fighting spirit. They kept up their friendships throughout their Navy years.[19]

Among his acquaintances Fuchida could count a slim, handsome cadet from a small town near Hiroshima. Minoru Genda came from an ancient samurai family.[20] He was one of the brightest in the group, and his future course would often parallel Fuchida's.

In his second year at Eta Jima an incident occurred that shifted the entire focus of Fuchida's life. To overcome his shyness, Fuchida forced himself to raise his hand before anyone else whenever an instructor asked a question. Sometimes his hand shot up before he bothered to think about the answer. One day two flying boats touched down at Eta Jima. All the cadets lined up on shore to watch them land and take off. Before the demonstration the flight chief, a second lieutenant named Miyazaki, explained the mysteries of the plane. "Is there any cadet here who aspires to become a flying officer?" he asked at the close of his briefing. "If so, he may ride with me in the demonstration."

Before Miyazaki had closed his mouth, Fuchida flourished a hand. "Hi!" he shouted. The idea of becoming a flier had never crossed his mind; he raised his hand from force of habit. Thus it happened that he climbed aboard the F-5 for his first flight. The pontoons had scarcely left the water when Fuchida knew that he had found his calling. Genda, who watched the demonstration with fascination, likewise decided to become an airman. From that time on he and Fuchida became close friends, drawn together by their interest in aviation.[21]

On 1 September 1923, at the beginning of Fuchida's third year at the academy, the Great Earthquake struck Japan. This catastrophe affected him deeply; suddenly he realized the fragility of his beautiful homeland. "All our efforts to build cities, landscapes, or seascapes used to be destroyed instantaneously by earthquakes or typhoons," he mused in later years. But he came to believe that disasters helped build national character, teaching the Japanese fortitude, patience, and diligence.

Fuchida's class graduated on 24 July 1924.[22] But before they became fullfledged midshipmen, they had to complete a long training cruise that would take them as far as San Francisco.

Fuchida was aboard the *Yakumo* when she and her fellow cruisers *Asamu* and *Izumo* sailed into San Francisco Bay under the escort of the battleships *West Virginia, Colorado,* and *Maryland.* "All the midshipmen and the crews were lined up on the upper decks, and all of them were startled to see the gorgeous demonstration," Fuchida remembered. Comparing the huge American battleships with his "old smoky tub squadron," he burned with shame and wounded pride.[23] But most of his shipmates were thrilled. This was only the start of a full week of receptions and sightseeing. The U.S. Navy and San Francisco rolled out the red carpet for the midshipmen.

One newspaper story pointed to the "almost unprecedented" courtesies extended; the United States, it suggested, was trying to demonstrate that the discrimination clause in the Immigration Law was not based on racial contempt.[24] Fuchida became aware of this thorny issue for the first time shortly after the *Yakuma* docked, when a number of Issei—first-generation Japanese living in the United States—came aboard to visit. He was detailed to guide them around the ship. One of them pointed to the *Maryland,* anchored in pair with the *Yakumo,* and asked, "Midshipman, are there any battleships like that in Japan?"

"Yes," Fuchida replied proudly, "we have two named *Nagato* and *Mutsu* just the same size as that."

"Oh, my! How wonderful!" the Issei exclaimed. Then he added, "Why don't you come with those two big battleships to the United States? Every time the Japanese training squadron visits the United States, it always uses these old tubs. As a result the American people discriminate against Japanese immigrants."

"Is there any discrimination toward Japanese immigrants?" Fuchida asked in surprise. "How come?"

Evidently the visitor did not know the reason. Somewhat evasively he mentioned the Immigration Law.[25]

Each of the U.S. battleships took a Japanese cruiser under her wing, and on Monday, 26 January, the *Maryland*'s officers invited the midshipmen from the *Yakumo* to dinner. Most of the visitors scrutinized the *Maryland*'s eight 16-inch guns cocked at their maximum angle, for at that time the Japanese navy was working on a way to outrange these guns. Fuchida and Genda, however, were much more interested in the scouting planes on the host battleships. Ever alert to innovation, Genda was surprised to see that the

American equipment ran by electricity. And both men took due note of the battleship's thick deck and side armor. Who knew, Fuchida reflected, when he might be called upon to bomb or torpedo that battleship.[26]

The visit to San Francisco marked a change in Fuchida's thinking. Throughout his years in Eta Jima the instructors had stressed that the United States was Japan's potential enemy, but this had been just an abstract concept to Fuchida. Now he felt in his heart that at some time the United States and Japan might indeed come to blows.[27]

From 1924 through 1927 Fuchida did not give his best efforts to his shipboard duties, for he wanted to go to Kasumigaura, Japan's naval aviation center, comparable to the U.S. naval base in Pensacola, Florida. He begrudged time spent on activities not related to flying. At that time his ship, the *Yahagi,* was a training vessel for cadets at the naval academy at Etauchi. The *Yahagi*'s assistant skipper, a commander named Madarame, was a gunnery officer and a zealous seaman. He had a perennial bone to pick with Fuchida. "You young officers of this training ship should be a model for the cadets of the academy," he would say accusingly. But the reproaches ran off Fuchida like sea water off a deck. He continued to neglect seamanship and devoted his time to learning what he could about aviation.[28]

At the end of each year, reports similar to the U.S. Navy's officer effectiveness reports went to Japan's Bureau of the Navy. One day Madarame asked Fuchida, "What field would you like to specialize in—gunnery, torpedo, navigation, communications, or submarine?"

"None," Fuchida replied emphatically. "I want to be a flier."

"I advise you to change your mind," Madarame answered gravely. "With your ability it would be better to choose anything else than becoming a flier."

The commander meant well, for Japan's naval air arm ranked very low on the navy's scale of prestige at the time. Madarame, Fuchida also suspected, thought that aviation should be the preserve of "nasty officers" whose early removal from the scene would be no great loss to the navy.[29]

About a year after this encounter, when the next appointments were due, the *Yahagi*'s skipper, Captain Kawamura, summoned Fuchida and greeted him with a beaming smile. "Well, Lieutenant, I've heard you're going to be a flier. That is excellent! Hereafter, able young officers like you should go to the air arm, and air power should be the main striking force."

Had Kawamura proclaimed that the navy's future lay in bank robbery, Fuchida would only have been a little more astonished. The skipper had never had a good word for air power before.

"I wish to study recent aviation developments," Kawamura continued. "So please bring me all kinds of books concerning that subject from the library."

One of Fuchida's tasks as assistant navigator was management of the ship's library. Bemused but happy at this conversion of a heathen, Fuchida hastened to gather an armload of books for the skipper. On 1 December 1926 when transfers came out, he discovered the reason for the aboutface: Kawamura was to take command of the *Hosho*, Japan's first aircraft carrier.[30]

Fuchida, however, had to remain patient. He spent three months at gunnery school and another three months at torpedo school at Yokosuka, then was assigned to the destroyer *Akikaze* as navigator. During his tour of duty the ship served as an escort for the emperor's cruise through the Ryukyu islands. His Majesty sailed aboard his favorite battleship, the *Hiei*. The *Akikaze* followed directly aft, and from the bridge Fuchida could see the imperial flag fluttering from the battleship's topmast. His heart swelled with loyalty for the young emperor and with pride for being an officer in Japan's navy.

While he was yet an ensign, his mother died of cancer. She had suffered for a period of several years during which she seldom left her sickbed. Gradually she weakened, bearing her pain as stoically as any warrior. "If I have something of the samurai in my nature, I owe it to my mother's physical discipline," Fuchida wrote many years later.[31]

His mother and father had united in urging their son against the air arm and the submarine service. Even in peacetime, both were dangerous. But the call of the sky was too strong for parental fears to quell. On 1 December 1927, Fuchida was promoted to sublieutenant and ordered to the navy's flight training school at Kasumigaura, about seventy miles northeast of Tokyo. His Eta Jima classmate, Eijiro Suzuki, entered Kasumigaura at the same time. They preceded Genda by one year.[32]

Fuchida's introduction to Kasumigaura was inauspicious. He and his nine classmates were attending the entrance ceremony when two planes crashed. One, a fighter, fell out of an acrobatic loop, killing the pilot. Another flier was seriously injured when a training craft overshot the landing and collided against a row of pine trees. This concrete demonstration of how dangerous aviation could be jolted Fuchida, but not enough to shake his resolution. And in the future he would need that resolution. Two of his classmates were to die in accidents before their graduation. Of that Kasumigaura class, only three—Fuchida, Suzuki, and Captain Shotaro Yamanokami—would survive the "China Incident" and the Pacific war.

At Kasumigaura the students rose early each morning, gulped down a hurried breakfast, and then in flying caps and overalls clambered into a truck and hastened to the airfield. In the morning they practiced flying, usually two sessions of twenty to thirty minutes each. In the afternoon they studied tactics in the classroom. Flight instruction was basic, with no specialization.[33]

Fuchida's instructor was a second lieutenant named Takahashi, one of the best on the base. They treated one another with super-politeness because Fuchida ranked him on the promotion list, while he was the teacher and Fuchida the student. Takahashi permitted his charge to solo after only fourteen hours of instruction—the fastest case in the history of Kasumigaura to that date—and took great pride in his student's progress.

Fuchida approached his first solo rather matter-of-factly, finding the experience little different from his dual-control training flights. He never became a daredevil pilot; he and his plane were a team not unlike an American cowboy and his horse. There was mutual understanding between them.

Innate practicality allied with enthusiasm led Fuchida to challenge Kasumigaura's approach to flying and fliers. Instructors set such unrealistic standards and enforced them so stringently that many a potential pilot fell by the wayside. Their objective was an elite corps. Fuchida believed that Japan needed swarms of pilots and that the severe entrance requirements should therefore be relaxed. It was nonsense, he proclaimed, to expect a prospective pilot to be "next to God." Any man of average intelligence, even a physically handicapped man, could win his wings with proper training.

No one in authority paid any attention to these suggestions from a brash young trainee. Fuchida's ideas were almost fifteen years ahead of his time; the Japanese navy did not institute a mass pilot training program until after Pearl Harbor.[34]

From Kasumigaura orders took Fuchida to the cruiser *Aoba*. This uneventful tour of duty ended in November 1929, when he transferred to the big carrier *Kaga*. The crew took great pride in the grand ship and in their esprit de corps.

During Fuchida's year aboard, the *Kaga* participated in a training cruise in the South China Sea. One foggy day he took off as an observer on a reconnaissance sweep, with Lieutenant Kiyoshi Katsuhata at the controls. In those days before radar, it was all too easy to lose oneself in the vastness of the ocean's surface. When they reached the limit of their search arc and returned to where the *Kaga* should have been, the carrier was nowhere in sight.

They circled aimlessly, seeking the missing mother ship. Suddenly Katsuhata said, "We have only ten minutes of fuel left. What'll we do?"

Fuchida peered downward. They were flying at about 1,500 feet under a layer of thick clouds. Ragged blankets of fog lay along the water and all they could see were intermittent glimpses of white surf. This might be a date with eternity, he thought.

He hesitated. An inner voice seemed to say, "Climb up!" Immediately he turned to Katsuhata. "Take the plane up as high as you can until we run out of fuel."

"Why?" asked the pilot uneasily. "That thick cloud overhead . . ." With clouds as well as fog below them, visibility would be even worse than it was at 1,500 feet.

Fuchida couldn't explain, for he didn't know why either. He simply directed Katsuhata to do as he was told.

Gradually the plane spiraled upward until, at 8,000 feet, the engine sputtered and died. They were out of fuel—but they were also out of the overcast. Through a break in the clouds Fuchida swept the ocean below with his field glasses. Off toward the horizon he saw a white dot floating on the sea. A Chinese junk! "There is your target—that white junk," he told the pilot. "Glide toward it." A plane would normally glide four times the length of its height, he calculated, which should be plenty to land them near their objective.

Katsuhata did a masterful job of coaxing the powerless aircraft into position. It splashed down almost alongside the junk, flipping over on its nose. Fuchida struck something, possibly the instrument panel, and gashed his right cheek. He bore the scar for the rest of his life. The aircraft began to settle into the water, the junk swung alongside, and the captain, a man named Kwa, fished the two Japanese aboard his junk.

After Fuchida and Katsuhata had been delivered to the *Kaga*, everyone congratulated them. "How did you happen to think of telling the pilot to climb up?" they asked Fuchida. He merely smiled and shrugged off the queries. He had not thought out the maneuver, simply obeying the inner voice and in his desperation abandoning logic for intuition.[35]

More than once over the years Fuchida's intuition saved him in a crisis. Call it God, his guardian angel, his subconscious mind, or what you will—he never disobeyed it, and it never let him down.

"Take the Cake"

2

ON 1 DECEMBER 1930, Fuchida transferred from the *Kaga* to Sasebo Naval Base in western Kyushu. He was promoted to lieutenant on 1 November 1931. Having received two weeks' winter leave effective 15 December of that year, he journeyed to Kashiwara, his father's ancestral home, to visit relatives. It was in their home that his cousin's wife deftly whispered, during a pleasant but aimless family chat, "There is a nice girl in a nearby village." Fuchida concealed a grin, for the comment hinted at volumes left unsaid.[1]

Up to this time Fuchida had not considered marriage, although he found women attractive, and women found him so. He had been too absorbed in his career to think seriously of establishing a home and family. But he had just turned twenty-nine, and time was marching on. What could he lose by looking over this "nice girl"?

The next morning, his cousin's wife took him to the home of a well-respected, prosperous farmer named Matachiro Kitaoka. Kitaoka owned an estate of a hundred *tan*—about 25 acres—a sizable tract of land in Japan. In the middle of his fertile fields sat a spacious and sunny house. There Fuchida met the Kitaoka's daughter, Haruko, and the other members of the family. This sort of a meeting was called a *miae*, or "looking at each other." It usually took place at a restaurant or theater so the atmosphere would be impersonal, and no one would be embarrassed if the couple did not respond to each other.

Bowing to the daughter of the house, Fuchida saw a medium-sized young woman dressed in a beautiful kimono. Heavy jet-black hair crowned a sweet face still as unlined as a child's. Soft brown eyes looked at him shyly, yet with a hint of humor. She was not pretty, but her face showed character and kindness, and overall she conveyed an impression of sensible good nature.

When the time came for the visitors to leave, Fuchida's cousin-in-law asked, "Would you like to take a piece of the cake with you?"

"Yes, take the cake," he replied, rather puzzled. He hoped he had said the right thing. When they reached home his sponsor said, "If a man takes a piece of cake home with him from a *miae*, it means he likes the girl." Unwittingly, he had virtually committed himself to an engagement.

Thinking the matter over, he discovered that he did not object to the idea. Haruko was well brought-up, quiet, and dignified. She was twenty-five years of age, just right for him. She had a good education, with four years in the Osaka girls college. Her family seemed to like him, and it was high time he married and produced a son to carry on his line.[2]

Having made up his mind, he wanted to conclude the formalities as soon as possible. An engagement usually lasted three to six months, but Fuchida had to return to Sasebo shortly, and a year might elapse before he saw Haruko again. So the next day his cousin visited the Kitaokas to sound them out. No one had any objections to Fuchida, and all concerned agreed to a wedding date of 7 January 1932. This day, called *Daian* (great peace), was and still is considered particularly auspicious for weddings.*

Fuchida applied to the Navy Ministry for permission to marry. Then he sent to Sasebo for his ceremonial naval uniform with its long sword, the customary marriage garb for an officer. He told himself that if it did not come in time, tradition be hanged—he would wear a formal civilian kimono. The uniform arrived safely, but not until the sixth, and the ministry's permission did not come until after the ceremony. Fuchida took the chance of going ahead, confident that approval would come sooner or later. There was no reason why it should not; there could be no objection to Haruko or her family.[3]

These marital arrangements, rather cold and certainly unromantic by Western standards, followed Japanese custom. Fuchida married a good, healthy young woman who would make him a comfortable home and who would give him children. Haruko gained the security and dignity that only an honorable marriage could bring. If love grew between the two, that would be a bonus of fortune. In the meantime mutual tolerance, courtesy, and thoughtfulness could work wonders.

So Fuchida and Haruko were wed in the Kashiwara shrine complex in

---

*By a curious coincidence, the Roman Catholic church observes this same day (January 6 in the Occident) as the traditional date of the marriage feast at Cana, which Jesus attended.

Shinto style. About sixty people attended the ceremony, evenly divided between the two families. The Fuchida delegation included the groom's father, brother, and sisters. None of his navy friends was present, although this was customary. "It all happened so suddenly," said Fuchida, with a grin, "just like a surprise attack!"[4]

That night Haruko's parents gave a big wedding party, and the next day the newlyweds started out for Sasebo. Haruko's grandmother, over eighty years of age but spry as a cricket, went along. She would stay until satisfied that Haruko, still a baby in her eyes, was well launched as a homemaker.

This proved to be an excellent arrangement, for Fuchida's work as aviation officer in the submarine tender *Jingei* left him little time at home. The *Jingei's* captain had nine submarines under his command, each carrying a seaplane. In addition, the tender housed three large seaplanes. Fuchida's job was to take care of these aircraft.

Soon he decided to send Haruko and her grandmother back to the Kitaoka's home until his next shore assignment. Family life for a Japanese navy officer could be erratic. A typical year worked out something as follows: At the end of February Fuchida went to sea with the fleet, staying until the last of April. During May he was ashore, then June through October the fleet sailed out again. From November through February he could join his family.

Haruko was fortunate at having a family who welcomed her home during her husband's absences. She would have been lonely otherwise. Japanese officers' wives enjoyed little of the socializing that marked relations between their American counterparts. They usually associated only with the wives of officers from the same Eta Jima class as their husbands.[5]

On 1 November 1932 Fuchida became a student in the Yokosuka Air Corps, the organization that gave navy pilots their specialized training. For six months he studied horizontal (high-altitude) bombing. The Japanese had no mechanical bombing aids; results depended upon a sense of timing, dogged practice, and a large helping of luck. When successful horizontal bombing could be very effective, but the navy needed a supplemental technique for low-level strikes. Fuchida thought about dive-bombing, only recently added to the curriculum; however, the course emphasized torpedo bombing.

At Yokosuka Fuchida's path once more crossed that of Genda, who spent the same six months there as an instructor.[6] During this period Haruko joined Fuchida and they lived at Zushi, a summer-resort town nearby. Then on 25 May 1933 Fuchida graduated and received his assignment to the light cruiser *Natori*. Once more Haruko went back to Kashiwara, this time carrying their first child. There at her family's home a son was born on 25 September 1933. Fuchida had been at sea all summer. Fortunately the fleet anchored in Ise Bay for a short time in September, so he arranged shore leave and hurried to Kashiwara for the great event. "I wanted a boy," said Fuchida, his eyes lighting up at the memory.[7]

Who but one who has held his first-born son in his arms could understand the depth of Fuchida's joy? He had become a man in the fullest sense of the term, a participant in the act of creation. For Haruko, too, the birth of her son held a special meaning. She had met the challenge of the Japanese wife and won. She had brought forth a boy, and now she could look the whole world in the eye.

Long before, Fuchida and his brother had decided that the names of any children they might have would incorporate the Chinese character *ya* in honor of their father Yazo. This ideograph has a number of meanings, all connoting betterment. So Fuchida named his son Yoshiya, which means something like "striving for goodness." He chose well, for in the years to come Yoshiya became a devoted exponent of self-improvement, always reaching toward new horizons.[8]

At the time of Yoshiya's birth, Fuchida did not have long to become acquainted with him. He had to return to sea, joining the cruiser *Maya* on 3 October 1933. Once more he left Haruko with her family and the baby. Thus it came about that Yoshiya spent much of his boyhood at his mother's girlhood home.

Fuchida's thirteen months aboard the *Maya* and a subsequent tour of eleven months with the Tateyama Air Corps passed smoothly. On 1 October 1936, he returned to the Yokosuka Air Corps, this time as an instructor in horizontal bombing. He was still unsatisfied with this technique, which had not proved very accurate against moving or stationary targets in simulated aerial warfare at sea. He studied the problem carefully and eventually developed a formation of nine planes to cover the target at one time—three units of three aircraft each, flying in echelon like big arrowheads. The Japanese navy later used this formation in war.[9]

Two honors came to him on 1 December 1936. Fuchida moved up the ladder to the rank of lieutenant commander and was selected to attend the Naval Staff College in Tokyo. Advance to the navy's top grades depended in large measure upon graduation from this institution, hence hundreds of applicants came forward for each class of only twenty-four. This meant that numerous good officers had to be weeded out of the competition by severe examinations. A candidate could take these tests three times; after the third strike out, he could not come to bat again.[10] Fuchida's selection was a tribute to his skill and dedication.

Genda had come to the staff college approximately one year before Fuchida, and for some seven months they served together once more. Fuchida's class included such old friends as Eijiro Suzuki and Takeshi Naito, classmates from Kasumigaura. Fuchida became friendly with Suteji Muroi, Hiroshi Kogure, and Yoshimore Terai, the latter destined to become a vice admiral in Japan's postwar Self-Defense Force.

Studies centered around the classic naval doctrine of the time, *Kantai Kessen*—the final all-out battle in the western Pacific, probably off the Marshall Islands, between the Japanese and U.S. navies. According to the blueprint, the American fleet would sail westward while Japanese submarines whittled away at it. When the depleted U.S. force reached the spot where the Japanese main fleet lay in wait, the two armadas would slug it out. Japan, fighting in home waters on its own terms, would emerge the victor.[11]

Fuchida entertained serious doubts about this strategy, which he believed did not take into account American industrial potential. Even if the Americans were obliging enough to behave exactly as anticipated and Japan won the engagement, this would be at best a temporary advantage. Inevitably, Japan would lose some ships, too, and the United States could replace sunken vessels much more rapidly and in greater number than the Japanese. Fuchida and his fellow airmen placed their faith in Japan's potential naval air power, participating in many talks and conferences on that subject. The battleship admirals opposed these meetings. Significantly, no first-class fliers taught at the Naval Staff College, although it had excellent instructors in gunnery, torpedo warfare, and submarines.[12]

During Fuchida's stay at the staff college, Haruko and Yoshiya lived with him in Tokyo. There on 9 March 1937 a baby daughter completed the family circle. Haruko's older brother, a doctor, came to take care of Haruko and deliver the child. Fuchida was delighted, for now he had both a boy and a girl. Again he pondered what to name the baby. Again, it must contain the syllable *ya.* He settled upon Miyako, a favorite name in Japan for girls. There is no English equivalent for the name, which consists of three characters—*mi* (beauty), *ya* (which, as indicated, connotes betterment), and *ko* (child). *Ko* is often used as the final syllable of a female's name, in which context it is an affectionate diminutive on the order of the French *ette* and the Spanish *ita.* The nearest one could come to Miyako in English would be "child growing in beauty" or, more simply, "pretty little girl."

There are several ways of writing the name in Japanese, some using Chinese characters and some Japanese ideographs. Fuchida and Haruko consulted a fortune-teller to choose the version based upon the number of favorable strokes in the characters. In later years Miyako acknowledged that this must sound ridiculous to Westerners, but Japanese children were often named in this manner.[13]

Haruko was a good mother. She reared the children not only with tenderness and care but also with genuine interest in them as persons. They responded like flowers to the sun. The children shared many qualities. Both were healthy, intelligent, and well-mannered, their expressive features mirroring now their father, now their mother. In personality they were surprisingly different.

Yoshiya developed into a quiet and rather solemn little boy. He played alone for hours at a time, especially when he got his hands on anything he could take apart. No radio, clock, or toy was safe from his inquiring mind and questioning fingers. As he grew, this instinct turned constructive. In the primary grades he made a radio, in high school a television set. An introspective boy, he needed no one's company but his own.

Miyako, on the other hand, was an extrovert who never met a stranger. The more people she could draw into her little circle, the better she liked it. As she grew, her abundant energies found creative outlets. She taught herself to paint and to type and attended sewing school. Haruko always wondered what Miyako would get into next.[14]

The promise of Fuchida's auspicious wedding date was being abundantly fulfilled. If he took his wife's devotion and the household she ran so smoothly as no more than his due, in this he differed little from many Japanese men of his generation. He loved his children dearly. And he was attending the Naval Staff College, a sure indication that his superiors considered him a man of promise in his chosen profession. In the words of a later generation, Fuchida had it made.

3

"Flying High"

FUCHIDA had no moral qualms over the "China Incident,"* which began in July 1937 at the Marco Polo Bridge. He firmly believed that the Japanese were the master race destined to dominate Asia. But to him this latest army venture had less to do with the glory of the Japanese empire than with the army's inflated self-image. He had the impression that that service was deliberately plunging Japan into war with China to consolidate political power.[1]

The difference in strategy between Japan's army and navy was surprisingly fundamental. The navy thought in terms of the great all-out battle with the United States; the army pointed toward a major land conflict with the Soviet Union. Moreover, the army brass did not believe that the army existed to protect and serve the Japanese people; they felt the people existed to support and serve the army.

Few Japanese doubted the ability of the Japanese tiger to take on the Chinese dragon. With all due respect to the courage and tenacity of the Chinese people, Fuchida believed that the Japanese army had the power to conquer Nationalist China in fairly short order. In his opinion, the army's strategists let the fighting drag on because as long as the nation was at war, the army called the shots.

Broadly speaking, therefore, the struggle in China was an army show. No

---

*The China Incident was what the Japanese called the long, bloody war between China and Japan that lasted from July 1937 until the end of World War II.

17

major naval battles thundered along the China coast, and Japan's surface ships had little difficulty dominating what action there was. The naval air arm, however, found many opportunities for service from land bases or from carriers. Indeed, China became the proving ground where airmen obtained the combat experience that made them superior during the first months of the Pacific war. Not all of them lived to profit by it. Three of Fuchida's Kasumigaura classmates fell from the China sky to their deaths.[2]

In that summer of 1937 Fuchida was a solid citizen of thirty-five, lean and hard, quick of step and movement. The years since his marriage had brought him only one personal sorrow, the death of his father. And that sorrow was mitigated by understandable pride in Yazo's life and influence. With each passing year, his father had endeared himself more and more to his fellow villagers and to his students—he was a sort of Japanese Mr. Chips. The grateful townspeople erected a statue in his honor that stands to this day.

As an officer, Fuchida set high professional standards for his subordinates. Knowing that he asked no more of them than he did of himself, they gave him their respect and allegiance. To his superiors, he in turn was loyal and enthusiastic without being servile. Whether he agreed with them or not, once they made their decisions, he carried out orders promptly and conscientiously. The naval air arm counted him as one of its most diligent officers. No task was too great or too small to command his best efforts, and under a deadline he would work all night if necessary to submit his report on time.

For all his ardor, fate bequeathed him a practical nature. Fuchida was well known for his sound, objective judgments. An incorrigible optimist, he expected the best and usually received it. Withal, he was a gregarious soul who loved life and his fellow man. Well-intentioned and kind, he wished ill to no one. Yet he was a rampant nationalist who supported to the hilt his country's expansionist ventures.[3]

Fuchida became involved in the China Incident after Japanese fliers pounced on the U.S. gunboat *Panay* in the Yangtze River near Shanghai in the early afternoon of 12 December 1937. Colonel Kingoro Hashimoto, a notorious army firebrand who had been involved in more than one unsavory incident, was responsible for the attack. The affair caused a diplomatic crisis, but serious trouble between Japan and the United States was averted when the former officially offered apologies and reparations. The United States promptly accepted, and Vice Admiral Isoroku Yamamoto, the navy's vice minister, followed up with his personal and public thanks to the Americans for accepting Japan's gestures in a generous spirit.[4]

Ripples from the Yangtze reached Fuchida while he was at the Naval Staff College. One day, much to his surprise, he received emergency orders to report as chief flight officer to the Thirteenth Naval Air Corps at Nanking.

The very day the orders came, Rear Admiral Zenshiro Hoshina, chief of the Navy Department's administration, summoned Fuchida to headquarters and explained them.

"An event like this *Panay* incident is seriously detrimental to our war effort," he emphasized. "It appears that two young lieutenants named Murata and Okumiya were among the ringleaders. You will be responsible for controlling these undisciplined officers by all means. They must not get out of hand again and upset our critical international relations."

"Yes, sir, I understand," Fuchida answered.[5] Tokyo wished for no repetition of an incident that forced an official apology to the United States. More important, Japan was not ready to challenge the United States economically or militarily, and another such venture would be much more difficult to smooth over.

Fuchida would have been more than human had he not departed on this assignment with mixed feelings—flattery at being entrusted with such a delicate mission, and resentment at having to leave his work at the Naval Staff College to go to China and ride herd on a brace of irresponsible mavericks.

Whatever his sentiments toward the two fliers at the time, Fuchida soon counted them among his friends. Lieutenant Masatake Okumiya was a dive-bomber pilot, short, sharp-eyed, and intelligent. He developed into a shrewd appraiser of the naval air scene and in the future would collaborate on several books about the Pacific war, one of them with Fuchida.

Fuchida described Lieutenant Shigeharu Murata as "small and slim; a real comedian. Everyone liked him. He had a smooth, unruffled disposition and could melt any tense atmosphere in a minute." At the time of the *Panay* incident, Murata specialized in high-level bombing, but shortly he turned to the aerial torpedo and became Japan's ace of aces in that field.[6]

During Fuchida's stay at Nanking, he frequently led bombing missions over China, mostly in the Hankow region. Fortunately the navy considered this assignment temporary duty and did not cancel out his Naval Staff College experience. Therefore, as his records show, he completed his studies on 15 September 1938.[7]

In 1938, Asia's zodiac came full circle once again to Fuchida's Year of the Tiger. Perhaps the beast of good fortune felt well disposed toward him, for he weathered his temporary duty without mishap. Upon graduation from the Naval Staff College he joined the small carrier *Ryujo* as a squadron commander, in which ship he served through the Canton campaign.

Fuchida had little to say about his experience in China, beyond the fact that he had served at Shanghai and on Hainan Island as well as at Canton, always emerging from combat intact.[8] Despite the inherent dangers of wartime, he considered his missions routine, not worth remembering.

What he never forgot was an odd little incident in the homeland after he had transferred on 1 December 1938 to Sasebo Naval Base. One day as he strolled through the city, he spotted a large Catholic church located on high ground not far from the base headquarters. The structure loomed up against the sky, its Gothic architecture as alien to Japan as the three crosses it lifted atop triple pinnacles like inverted ice-cream cones. A visitor to the church reached the gray stone structure by mounting two series of steps. At their top stood a large white statue of the Virgin Mary. Fuchida had no idea who she was. With her outstretched hands and maternal smile she looked somewhat like a European's idea of Kwan Yin, the Goddess of Mercy so popular with Japanese and Chinese women.

In Fuchida's opinion, this Christian church stood in much too strategic a position for the comfort of a good son of Dai Nippon. On any clear day an enemy agent could climb the middle steeple and enjoy an unparalleled view of the city, the base, and the comings and goings of the warships. He would not even need field glasses.

"If I had my way, I would tear that church down and put the area off limits to foreigners," Fuchida said to himself. "And I would never again permit Christians to erect a church in such a perfect location for espionage."

What little Fuchida knew about Christians he didn't like. They spoke of Christ as O Gimi (great master), a title Shintoists gave the emperor. When someone asked a Japanese Christian, "Who is O Gimi, the emperor or Christ?" the Christian would say something like, "Only Christ is O Gimi, for he is the divine savior and the emperor is human."

Fuchida considered Hirohito to be just like a god. The Christian attitude smacked of treason and blasphemy, and he did not believe that Christians could be trustworthy subjects of the emperor. Christianity in his mind was one with Western civilization, especially with Japan's predestined enemy, the United States.[9]

Like most of his fellow officers, Fuchida was a Shintoist because Shinto was the state religion. But he was loyal rather than devout. He had no belief in an afterlife. He knew that he stood an excellent chance of dying in combat, and he accepted the prospect without fear. If he did his duty well and died for the emperor, people would remember his name. That was all the immortality he could expect or hope for. Somewhat paradoxically, he often visited the nearest Shinto shrine to worship the emperor and his ancestors.[10] Presumably he rationalized that the emperors of Japan, being divine, had spirits that survived, a distinction denied to lesser mortals such as Fuchida.

Quite frequently in Japan, Shinto and Buddhism share the same temple. Many Japanese are both Shintoists and Buddhists and feel no sense of incongruity. Fuchida was not one of them, for he had no inclination toward Buddhism. His wife, however, was a staunch Buddhist with a firm belief in the goodness of the Buddha and in the efficacy of prayer. Haruko often went to the temple where she secured prayers for her husband's safety. Haruko took the prayers, printed on thin sheets of paper, and slipped them into the pockets of Fuchida's uniform. But her skeptical husband never bothered to move them from his uniform to his flying suit. "I was flying high all the time with no prayers in my pocket," he remembered.

Then one day Haruko visited his air base, and Fuchida, being too busy to do the honors, had his orderly show her around. It was then that she discovered the prayers forgotten in the pocket of his uniform. That night when Fuchida went to bed, he felt a mysterious crackling in his night robe. Exploring, he found that Haruko had sewn prayers into it. Determined to protect her husband in spite of himself, she had also sewn them into his flight uniform.

Fuchida regarded such measures with half-amused, half-contemptuous tolerance, as fit only for superstitious women. As time went on and Fuchida seemed immune to the dangers of his career, Haruko took this as evidence that Buddha had heard her prayers, and became even more firm in her faith.[11]

On 1 November 1939, Fuchida transferred from Sasebo to the big carrier *Akagi* as a squadron commander. The ship had been completed in 1927 and modernized ten years later. When he joined her, the *Akagi* was comparable to the USS *Lexington*. To men of the sea, each ship has her own personality. The *Akagi* and Fuchida were compatible, and he came to regard her with a special affection.

He liked and respected her skipper, Captain Ryunosuke Kusaka. Their paths would cross throughout the war and later. Although not a flier, Kusaka had been associated with the air arm off and on since his graduation from the Naval Staff College.[12] Fuchida did not consider him "a real warrior," but what he may have lacked in fire he made up with a calm self-possession developed over many years with the study and practice of Zen Buddhism.[13]

Also aboard the *Akagi* was Fuchida's comrade of China days, Murata, nicknamed *Butsu-san* (Buddha) because of his perpetual good nature.[14]

Fuchida's specialty aboard the *Akagi* was torpedo bombing, which he and his associates practiced at night. During practice sessions the *Akagi* left inland waters for the open sea. During one such exercise, Fuchida met Admiral Isoroku Yamamoto for the first time.[15]

On 30 August 1939, Yamamoto had become commander in chief of the Combined Fleet. A stocky man a few inches shorter than Fuchida, neat as a cat in his spotless uniform, Yamamoto exuded confidence and inspired it in others. He was a man of much charm who commanded the loyalty and affection of his officers and returned it unstintingly.

Much too large-minded to consider himself above learning, Yamamoto solicited opinions and listened to anyone with something intelligent to say. He had worked on the development of Japan's naval aviation and once skippered the *Akagi.* Therefore the admiral and Fuchida had interests in common, and they often talked together long and earnestly about naval air power. Small wonder that Yamamoto pulled Fuchida into his orbit and won his lifelong devotion.[16]

Fuchida had another—but less admirable—hero in those days. Adolf Hitler's rise to power intrigued him. The elements of surprise, dash, and decision that characterized Germany's campaigns against Poland, Norway, and especially France were impressive, he felt. Peering into his mirror to shave, Fuchida fancied he saw a resemblance to *der führer.* He emphasized this likeness by sprouting a little moustache and cultivating a mesmeric stare. Sometimes he let a lock of hair fall dankly over his forehead.

He thought Hitler invincible and was enthusiastic about his *Dengeki Sakusen* (thunder and lightning operation), as the Japanese called the *blitz-krieg.* So it surprised him when the summer of 1940 came and went without Hitler's invading England, as he and many others had expected. Late in September he had the opportunity to discuss this with Genda, who had just spent a year in England as assistant naval air attaché.

"How are things going over there?" Fuchida asked him. "And why doesn't Hitler invade England?"

"There is one important reason Hitler did not invade England," answered Genda in his direct fashion. "He doesn't have control of the air over England. And the only reason he doesn't have it is the superiority of the RAF fighters."

Genda being an expert on fighter aircraft and their tactics, his opinion carried weight. Furthermore, he spoke with admiration of the dogged British resistance and will to fight. For the first time, a cloud of doubt about final German victory scudded across Fuchida's mind.[17]

On 15 November 1940, Fuchida became air staff officer for the Third Air Squadron, comprising the small carriers *Ryujo* and *Shoho.* Rear Admiral Kakuji Kakuta, a battleship gunnery officer, commanded this squadron. The assignments of Japanese high brass revealed a blissful disregard for qualification, being strictly by the numbers. Fuchida liked and respected Kakuta enormously, however, and entertained private hopes that some day he might convert him to the true faith of naval air power.

In staff discussions the question constantly came up: "How many planes do we need to protect our battleships?" Fuchida thought this silly. In his opinion, the idea of using carriers as defensive weapons was *abe kobe,* as he put it—"upside down." "Aircraft carriers should not protect battleships," he insisted. "It should be the other way around. Japan should gather all her carriers into one great squadron for massive air striking power. The battleships, cruisers, and other ships should protect the carriers."[18]

This shocked the navy's traditionalists. But Kakuta, though a battleship admiral, had an open mind. So rather gingerly he presented Fuchida's heretical idea to Yamamoto and found to his astonishment that Yamamoto agreed.[19] What neither Kakuta nor Fuchida knew was that the commander in chief had already been thinking about a task force along just such lines as Fuchida had proposed.

4

"To Be Flight Leader"

"I CAN'T UNDERSTAND IT, sir," Fuchida said to Kakuta one day in mid-August 1941. He handed the admiral the telegram he had just received ordering him back to the *Akagi* as a flight commander. He had only been with the Third Carrier Squadron for nine months, and the normal tour of duty was at least a full year, probably two.

Kakuta lifted his brows in surprise. "You served in that post last year, didn't you?"

"Yes, sir," replied Fuchida.

"And you expect to be promoted to the rank of commander this October, don't you?"

"Yes, sir."

Fuchida had been in grade for five years and his record was superior. Neither of the men had ever heard of a flight leader with such high rank. Kakuta shrugged resignedly, the universal gesture of a field commander confronted with the inscrutable headquarters mentality. "There must be some mistake somewhere."[1]

There had been no mistake. Fuchida owed his transfer to Genda, who on 10 April 1941 became air staff officer of the newly activated First Air Fleet. Working on a top-secret project, Genda had been deftly skimming the cream of Japan's naval air arm. Such was his standing that he had little trouble securing the men he wanted.

"Fuchida had a strong fighting spirit—his best quality," reminisced

Genda later. "He was also a gifted leader with the ability to understand any given situation and to react to it quickly. He was not only our best flight leader but also a good staff man, cooperative and clearheaded. He got along well with people and commanded the respect of his subordinates and superiors."

His Eta Jima classmate had one weakness, which Genda recognized—drink.[2] Fuchida did his part to support Japan's distilling industry. But his imbibing was social, not compulsive. Many of his colleagues drank heavily; it was part of the "macho" image. A notable exception was Yamamoto. He became a teetotaler early in life after discovering that one or two drinks deprived him of full command of himself.[3]

Having received his mysterious orders, Fuchida hastened to Kagoshima Air Base, where, rather than aboard the *Akagi,* he would be billeted. He felt as if he had come home, and his old associates seemed as happy to see him as he was to be there. Murata, the torpedo ace, mockingly commiserated with him on having the same job again.

"Yes, Butsu-san, I'm back," said Fuchida, "and I want your assistance."

Several days later, he received orders from the office of Vice Admiral Chuichi Nagumo, commander in chief of the First Air Fleet. Fuchida knew him vaguely but had never served under him. He respected Nagumo as a fine officer with a thorough knowledge of torpedo warfare. But what was Nagumo doing at the head of an air fleet? He had never had the slightest connection with naval aviation.

The orders made Fuchida senior flight commander in charge of the First Air Fleet's airmen. This meant he would have responsibility for training the air crews of four carriers—the *Akagi* and *Kaga* of the First Carrier Division and the *Soryu* and *Hiryu* of the Second Carrier Division. He would also command all the fleet's air forces when they were used as a group.

"Butsu-san, I've been given a big order," he remarked, showing the document to Murata.

"I thought there was something behind your appointment," his friend remarked. "From now on, let's call you the general commander!" Fuchida grinned.[4]

He realized that something was in the wind, if only because of the caliber of the top airmen who would be working with him at the air bases scattered about southern Kyushu. He would have direct charge of the First Carrier Division's horizontal and torpedo bombers assigned to Kagoshima. At Tomitake, that division's dive-bombers practiced under Lieutenant Takehiko Chihaya, twenty-eight years old and three years out of Kasumigaura. Chihaya's present position testified to his ability. Considered one of the navy's best observers, he was a thoughtful type and a fearless flier.[5]

The Second Carrier Division's horizontal and torpedo bombers trained out of Izumi under the expert eye of Lieutenant Commander Masashi Kusumi. Kusumi had been an air officer since graduating from Kasumigaura in 1933. His experience was broad. Fuchida's special friend among the leaders was Lieutenant Commander Takeshige Egusa, in charge of the Second Carrier Division's dive-bombers at Kasonohara and whom Genda considered "the number-one dive-bombing pilot in all Japan" as well as "a good tactician in the air."[6] Good-natured and trustworthy, Egusa was a soft touch for any friend in need of a cash to tide him over until payday, so much so that Fuchida often had to come to Egusa's financial rescue.[7]

Fuchida had little contact with the fighter pilots training at Saeki. One of the best fighter pilots in the navy, Lieutenant Commander Shigeru Itaya, was in charge of them.[8] Fuchida never became close to Itaya. He didn't have much fellowship with his colleagues and wasn't well liked. He preferred to be left alone with a book.[9]

With these men and others Fuchida kept busy for the next month, moving from base to base, supervising, advising, refining techniques, and getting to know his men—without any idea of the ultimate aim. Obviously, however, Genda was deeply involved, and no dish of his cooking would ever lack spice.

Both men were so busy they had scarcely seen one another since Fuchida's arrival. So Fuchida was delighted when a sailor announced Genda near the end of September. After a brief greeting, the air staff officer got down to basics.

"The situation with the United States is getting worse. In case of war, Yamamoto plans to attack Pearl Harbor," he announced briskly.

Fuchida's jaw dropped and his eyes popped.

"If the plan is approved," Genda continued, "you are to be flight leader of the attack force. I recommended you for the job, and Yamamoto himself agreed. So I went to the navy minister and said, 'We want Lieutenant Commander Mitsuo Fuchida for this assignment.' "[10]

He was thrilled by this honor. No moral qualms assailed him. Japan had a long tradition of opening hostilities by surprise attack. Anyone who read the newspapers or listened to the radio knew that relations between Japan and the United States were worsening. In Fuchida's opinion, if the American forces on Oahu could be caught napping—the crucial if—they deserved everything they got. So he felt unalloyed admiration for Yamamoto's daring and fortitude and a sense of destiny at being slated to put Genda's ideas into practice.

Genda hustled Fuchida to the *Akagi* to draw him into the center of the project. Much planning had been completed, but details, especially of the air strike, had yet to be refined. The two men went directly to the chief of staff's cabin. There a number of officers were gathered around two large platforms. Nagumo was among them, as was his chief of staff—none other than Fuchida's former chief Kusaka, now a rear admiral.

The officers looked Fuchida over appraisingly. Kusaka motioned him to come close to the platforms, one of which held a model of Oahu, the other a mock-up of Pearl Harbor. Kusaka filled him in briefly on the plans and concluded, "We want you to begin special training for this purpose. This plan must be kept absolutely top secret."[11]

Nagumo and his staff wanted Fuchida's immediate opinion. He protested mildly. The models were excellent visual aids, but they gave no figures. So he asked to see a chart of Pearl Harbor. Genda's assistant Lieutenant Commander Chuichi Yoshioka pulled one out, and Genda explained where each type of U.S. warship customarily docked. The attack plan would rely primarily upon aerial torpedoes.

Fuchida knew that he lacked Genda's brilliance and creative imagination; he also knew that those traits needed occasional checking. "Genda was a very bright officer," he said in retrospect, "but once he got a plan in his head he did not always consider its application."

Fuchida raised a practical point: The water in Pearl Harbor was only some forty feet deep, much too shallow for a torpedo run. Genda took immediate issue. "A torpedo attack is essential. It will inflict much greater damage than bombs."

"But Japan has no torpedo that can run closely enough to the surface to hit the target and not sink into the mud of such shallow waters," Fuchida protested.

"Do it anyway!" Genda replied.[12]

That was characteristic of Genda. Once he made up his mind that torpedoes would provide maximum destruction, he planned on torpedoes. The fact that a suitable missile had not yet been invented didn't deter him. If Japan needed them, somehow they would be forthcoming. Perhaps such dynamic faith generates its own positive responses, for technical skill plus intensive training eventually produced the modified torpedoes for Pearl Harbor and Japanese ability to use them.

Having agreed, with reservations, to include torpedoes, Fuchida insisted that other weapons be added. Even if shallow-running missiles were available, two other factors had to be considered. The first was torpedo nets around the targets. Genda discounted the possibility, but Fuchida could not believe the Americans would fail to take such elementary precautions. His next argument was more potent: U.S. ships would be double-berthed in Pearl Harbor. The inside ship could not be attacked by torpedoes. This was undeniable. What about using only dive-bombers, Nagumo wanted to know. Fuchida explained that dive-bombing could not penetrate the heavy armor of American battleships; for that they must rely on high-level bombers. Wouldn't dive-bombers be effective against carriers? Nagumo knew enough about carriers to recognize that they were particularly vulnerable to dive-bombing.

This was one of his few contributions to the discussion. Several times Nagumo asked, "Is everything going to be OK?" Fuchida had the impression that he would welcome a legitimate excuse to call off an operation with so many built-in risks.

"I can't tell you at this time, sir," Fuchida answered. "Everything depends on our training from now on."

Genda had almost given up on horizontal bombing, Fuchida's specialty, because the Japanese navy had a terrible record of hits using this technique. Fuchida, however, didn't have to twist his arm to reinstate the program.

As the conference drew to a close, Kusaka said, "Let me repeat that this business must be kept extremely secret at all times. This is the most secret thing of all secrets." Even the flying crews must be kept in the dark. The meeting disbanded in a sober mood.[13]

Fuchida soon realized that of the First Air Fleet Staff only Genda was truly enthusiastic about Operation Hawaii, though he did have a staunch ally aboard *Soryu,* Rear Admiral Tamon Yamaguchi, commander in chief of the Second Carrier Division. Technically, Yamaguchi was no more an air admiral than Nagumo, but he had studied air power closely. He was a friend of Yamamoto's and backed his plan to the last inch. "This is an invincible striking force," he said to Fuchida more than once. Fuchida came to respect Yamaguchi second only to Yamamoto, and once or twice told Genda that he should be in command of the Pearl Harbor task force. "He was a real samurai with a real fighting spirit."

Yamaguchi's air staff officer was Lieutenant Commander Eijiro Suzuki, who had been Fuchida's classmate at Eta Jima, Kasumigaura, and the Naval Staff College. Now they were together again to learn and teach new lessons.[14]

The ban against total secrecy didn't last long. Quite soon certain key fliers had to be told their objective in order to get the best out of them and their men. Fuchida drew to himself a triumvirate of unofficial personal staff. These were Murata, the torpedo ace; Egusa, the dive-bombing expert; Lieutenant Izumi Furukawa, a particular favorite of Genda, who had been one of his instructors at Yokosuka.[15] "He was the best in the Japanese navy," said Genda later. "He was to the horizontal bomber what Murata was to the torpedo bomber." Under Furukawa's tireless direction, his men had already made remarkable progress before Fuchida arrived.[16]

When the Fifth Carrier Division, consisting of the new flattops *Shokaku* and *Zuikaku*, joined the First Air Fleet in October, Fuchida gained two valuable friends and assistants. Lieutenant Commander Shigekazu Shimazaki had joined *Zuikaku* as a squadron commander on 10 September 1941. A big man and a judo expert, Shimazaki was not particularly bright, but he was "a good solid type with a fine sense of humor." More to the point, he excelled in all three forms of aerial bombing—torpedo, horizontal, and dive.[17]

Fuchida was also close friends with Egusa's brother-in-law, Lieutenant Commander Kakuchi Takahashi of the *Shokaku*. Since Takahashi outranked Egusa, he took over the lead of the dive-bombers. He struck Fuchida as rather stupid. He never saw the point of a funny story until all the others had laughed and started talking about something else. But he was honest, good-natured, "solid, sound, and dependable."[18]

Fuchida took particular pride in the progress of horizontal bombing. They had fifty bombers available, so he changed the conventional nine-plane formation to five. This gave them ten strike units flying in sharp echelon for greater accuracy. By the end of the training period the record of hits had increased by 70 percent—a tribute to patience and determination, for Japan still had no mechanical bombsight. For dive-bombing, Fuchida's old nine-plane formation was satisfactory, and once suitable bombs became available they worked up to 40 percent hits, a very good record.

During this training blitz, a long promotion list came out. Murata became a lieutenant commander and Fuchida moved up to full commander.[19]

Here, there, and everywhere, Genda rode like a surfer on the crested wave of his enthusiasm. He checked training progress, cast an X-ray eye over dress rehearsals, attended conferences, and prodded the technicians. Kusaka was a tower of strength. On his shoulders fell the problem of surface ships, of which the airmen knew little or nothing.[20]

By early November 1941, Fuchida had honed Nagumo's pilots to a cutting edge. He and Genda had organized the air strike in two waves, for not all the aircraft could take off at once from the six carriers, and it took time to make formation.[21] Now they decided that the time had come for final dress rehearsals. A few problem areas remained, but on the whole the mock attacks were satisfactory.[22]

In midafternoon of 17 November, with the task force ready to sail to the rendezvous point—Hitokappu Bay on the island of Etorofu in the Kuriles—Yamamoto boarded the *Akagi* to wish them luck. The admiral was rather subdued. Evidently he feared that the men of the task force might underesti-

mate the Americans, whom many Japanese believed soft and disunited. He
spoke earnestly: "Japan has faced many worthy opponents in her long history—Mongols, Chinese, Russians—but the United States is the most worthy of all. You must be prepared for great American resistance. Admiral
[Husband E.] Kimmel, commander in chief of the Pacific Fleet, is known to
be farsighted and aggressive, so you cannot count upon surprise. You may
have to fight your way in to the target."

Stepping up to Fuchida, Yamamoto grasped his hand in silent farewell.
Then he was gone, leaving his audience to digest his ominous words.[23]
Neither Nagumo nor Kusaka had really believed they could achieve surprise,
but Fuchida and Genda had predicated their tactical plans upon catching the
Americans unawares. Not that any of the key airmen expected to escape
unscathed. In fact, the previous day Fuchida and Murata had purchased
bright red underwear and shirts, having decided that if they should be
wounded, the sight of their gore might dismay and discourage their men.
During the attack they would wear these garments, which would not show
blood.[24]

With Yamamoto's words ringing in their ears, Fuchida, Genda, and
Murata worked out a new scheme. If Pearl Harbor's antiaircraft defenses
should indeed be alert and waiting, the horizontal and dive-bombers
would hit first, not the slow torpedo planes. This did not suit Murata at
all. Like the French general with a similar name, Murat, he preferred to
dash off in the lead. Fuchida and Genda overrode his objections. The
three arranged a signal by smoke pistol: If the Americans were unpre-
pared, Fuchida would fire one rocket. In that case, Murata and his tor-
pedomen would lead off as originally planned. But if he fired twice, this
meant the enemy was on the alert, and Murata must wait until the other
groups went in.[25]

As the *Akagi* and her two escort destroyers slipped northward toward
foggy Etorofu, Fuchida could congratulate himself on a job well done—so
far. He could tie up no more loose ends until all the carriers assembled in
Hitokappu Bay. There for the first time all hands learned of their destina-
tion. Fuchida talked himself hoarse thanks to numerous briefings.[26] He
and his colleagues had done all they could to insure the success of their
mission. Many factors would be beyond Japanese control—the movements
and defense measures of the U.S. Pacific Fleet, the weather, and so on—
but as the ships weighed anchor in the cold gray dawn of 26 November
1941, Fuchida's natural buoyancy surfaced. Who could be more lucky
than he?[27] He was aboard his beloved *Akagi;* with her, and on the other
flattops, were the best of companions, handpicked for their expertise and

bravery. And the Imperial Japanese Navy had found him worthy to lead them.

As the *Akagi* slipped out to sea, her young crewmen shouted *"Banzai!"* at the top of their lungs. Morale was high and determination firm.[28] But not even the most optimistic of them could have anticipated the success that would be theirs.

5

"Tiger! Tiger! Tiger!"

O N THE VOYAGE to Hawaii, Fuchida found plenty to occupy his mind. He kept his airmen busy studying mock-ups of Pearl Harbor and Oahu, along with models of American warships, going over every angle of the tactics again and again until each man's part became second nature to him. The ships, though they maintained radio silence, received daily intelligence data relayed by Tokyo from the consulate on Oahu. Nagumo fretted over the possibility that American submarines might be stalking the task force. Fuchida worried lest the admiral's attitude dampen morale. But, off duty, the airmen played games and drank sake or beer as if on a routine training mission.[1]

The long-awaited message from Combined Fleet headquarters told the Nagumo force that Japan had decided the war would begin on 8 December 1941 Japanese time. In a way, the news came as a relief.[2] Had Tokyo and Washington effected a reconciliation at the last minute, the letdown would almost have been unbearable.

The nearer they sailed to their objective, the warmer the weather grew. Officers and men shed winter clothing and took to shorts and shirts, spending as much time as possible above decks enjoying the fresh salt air. The sun shone only rarely. "The weather and the condition of the seas were so obviously in our favor that most of the officers considered it a special dispensation of providence," Genda remembered. The spiritually oriented Kusaka repeated frequently, "This is the hand of God." Even Nagumo observed more than once, "When men work as hard as we have on this operation, Providence will favor them with its blessing."[3]

Half the crews stood at battle alert. The chances of discovery increased with every plunge of the bows toward Hawaii. Fuchida moved among his airmen, distributing words of encouragement, answering questions, intervening with a smile at the slightest hint of disagreement or pessimism. Murata seconded his efforts with alacrity and kept everyone laughing.[4]

The task force began refueling for the last time before the attack at 0830 on Saturday 6 December (local time). These were the most dangerous hours of the voyage, with the ships cruising at reduced speed far into enemy waters. So Nagumo ordered an all-out alert. When the last tanker steamed away for the postattack rendezvous point, the final link with home appeared to be severed.

But no one had time to brood. At 1130 the task force changed course to due south and increased speed to twenty knots.[5] That night, after talking over various aspects of the attack for about an hour, the meeting of the staff and key airmen broke up in a mood of optimism, ready to accept whatever fate befell them. Nagumo and Kusaka stayed up most of the night in the operations room. Fuchida advised his flight leaders to get a good night's rest. Then he threw himself down on his bunk for a few hours. "I slept soundly," he recalled. "I had set up the whole machinery of the attack, and it was ready to go. There was no use worrying now."[6]

He jumped out of bed at about 0500 and pulled on his long red underwear, red shirt, and then his flying suit. Then he ate a quick but hearty breakfast. The *Akagi* pitched and tossed in the heavy seas. On a training maneuver Fuchida would not have permitted his pilots to take off. But this was a real operation, timed to the second. Throughout the Japanese empire the armed forces waited. Danger or no danger, they must get off the carriers.[7]

On his way for a final report to Nagumo, Fuchida passed Genda in the gangway. For an instant they looked at one another. In that arrested moment, half a lifetime of understanding flashed between them. They smiled, and then Fuchida hurried to the flight deck for takeoff.[8]

As Fuchida prepared to climb into his plane, the *Akagi*'s senior maintenance crewman handed him a white scarf. "All of the maintenance crew would like to go along to Pearl Harbor," he shouted above the roar of the engines. "Since we can't, we want you to take this *hachimaki* as a symbol that we are with you in spirit." Touched, Fuchida tied the scarf samurai-fashion around his flight helmet and scrambled into the aircraft.[9]

Although the carriers bucked like broncos, takeoff met with surprisingly few mishaps. At about 0615 Fuchida signaled the circling aircraft to follow him south to the target. Even as his formation winged away, the mechanics were working frantically to bring the second wave of aircraft up to the flight decks. All told, the task force would launch 353 aircraft in this, the largest naval air armada ever sent aloft to that date.[10]

As they flew toward Oahu, the first rays of dawn crept over the horizon. Then came the great red disk of the sun, looking like a huge Japanese naval flag. A chill of awe ran through Fuchida. He pushed back his canopy. The wind beat against his face and sent his *hachimaki* streaming out behind him like a banner. Behind him thundered the first attack wave, the rising sun glittering on its wings.

It was a glorious, inspiring sight. He was proud to be a man living at that time. The destiny of his country rested on his shoulders. O glorious dawn for Japan! he thought. Raising both arms, he waved exultantly to his air fleet. Some of the men saw the gesture and waved back.[11]

Closing his canopy, he settled back to scan the sky for enemy aircraft. Clouds billowed below so thickly that he feared his pilot, Lieutenant Mutsuzaki, might overfly Oahu. He also worried about the weather obscuring the target. At that very instant, Honolulu radio obligingly gave his radioman a weather report indicating perfect visibility. This was followed with music to home in by. About 0730 Fuchida saw land below, all green foliage and white sands next to the sparking blue sea. "This is the north point of Oahu," he said to Mutsuzaki.

As they flew on, Fuchida cried, *"Tenkai!"* indicating take attack position, and instructed Mutsuzaki to watch for enemy interceptors. So far, everything had worked out perfectly. By all the canons of the war gods, a snafu was long overdue. Fuchida could see no American patrol activity at sea or in the air, nor any sign of preparations for an attack.

Almost sure that the strike would come as a surprise, he fired a single Black Dragon rocket. Murata saw it and swung low toward the target. But Lieutenant Masaharu Suginami, a fighter-group leader, kept his aircraft in cruise position. Thinking he had missed the first rocket, Fuchida fired another. Then he groaned—Takahashi, mistaking the second rocket for the double signal meaning that the enemy was on the alert, swooped in with his dive-bombers. Fuchida ground his teeth in rage. Soon, however, he realized that the error made no practical difference.[12]

Through his binoculars he looked at Pearl Harbor. What a majestic sight! There lay the beautiful harbor with all the great ships at anchor, so much like the model in Kusaka's cabin that it seemed unreal. Fuchida saw seven battleships, though according to the latest intelligence reports nine were in harbor. Undoubtedly someone had counted the old *Utah*, now a target ship. Fuchida didn't yet know that the flagship *Pennsylvania* was in dry dock. He was in no mood to quibble over a battlewagon or two. To his disappointment, there were no carriers in port. Preattack reports had indicated this, but he had hoped they were mistaken.

At 0749, somewhat off Lalalahi Point, Fuchida grabbed the intercom and gave Mutsuzaki the attack signal: *"To! To! To!"* Then he ordered the radio-man, First Flying Petty Officer Tokunobu Mizuki, to transmit the order to all pilots. The air fleet broke into its assigned parts. Fuchida's plane sped around Barbers Point. Certain now that they had caught the enemy una-wares, Fuchida shouted, *"Tora! Tora! Tora!"* (Tiger! Tiger! Tiger!)—the code word signifying that they had achieved surprise.[13]

For a fleeting moment, the tableau of the ships appeared fixed in time. Then events unwound at a furious pace. Suddenly the air was a confusing crisscross of planes as the first wave plunged down upon its targets. But no collisions marred the attacks. The men knew exactly what they were doing and went to work with ruthless precision.

Itaya's Zeros zoomed around like teams performing aerobatics, shooting up everything in sight. Takahashi's dive-bombers swooped down on Ford Island, exploding fires, erupting huge billows of smoke, loosing debris in every direction. At Battleship Row, Murata's torpedo bombers dropped so low it seemed they might tangle with the ships' superstructures. Fuchida was anx-ious about the torpedo attack, because the success of the plan depended heavily on it. He adjusted his binoculars, and the scene sharpened into focus. Murata and his men were splashing their deadly fish into the water, sending huge geysers shooting skyward.

Then Fuchida's own horizontal bombers swung over Battleship Row and he cried, *"Tsu! Tsu! Tsu!"* the order for them to go into action. Already antiaircraft bursts were dotting the sky. Fire came from the ships, and Fu-chida felt a flicker of reluctant admiration. Just like Americans! he thought. If this were the Japanese fleet, it wouldn't have reacted so quickly. The Japanese are cut out for the offensive, not for the defensive.

At that moment, his plane quivered from a direct hit. Mutsuzaki assured him that everything was all right. No sooner had the words left his mouth than the plane rocked again, this time from a near miss. Reflecting on the need to overfly battleships at three thousand meters in the face of such fire, Fuchida wondered if his luck was not about to run out.[14]

After three runs to ensure a good sighting, he dropped his bomb on the *California*, moored singly somewhat to the south of the double row. During his second run, he saw a terrible explosion. "The flame and smoke erupted skyward together," he recalled. "It was a hateful, mean-looking red flame, the kind that powder produces, and I knew at once that a big magazine had exploded." His plane shuddered in the suction of the after-blast, but Mutsuzaki, skillful as he was brave, kept the damaged aircraft on an even keel.

Fuchida didn't know that he had witnessed the destruction of the *Arizona;* he only knew that at least one American battleship was out of action for good. Joy and gratification filled his heart; the mission would be a success.[15]

Having dropped his single bomb, Fuchida fell back and exchanged places with his number-two aircraft. Henceforth his prime responsibility was to assess the damage for a report to Nagumo. Hovering out of range of antiaircraft flak, he looked down on a scene of desolation. The shattered hulk of the *Arizona* blazed like a forest fire, the *Oklahoma* had turned turtle, and the *California* and *West Virginia* were slowly settling. On the far side of Ford Island, the old *Utah* lay on her side, the victim of a mistake; the Japanese never intended to waste a precious torpedo on her. Across the channel near the navy yard and dry docks, the light cruiser *Helena* lay crippled.

Rolls of heavy smoke boiled up from Ford Island and Hickam and Wheeler Fields. Takahashi and Itaya had succeeded in pinning down Oahu's air power. The almost complete absence of American military aircraft in the skies told Fuchida that outlying airfields had suffered the same fate. The Japanese had complete control of the air over Oahu.[16]

At about 0840 Fuchida saw Shimazaki's second wave thundering over the sea in perfect formation, on course and on schedule. Originally Fuchida had planned to take over the leadership of this wave, but soon he saw that Shimazaki was doing fine without his help. So he continued to observe the action and to record the damage.

Shimazaki's force did not include torpedo planes, which would have been highly vulnerable once the Japanese lost the vital element of surprise. This arrangement proved wise, for the second wave had a much rougher time than the first. Fuchida could see the muzzle flashes of antiaircraft guns belching black puffs of flak. From time to time, it chewed into the attacking planes and forced the pilots to maneuver out of its way. And a few American fighters buzzed into the second wave, doing well in view of the odds. Then there was the smoke rolling skyward from stricken ships and wrecked airfields, which made bombing difficult and hazardous.

Most of the power of the second wave rested in Egusa's capable hands. His men pounced on the *Nevada* as she tried to escape the deathtrap. This was the opportunity for which the Japanese longed—sinking a big ship in the narrow channel and bottling up Pearl Harbor. But the beleaguered *Nevada,* in spite of the blistering attack, crept down channel and beached near Hospital Point.

Behind the damaged *Pennsylvania,* in dry dock, Fuchida spotted two destroyers collapsed against one another like broken toys. Smoke seriously hampered his view.[17] He hovered over the scene of destruction until certain that all his aircraft still skyborne had cleared the area. After making one final check of the damage, he instructed Mutsuzaki to go to the rendezvous point.

In those days it was easy for a single-seated fighter plane to get lost on long overwater flights. Therefore, the Japanese had designated a rendezvous point for all aircraft off the northwest coast of Oahu, from which the bombers could guide the fighters to the carriers. There Fuchida's plane picked up a straggler or two and headed back toward the task force.

Remembering the grueling training he had put his men through, Fuchida's heart warmed. Those who attempted to accomplish the impossible had reaped their reward. And he felt a certain contempt for the U.S. Pacific Fleet. In a time of crisis threatening war, it had neglected to place antitorpedo nets around its battleships.[18]

He was filled with pride of his men and of himself, and from his standpoint he had every right to be. The airmen had succeeded beyond all expectation. Years would pass, however, before Fuchida understood that he had left behind more than smashed ships and aircraft and dead and wounded men. He also left behind a nation welded together by the fires he and his men had set—a United States that would not rest until the Japanese had paid in full for their morning's work.

6

"Japan Once More!"

WHILE Fuchida's plane devoured the miles between Oahu and the waiting task force, he thought of ways to exploit the unexpectedly favorable situation. His men had accomplished wonders, but for maximum destruction much remained to be done. A third and even a fourth wave could polish off those damaged battleships, strike some of the lighter ships that had escaped, and take another crack at the airfields. When surveying results Fuchida had spotted the U.S. Navy's huge fuel tanks, which he didn't attack because the ships were his assigned mission. What a tempting target they were! If the Japanese could have ignited those tanks, American naval strategy for the Pacific would have gone up in smoke.[1]

His plane touched down on the *Akagi*'s flight deck sometime after noon. There awaiting him was Genda, smiling in triumph. Both men quickly sobered. "How many planes were lost?" Fuchida asked.

"About thirty," replied Genda. "Some of *Akagi*'s planes are missing."

"No more will return," Fuchida told him. "Mine is the last." Whereupon Genda hurried to the bridge.

Genda's calculation took into consideration only those aircraft—twenty-nine to be exact—lost in direct combat. An additional ten or fifteen were so badly damaged they had to be pushed overboard to make room for other incoming planes to land. Another forty or forty-five were damaged but reparable.[2]

There was a frenzy of shipboard activity. Engines were being checked, planes fueled and armed. The aircraft had to be ready to attack in the event that the Americans discovered the task force. The horizontal bombers were converted into torpedo planes—more effective at sea but useless for another strike at Oahu now that surprise had been lost.[3]

Genda had scarcely vanished when a sailor rushed up: Admiral Nagumo wanted to see Commander Fuchida right away. Fuchida decided to risk a delay in the interests of an accurate report. He hurried to the operations post to check his observations against those of the flight leaders. A cup of tea in one hand and a slice of bread in the other, Fuchida listened to their reports and checked the figures posted on the blackboard. These conformed closely to his findings. He would be able to give Nagumo a fairly reliable interim report. Meanwhile, the sailor returned with Nagumo's orders to come on the double.[4]

He hurried to the bridge, where Nagumo, Kusaka, and other staff officers were waiting for him, and saluted the *Akagi*'s skipper prior to making his report.

But Nagumo interrupted. "Many, many thanks, Flight Commander! What was the result of the action?"

The skipper, Captain Kiichi Hasegawa, signed to Fuchida that he should report directly to the admiral.

"Four battleships sunk," responded Fuchida. "I am confident of this from my personal observation."

"Four battleships sunk!" repeated Nagumo. He seemed to roll the figure around on his tongue, savoring it. "Good! What about the other four?"

"There hasn't been time to check results precisely, but it looks like three were seriously damaged, the other somewhat damaged although not quite so badly." He went on to list the other ships struck, using a berthing chart.

When he had finished, Nagumo asked the key question: "Do you think that the U.S. fleet will be able to operate out of Pearl Harbor within six months?"

That had been the object of the attack—to immobilize the fleet for at least half a year. If Fuchida replied in the affirmative, it would mean that the airmen had accomplished their mission. He saw the direction of Nagumo's thinking and felt a momentary twinge of alarm. But he had to tell the truth. "The main force will not be able to come out within six months."

Nagumo beamed. "A lot of light cruisers and other vessels remain in the harbor," Fuchida hastened to add, "It would be worthwhile to launch another attack."

Kusaka ignored this suggestion. "What about the air bases?" he asked.

"Heavy smoke made observation difficult. As best we can figure, we destroyed almost all the aircraft parked on the ground, and probably half of those in the hangars. Still," he cautioned, "it would be wise to assume that many remain operational."[5]

"Could land-based bombers counterattack our task force?" Kusaka asked. His query reflected conventional wisdom: Carrier-borne planes could not compete with land-based aircraft. Nagumo and Kusaka subscribed to that tenet, and dreaded the possibility of American heavy bombers such as the B-17 attacking lightly armored carriers.

Fuchida had no doubt that the Japanese ruled Hawaii's sky, though he couldn't offer definite proof. So he answered honestly, "That's a possibility that has to be considered. I believe we destroyed a lot of enemy planes, but I don't know how many serviceable aircraft remain. Some could probably get into the air and seek us out."

"There's no use worrying about that," said Genda. "Our fighter cover will be able to shoot down those heavy bombers."

The senior staff officer, Commander Tomatsu Oishi, asked about antiaircraft fire. The American response had been unexpectedly quick, Fuchida admitted. With the second wave, it was even faster.

The amount of enemy resistance was an important factor in considering further strikes. Would results be worth the anticipated losses?

"If we attack again, what should the targets be?" asked Kusaka. Fuchida had no difficulty in answering, having thought of little else all the way back to *Akagi*. "The damaged battleships and the other vessels in harbor, the dock yards, and the fuel tanks," he informed them.

At this point Nagumo, who had been silent, spoke. "Where do you think the missing U.S. carriers are?"

Fuchida could only give an educated guess. "I didn't see any U.S. Navy fighters or bombers over Pearl Harbor," he said. "The carriers are probably training somewhere at sea. By this time no doubt they know about the attack, and they're searching for us."

This admission made an unpleasant impression on everyone but Genda, who, like Fuchida, hoped for an encounter with the American flattops. In any case, their inability to pinpoint the whereabouts of the carriers underlined what Fuchida considered a major weakness in Japan's tactical planning for Operation Hawaii: No provision had been made for postattack aerial reconnaissance.[6]

Nagumo made no immediate decision, dismissing Fuchida with a word of praise. As soon as he departed, Genda took up the battle. Nagumo shouldn't leave without making every possible attempt to locate and sink the enemy carriers, if necessary remaining in the area for several days. However,

Nagumo refused to attack Pearl Harbor again or to hunt for the elusive flattops. He had accomplished his mission, he felt. And the longer the American carriers remained out of sight, the better. Having expected from one third to one half of his ships to be sunk or damaged, Nagumo had no desire to tempt fate further. His immediate concern was to preserve his task force.[7]

In the meantime, Fuchida returned to the command post for a lunch of *botamochi*, rice cakes with bean paste. While he was eating, an order came down: "Preparations for attack canceled."

The *Akagi* hoisted a signal flag indicating retirement to the northwest. Upset, Fuchida scrambled to the bridge.

"What's happened?" he asked Genda.

His classmate shrugged. "It can't be helped."

That wasn't good enough for Fuchida. He turned to Nagumo, saluted, and asked bluntly, "Why aren't we attacking again?"

Kusaka forestalled whatever reply Nagumo might have made. "The objective of the Pearl Harbor operation is achieved," he said. "Now we must prepare for future operations."

Silently, Fuchida saluted and stalked off the bridge. "I was a bitter and angry man," he recalled, "for I was convinced that Nagumo should have attacked again."[8]

He went back to the more congenial company of his fellow flight leaders, who had been eager to enplane for another strike. The decision to withdraw disappointed and angered them, especially Murata. "Now all of us pilots can live to be a hundred years old!" he remarked sarcastically. This was a crack at Kusaka, who practiced daily calisthentics, telling the grinning young men who watched him that by such means he planned to reach the century mark. But the junior officers had been trained to respect authority. They didn't openly criticize their superiors.

Back on the flight deck, Fuchida took a quick look at his aircraft. American antiaircraft fire had punctured about twenty-one large holes in the port side, and the control wire was held together by a whisker-thin thread. It was impressive. On the first day of the Pacific war, he had experienced the first of many narrow escapes from death that would checker his wartime service, that gradually convinced him that Somebody up there liked him, that his good fortune rather than poor American marksmanship accounted for his safe return to the *Akagi*.

For him nothing remained of the great adventure but to collect attack photographs. That night he and the other flight leaders studied the results. The next morning he sent Nagumo his definitive report, which turned out to be fairly accurate by later American figures.[9]

Japan learned almost immediately that its naval airmen had made a daring attack on Pearl Harbor. When the news came over the Fuchidas' radio, Haruko turned to Yoshiya and Miyako and said with quiet confidence, "That is your father." Fuchida had never mentioned Operation Hawaii to her, but she knew that he and no other had led Japan's fliers.[10] During the ensuing weeks the Japanese press lauded its navy and mocked the Americans. Could the average citizen be blamed for thinking it was all over but the shouting?[11]

Fuchida knew nothing of the publicity boiling at home. The Pacific Ocean was doing a little boiling of its own. As if to charge the Japanese for the good weather they had enjoyed on the outward voyage, the sea erupted into mountainous waves that lasted from 11 December to the thirteenth. Several crewmen were swept overboard. The task force would have been in real difficulty had the Americans attacked during this critical period, for fighters could not have taken off, and antiaircraft fire would have been inaccurate.[12]

Within a few days the Japanese discovered that the American garrison on Wake Island was proving unexpectedly tough. Yamamoto directed Nagumo to help the attacking forces.* Thus on 16 December Nagumo detached the carriers *Soryu* and *Hiryu,* the cruisers *Chikuma* and *Tone,* and the destroyers *Tanikaze* and *Urakaze* to reinforce the ships operating against Wake. The rest of the task force continued steadily toward Japan.[13]

On 22 and 23 December, in groups of ten and twelve, airworthy planes from *Akagi, Kaga, Zuikaku,* and *Shokaku* flew to their land bases for repairs and renewed training exercises. Their secondary mission was to sweep ahead of the task force in search of American submarines, a subject of much concern.[14]

One of the last to depart was Fuchida, who headed for Kagoshima. As the home island of Kyushu came in sight, he experienced a moment of understandable emotion: "Japan once more! I never thought I would see it again." After landing he walked straight into the arms of a delirious reception. When the first planes had flown in, the citizens of Kagoshima didn't know what was happening. By the time Fuchida arrived, word had spread that the men who attacked Pearl Harbor were returning. When Fuchida arrived, to his bewilderment he found the mayor of Kagoshima City, the governor of Kagoshima Prefecture, a pretty girl bearing flowers, wide-eyed schoolchildren, and a horde of screaming townspeople greeting him.

Up to this time Fuchida, surrounded by his fellow servicemen, had consid-

---

*The initial Japanese force attempting to take Wake Island was much too weak and was repelled.

ered the attack solely in the light of a naval air operation, albeit an unusually daring and successful one. Now he began to realize how much this demonstration of Japanese prowess meant to his countrymen. "Thank you for your wonderful welcome," he said when he could make himself heard. "I'm sorry that, for security reasons, I can't give you an account of the operation." Whereupon the crowd went wild again.

They seemed to feel that they had shared in the adventure. In a way they had, for much training had taken place in their city. Earlier, some had complained of the disturbance. Now they joked; all was forgiven.

That night the governor and other officials held a dinner in honor of Fuchida and the other aviation officers at the *Aoyagi* (blue willow) restaurant. A special type of fish called *tai* was served, usually eaten only in celebration of some great event. Sake and beer flowed freely. The enlisted men were not forgotten; they were swept off to a celebration of their own.[15]

During dinner a messenger handed Fuchida a telegram: "Commander Fuchida return to *Akagi* tomorrow." So the next morning he made a solo flight to Hiroshima Bay. The *Akagi* was swarming with top brass, headed by Chief of the Naval General Staff Admiral Osami Nagano and some of his officers. From the Combined Fleet came Yamamoto, his chief of staff Rear Admiral Matome Ugaki, and other staff members. At luncheon ceremonies the dignitaries insisted that Fuchida and Murata join them at the head table, where each admiral in order of rank passed his sake cup to Fuchida.

Yamamoto was more than ceremonially gracious to Fuchida, for he was genuinely fond of him. "I listened on the radio during the whole attack," the admiral said. "I heard your order, 'All forces attack.' When I heard that, I needed no report to tell me that the attack would be successful." He smiled reminiscently. "I also heard your signal that you had achieved surprise."

The moment of the day Fuchida cherished most came when Yamamoto presented him with a beautiful *kakemono,* * which the admiral had brushed out the very day of the strike, December 8 (Japanese time). It read: "Message of 'Attack!' reaches my ears from more than three thousand miles away—a message from Hawaii. Thinking of Flight Leader Fuchida's brilliant action on the early morning of 8 December, so writes Isoroku Yamamoto." The bold, generous calligraphy seemed to typify Yamamoto himself in all his breadth of character, his kind expansiveness.[16]

As if this were not enough, Genda relayed to Fuchida a message that the

---

*A long, narrow scroll with either painting or calligraphy to be hung on a wall and rolled up when not on display.

emperor wanted to hear about the operation from participants. Fuchida and Shimazaki were to report to Tokyo on 25 December in preparation for an imperial audience the next day.

Staggered by this unprecedented honor, Fuchida spent the next two days and nights preparing for the great event. High-flown generalities would not be good enough for His Imperial Majesty; the presentation must be detailed, factual, and organized. This meant that Fuchida would have to write Shimazaki's report as well as his own.

Shimazaki was fully aware of his deficiencies. Like many men of action, he detested paperwork and was much better at fighting than at recounting his exploits. So he was perfectly content to have Fuchida tell him what to say.[17]

While Fuchida was thus engaged, a brief tempest stirred the court teapot. Nagano and Nagumo would also appear before Hirohito. This presented no problem, since both were flag officers. But the low ranks of Fuchida and Shimazaki threw the guardians of rigid court etiquette into a dither. Someone came up with the expedient of making the two fliers "special assistants to the chief of the Naval General Staff," thus saving the situation.[18]

Early in the morning of 26 December, Fuchida and Shimazaki met with Nagano and Nagumo at the Navy Ministry. There the two airmen gave a brief official report to the Naval General Staff and received last-minute instructions on how to conduct themselves before the emperor. Nagano stressed that the emperor might ask questions directly, but they were not to answer directly; they would reply through his aide-de-camp.

Then the four officers got into limousines. Shortly after 1100, they entered a rather small room in the palace. Across one end ran a narrow platform some two feet high, in the center of which stood the emperor's seat (see the figure).

As the men arranged their maps and charts on a large table in front of the dais, an official of the imperial household, in formal morning dress, entered the room, a small censer cupped in his hands. Silently he walked a full circle around the emperor's chair, the sweet, heavy fragrance of incense wafting in his wake. Then he departed, still without a word. This ceremony increased the tension. Even Fuchida, the fluent extrovert, felt ill at ease, and the inarticulate Shimazaki quivered with awe.

A moment of dead silence, a whisper in the adjoining room, the sound of footsteps—then the emperor entered, followed by his aide, Major General Shigeru Hasunuma. As Fuchida described the scene, Hirohito "walked in slowly with quiet dignity. He wore the uniform of a naval generalissimo. . . . A medal adorned the left side of his chest and a sword hung by his side.

IMPERIAL BRIEFING
27 December 1941

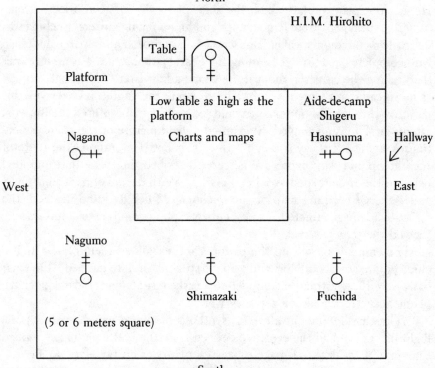

As he entered, everyone bowed low. Then the emperor sat down in his chair on the raised platform."

Hasunuma nodded to Nagano to begin. The latter introduced Nagumo, who outlined the background of the attack and gave a brief summary of the strike. He emphasized that the operation must have been blessed by heaven. The auspicious weather, the enemy's failure to discover the task force, the clouds that had first screened the approach, then miraculously parted at the perfect moment—such a combination of circumstances was proof of divine power, operating through the instrument of the emperor.

During this brief speech, His Imperial Majesty nodded approvingly several times but said nothing. Nagano next introduced Commander Fuchida. He would explain the attack on the ships of the U.S. Pacific Fleet. Accustomed to speaking before large groups and high-ranking officers, Fuchida was normally a confident speaker. But who could approach an imperial audience with complete equanimity? Leading the Pearl Harbor attack was much easier than telling the emperor about it, he would admit later.[19] His fingers shook as he spread out a large map of Oahu. Despite the handicap of relaying his narrative through Hasunuma, he could see that he had captured the imperial attention. Thus encouraged, he painted a vivid picture of the plane formations winging their way through a thick overcast. He outlined the route of each group and with expressive gestures described the scene that unfolded below as the aircraft sped over Pearl Harbor. With the aid of a tracking chart and a special berthing map of the anchorage, Fuchida listed in detail the estimated damage inflicted. Twelve enlarged photographs taken on the scene showed the targets struck.[20]

The emperor picked up the pictures and examined them closely as Fuchida pointed out bomb hits and torpedo strikes. Hirohito queried, "On what basis were these estimates compiled?" he asked, studying the damage chart. "How accurate would you say they were?"

"The charts represent a careful synthesis of all the reports made by the flight officers and all the evidence derived from the battle pictures," replied Fuchida. "I think the damage estimates are about 80 percent correct."

Reading down the neat tables of battle results, Hirohito pointed to the figures for aircraft damage. "We note that about fifteen enemy planes were shot down in the air. Were any civilian planes hit?"

"Three or four of the planes hit were unarmed training planes," answered Fuchida, "and one green-colored aircraft was shot down in flames. This could possibly have been a civilian plane."

"I hope it wasn't," said the emperor.*

---

*It was; however, the pilot bailed out safely.

At one point he inquired, "Did you definitely identify the American ships before you ordered the attack? Were there any hospital ships in Pearl Harbor, and did you by chance make a mistake and hit such a ship?"

"Most of the ships were clearly recognizable," Fuchida explained. "No hospital ships were sighted."*

"What was the initial reaction of the Americans?" asked His Imperial Majesty.

"Two minutes after our first bombs were dropped, we received heavy bursts of antiaircraft fire. In truth, we were surprised that the Americans could recover so quickly."

"Were any of our planes shot down because of their inability to return to the carriers?" the Emperor queried.

Fuchida explained the rendezvous arrangement, adding, "I remained in the area some time and led one or two fighters back."

In short, the emperor was so interested that time slipped by, and Fuchida's allotted fifteen minutes more than doubled.[21]

Shimazaki took the floor next, stammering out a brief description of the damage done to Oahu's airfields. He was only too happy to stick to his scheduled ten minutes. When he had finished, Hirohito picked up a picture of Wheeler Field showing American planes burning on the parking aprons. "Were those planes manned or not?" he asked.

"I don't think so," answered Shimazaki. "These planes were merely lined up in front of the hangars."

After a few more questions a heavy and long silence fell. Nagano started to rise. Suddenly the emperor inquired, "Was any damage inflicted other than on ships, planes, and airfields?"

Nagano asked Fuchida to answer. In his earnestness addressing Hirohito directly—a serious lapse of etiquette, which was graciously overlooked—Fuchida replied in the negative. "The airmen were very careful to bomb only military targets."

Hasunuma bowed to Hirohito to indicate the audience was over. The emperor was preparing to rise when a thought seemed to strike him. "Are you going to take these pictures with you?" he inquired of Nagano.

"They are to be placed in an album and presented to Your Imperial Majesty."

Hirohito hesitated a moment, then said, "We would like to have the pictures remain in the palace, as we wish to show them to Her Imperial Majesty the Empress." And after that he retired from the room, to deep bows.[22]

---

*Fuchida overlooked the *Solace,* which was anchored north of Ford Island. Although rocked by near misses, she suffered no damage.

Gratifying as the audience had been, a certain strain had hung over it. His Imperial Majesty had displayed natural interest in a great naval operation, the concern of a decent man for noncombatants, and the instinct of a husband to share an experience with his wife. But he showed no sign of exultation.

Fuchida left the imperial palace with his head in the clouds at the overwhelming honor of having met and talked with his emperor. Little *Tako*, the Octopus Kid, had come a long way!

7

"We Should Face East"

THE MORNING AFTER the imperial briefing, Fuchida tumbled to earth with a jarring thud. At Naval General Staff headquarters, he had a long talk with Rear Admiral Shigeru Fukudome, chief of the First Bureau (operations). Fukudome was efficient and knowledgeable about the surface navy but knew little about air power. To Fuchida's inexpressible shock, Fukudome told him that the First Air Fleet would be broken up. "The *Shokaku* and *Zuikaku*—the Fifth Carrier Division—will remain together and operate eastward. The other four carriers will operate as a unit to the south and west. Twenty percent of the flight personnel will be transferred to Kasumigaura as instructors for the new pilots being incorporated into our air arm."

Fuchida objected vigorously. He was much too disturbed at the time to recall in later years exactly what he said to Fukudome, but his plea went something like this: "The First Air Fleet has proved its worth! By all means the carriers should stay together, and the flight personnel should not be reduced. Let some other source send instructors to Kasumigaura. Any competent pilot can teach beginners; the First Air Fleet crews are irreplaceable combat veterans."

Building up steam, he continued. The six carriers should stay together as the main striking force of the navy, he argued. They shouldn't be reduced under any circumstances; on the contrary, two more should be added. What's more, the carriers shouldn't turn southward and westward. They should face east, against the remaining strength of the U.S. Pacific Fleet.

Fukudome, knowing that Fuchida had the good of his country at heart, didn't slap him down for insubordination. He made delicate soothing noises. "General Headquarters greatly appreciates the wonderful work of the pilots at Pearl Harbor," he said, "but their mission has been accomplished. We have nothing to fear from the east now. So the aircraft carriers—four of them—will now join the main Japanese operation to the south."

Fuchida left Fukudome with the deepest misgivings. "The doom of Japan began on that day, 27 December 1941," he said as he looked back. "Here was an example that General Headquarters didn't understand the war in the Pacific."[1]

His was no sudden protest. Already he had suggested to Kusaka that the six flattops be kept together and the Fourth Carrier Division (the *Ryujo* and *Shoho*) added to them. This would have been an invincible armada, an unbeatable combination. The original six Pearl Harbor carriers could be used to strike the enemy, and the *Ryujo*'s and *Shoho*'s planes could be used to protect the carriers in battle.[2]

If Fuchida's reaction was predictable, so was the action of the Naval General Staff. One of that organization's conditions for approval of Operation Hawaii had been that the First Air Fleet would be available for the Southern Operation as soon as possible.[3] This, in turn, reflected a tendency firmly rooted in Japanese thinking—the inability to exploit an unexpected advantage. Nagumo's and Kusaka's refusal to send a third attack wave over Pearl Harbor was only one of many examples. This sort of thing happened so often in the Pacific war that Commander Masataka Chihaya, brother of Fuchida's Pearl Harbor comrade, decided that some racial characteristic, some mysterious flaw deep in the genes, must be involved. "The Japanese navy just cannot help stopping the chase. It just cannot go the limit."[4]

Swallowing his dismay as best he could, Fuchida went with Fukudome to a champagne luncheon at the official residence of Navy Minister Admiral Shigetaro Shimada. An impressive array of top brass attended. They called upon Fuchida to explain the Pearl Harbor operation, which he did in much greater detail than he had for the emperor.[5]

The following day, 28 December, he briefed an assembly of several princes of the imperial family and their wives. It was an awe-inspiring gathering, for most of the princes were members of the armed forces in full uniform and their wives were wearing the beautiful national kimono. Having just faced the emperor, Fuchida was not as nervous as he might have been in other circumstances. Moreover, the event took place under the sponsorship of his Eta Jima classmate, Commander Prince Takamatsu, then a member of the operations section of the Naval General Staff. Quite aside from his royal blood, the prince was a first-rate officer, clear-headed, professional, and popular with his colleagues.[6]

That night at the navy club, Fuchida gave an interview to one of Tokyo's leading correspondents. After being censored by Commander Toshikazu Ohmae of the Navy Ministry, it appeared in English on 2 January 1947, in the Foreign Office's mouthpiece, *The Japan Times and Advertiser.* Entitled "Brilliant Account of Hawaii Bombing Attack Given in Report by Air Squadron Commander," it identified Fuchida only as "Commander X of the Japanese navy."[7]

How much of the story was genuine Fuchida and how much lily-painting on the part of an overenthusiastic reporter or censor is questionable. Fuchida was an articulate speaker who illustrated his rapid-fire narratives by gesturing with his arms and his long expressive fingers.[8] His language was usually straightforward; much of the newspaper story was uncharacteristically grandiloquent.

At last he was free to snatch a few days' leave to visit Kashiwara, where Haruko was staying with the children at her girlhood home.[9] At eight years of age Yoshiya was old enough to sense the doubt some Japanese felt about what Japan was getting into by taking on giant powers. But the townspeople did not allow such considerations to influence their joy in the military victory. Yoshiya's father was the hero of the hour, and the boy glowed with pride.[10]

Miyako didn't quite know what all the fuss was about, but she too was proud to walk beside her father as he strolled down the street in his smart navy uniform. Whenever a passing soldier or sailor saluted him, Miyako raised her small hand to her forehead in imitation of her father's acknowledging salute.[11]

The citizens overwhelmed him with courtesy and honors. He addressed a packed house of about four thousand in the Kashiwara auditorium, telling them in general terms about the Pearl Harbor attack. They cheered him vociferously.[12]

The adulation of the populace, the approval of his superiors, the admiration of his comrades in arms, the devotion of his wife, the adoration of his children—it was a rich, creamy dish that life set before Fuchida in those days. And he lapped it up.

Fond as he was of his family, he was never sorry to slip back into the harness. Soon he returned to his duties. He still brooded about the proposal to break up the First Air Fleet. But he told himself that Yamamoto would soon put an end to it. Imagine his intense disappointment and disillusionment when he discovered that Yamamoto not only failed to protest, he agreed with the idea.

At that time Fuchida loved and admired Yamamoto above all men. After this decision, he had to admit to himself that the admiral, although sympathetic toward the naval air arm, did not comprehend the ramifications of the new force he himself had done so much to encourage. Fuchida began to think that the formation of the First Air Fleet had been a freak of nature, a two-headed calf and not an evolutionary step forward. Pearl Harbor had been only a sideshow. Yamamoto was deeply committed to the supremacy of the Southern Operation.[13]

Fuchida did not disagree with Japan's driving ambition to extend the empire over Malaya, the Philippines, and the Netherlands East Indies. Japan desperately needed the raw resources of that vast treasure house, and he saw no reason why his country should not take them if it had the strength to do so. But Japan's strategists seemed to be taking the hard road.

Fuchida, along with Genda and a few other dedicated airmen, had believed all along that the Pearl Harbor operation should have been an all-out attack—even an invasion and occupation of the Hawaiian islands. The U.S. Pacific Fleet formed the keystone of the Allies' power posture in the Pacific. If that fleet could be blasted out of the area or put out of action for a sufficiently long period, and if Japan held the Hawaiian chain, all other steps would require far less military effort than envisioned in Japan's southern strategy.[14]

He did not deceive himself that this would be an easy course. He realized, and cautioned his fliers, that they had met the Americans under unusual circumstances that did not permit a true evaluation of their fighting power. "The time will come," he told them, "when the Combined Fleet will meet the U.S. Fleet in open combat in the Pacific, and for that day everyone now must train and be prepared."[15]

The failure to follow through at Pearl Harbor was now part of the irretrievable past. But, Fuchida felt, the Combined Fleet could learn from this mistake and not compound the error. Before time ran out they should go back east and finish the job—the immediate and complete destruction of the U.S. Pacific Fleet, followed by the occupation of Oahu. If they succeeded, the United States would have to withdraw from the central Pacific. In which case China's main lifeline would be severed and that country might have to abandon its stubborn resistance. Cut off from American supplies and reinforcements, the Philippines and Australia would wither away. France and Holland, under Hitler's heel, could not bolster their tottering Asiatic empires. Britain carried the full load in western Europe, and her far-flung possessions were stirring restively.

In brief, Japan would have no need to hurry men and matériel to Southeast Asia. "The theater for the Southern Operation . . . would have fallen by itself if the Pacific Fleet had been completely destroyed," said Fuchida. This was his idea of a strategy that made sense. Now it seemed to him that Japan was preparing to fight the war in reverse.[16]

Despite the victory at Pearl Harbor and the exploits of the Eleventh Air Fleet's land-based planes in sinking the British men-of-war *Prince of Wales* and *Repulse* a few days later, the navy's high command still did not understand the revolution in warfare. Its strategy was illogical even by conventional standards. Instead of sending his battleships east to seek out and destroy the major foe, Yamamoto kept the main body of the Combined Fleet in the Inland Sea, an object of amusement to Fuchida's airmen, who joked about the "Hashirajima Fleet." These vessels were intact and fit for battle. But according to Fuchida, "They didn't do a damn thing in the early part of the war. This was a very serious mistake. The Japanese battleships were about as useless as the U.S. battleships." They were sitting around waiting for their American counterparts to be repaired and reconditioned. No amount of personal affection for Yamamoto could get around the stupidity of this strategy.

Fuchida had hoped that Yamamoto would join the main body of the intact First Air Fleet and sail first to Truk and then to the Marshalls, positioning themselves to engage the Americans. As time passed without a move in this direction, some of the airmen, Fuchida included, asked each other, "Who is Japan fighting, anyway?"[17]

Fuchida always believed that the Japanese navy made four major mistakes in rapid succession in the early days and weeks of the Pacific war: not finishing the job at Pearl Harbor; breaking up the First Air Fleet; hoarding battleships in home waters; dispatching the major carrier force south and west instead of eastward to seek out the Americans. "Had we gone after the U.S. Pacific Fleet at once after Pearl Harbor, the course of the war in the Pacific would have been vastly different," Fuchida lamented in retrospect. "Then there would have been no Battle of the Coral Sea, no Battle of Midway, no Guadalcanal, and the United States would have been in a hell of a fix."

As if to add insult to injury, Yamamoto moved his flag early in the year from the *Nagato* to the new superbattleship *Yamato,* pride and joy of the surface navy and a masterpiece of shipbuilding and armament. But where was this terror of the deep? Anchored in Hashirajima Bay in the Inland Sea along with a number of other battleships of the main body! The *Yamato* symbolized the frustration of Fuchida, who referred to her as a big hotel. He waxed sarcastic about her living quarters. "We in the air force never had such fine quarters and accommodations!"[18]

Indeed, the Japanese had produced, on paper, the most formidable battleship afloat, yet at her Inland Sea base and in her capacity as Yamamoto's flagship, the *Yamato* was scarcely more than a floating hotel and office building for the Combined Fleet staff. This frittering away of the *Yamato*'s immense potential typified Japan's failure to seize advantages. One can readily understand why Fuchida thought this was no way to fight a war.

Not surprisingly, the exhilaration and mystic sense of mission Fuchida had brought to the Pearl Harbor project were missing when early in January 1942 the Nagumo force sortied from Hiroshima Bay. At its heart sailed the *Akagi, Kaga, Shokaku,* and *Zuikaku.* The presence of the last two flattops betokened no change of mind in the Naval General Staff. Rear Admiral Chuichi "King Kong" Hara's Fifth Carrier Division was substituting temporarily for the *Soryu* and *Hiryu,* which required replenishing and whose crews needed rest following their Wake Island adventure. This time the task force was to cover assaults in the vast area over which Japan was spreading its net of conquest—Malaya, the Philippines, the Netherlands East Indies, New Guinea, and the large islands off its eastern shore.

On 22 January Fuchida led about ninety fighters and bombers in heavy strikes against Rabaul, the advanced Australian air base at the northern tip of New Britain Island. Rabaul had only a token garrison, and Fuchida felt like a hunter sent to stalk a mouse with an elephant gun. Hoping to find an enemy worthy of the name, he discovered neither targets nor opposition. And when his bombers could not return to their carriers with a heavy bombload, he had to order some of them to jettison their missiles over the jungle. He felt deflated. They had wasted a large investment in time, gas, and bombs, none of which Japan had to spare.[19]

Rabaul fell, as Genda put it, "with ridiculous ease." The use of four carriers for such a routine mission was so obviously redundant that he thought something must have gone wrong in high places.[20]

As soon as Fuchida's plane touched down on the *Akagi,* he sought out Nagumo. It was ridiculous to use all of these aircraft in such an operation, he informed the admiral. When he explained the situation at Rabaul Nagumo heartily agreed. The next day, after amphibious forces of Japan's Fourth Fleet landed, Nagumo sent word to Yamamoto that the task force had encountered no opposition. Yamamoto replied by ordering the carriers back to Palau, hundreds of miles westward.

In Fuchida's opinion, this action only exchanged one mistake for another. Palau, a small atoll at the end of the southwestern chain of the Marianas, was over three thousand miles from Oahu. Six weeks had elapsed since the Pearl Harbor attack, and Fuchida could not delude himself into thinking that the Americans were wasting time getting their ships back into action.[21]

The day after Fuchida's planes attacked Rabaul, aircraft from Yamaguchi's Second Carrier Division (*Soryu* and *Hiryu*) hit Ambon in the Netherlands East Indies.[22] At the same time, Japanese forces occupied Kendari on Celebes Island, rapidly putting it into commission as an air base.[23]

For the Nagumo force, the next major action came when Yamamoto ordered the carriers to join forces with Admiral Nobutake Kondo's two battleships and three heavy cruisers to sail to northern Australia and attack the coastal city of Darwin. The Combined Fleet had received a report that Allied ships had concentrated at Darwin and that reinforcements were arriving there. The raid, the top brass believed, would have a demoralizing effect on Australian morale.

Again Fuchida considered the mission nonsense, not Japan's main operation. Yamamoto and Nagumo, however, believed that the navy must cooperate with the army to take Southeast Asia while the taking was good and thus put Japan in the best possible strategic position. Dropping the Fifth Carrier Division, called back to Japan to protect against American task forces that might venture near the homeland, but picking up the Second Carrier Division, the Nagumo force proceeded to its target area.

The intelligence report about Darwin had made no mistake—the harbor was tailor-made for an air attack, jammed with an unusually heavy assortment of Allied shipping. Two Australian transports, a troop ship, a freighter, a corvette, and a hospital ship lay in harbor on 19 February, along with an American destroyer, aircraft tender, two transports, and a few other craft of various registry. Nevertheless, in Fuchida's opinion these were small fry, not targets worthy of the First Air Fleet.

He led his usual complement of approximately 180 planes, and by some freak of fortune they approached without the defenders' receiving any warning. A cloudless sky provided excellent visibility. The Japanese inflicted severe damage to the huddled shipping, destroying about a dozen vessels, then shot up the town so thoroughly that it had to be abandoned temporarily. Fuchida did not recall seeing more than five or six Australian aircraft on the ground and in the air. Allied records indicate, however, that a force of approximately ten American planes engaged his aircraft, and that his force destroyed eighteen Allied planes.[24]

Returning from this mission, Fuchida found Nagumo fired up to make a second strike against Darwin. Half amused, half irritated, Fuchida reflected that at Pearl Harbor when Nagumo should have launched an additional attack, he could not get away fast enough. Now at Darwin, with no earthly reason to strike another time, he champed at the bit. "It isn't necessary to repeat the attack," he informed the admiral. "There are no enemy forces. It isn't worth it."[25]

Again he stressed that Japan's naval air power greatly exceeded the needs of this region. "Don't swing such a long sword!" he said to Nagumo, half seriously, half in jest. This struck the fancy of the airmen and became a catchword among them. They derided the quality of the opposition encountered so far, laughed and joked about poor enemy resistance or no enemy at all.[26]

Nagumo was a happy man these early days of 1942. He swaggered as he walked on deck and his hat rested on his head at a jaunty angle. Relations between him and Fuchida were rather peculiar. Personally they got along. In fact, Nagumo loved Fuchida like a son, and Fuchida felt a sincere affection for the admiral. But professionally they generated a certain friction. Nagumo was out of his element as commander of an air fleet. As his flight commander, Fuchida had a duty to tell him the facts of life. Nagumo had Genda to school him in tactics, but Fuchida actually flew the missions and saw the situation firsthand. Nagumo didn't relish Fuchida's pointing out that their more recent victories amounted to no more than snatching a fan from a geisha.

To a degree, Yamaguchi egged Fuchida on. In the first place, the admiral agreed with Fuchida's views and wanted to encourage him. In the second, he lost no love on Nagumo and didn't mind helping to administer an occasional pinprick. Fuchida admired Yamaguchi and looked forward to seeing him command the Combined Fleet or head the Naval General Staff in the future. Although not a pilot himself, Yamaguchi's aggressive nature appealed to his airmen, who thought him tops.[27]

After Darwin, the Nagumo force returned to its anchorage in Staring Bay near Kendari on Celebes to prepare and train for the invasion of Java. On 3 March Fuchida led a group of 180 planes against Tjilatjap on the southern coast, heavily damaging Allied shipping.[28]

During the mission, Fuchida's plane, with Murata at the controls, caught some flak. Fuel began to spurt from a wing tank. Murata did his best to coax the damaged aircraft over Borneo and back to the nearest Japanese base. The peaks of a high mountain range loomed ahead. To lighten the plane, they jettisoned everything not essential. These measures were not enough; Murata had to crash-land in the Borneo jungle. The radio operator died instantly. Fuchida and Murata crawled away from the wreck battered but alive. Again Fuchida had evaded the clutches of death.

After burying their fallen crewman, the two fliers set out in search of civilization. They might have dropped out of time as well as out of the skies. The steaming jungle showed little sign of having changed since the age of the dinosaurs. If any settlements had ever existed here, jungle vegetation had long since obliterated them.

Fuchida and Murata tried to get their bearings. Knowing the sea to be fairly near, they set off toward the coast, where they would stand a good chance of rescue.[29] For three days they wandered through the jungle. At night they climbed trees and lashed themselves to sturdy limbs. There they tried to snatch a little sleep, out of reach of the prowling animals below. At length, weary, sweltering, maddened by insects, and nearly starved, they clambered up a hill. In the distance they saw the wreck of a Japanese aircraft. Hoping to find survivors and food, they hurried toward it, shouting a greeting. Only whistling, crackling sounds of the jungle answered. When they neared the aircraft, its number read 301. "Our own plane!" exclaimed Murata. They had walked in a circle for three miserable days and were right back where they started.[30]

This is the end, they thought. For a few minutes they sagged in discouragement. But soon they summoned up courage to leave the scene and start all over again. This time Fuchida surveyed the terrain with extreme caution. Some distance away lay a beautiful valley. "It looked like a primitive Garden of Eden," said Fuchida. Once again at a moment of crisis a voice sounded in his inner ear. This time it seemed to emanate from the valley: "Come!" And then from far off the men heard the roar of a waterfall. A waterfall meant a river, and rivers lead to the sea. Hope strengthened their legs. About six hours later they penetrated the valley to the banks of a fast-flowing stream.

They tied their valuables on top of their heads and tugged a large log into the water. On this they floated downstream, clutching its bark. Abruptly the night settled over them. The darkness came alive with the screams and chattering of strange animals and birds, with rustlings and splashings all the more ominous because the men could not see their source. Occasionally crocodiles investigated the log and its passengers, frightening them badly.

Eventually, the long night ended, and with it the jungle. They emerged at a point where the river joined the ocean. Close by stood a Chinese establishment of some sort, evidently a small trading post. Its proprietor allowed the two Japanese to charter a junk. After securing much-needed rest and food, they sailed back to Kendari.[31]

8

"Here Was Our Real Enemy"

F OLLOWING the Java campaign, the Nagumo force returned to Staring Bay for refueling and to incorporate the Fifth Carrier Division into the task force once more. The *Kaga* had scraped a reef, damaging her bottom, and had to return to Japan for repairs. The next major task for the remaining five flattops commenced when Yamamoto ordered the Nagumo force to support the upcoming invasion of Burma. The mission was twofold: to cut off British supplies to Burma, and to seek out and destroy all British fleet units operating in the Indian Ocean.[1]

The task force that sortied on 26 March 1942 headed for Ceylon looking like a reunion of Pearl Harbor veterans. Five of the original sextet of flattops were present, the battleships *Haruna* and *Kongo* were reinforcing the Pearl Harbor support ships—the battleships *Kirishima* and *Hiei,* the heavy cruisers *Tone* and *Chikuma,* and the light cruiser *Abukuma*—and nine destroyers prowled on the flanks.

The British had a strong force in the Indian Ocean—five battleships, three carriers, and a number of cruisers and destroyers.[2] A direct confrontation might well throw a monkey wrench into Japan's strategic machinery. The Japanese hoped to catch the British by surprise, but could not afford to underestimate British seamen. They were like junior diplomats about to negotiate with Elizabeth I in her old age—vigorous and optimistic, but wondering uneasily just how many aces the old girl had up her sleeve. She was still the Sea Queen, schooled in naval warfare, sharp as a cutlass, with "the heart and stomach of a king, and of a king of England, too!"[3]

Nagumo's luck held. On 4 April the task force spotted a British reconnaissance plane. Quickly they launched a few Zeros, which made short work of the intruder. The scout, however, had had time to radio a warning, so Nagumo did not catch enemy aircraft on the ground. For all practical purposes this made little difference. At 0800 on Easter Sunday, 5 April 1942, Fuchida's men struck Colombo, one of Britain's main naval and air bases. They hoped to find British fleet units there. Instead, the place was jammed with merchant ships.

The Zeros under Itaya's leadership disposed of virtually every RAF aircraft that challenged them. While the aerial fight raged, dive-bombers and horizontal bombers smashed the shore installations. In the harbor the Japanese hit only an armed merchant cruiser and a destroyer, because advance warning had permitted the other craft to work up steam and escape. And though victorious, Fuchida's men paid a price—a number of aircraft failed to return to their carriers.[4]

Following the raid, Fuchida flew back to the *Akagi* and reported to Nagumo. After sketching out the results, he advised that they begin searching for any British that had fled. Nagumo agreed, and reconnaissance planes were launched at once.

This search soon paid off. Around noon the planes discovered two British heavy cruisers, the *Dorsetshire* and *Cornwall,* headed for a rendezvous with Britain's Eastern Fleet.

As flight commander Fuchida directed the attack, but he left the actual leadership to Egusa from the *Soryu.* Fuchida remained aboard the *Akagi,* standing by with decks full of aircraft in case another strike on Colombo was called. He busied himself preparing torpedo planes for takeoff to help dive-bombers sink the heavy cruisers. It proved unnecessary to launch them. Egusa's bombardiers sank the *Dorsetshire* and *Cornwall* in what Fuchida estimated to be twenty minutes. "The surface vessels did not have a chance against our striking force. It was like turning a hand, it was so easy," Fuchida later remarked.[5]

When he reported to Nagumo on the sinking of the cruisers, the admiral swelled with pride. But the surface fleet commanders were discomfited, almost angry. They didn't like the naval air arm being so powerful.

This time the First Air Fleet's planes had sunk two men-of-war in motion, not trapped and immobile like the ships in Pearl Harbor. The advocates of heavy surface ship supremacy had no alibi left. "Sea power had changed and a new era had begun," said Fuchida. "This was the victory of naval air power."[6]

Nagumo next swung his ships around the southern end of Ceylon and headed northward to strike Trincomalee, Britain's second principal base on the island. Again an enemy reconnaissance plane warned the defenders of the Japanese approach. Most of the ships had already sortied when by 0725 on 9 April Fuchida led his team of about one hundred aircraft into action.

Eleven Hurricane fighters bravely rose to meet the attack; nine paid the penalty. While the dive-bombers concentrated on demolishing parked aircraft, the high-level bombers buried their missiles in shore installations. Buildings exploded in geysers of flame and smoke. The planes also sank one merchant ship.

Fuchida decided to leave the remaining vessels to Egusa's second-wave dive-bombers. Radioing his decision to the *Akagi,* he shepherded the first wave back to the carriers. Not all who had winged in would follow him; about twenty had been shot down. On the way back, he intercepted a report from one of the First Air Fleet's scout planes that an enemy carrier was heading south with its escort destroyer. As the first wave no longer had the firepower to tackle a flattop, Fuchida and his men sped back to their mother ships.[7]

By the time Fuchida touched down, the Japanese had identified the British ships as the old carrier *Hermes* and her escort destroyer *Vampire.* This duo being a much more important target than the stray vessels in Trincomalee Harbor, Egusa was already spearheading his second wave toward the *Hermes.* Maintenance crews hastened to refuel and rearm Fuchida's first-wave planes, fitting the level bombers with torpedoes in case they had to go to Egusa's aid.

While this was going on, nine British Blenheim bombers attacked the *Akagi.* They inflicted no damage. Between the Zeros' cover and the carrier's antiaircraft fire, the *Akagi* destroyed five of the Blenheims and damaged the rest. Leaving his bombers aboard the carrier, Fuchida led a group of Itaya's fighters in pursuit of Egusa, in case he required assistance against the *Hermes*'s interceptors. But Egusa did not need help. He had about eighty dive-bombers, nearly all of which had direct hits on the *Hermes.*

When Fuchida arrived the carrier was already sinking, lost within fifteen or twenty minutes of the first bomb. He noticed Lieutenant Shokei Yamada, who led the *Akagi*'s dive-bombers, gesticulating urgently, so Fuchida flew alongside his plane. Yamada pointed at his nose, then downward, and smiled. Fuchida followed the finger, and there below him the *Vampire* trembled in her death throes. Then Fuchida understood: Yamada had set his heart on bombing the carrier, and rather than waste his bomb had dropped it on the destroyer instead.

When Fuchida saw how easily his airmen had sunk a British carrier and destroyer, again he reflected to himself, We are using too much power on secondary missions. The First Air Fleet should be in the Pacific, fighting the number-one enemy. While his radioman took official pictures, Fuchida observed the action. How powerful is the Imperial Navy! he exclaimed inwardly as he watched *Hermes* sink under the hail of bombs. He who controls the air controls the sea—and the world. Conventional navy vessels do not have a chance against air power. It is sad to see them sink so helplessly.[8]

Something like nostalgia seized Fuchida. This is the end of the British Empire and British sea power, he mused. What a pity—an era of world history lay dying before his eyes. Japan's first great naval vessels had been built in British shipyards; its first instructors hailed from Britain; the very bricks of the naval academy at Eta Jima were baked in British kilns. The British were not popular in Asia, but no one could deny they were expert seamen and brave fighters. How strange that Fuchida, a navy man who loved the sea, had helped write this sad chapter in the saga of British sea power.[9]

The Indian Ocean campaign over, Kondo and Nagumo turned prows eastward en route to Japan for refurbishing and refueling. Fuchida was glad to leave the area where the Nagumo force had been wasting its time.[10]

The First Air Fleet's support of the Southern Operation had cost Japan more than squandered days and weeks. Every raid took its toll of planes and fliers. Airmen for Nagumo's fleet were virtually handpicked, being either combat veterans or the cream of the young crop. When one of these precision instruments crashed, it left a gap in Japan's shortest of all short supplies— skilled manpower.

Moreover, as it worked out, time, fuel, and personnel losses were just enough that a full carrier complement would not be available for the Battle of the Coral Sea—only the *Shokaku* and *Zuikaku*. And because of their participation in that battle, the *Shokaku* would suffer severe damage and the *Zuikaku* would have to be restocked and remanned. They would miss the Battle of Midway. Though unquestionably the Nagumo force had scored tactical victories, they were links in a chain reaction of disaster.

No such thoughts troubled Fuchida's aircrews as the carriers steamed toward Japan. Confident that they could beat all comers anywhere at any time, they swaggered about singing and wisecracking. These young men had not only fulfilled their assigned missions brilliantly, they were going home to bask briefly in their families' love and to sip the heady brew of public acclaim. As intoxicated with success as the greenest airman, Nagumo beamed on them all with paternal gratification.[11]

Who shall say he did not have just cause? Beginning with Pearl Harbor, he had racked up an awesome score, while enemy action had not sunk or even damaged a single ship under his command. With the hopes of Japan nailed to his masthead, he had written in fire a record few sea captains ever compile in a lifetime.

En route to Japan, the First Air Fleet stopped at Singapore. Just a few months before the city had been proclaimed Great Britain's outpost of the empire, the Gibraltar of the Orient. Yet the Japanese had plucked this plum with comparative ease.

During his stay, Fuchida paid his respects to Vice Admiral Jisaburo Ozawa, in command of Japan's naval forces in that area. As his only flattop strength consisted of the lightweight Fourth Carrier Division (the *Shoho* and *Ryujo*), Ozawa was glad to see the First Air Fleet. Fuchida hastened to reassure him. "You needn't worry," he said. "Your Fourth Carrier Division is strong enough to take care of the Indian Ocean now."

Sure of a sympathetic ear, for Ozawa was a longtime friend as well as a solid proponent of air power, Fuchida spoke of his displeasure with Japan's naval strategy. "What's the difference," he asked, "between the U.S. battleship force destroyed or damaged in Pearl Harbor and the Japanese battleship force anchored in the Inland Sea doing nothing? It looks as though we want the U.S. Pacific Fleet built up again before we go out to strike it. We're wasting time. We must go east as soon as possible and attack the main enemy."

But Ozawa refused to be drawn. Like most of Japan's top naval brass, he thought largely in terms of the Southern Operation.[12]

Once more homeward bound, the First Air Fleet received orders detaching the Fifth Carrier Division, which was to sail to Truk in anticipation of the struggle for Port Moresby. This developed into the Battle of the Coral Sea.[13]

The rest of Nagumo's carriers proceeded as scheduled. As they plunged through the China Sea, Fuchida continued to fret that the United States was growing stronger every minute Japan frittered away. To his relief, on the cruise back to Japan the brass finally began to consider future operations against the U.S. Navy.

He wholeheartedly supported a plan called the *Bei Go Shadan Sakusen*—the United States–Australia Cut-Off Operation. The strategy, which originated in the Naval General Staff, called for a campaign in the Fiji area to isolate Australia from the United States. This accomplished, the Japanese navy would keep moving eastward and eventually occupy Hawaii. Originally, Yamamoto was receptive to this idea, but two events settled his future strategy and ruled out the operation—the Doolittle Raid against Japan, and the Battle of the Coral Sea.[14]

The uninterrupted chant of Japanese victory struck a sour note on 18 April 1942. Early that morning, a picket boat on patrol duty sighted Vice Admiral William F. Halsey's task force moving toward Japan. Nagumo's force received the news approximately midway between Formosa and the Philippines. An order came through from the Combined Fleet to chase an

American force consisting of a carrier, a cruiser, and some destroyers located about eight hundred miles off Japan.

Nagumo and Fuchida blazed with anticipation. "Here was our real enemy, the U.S. Navy," reflected Fuchida, "especially carriers—the warships we wanted to destroy the most." Of course, Japanese planners had antici- pated that the Americans would try to bomb the homeland, but they es- timated that a carrier must come within a three hundred-mile circle of the target before launching. Otherwise the attackers would be too far offshore to recover their planes. Therefore Nagumo and his airmen were sure that they had at least a full day's grace. With any kind of luck, they might intercept the American task force in time either to prevent the raid or to exact revenge for it.

The *Akagi, Soryu,* and *Hiryu* sped toward the estimated American course at 24 knots. Then reports came in from Tokyo that American B-25 bombers had attacked the home islands. Where had these land-based bombers come from? Fuchida wondered. He knew of no base remaining in American hands nearer than Midway, and that was too far away. The B-25s could not have been launched from a carrier. A raid by naval aircraft must still be in the making. So the Nagumo force continued to pour on the oil.[15]

Genda was not aboard the *Akagi* to participate in the excitement and discussions, for he had temporarily parted company with the First Air Fleet at Singapore. He flew back to Japan, landing at Iwakuni that very day, 18 April. But it is doubtful if he could have added anything constructive. Even he, with his far-ranging mind, had never hit upon the idea of launching army bombers from a carrier. Nor had anyone else in the Japanese navy.[16]

But that was precisely what the Americans had done. Thanks to the tactic, the *Hornet* only had to come within 700 miles of Japan, well out of range of Japanese land-based fighters. It also threw the air-raid defense off schedule, because the defenders expected the American planes to appear on the nineteenth.

There were some Japanese fighters patrolling at about 10,000 feet. But Lieutenant Colonel James H. "Jimmy" Doolittle's sixteen B-25s flew in at roughly 150 feet, right under the fighters. They bombed Tokyo, Yokosuka, Nagoya, and other locations, causing relatively little damage. In Tokyo they also strafed, accidentally machine-gunning two grammar-school students. Their deaths formed the core of the prosecution of the captured members of Doolittle's raiding party.

The following day, Japanese headquarters at Shanghai informed Tokyo that two U.S. bombers had crashed not far from Hankow. Then Japanese airmen realized that the raid was a true one-way attack. Army bombers could take off from a carrier deck, but there was no way they could land on one.

Obviously Nagumo would not be able to run down a task force already steaming far to the east. Yamamoto ordered Nagumo to abandon the chase and proceed to Hashirajima. By this time the First Air Fleet had almost reached Yokosuka, so Nagumo turned it around and sailed for the Inland Sea, minus the *Akagi*, which went on to Kure.

Fuchida and his fliers admired the valor of the Doolittle pilots. Previously they had not credited the Americans with having so much courage.[17] The raid also fascinated Fuchida. He felt an affinity with those Americans who, like his own Pearl Harbor team, had not hesitated to fly into the tiger's den. Through the war and after it, he made a special study of the operation.

He had more regard for the brave men who had bombed Japan than for the Japanese army responsible for defending it. He had little use for or faith in the army. In this instance, army spokesmen announced that the raid had done no damage and that army fighters had shot down nine of the attacking planes. Fuchida knew quite well that not a single B-25 had been brought down over Japan.

Later he learned that the wrecks of two B-25s that crashed in China had been hauled to Tokyo and piled in front of the Yasukuni Shrine as evidence that the army had indeed bagged enemy bombers as claimed. To thus use the most sacred shrine of Japan's honored dead shocked Fuchida to the core. He was ashamed that the army would so mislead the Japanese people.

The armed forces hushed up the Doolittle incident. For many in Japan the raid caused only a ripple of interest. But the whole truth could not be hidden. In Tokyo especially it came as a great surprise to citizens who until then had heard about nothing but one Japanese victory after another. Nor had the general public been alerted to expect hit-and-run raids, which the armed forces always believed might occur. Some were a bit disillusioned with the navy for letting Americans sail so close to the sacred shores. Little wonder that Yamamoto received a few nasty letters with his usual laudatory fan mail.[18]

"The Doolittle Raid hurt Yamamoto's pride," reminisced Fuchida. "He loved the emperor . . . and wanted to insure his safety in Tokyo. So he determined there must never be another Doolittle Raid on Tokyo again."

Between wounded vanity and anxiety over the emperor's safety, Yamamoto lost his judgment. He hastened to initiate the strategy that led to the Japanese disaster at Midway.

As mentioned, work had recently started on a strategy to sever all communications between the United States and Australia, blocking General Douglas MacArthur's supply of men and matériel so that eventually he would wither on the vine. Under those circumstances, the Americans would not be able to move up from Australia into New Guinea and then to the Philippines. The plan called for Nagumo's airmen to attack Allied air bases near Canberra, to bomb Sydney Harbor and all the naval vessels therein, indeed to hit every worthy target available in eastern Australia. Then they would turn eastward and occupy Fiji, Samoa, and eventually Hawaii. Fuchida believed this concept to be the sensible, logical move and had every confidence in its success. Along with the rest of Nagumo's staff, he was eager to get the plan under way. The American attack, Fuchida felt, caused Yamamoto to recoil from it. "Had the raid not taken place, the Japanese navy would have moved south to Fiji," Fuchida lamented in later years.[19]

Genda did not go that far. He had heard about the Midway plan on 19 April, the day after the raid, in the Combined Fleet's staff room aboard the *Yamato.* Obviously, the strategy had been under study for some time. But he agreed with Fuchida that the raid worried Yamamoto no end. In his opinion, the admiral made his big mistake updating the Midway schedule, rushing it through before the First Air Fleet had had sufficient time to prepare for such a massive operation.[20]

Yamamoto decided upon the plan to occupy Midway and the Aleutians because he was obsessed with protecting the homeland, above all the emperor. He was determined to form a protective shield around Japan so far north and so far east that never again could the United States attack the main Japanese islands.

Fuchida was devoted to Yamamoto; still, facts were facts, and when he heard of the admiral's latest scheme he labeled it grammar-school strategy. This was defensive psychology, to keep the United States from striking Japan instead of carrying the war into the American camp. To occupy Midway would decide nothing as long as the United States held Hawaii. Fuchida understood that Yamamoto and his backers hoped the attack on Midway would force the U.S. Fleet to come out and fight, hence give the Japanese the chance to destroy it. But this was secondary to the occupation of Midway.

The strategy had an important flaw: it revolved around a limited objective—the protection of the emperor and the imperial family. "This is nonsense!" said Fuchida irritably to Genda. "Of course Tokyo will be bombed again. If necessary, the emperor should be moved to Kyoto or Nara." Either of those historic cities would be less accessible to enemy bombers than huge, sprawling Tokyo, with its readily visible imperial compound.[21]

At the time of the Doolittle Raid, many Americans criticized it severely as at best premature, at worst a criminal waste of brave men and much-needed planes in an empty gesture of bravado. It is doubtful if Doolittle himself ever expected any such far-reaching consequences as his brief bombing expedition triggered. His raiders had accomplished what the whole Japanese naval hierarchy could not: They had made Isoroku Yamamoto lose his cool and plunge precipitously into an ill-considered course of action.

9

"Go to Midway and
Fight"

As soon as the First Air Fleet returned to Japan on 22 April, Yamamoto ordered Nagumo and key members of his staff to report to the *Yamato*. There for the first time they heard about the Midway scheme. The plan aimed first to occupy Midway, and second, in doing so, to lure the remaining ships of the U.S. Pacific Fleet beyond the atoll where Japanese forces could destroy them. The First Air Fleet would cover the landing and act as the advance escort for Yamamoto's main body. The latter, an assemblage of battleships, cruisers, light carriers, and destroyers, would stay 300 miles in the rear, then at the strategic moment thunder forth to annihilate whatever American ships escaped the Nagumo force. Meanwhile, another major aggregation of ships would attack American forces in the Aleutians.

The high brass assigned Nagumo an important mission but allowed him no hand in the planning. Most of his staff disapproved. As spokesman, Kusaka tried to explain that the task force could not yet undertake another major campaign. The ships required overhaul, and the crews needed rest after being on the go for so long. He wanted time to train new air crews before starting out again.[1]

Genda did not oppose the plan as such. He could see its possibilities, if carried out properly. Here was the long-awaited chance to force a decisive battle with the American main force. But he, too, strongly urged postponement. Upon return from the Indian Ocean, many veteran pilots had been whisked away to land bases. Lacking them, Genda at the very least would need time to train their replacements. He also recommended that the Aleutian portion of the plan be scrapped, since it split the Combined Fleet's strength.[2]

On behalf of his Second Carrier Division, Yamaguchi strongly supported Genda's position. When overruled, he became one of the Midway plan's most ardent advocates.[3]

Fuchida vigorously opposed the idea. His exhausted men needed rest, and the ships and planes needed overhaul. Midway would be useless for the Japanese, not worth fighting for. Even if they could occupy the base, they wouldn't be able to maintain it. As for luring out the U.S. Pacific Fleet, that had been Fuchida's primary idea ever since Pearl Harbor, but the United States–Australia Cut-Off Operation would accomplish that purpose and still give the First Air Fleet time to prepare men and matériel for a major battle.

In short order Combined Fleet headquarters made it clear that they had already settled on the plan and expected the carrier men to agree, not argue. The memory left Fuchida torn between anger and bitter laughter: "It was like this: 'This is your duty. Go to Midway and fight.' There was no real planning, preparation, or thinking—all nonsense!"

Fuchida made one forlorn attempt to reach Yamamoto through an air staff officer, Commander Akira Sasaki. When he boarded the *Yamato*, he discovered that Sasaki backed Yamamoto's Midway scheme to the letter, which was not surprising. Once Yamamoto made up his mind, his fiercely loyal staff stuck to him like barnacles.

"We'll occupy Midway and thus force the U.S. Pacific Fleet out in the open," Sasaki told him. "After Midway we'll occupy Hawaii."

"Forget about Midway," Fuchida urged. "The base is no good, and this is all a waste of time. We should move at once against the Fijis and Samoa, then Pearl Harbor. The U.S. Fleet will come out anyway to keep Australia from being isolated. When it does, we can destroy it."

Fuchida had the feeling that Sasaki, a career naval aviator, was more or less of the same mind but could not openly disagree with Yamamoto. So instead he went and talked to Kuroshima.[4]

Fuchida was no admirer of Captain Kameto Kuroshima, Yamamoto's senior staff officer. He considered Kuroshima to blame for the insistence upon maintaining supremacy of the Southern Operation in the face of the unexpected success at Pearl Harbor. Now he hunted up Kuroshima in the latter's messy cabin. The Japanese navy was never quite as devoted to spit and polish as its American counterpart, but Kuroshima carried indifference to majestic heights. Papers all over the place, Fuchida had to pick his way through an obstacle course of dirty dishes and sticky glasses full of cigarette butts.[5]

A lean, bald, taut-faced man usually enveloped in cigarette smoke, Kuroshima had a sharp and introspective mind, but he didn't understand air power. "He was a gunnery officer," said Fuchida, "and he wanted to fight the Battle of the Japan Sea* at Midway." So Fuchida didn't waste his breath talking to him about the First Air Fleet's assigned duties; he confined his arguments to the proposed use of Yamamoto's main body.

"If the battleships are to stay three hundred miles behind the carriers, what good are they?" Fuchida asked. "Why bother to sortie at all if you're coming out only to watch? Who do you intend to fight? Who is your enemy?" he prodded.

Kuroshima only shrugged his thin shoulders and replied, "No enemy," quite confident that the Pacific Fleet didn't amount to much.[6]

All the logistical arguments the First Air Fleet staff could muster bounced off the Combined Fleet staff like buckshot off the *Yamato*. But not one of Nagumo's officers opposed Midway because they thought it might be too risky or that they might lose the battle. It never occurred to any of them that the First Air Fleet couldn't handle the entire mission by itself. "This smug confidence," recalled Fuchida, "was the beginning of the Japanese defeat at Midway."[7]

On 28 and 29 April at a big conference aboard the *Yamato*, representatives of the Naval General Staff, the Combined Fleet, and the First Air Fleet reviewed the exploits of the Nagumo force and discussed the lessons learned. As principal speaker, Genda explained operations up to that time. The brass-heavy audience bubbled with praise. This was more pleasant than helpful. What ideas for improvement came up originated with the carrier men. Yamaguchi suggested that the Combined Fleet be reorganized into three task forces, two for immediate use, a third to be ready at the end of the year.[8]

Fuchida urged that the First Fleet, as the main body was often called, and the First Air Fleet be combined into one superforce under Yamamoto's personal command, with six carriers at the center and all the vessels of the First Fleet as support. "If the two fleets fight as one unit they will be practically invincible. But this can't be if the *Yamato* and the rest of the main body trail 300 miles behind the First Air Fleet."[9]

Fuchida was quite naive to think that Yamamoto, with such staff officers as Ugaki and Kuroshima, not to mention a solid backlog of battleship admirals, would adopt his idea. In effect this combination would be a super task force and would reduce all the Main Body's battleships, including the mighty *Yamato*, to the level of escort vessels. The thought patterns of generations are not so easily set aside.

Next Fuchida brought up the matter closest to his heart, a plan which

---

*I.e., Tsushima, where the Japanese defeated the Russian fleet in 1905.

he called the flight concept. It was high time that the Japanese navy ceased thinking of pilots as belonging to individual carriers; crews should be assigned to a flight and used on any flattop, depending on need. The best trained pilots from all the carriers should belong to one flight, which would battle the enemy at sea. Back in the homeland, new pilots would be trained not only in operational techniques but also to think in terms of the flight. These men would constitute the second team, ready to go to sea and fight when necessary.

This was a revolutionary idea. Throughout naval history, the ship had been the basic unit to which men were assigned. Their captain led them into battle. Fuchida didn't see how this made sense applied to a carrier. Skippers of flattops were not combat leaders. "They were only hotel managers," said Fuchida. Each aircraft should be free to operate as part of a mobile flight. Fliers shouldn't consider themselves *Akagi* men or *Hiryu* men. They should be able to function anywhere without getting tangled in red tape or hampered by false sentimentality.

Yamaguchi and Genda supported Fuchida's proposal. Kusaka agreed that it had possibilities; however, he wanted to give higher authority plenty of time to think it over. "This is too big a problem for a quick decision," he said. "We'll have to wait." The postponement disappointed Fuchida, for he had hoped his plan would be adopted in time for Midway.[10]

A few days after this conference, Fuchida's stomach began to bother him and he went on sick call. As Kagoshima had no navy hospital, the base doctor sent him to the nearest army hospital for X-rays. There he remained for about two weeks under observation. Finally the doctors told him that he had a stomach ulcer and ordered him to give up drinking. He did so, with great reluctance.[11]

During his stay in the hospital, the Battle of the Coral Sea was fought on 7–8 May. General Headquarters announced it as a major Japanese victory, and the press outdid itself with flowery articles of praise and exultation. But Fuchida and other knowledgeable airmen couldn't rejoice. True, the Japanese had sunk the U.S. carrier *Lexington* and mauled the *Yorktown*, but the Americans had sunk the light carrier *Shoho* and damaged the *Shokaku*. In addition, the Fifth Carrier Division's plane losses were heavy.

Tactically, Japan scored higher in carrier action. Nevertheless, it is a peculiar sort of victory to lose twice as many men as the enemy and not to achieve one's strategic objective. When Fuchida returned to duty and talked over the battle with Genda, they had to admit that the Japanese suffered a strategic defeat at Coral Sea. Moreover, it meant that before the Midway operation even started, two of Japan's best carriers—the *Shokaku* and

Zuikaku—would have to be scratched. They couldn't be repaired and refitted in time to participate.[12]

The obvious course would have been to postpone the operation, at least until the *Zuikaku* was ready to participate. Yet the loss did not cause the Combined Fleet to take a second look at the Midway scheme. In almost every way, planning and preparation for this battle fell below the standards set for Operation Hawaii. Security especially suffered in contrast. Genda discovered that even forces not scheduled to take part knew about the plan.[13] One day in a conversation with several other officers aboard the *Akagi*, Takehiko Chihaya remarked that in Kure such men as "barbers and masters of small drinking places have known that we are going to head for Midway this time."[14]

A particular source of annoyance to Fuchida was Kusaka's absence. Instead of being available to work on the coming campaign, he was trying to obtain double promotions for the fifty-five officers and men of the naval air force who had been killed at Pearl Harbor. Such double promotions had been immediately awarded to the nine midget submariners who had died in that attack.[15] On 36 March 1942 Tokyo had announced "the heroic achievements of the Special Attack Flotilla." The navy's publicity spokesman, Captain Hideo Hiraide, never at a loss for words, eulogized the nine heroes as the "guardian gods of Japan" in a radio address more remarkable for eloquence and imagination than for accuracy. He went so far as to credit a midget submarine with sinking the *Arizona*.[16]

Having seen that battleship blow up practically under his nose, Fuchida knew better. Like many men of the First Air Fleet, he resented the fact that the navy seemed to have forgotten the fifty-five airmen, equally brave and equally dead, who with their comrades accounted for all the damage at Pearl Harbor. Still, he was not one to linger in the past. "Let the midget sub men have credit for the *Arizona* if it will keep the peace," he said. The First Air Fleet had a new campaign on its hands and needed its chief of staff.[17]

The air fleet sortied from the Inland Sea on the morning of 27 May, Japan's Navy Day. As the fleet was passing through Bungo Channel, Fuchida doubled up in excruciating pain. He called out to his orderly to get the flight surgeon at once. At first, the *Akagi*'s surgeon, Dr. Tamai, thought like the army doctors that Fuchida's stomach was protesting against too much alcohol. But when Fuchida's pain intensified, there could be no question of the diagnosis—appendicitis. "You must have immediate surgery," he said.[18]

He broke the news to Fuchida's superiors. Nagumo, Kusaka, and Genda hurried to his cabin and held an impromptu consultation around his bunk. They wanted to send him by destroyer to the naval hospital at Beppu, a few hours' voyage from the carrier. But Fuchida put his foot down. The *Akagi* served as the task force's floating surgery, and her medical complement was perfectly capable of handling an appendectomy. Besides, even if he couldn't actively participate in the forthcoming battle, at least he would be available for consultation if needed and in place for the post-battle plan. Nagumo agreed to let him stay. He wasn't sorry to keep his veteran flight leader on tap, and his good sailor's heart told him how much being present meant to Fuchida.

They discussed what type of anesthesia would be best. Dr. Tamai preferred a general anesthetic, but Fuchida held out for a local in order not to lose hours of consciousness and to encourage a quick recovery. He couldn't avoid missing the Midway action, but he had no intention of missing the next campaign. With a local, he would be back in harness in two weeks.[19]

Dr. Tamai operated at about 2200 on 27 May. For the next two days he permitted Fuchida neither food nor drink. For a hearty trencherman this enforced diet was an ordeal, but hunger and postoperative aches were not nearly so painful as being cheated out of the forthcoming battle. He cursed his luck.

Understanding friends visited him daily, briefing him on the course of events. From their conversation he had a good idea of what was happening during the voyage eastward. After a few days, Genda joined the group of patients in sick bay. Weakened by work over a long period, he came down with a feverish cold that threatened to develop into pneumonia.

On the morning of 4 June Japanese time (3 June local), the surgeon removed Fuchida's stitches. That evening he walked to the head and back, feeling wobbly. Thankfully he sank back into bed. He knew it was no use trying to rush nature's work. At any rate, he had won his battle to stay aboard the *Akagi*. How could he know that this would be his last night aboard that grand carrier he loved so much?[20]

10

"A Hell of a Time"

ARLY THE NEXT MORNING Fuchida awoke to the sound of aircraft engines. Sick bay lay well below the waterline, so he could see nothing, but he knew that topside his men were preparing for takeoff. He looked around the curtained-off corner of sick bay, which he shared with two junior officers—the first a nisei who had cast his lot with Japan and served as an interpreter, the second an assistant paymaster. Both young men appeared to be sleeping. Well, that was all right. Neither of them would be participating in the day's action. But what about Mitsuo Fuchida?[1]

"The chief flight commanding officer got sick and couldn't participate in the big battle: So I was ashamed." He knew then that he couldn't remain in bed lapped in comfort and self-pity. His place was with his men. "Even if I couldn't fly with them, I could encourage them by waving my hand as they took off. That was the least I could do."[2]

Dr. Tamai had not given Fuchida permission to leave sick bay, but what the surgeon didn't know wouldn't hurt him. Tentatively, Fuchida slid out of bed. He would have to reach his cabin and change into uniform before presenting himself on deck. He wobbled across the room and tried the door. As he suspected, crewmen had fastened the doors and portholes for watertight integrity. Each door, however, contained a manhole for use in emergency. A large crank opened it.

Fuchida gripped the crank and applied all his strength. Slowly it began to turn. Cold sweat poured down his face. Finally the cover opened just enough to let him through. Then he had to do the whole business over again in reverse to maintain watertight security.

The gangway Fuchida thus entered was also sealed off. By climbing a small ladder, he reached another manhole leading up to the cabin area. This one proved much more difficult to open. The ladder provided but a slim foothold and Fuchida had used up much strength already. Then, too, being in such a hurry for fear his men would take off before he reached the flight deck made him clumsy. When he finally crawled through, his muscles were quivering. But the struggle had only begun, for he had to open and close a total of ten manholes to reach his cabin. Several times he almost fainted.[3]

Exhausted and drenched with sweat, he had to rest in his cabin until his legs would support him again. Then he washed, shaved, and put on his uniform, feeling much better. Then he proceeded to the flight deck. Most of his comrades were too busy to pay more than passing attention to him. Commander Shogo Masuda, the *Akagi*'s air officer, threw him an anxious "Are you all right?" and Fuchida smiled in answer.

In the command post, he joined the flight officers gathered to await takeoff and buttonholed Furukawa, torpedo squadron commander at Midway.[4] Furukawa was so handsome that Teiichi Makajima, a news photographer assigned to the *Akagi* to cover the battle, mentally tagged him Sanae Takasugi, the name of a noted movie actress. To sort out the officers aboard the carrier, Makajima gave a number of key personnel unspoken nicknames for his own use. Fuchida was "Hitler."[5]

"Have our reconnaissance planes already left the *Tone* and *Chikuma*?" Fuchida asked Furukawa.

"Not yet. They'll take off at the same time as the launching of the first attack wave."

Furukawa briefed him on the search pattern. Something about it made Fuchida uneasy. The search wasn't complete. Gaps much too large for security existed between each segment of the search arc.[6]

But there was nothing Fuchida could do about it, and realizing that he was underfoot at the command post, he climbed down to the flight deck. There, weary from his efforts, he lay down. One of his comrades, seeing him thus sprawled out, brought a parachute, which Fuchida tucked behind his head. Then he fished some paper and a pencil out of his pocket and prepared to take notes.

He was in a perfect position to do so. All the other officers had duties that absorbed them; Fuchida could survey the scene without distraction. From his vantage point just below the command post, he could hear the shouts from above, watch the planes overhead, see the action on the flight deck. He had a good view of the bridge and could catch snatches of conversation going on there. He was pleased to hear Genda's crisp accents.

These two men whose careers had followed such parallel paths reacted identically in this urgent hour. No more than Fuchida could Genda remain in sick bay when important duties awaited him.[7]

"Start engines!" Masuda ordered. With a flurry of excitement and a deafening roar, the first wave of fighters and bombers thundered off the *Akagi* to attack Midway. Replacing Fuchida in overall command was Lieutenant Joichi Tomonaga, head of the *Hiryu*'s air unit.

Of the exceedingly complicated battle action that ensued, Fuchida had direct knowledge only of what took place aboard and near the *Akagi*. But that was quite enough to fill his eyes, ears, and notebook. During the early morning, several types of American land-based aircraft found the Nagumo force. They inflicted little damage, although their bombing disrupted fleet formation and their strafing killed a number of crewmen aboard the carriers. The speedy Zeros, backed by antiaircraft fire, shot them down like clay pigeons. Unquestionably these American airmen had courage. They flew right into that murderous fire. But their planes were obsolete, their bombing and torpedoing techniques were not too good, and they had no fighter cover.

One B-26 missed the *Akagi*'s bridge by about ten meters, sped on toward the *Hiryu*, then plunged into the sea. Many of those watching jumped for joy. "This is fun!" exclaimed Fuchida. But Murata, waiting to lead his torpedo bombers in a second wave, took no part in the jubilation. He usually met any situation with a joke; this time he stood silently watching the death of a brave enemy.

Makajima noted that Fuchida's face was pale, and asked, "Are you all right, *Sotaicho* [overall commander]?"

"I'm all right," he replied. "Anyway, I can't be in bed under such circumstances as this."[8]

Meanwhile, Japanese reconnaissance planes reached their outward search limit without sighting an enemy ship. According to Japanese estimates, the Pacific Fleet would not know of the Nagumo force's presence until the capture of Midway drew American ships out. Just in case, Nagumo retained a good force of bombers armed with torpedoes.

Although Tomonaga's attack on Midway had inflicted considerable damage, both in the air and on the ground, it had by no means put the base out of operation or destroyed its defenses. Dissatisfied with these results, Tomonaga radioed his recommendation for a second attack. Nagumo decided to comply. this meant that second-wave planes loaded with torpedoes for attacking ships had to be rearmed with bombs for use against ground targets. The maintenance men hurried with this work, because Nagumo wanted to send Murata and the rest off to Midway in time to catch the American land-based planes when they touched down on the runways.

About halfway through the changeover, a scout plane reported ten American surface ships. After a quick plotting of their position, Nagumo hastily belayed the order to exchange torpedoes for bombs. If the American force contained no carrier, his aircraft could hit Midway again and take care of these ships, too.

While all this was going on, Midway-based planes attacked two more times. But like the other strikes, they inflicted little damage. They only reinforced the smug belief of the First Air Fleet's men that the enemy bombardiers were poor marksmen and that in all probability the Americans had no carriers in the area. If one lurked nearby, why had it not sent fighters to cover the bombers?

The scout's follow-up report about a carrier accompanying the U.S. surface force reached the *Akagi* about the same time Tomonaga's first wave appeared for landing. To save those fliers from ditching, Nagumo, on the advice of both Kusaka and Genda, decided not to launch an attack on the American carrier until after recovering the first-wave planes. This involved clearing the decks and reequipping with torpedoes the aircraft already loaded with land bombs.[9]

Chihaya—"Beethoven" to Makajima—wore a scowl as he strode across the flight deck with his fellow dive-bomber commander, Lieutenant Shohei Yamada. Both men were furious because the First Air Fleet's antiaircraft had at first mistaken Tomonaga's incoming flight for more Americans and shot at them. Avid for details of the action at Midway, Fuchida asked them if enemy fighters had come out.

"About ten minutes before we reached the island, Grummans came out to give us a hell of a time," Yamada replied. Asked about antiaircraft fire on the island, he added that this was "fiercer than expected."[10]

Meanwhile, maintenance men below decks unloaded big 800-kilogram bombs. In their haste, they piled them near the hangar instead of returning them to the magazines.

Just as the last first-wave plane touched down, another attack group roared overhead—the first American carrier-based planes the Nagumo force had seen that day. So the report of an enemy carrier proved correct.

Unescorted by fighters and using primitive tactics, the torpedo bombers pressed their attacks bravely but had no more success than the aircraft from Midway. Bomber after bomber spun, wobbled, and dropped into the sea. One of them seemed bent on crashing into the *Akagi*'s bridge, but it, too, missed its mark to fall into the sea.[11]

Throughout the torpedo attack, preparations continued for launching the *Akagi*'s second wave. The first Zero took wing. At that moment, Fuchida saw the approach of American Helldivers. He yelled a warning to the command post, and the *Akagi*'s machine guns and antiaircraft barked into fire. The first bombardier appeared off target; Fuchida figured that he would miss. Sure enough, he came into his glide too far out and his bomb hit about ten meters from the carrier on the starboard side, sending a huge geyser of dark gray water high in the air. Some of it poured down on the *Akagi*, dousing the bridge and blackening the faces of everyone there.[12]

Close on the tail of the first Helldiver came a second. The thought flashed across Fuchida's mind: This one will adjust on the leader and will be much nearer the target. As if in answer, the American swooped in and released his bomb. It struck close to the elevator amidships, twisting it grotesquely and dropping it into the hangar. Bright yellow light blazed into Makajima's face and the blast smashed him against a steel bulkhead. His body felt as if it had been torn apart, but miraculously he was uninjured.

Fuchida saw the explosion. Terrible! he thought, but the flight deck hasn't been hit.[13] He screwed up his eyes against the bright sunshine and watched a third dive-bomber follow in some distance behind the second. "This one will make adjustments too and probably hit the flight deck," he told himself apprehensively. So he rolled over on his stomach, pressed his face tight against the deck, and linked his hands over his head. The bomb struck near the port flight deck and crashed through it into the hangar. Fuchida estimated the bomb to weigh about 250 kilograms. Usually one of this size would do comparatively little damage, but two circumstances made this an exception.

First, the bombs from all the changeabouts clustered around the hangar deck. When the American missile penetrated, it landed in the middle of a stack of bombs. One set off the next and they exploded at the rate of one or two a minute. Second, fully armed aircraft crowded the flight deck. These caught fire from the blaze below, each plane igniting the other until the deck became a sweeping sea of flame.[14]

Realizing that the blazing flight deck was no place for him, Fuchida moved to the briefing room. There haste matched confusion, with sailors hauling in the wounded and disposing of them as best they could. Fuchida stopped one rescue worker to ask, "Why aren't you taking the wounded down to sick bay?"

"The entire ship is on fire and no one can get through," he replied. Horror-struck, Fuchida recalled the thirty-some men still in sick bay, now hopelessly trapped. He reeled out of the briefing room with the idea of reaching his cabin to salvage what he could, but fire and smoke turned him back.[15]

Well might Fuchida reflect on the interweavings of fate: If he had not been so eager to watch the takeoff and send his comrades away with a personal good wishes, he would have burned to death, either in sick bay or in his cabin. He had received a sobering lesson in the limitations of common sense. The human spirit has a built-in wisdom of its own. Reason dictated that he stay below, recuperating. Yet something beyond reason sent him topside. And that *same* "something" had brought Genda from certain death.

Up to this moment, Fuchida had been so preoccupied with events aboard the *Akagi* that he had not noticed what was taking place elsewhere. Now, headed for the bridge, he looked across the sea and stopped dead. The *Kaga* was a huge ball of smoke and fire. And off in the other direction flame and smoke enveloped the *Soryu.* He knew then that the Japanese had lost this battle, which he had opposed in principle but never doubted they would win. The First Air Fleet had gone, and for what? Even the capture of Midway would not have been worth this price. Perhaps the *Hiryu*'s planes, the surface force, or the submarines could snatch something from the wreck, but this was defeat.

Fuchida wandered to the bridge in a daze. Although his brain was numb, his legs kept moving, taking him instinctively to the one man on Nagumo's staff who could realize the full magnitude of the disaster. Wordlessly he faced Genda. Haggard and stiff with grief, his friend shot him a look and spoke one word: *"Shimmata.* " (We goofed.) No one else said anything, or needed to.[16]

By this time smoke and flames had reached the bridge. Kusaka urged Nagumo to leave the ship with his staff and establish headquarters elsewhere. At first Nagumo resisted, preferring to go down with the *Akagi* in the traditional gesture. But Kusaka, who had little use for futile dramatics, persisted. "The *Hiryu* is still intact. We must continue fighting with her." At last Nagumo agreed that his larger duty lay with those still living. He ordered his aide to contact the light cruiser *Nagara* and send over three small boats for the First Air Fleet staff.[17]

Meanwhile fire and smoke had sealed off egress from the bridge to the deck; the officers on the bridge had to leave by climbing out a window and sliding down a rope to a small deck adjacent to the briefing room, on which stood a machine-gun battery. They hurried for the machine-gun deck was already awash in flames. Nagumo and his staff swarmed down that rope like Eta Jima cadets. Kusaka, who was quite stout, almost stuck in the frame. About halfway down his scorched hands lost their grip and he fell to the deck, spraining both ankles and burning one leg.[18]

Fuchida was the last man off the bridge. The operations room directly under him was hot as a chimney. The end of the rope caught fire as he worked his way down. All this time, the unending chaos of violence below decks shook the *Akagi* like cobblestone streets jolting a baby carriage.

Just as his feet touched the deck, a thunderous explosion hurled him eight or ten feet in the air in a wide parabola. He landed on the flight deck with a crunching smash. Stunned by the explosion and the fall, he attempted to struggle to his feet, but both his legs had been broken. Once more he attempted to rise, but could not. Demoralized and shattered, he relapsed into a sitting position.

"I was weary from my operation," he recalled. "I kept getting weaker; sweat was pouring down my face. Black spots moved before my eyes, and I was afraid I might faint." Swirls of smoke and little tongues of flame crept closer. His brain told him to crawl along the deck to the bow, which had not yet caught fire, but in his weariness and pain it seemed like too much trouble. Mentally Fuchida squared his shoulders and lifted his chin. "All right!" he told himself. "If this is the end of my life, I am ready to go."

His clothes began to smolder and smoke stung his eyes. At that propitious moment two enlisted men raced by and spotted him. They scooped him up and carried him down to the outside passage. Just as they reached the anchor deck, the last boat carrying Nagumo's staff pulled off. "Wait, come back!" the sailors yelled, and it swung about. His rescuers put Fuchida in a big net sling and lowered him carefully into the small boat.[19]

As the craft cut through the sea away from the *Akagi*, Fuchida raised himself for one last look at the grand carrier. His thoughts turned in grief to the officers and men already killed and those who would still die aboard her and the other carriers. Then he reflected that on this day he had escaped death twice by the narrowest possible margins. "*Sotaicho*, you must lie down," Dr. Tamai cautioned him. Fuchida nodded and obeyed.

As the boat nudged against the cruiser *Nagara*, sailors lifted Fuchida out and carried him aboard. There he saw many wounded stretched out on blankets on the main deck. Sympathy and distress welled up in him as his bearers bore him past his old shipmates, some covered with blood, some with mangled arms and legs, some frightfully burned.

The men hurried Fuchida straight to a hospital room. The surgeon, a lieutenant, was already swamped with work, but he wanted to drop everything and care for Fuchida, who bore the rank of commander and was well known. This he would not allow. "My injuries are not serious, just broken legs," he said. "Those up on deck need help much more than I. Take care of them first, then come to me."

So his bearers took him to the officers' quarters, a compartment of four bunks, and deposited him gently in an upper one. Opposite him lay Kusaka, his hands, feet, and ankles bandaged.

Later in the hospital room the surgeon carefully examined and X-rayed Fuchida. The pictures showed both legs broken around ankle and arch. One break was a simple fracture, another showed a clean break with the bone slightly separated, and in a third the bone was twisted. "The first two should mend within a few months," explained the surgeon. "The twisted bone will require at least six."

Fuchida couldn't complain; he was thankful to be alive. The lieutenant set his legs, put them in casts, then treated him for burns on the neck and hands.[20]

Several times that evening Genda came to the compartment to report to Kusaka. Fuchida heard him tell Kusaka that Nagumo planned to seek out the enemy and destroy him in night action. Nagumo is deceiving himself, Fuchida reflected silently. How can he hope to defeat the Americans without air power?

By this time Fuchida knew that the *Hiryu* had also been bombed. Japan had lost not only four carriers but all their aircraft. Thanks to prompt action and fine rescue work, many of the air crews had been saved. But aside from these men, all that remained of the First Air Fleet was Nagumo, his staff, and the auxiliary ships.[21]

Early the next morning the Japanese had to sink the *Akagi* and *Hiryu* to keep them from falling into American hands. For Fuchida, except for the loss of the *Akagi*, the worst moment of the battle came when Yamaguchi went down with the *Hiryu*. His staff begged him to leave the doomed vessel, but he refused. Fuchida didn't blame Yamaguchi for adhering to Japanese tradition. In his place Fuchida would have done the same. But he knew that Yamaguchi would have served Japan better by living, to give his country the continuing benefit of his experience and inspirational leadership.[22]

Genda was terribly upset over the loss of the carriers.[23] Fuchida tried to cheer him up. "Don't worry too much. We still have most of our ships and our land-based air power on our islands in the Pacific. These are aircraft carriers too, though they're stationary. We can't carry on offensive operations without floating aircraft carriers, but we can defend ourselves against the enemy with land-based aircraft." All of which was whistling in the dark. Wars are not won from defensive postures, and no one knew it better than Minoru Genda and Mitsuo Fuchida.

Up to and including Midway, the keynote of Japanese naval strategy had been aggressive operations, *shinko sakusen*. After Midway, the Imperial Navy had to adopt defensive operations, *yogeki sakusen.* This was the real meaning of the battle. The United States had snatched away the initiative that Japan had seized at Pearl Harbor, and throughout the agonizing months ahead would never let it go.[24]

11

"It Was Ridiculous!"

URING THE VOYAGE back to Japan, many of the wounded transferred to battleships of the Main Fleet, which had better medical facilities than the rescue cruisers and destroyers. Fuchida, however, remained aboard the *Nagara* with Nagumo's staff. He had always been an operations type; now, with both legs sunk in plaster, he became in effect a staff officer, though not by official orders.[1]

His friends kept him informed of events during the cruise homeward. Nagumo was in a black depression. Onishi came to Kusaka to say that all of the First Air Fleet staff were prepared to commit suicide to atone for Midway, and he subtly but unmistakably hinted that Kusaka should urge Nagumo to do likewise. Whereupon Kusaka laid Onishi out in no uncertain terms: This was no time to think of suicide. Their duty was to live, fight, and win future victories.

Kusaka reported this conversation to Nagumo. The latter had to agree with Kusaka's reasoning, but he added despondently, "Matters often don't follow logic." Only with difficulty did the chief of staff extract the commander in chief's promise that he wouldn't commit "a rash act."[2]

Kusaka related the incident to Fuchida in the strictest confidence. "You said the right thing," Fuchida told him approvingly. Privately he felt a little impatient. In his opinion, hara-kiri was an individual matter, not a suitable subject for discussions with colleagues and friends. "If a man thinks he should commit suicide, okay," said Fuchida, "but he can't expect a friend to tell him to do it!"[3]

Genda gave him a spirited account of a conference held on the *Yamato* between key staff officers of the Combined Fleet and the First Air Fleet. Kusaka represented Nagumo and reported at length on the battle, pulling no punches. He closed by acknowledging that he and Nagumo bore a heavy burden of responsibility and stood ready to suffer the consequences; he asked that, if possible, both be given the opportunity to pay off the score in battle. This straightforward request so touched Yamamoto that tears filled his eyes, and he could only reply gruffly, "All right."

Kusaka also hinted that the question of suicide preyed on Nagumo's mind. Yamamoto settled the matter by stating forcefully, "No, Nagumo is not to blame. I take full responsibility. If anyone is to commit hara-kiri because of Midway, it is I."

"That was the type of commander Yamamoto was," Fuchida reminisced, "and that is why we officers served under him so willingly and respected him so highly."[4]

When Genda returned to the *Nagara,* she sped ahead of the *Yamato* bound for Kure, so that Genda and the rest of the First Air Fleet staff could begin working on a plan to reorganize Japan's remaining naval air power.[5]

From Kure, the *Nagara* proceeded to Hashirajima, where Fuchida and about five hundred wounded were moved to the hospital ship *Hikawa Maru.* All of those injured in the Midway battle were to be rounded up for treatment at the Yokosuka naval hospital. Kusaka had urged Ugaki to tell the Japanese people the truth, but the navy ignored this excellent advice. Newspapers and newscasts proclaimed Midway a great victory, and radio broadcasts began with the playing of the "Battleship March." If the wounded fanned out all over Japan, the truth about the disaster would inevitably leak out.[6]

The day before the *Hikawa Maru* sailed for Yokosuka, Yamamoto boarded the ship to visit the wounded. He came first to Fuchida's room for a long talk. Fuchida never forgot the sight of the admiral smiling down at him with fatherly affection. Having heard about Fuchida's appendectomy but not his crash landing on the *Akagi*'s deck, he was surprised and concerned to find the flier with both legs in casts. Not until he had satisfied himself with Fuchida's prógress did he get down to business.

"The Midway battle is lost," he said uncompromisingly. "Now what do you think of the situation?"

Fuchida replied along the lines he had followed with Genda. "We have lost four carriers and some other ships, this is true. But we still have all the big battleships, most of the cruisers, light cruisers, and destroyers. In addition, we have our unsinkable aircraft carriers—our island bases—for navy planes."

Yamamoto nodded in agreement; he knew even better than Fuchida that the Combined Fleet remained a force to be reckoned with. But Fuchida had more on his mind, and appreciated this unexpected chance to air his views without going through a maze of channels. He propped himself up as best he could and spoke.

"We are in an epoch-making period," he began slowly, feeling his way. "You see, all the battleships, many of the cruisers and destroyers scarcely got into battle at Midway. It was a fight between carriers in large measure. Now these big battleships like the *Yamato, Nagato,* and the rest of the main body went to Midway and back to Japan without seeing action."

This was not news to Yamamoto, but he listened intently while Fuchida marshaled his thoughts. It encouraged him to proceed. "Midway was a tragedy, yes, and we have come to the end of the battleship era. But all is not lost if we will learn the imperative lesson of Midway—the full and complete advent of naval aviation. We must accept the truth of Midway and plan toward the future accordingly. Japan must face the facts of naval air power."

A scene from the past flashed across Fuchida's memory. "Do you remember, Commander in Chief, that when I was air officer of the Third Carrier Division I advocated reversal of the roles of the carriers and battleships? You may recall that I used to describe the defensive role of the carriers as *abe kobe* (upside down)."

"I am very sorry that we did not make the change in naval air power several years ago," replied Yamamoto. Then he patted Fuchida's shoulder and added kindly, "Don't worry now, Fuchida—we will make all the necessary adjustments at once."

Fuchida was much relieved that his plain speaking had not offended the admiral and glad to hear his assurance of reform. "I am very happy to serve under such a great commander," he answered gratefully.

After Yamamoto left Fuchida's cabin he spent about three hours greeting the rest of the wounded. For every man he had a firm handshake and words of concern and encouragement. "Keep your spirits high! We have much confidence for the future," he said as he moved from bunk to bunk.

But what he said mattered little. His presence was the real morale booster. The sound of his light, quick footsteps, the sight of his stocky form, the impact of his dynamic personality zipped through these men like a shot of adrenaline. Every man wanted to rise and follow him back into battle.[7]

After Yamamoto was piped over the side, the *Hikawa Maru* weighed anchor and crept into Yokosuka. The ship laid off the harbor until dark so that area residents might not see so many wounded disembark. The sick and injured landed at the Nagaura pier, a back way into the base, smuggled like contraband down the road between a heavy escort of shore police. At the base hospital they were settled into two buildings, which were put under close security guard.

There they lived isolated from the outside world. Visitors, even wives, were prohibited, along with phone calls and letters. Just like an internment camp, Fuchida thought angrily. Trained to be stoical, Japanese men-at-arms could bear pain, discomfort, inconvenience, and tedium, but under this grim system they became demoralized. The spirit that made the First Air Fleet the terror of the seas and the pride of a nation faltered and would never completely revive.

Trust in the government shriveled into cynicism. From the newspapers and radio Fuchida soon understood that the wounded had been put under wraps to keep the real story of Midway from the Japanese public, even from most of the military. Up to this time, the press had reported naval actions rather faithfully. Beginning with Midway, however, the government initiated a policy of suppressing the truth.

Propped up in his hospital cot, rustling newspapers and twisting the radio dial, Fuchida asked himself, "What's the point? The enemy knows all about our losses and will soon tell the rest of the world." It would be much wiser if navy headquarters itself announced that Japan had lost four carriers and one heavy cruiser. That way, they would get the jump on the American press and prove that the government had confidence in the courage and strength of the Japanese people. Sooner or later the facts must come out; when they did, the public would be angry at the deception.

It was little short of torture for a man as gregarious as Fuchida to be locked up with only newspaper and radio propaganda for company. The situation might have been easier if he had been really sick, half-conscious and self-absorbed, but from the knees up he was perfectly well. By devious means, he managed to make a few phone calls. The authorities looked the other way, knowing him to be a favorite of Yamamoto. Fuchida counted on this. He had no qualms about using influence when it seemed effective.[8]

While Fuchida was thus immured, headquarters of the First Air Fleet moved to the battleship *Kirishima*. The photographer, Makajima, noted that Nagumo, Kusaka, and especially Genda looked worn out. "You can never go back to Tokyo," an officer warned Makajima. "If you did, you would be arrested by the *Kempeitai* [military police]." Makajima knew he would never be permitted on the loose in the nation's capital; he knew too much about Midway. So he asked to remain with the fleet, where he could die, if die he must, "in a respectable way." Rather than wait for the Third Air Fleet to be combat ready, he requested transfer to a cruiser headed for the Indian Ocean on a raiding mission.[9] Thus this keen observer passed out of Fuchida's ken.

During Fuchida's hospitalization, the Third Air Fleet came into being, with twenty-nine ships—six carriers, two battleships, five cruisers, and sixteen destroyers. Kusaka counted two pluses in this arrangement: the carriers had been brought together, and the fleet would be a permanent organization. But much to his disappointment, the navy did not abandon the big-ship-big-gun concept, as he called it. He was sorry to lose Genda, who became air officer of the *Zuikaku,* but found his successor, Commander Takeshi Naito, a satisfactory substitute. Naito had been a classmate of Fuchida's at Kasumigaura and the Naval Staff College.[10]

Of these developments Fuchida was unaware. Outside the hospital, no one knew where he was except the Navy Personnel Bureau. "It was ridiculous!" he fumed. After about a month of grinding boredom and official foolishness, he compared notes with Egusa, under treatment for burns on his hands and arms. Both were fed up. They decided on a jailbreak and began waiting for the right moment. When it came, Egusa telephoned for a taxi and boldly carried Fuchida to it on his broad back. They sped off to their families, Egusa to Kamakura and Fuchida to Zushi.

Haruko greeted her husband joyously, but with no surprise. At that time many navy families lived at Zushi and through the intraservice grapevine had a fairly good idea of what had happened at Midway. Haruko had heard that her husband was in the hospital, but she didn't know the extent of his injuries. Fearing he was in serious condition, she was relieved to find him with nothing worse than leg fractures.

The children whooped with delight and hung onto their father. Yoshiya was old enough to realize that Japan was at war and that his father had been injured during a battle. Miyako, five years old, only knew that once more she had both of her adored parents with her.

When the children were out of earshot, Fuchida spoke frankly to Haruko about Midway. She offered little comment beyond remarking, "I assumed that something had gone wrong." She sensed that he didn't want to discuss the battle further; he just needed to get it out of his system. With her air of reassuring calm, Haruko made an ideal audience. She was never too busy to listen when he wanted to talk and disappeared tactfully when he lapsed into brooding silence.[11]

All this pleasant comfort made Fuchida uneasily conscious of the gap between his situation and that of his comrades. And worried. Someone should put him on convalescent leave before he turned up on roll call as AWOL. But where exactly did he belong in the navy? Who was his commander? Seeking clarification, he wrote to Captain Taijiro Aoki, the *Akagi's* ex-skipper, asking permission to stay at home instead of returning to the Yokosuka hospital. He didn't like to bother Aoki, but he had to find out where he stood and protect his position.

Fuchida deserved a reprimand for going AWOL; instead, Navy Department orders came assigning him to Yokosuka Naval Base. He was to report to Hirayama Springs at Ito. In happier days, this beautiful hot springs resort on scenic Izu Peninsula had been a favorite vacation spot and health spa for the wealthy. Now he and ten or more patients took the baths for broken bones. Security being relatively light, his family could visit him. All things considered, his two months at Ito contented him. But he believed that the reason for his plush assignment was to keep him away from Yokosuka Hospital, where he might have led a revolt of patients and attracted public attention to their number.[12]

After his treatment at Ito, Fuchida returned home to Zushi. There he lived in semi-isolation, for he could not yet walk on crutches and never left the house. Not even his brother and sisters visited him, being unaware of the situation. So Fuchida talked with Haruko and spent time playing with the children. He tried his hand at oil painting. He and Yoshiya made many models of Japanese airplanes from balsa wood and rice paper. These they hung from the living room ceiling. Haruko accepted with equanimity such unorthodox additions to the house. Both Yoshiya and Miyako remembered those model aircraft long after other, seemingly more important matters had escaped them.

Fuchida devoured the newspapers. He didn't trust them, but they helped to pass the time. Out of his knowledge of the places and personalities in the news, he tried to piece together at least a general idea of what was happening in the outside world. He longed to recover and return to active duty, regretting that the whirlpool of events had spun him into this peaceful backwater.[13]

The long struggle for Guadalcanal dominated the last months of 1942. Slowly but surely the United States proceeded on the offensive. And then at the Battle of Santa Cruz in late October Nagumo restored much of the luster to his reputation. There Japanese forces destroyed the *Hornet* and damaged the *Enterprise*. But with good news came bad. Leading the torpedo plane attack, Fuchida's dear comrade Murata plunged to his death.[14]

Many leaves dropped from the trees before Fuchida received crutches. He hobbled on them with considerable difficulty, for he couldn't use either foot for balance. By the end of November he could get about quite well. Around that time, he received his first visitor, Captain Toshiyuke Yokoi, chief of instructors at Yokosuka. A pilot, a keen student of air power, and a brilliant man, Yokoi acted as something of a one-man brain trust for Rear Admiral Keizo Ueno, the installation's president.

Yokoi brought good news. He asked Fuchida to come to Yokosuka and assist him in making a survey of the Battle of Midway. Fuchida agreed enthusiastically. Yokoi assigned him quarters on base. Fuchida would stay there on weekdays and go home weekends, taking advantage of the transportation that Yokoi thoughtfully provided.

At Yokosuka, Fuchida studied not only Midway, but also the Coral Sea and Indian Ocean engagements. He didn't delve further into Pearl Harbor; Yokosuka already had studied it thoroughly. He stayed on this assignment from December 1942 to June 1943, working on his studies, doing research, and questioning survivors who came to Yokosuka to talk with him.

For each of these naval battles he wrote a pamphlet that the navy distributed for officers to study. In the case of Midway, Yokosuka authorized only six copies—the security lid remained clamped on that one. Fuchida regretted this, for he believed that the Japanese navy had much to learn from Midway. Some admirals didn't like his monographs because they were honest. Where Fuchida felt the Japanese had erred, he said so, and went into explicit, sometimes unpalatable detail. In all of his pamphlets he preached the gospel: "This is an epoch-making time. It may already be too late! We must have an up-to-date strategy."[15]

This quiet, scholarly interlude in Fuchida's life was a valuable experience. At the age of forty he was practically a graybeard by the standards of aerial combat. Even if he had never been injured, soon he would have been forced to leave the field of action to younger men. His injuries and convalescence permitted him to make the transition without regret. Here at Yokosuka, he had the priceless practice of presenting his ideas clearly, in logical order, and mastering his command of the language. Perhaps most important, although incapacitated for combat, he could still contribute to his nation's war effort.

12

"Into Dangerous Areas"

F UCHIDA had been in his new job for some months when he requested permission to go to the southwest Pacific to update himself on operations. Yokoi arranged for him to fly to Rabaul. At the airstrip Fuchida met Genda, who had been on the Naval General Headquarters staff since early December of 1942. He had come to Yokosuka to catch a flight to Rabaul. With him was an army officer, Lieutenant Colonel Masanobu Tsunji, who declaimed with the utmost seriousness, "I am a war god!" Fuchida had enough of a sense of humor to find amusing a man who could brag of his wartime exploits to the likes of Minoru Genda and Mitsuo Fuchida.[1]

Fuchida stayed in Rabaul for about a month and, for the first time since Midway, received a firsthand picture of Japanese operations. He held long discussions with some of his fellow Pearl Harbor veterans. The whittling away of Japan's irreplaceable first-string naval fliers deeply concerned and grieved Fuchida. During the Guadalcanal campaign, they had gone to Rabaul as land-based pilots against an enemy entrenched on the island. The toll had been alarming.

During this time Yamamoto came to Rabaul. Several times Fuchida had the chance to talk to him. Knowing his presence was a morale booster, the admiral avoided the navy's summer khakis and appeared always in impeccable whites. He was still full of fight but was as unhappy as Fuchida over Japan's dwindling supply of first-class naval pilots.

Nor was Yamamoto satisfied with the Third Fleet, now under the com-

mand of Vice Admiral Jisaburo Ozawa. Of the original main strength of the
fleet, the light carrier *Ryujo* and the battleships *Hiei* and *Kirishima* had been
sunk. The *Shokaku* had been badly damaged at Santa Cruz and was still out
of action. The light carrier *Zuiho* had taken two bombs in the same battle.
That left only the *Zuikaku* plus the light carriers *Junyo* and *Hiyo* in fighting
trim. Of aircraft, Ozawa had less than one hundred fighters, sixty-odd dive-
bombers, and a sprinkling of torpedo planes. As Yamamoto bluntly said to
Fuchida, "The Third Fleet is boneless."[2]

For the first time, little ghosts of doubt about the outcome of the war
haunted Fuchida. The situation was not yet hopeless, but he didn't see how
Japan could launch any major offensive in the foreseeable future. He pondered long-range plans. Gradually he developed the idea of a powerful line
of air and surface defense through the Marianas. There Japan must hold the
enemy.

It is ironic that in the spring of 1943 Fuchida was forced to advocate
much the same type of strategy for which he had faulted Yamamoto before
Midway. In discussions with colleagues, Fuchida recommended that the
Marianas Line be composed primarily of land-based naval air power. He had
little faith in the efficacy of the boneless Third Fleet. If the Americans took
over the Marianas islands, only 1,550 miles from Tokyo, they would be in an
excellent position to strike at the heart of the Japanese homeland. Aggressive
by nature and by training, Fuchida didn't relish the idea of a last-ditch
defensive policy. Nevertheless, Japan must base its strategy on the facts,
however unpalatable.[3]

Shortly after his last talk with Yamamoto, Fuchida returned to Yokosuka,
where he resumed work on his pamphlets in a thoughtful mood. When he
had finished all the studies, Yokoi called for a war-lesson survey. He presided,
and many officers attended from Yokosuka and the Naval General Staff. The
latter group included Genda, who had preceded Fuchida back to Japan.
Fuchida prepared the materials for discussion and acted as general secretary.
To the best of his knowledge, no real action ever came of this critique, but
everyone paid attention and looked at every aspect of the battles under
study.[4]

Fuchida was in Yokosuka for the first anniversary of the Doolittle Raid,
18 April 1943. On that day, fate struck Japan an infinitely more crushing
blow.

Yamamoto, his chief of staff Ugaki, and several members of the Combined Fleet staff took off from Rabaul en route to Buin by way of Japan's air
base at Bellale, off the island of Bougainville. Yamamoto and Ugaki flew in
separate planes, so that any mishap would not result in the loss of both the
commander in chief and his righthand man. Despite an escort of six Zeros,

a flight of American P-38s ambushed both aircraft. Ugaki's bomber crashed into the sea. He escaped with a broken arm and other relatively minor injuries. Yamamoto's bomber caught fire and smashed into the dense jungle of Bougainville.

"The body of the commander in chief was found on the seat outside of the plane still gripping his sword. It had not decomposed yet and was said to be in a state of great dignity. He must have been . . . superhuman." Thus wrote Ugaki a year later.[5]

The government withheld the official public announcement of Yamamoto's death for more than a month, but it had to inform the navy's higher echelons immediately. Along with the news came a brief announcement that Admiral Mineichi Koga, Yamamoto's friend and sometime confidant, would succeed him as commander in chief.

Yamamoto's death shook the navy from keel to mast. Fuchida was already depressed when he heard. His legs, still healing, hindered an otherwise vigorous body. The gloom and tedium of convalescence and inactivity weighed on him. And his doubts about Japan's fate undermined his morale. The report of his beloved chief's death flared through his thoughts like a meteor heralding doom.

Despite Fuchida's criticism of Yamamoto's tactics at Midway, and despite his post-Guadalcanal worries, he never lost the feeling that as long as Yamamoto commanded the Combined Fleet, somehow all would be well. With that steady, valiant hand no longer on the tiller, what would happen?

"I believed now that the war was entirely lost," said Fuchida. His physical and psychological condition probably accounted for part of this uncharacteristic surrender to pessimism. But he didn't stand alone. For the entire navy the admiral's death was an evil omen.[6]

Public announcement of the loss finally came on 22 May. Yamamoto's body had been cremated on the site of the crash, and a portion of his ashes buried there. Captain Yasuji Watanabe of Yamamoto's staff carried the remaining ashes to Tokyo, there to be divided between Tokyo and Yamamoto's home town of Nagaoka. The casket lay at Tokyo's navy officers' club until 5 June, when Yamamoto received a state funeral. Only once before had such high rites been granted a navy man—Fleet Admiral Heihachiro Togo. Yamamoto's ashes were borne slowly through the flag-lined avenues of the sprawling city in resplendent, solemn procession. Virtually the entire population except the emperor, who never attended funerals, crowded the route to the cemetery.[7]

Because of Fuchida's crutches, he could not participate personally. From the sidelines he watched the stately ceremonies. This will be the last state funeral, he thought grimly. There can be no more! The end will have come before there is occasion for another. He recalled Togo's victorious operations against the Russians, then Yamamoto's life of steady service to his country.

When the flood of shock and sorrow began to ebb, Fuchida and his fellow officers considered the conditions under which Yamamoto had been shot down. The Americans had pinpointed Yamamoto's position and concentrated their fire on his bomber. After hitting Ugaki's plane, they had left it alone when it crashed into the sea, as if the American gunners were fishermen contemptuously letting a little one get away. Among those who did not escape, however, was Commander Suteji Muroi, a promising member of Yamamoto's air staff as well as a Naval Staff College classmate and good friend of Fuchida's. Mercifully, he had been shot dead before the plane hit the water.[8] The logical conclusion, that the Americans knew which of the two bombers was Yamamoto's, was incorrect. They hadn't expected two bombers and had no idea which one held their prey. So they shot down both.[9]

Fuchida and his associates were correct, however, in agreeing that the pattern of the attack showed clearly that Yamamoto's death was no accidental bonus of a routine patrol. No P-38s were based nearer Bougainville other than the Thirteenth Air Force's fighter command detachment at Guadalcanal. The presence of double-boomed fighters so far afield was quite suspicious. Obviously, Yamamoto had fallen into a deliberate ambush.

This line of reasoning led to a disquieting conclusion—the Americans must have broken Japan's top naval code. The intelligence section of the Naval General Staff, however, refused to accept this. They had confidence in the code's invincibility. Once more the smug self-confidence, the incorrigible stupidity that had led to the disaster at Midway worked to Japan's detriment. The Americans had indeed intercepted a message from Japan's Shortland base announcing Yamamoto's schedule.[10]

About a month after Yamamoto's funeral Fuchida became senior staff officer of the new land-based First Air Fleet, under the command of his old boss, Kakuta. Captain Kazuo Miwa, a very able flier, was Kakuta's chief of staff. The new fleet roughly followed Fuchida's flight concept, being entirely divorced from ship assignments. It also operated free of any particular base. The First Air Fleet could and would move anywhere, without administrative entanglements.

At the imperial palace, the emperor himself invested Kakuta as commander in chief of the First Air Fleet. Fuchida was present as Kakuta's aide. After the ceremony, a group of approximately twenty newly assigned officers, among them Kakuta, Miwa, and Fuchida, lunched at the palace. The emperor sponsored the luncheon but did not attend.

As the group broke up, Miwa suggested thoughtfully, "It would be fitting if we three officers representing the First Air Fleet now visit Yamamoto's grave to pay our respects. We should promise his spirit that we will succeed in our mission."

This suggestion struck Fuchida as proper. At the grave he bowed his head in reverence and addressed Yamamoto's spirit: "It is now or never. If the new First Air Fleet can't do this job, that job will never be done. This is the last major naval air force we can muster to stop the United States. If we fail, all your heroic life, all my exploits under your command, all the pain and death have been in vain."

The motto at Yamamoto's funeral had been "Follow Yamamoto!"[11] Realistically, who could follow him? Japan had no other admiral who approached him in ability and leadership. The knowledge of this weakness in the Japanese navy's high command had been one factor in the American decision to ambush him. In effect, Yamamoto was an irreplaceable national asset.[12]

Admiral Koga, Yamamoto's successor, came to his new post as a full admiral with a variety of key positions behind him. He had every professional qualification it took to be an excellent commander in chief. He had the opportunity to profit by Yamamoto's mistakes and to rethink Japan's naval strategy. This, however, he did not do.

"There is only one Yamamoto and no one is able to replace him," proclaimed Koga when he took over his new command.[13] This wasn't just a tribute to his predecessor and patron; it was a summation of his own situation. After Yamamoto's death, the nation virtually canonized him. One suspects that this would have only amused and irritated him. Tremendous strength of character and originality of mind would be required to come up with a new strategy. And Yamamoto had groomed his heir-apparent to toe the line.

Koga believed that the Japanese navy must win a decisive battle with the Pacific Fleet in 1943, before the Americans could reach their full potential. He obtained permission from imperial headquarters to engage in such a battle if the opportunity arose. But by early autumn headquarters had postulated the New Operational Plan, which established a holding policy for 1943 in preparation for an offensive in 1944.[14]

The record of Japan's naval activities during Koga's command indicates that either he had no original contribution to make, or Yamamoto's personality and policies dominated him from beyond the grave. The Japanese navy retained the weaknesses of the Yamamoto regime without its saving dynamism and vital leadership.

Fuchida was still lunging about on crutches, but his bones had mended sufficiently to permit occasional trips to Tokyo, where he conferred with Genda. They discussed the new First Air Fleet that was being put together with headquarters at Kanoya in southern Kyushu. Its forces were to be spotted at various locations around that island, where personnel would undergo training similar to that used to prepare the old First Air Fleet for Operation Hawaii.

This organization came directly under Admiral Osami Nagano, chief of the Naval General Staff, rather than under Koga, as would be normal. The navy intended the new organization to be established as a sort of flying squad that could move rapidly and efficiently to any front at a moment's notice.

For Fuchida, the setup came as both triumph and disappointment. Its blueprint was basically the plan he and Genda had proposed earlier. He wished that the idea had been put into effect in April 1941 when Yamamoto called the original First Air Fleet to life. A task force with the freedom and flexibility of the new, combined with the scoring punch of the old, would have been the air fleet of his dreams.

But now that Japan had the organization, it lacked the ships.[15] No carrier available for immediate action compared with the *Akagi* or *Kaga*. Japan would have to use island bases—those unsinkable aircraft carriers of which Fuchida had spoken to Yamamoto and Genda after Midway. The trouble was that while an island was unsinkable, it was also immovable. An aircraft carrier's great advantage was mobility.

Nor could the naval air arm man its aircraft with crews of the caliber it had enjoyed in the past. The young airmen being sent to Fuchida were courageous and patriotic, but they lacked combat experience and adequate training. Normally pilots received a full year's special instruction after graduating from Kasumigaura; now they came directly to the fleet and went to work under seasoned instructors.[16]

The latter, too, dwindled alarmingly. Every engagement, whether a victory or defeat, cut into the reservoir of veterans. Fortunately for Fuchida, some of Japan's first-line pilots were available to help train the new ones. These instructors included Chihaya, so knowledgeable in the field of reconnaissance. The invaluable Furukawa taught torpedo bombing. This function became the new organization's specialty, because it visualized most of its future air operations as direct attacks on ships at sea. Here again one shortage compounded another. Every experienced airman assigned to duty as an instructor was one less experienced airman at the front.

In summer 1943, training was the First Air Fleet's primary mission; it wasn't ready for combat. Nagano wished to weld it into a mighty instrument to be turned loose only when fully prepared. Preventing premature commitment was one reason the fleet came directly under the Naval General Staff.[17] This policy made sense; on the other hand, no combat unit could be honed to a fighting edge at a training installation. There is no school like experience.[18]

That summer two air divisions of eighteen planes each from the Japanese Army joined the First Air Fleet. "However," explained Fuchida, "these army bombers came under the First Air Fleet for training purposes, not operational purposes." So in the event of an emergency call Fuchida couldn't count on them.

One of Fuchida's more painful headaches was the short supply of training aircraft and the poor quality of those available. Japan lacked the industrial capacity to produce quality planes in sufficient number, and the combat front siphoned off aircraft as soon as they left the assembly line. Being home-based and in a training status, the First Air Fleet ranked fairly low on the priority list. Fuchida estimated the total production of navy planes at that time as about five hundred per month, of which he received only thirty. The army, too, received approximately five hundred aircraft monthly, and he begrudged every one of them. The army's air power remained in the homeland or went to China, leaving the air war in the Pacific almost entirely up to the navy. "We Japanese were fighting the United States in the air with only one hand—the navy hand," recalled Fuchida. "The army hand was almost useless at this time."[19]

Another of his problems was the dearth of overseas air bases from which the First Air Fleet could operate when released for combat. To the airmen, this amounted to a national scandal. Advanced installations had been established with almost total disregard for the maximum radius of Japan's aircraft. The distance continually strained both planes and pilots to the limit of endurance.[20]

The task of scrounging around for suitable air bases fell to Fuchida. So in September 1943, still using crutches but able to pilot a plane, he flew from Kanoya to the Philippines. There he briefed Vice Admiral Gunichi Mikawa, commander of Japan's naval forces in that area. Mikawa had commanded the support group in the Pearl Harbor task force. He was still the same pleasant gentleman Fuchida remembered.

"By the end of the year, the First Air Fleet will be sending some 1000 planes into the islands," Fuchida explained. "We plan to concentrate the fleet in the Philippines and from there operate in any direction required. I estimate we require fifteen bases. Would you please have this number remodeled or built in time for the fleet's arrival?"

With Mikawa's green light, Fuchida prepared to fly around the Philippines on a two-week inspection tour to select sites for the new bases. Before he set out, members of Mikawa's staff warned him, "You will be going into dangerous areas, where bands of Filipino guerrillas lurk in the mountains, so be on your guard." Fuchida didn't worry too much about being ambushed, but he kept his eyes open wherever he went.[21]

He made a thorough search for abandoned American or Filipino bases. The Japanese could rebuild these more quickly and economically than they could construct new ones. After surveying the area around Manila, he asked for five bases north and west of the capital.

With this taken care of, he flew several hundred miles southward to Mindanao. There he requested construction of two bases near Batangas on the northern tip of Mindanao, to serve as auxiliary outposts for bases around Manila. Some of Japan's army forces, under command of a major, were stationed in Batangas, and the navy wanted to build its air bases as near as possible to army posts. The latter could protect aircraft against guerrillas. In selecting sites, Fuchida also had to consider convenience in unloading supply ships, because at that time Japan's oil came from Singapore and its weapons from the homeland.

He spent about three hours conferring with the major in Batangas, then continued on his journey. It was his first visit to this part of the world, and he enjoyed the dazzling beauty of the islands. But he had little time to delight in the landscape; he had to view everything in the light of its present or potential use to Japan's war effort. During his mission, he discovered that he no longer needed his crutches and thankfully discarded them.[22]

The almost unanimous hostility of the natives impressed Fuchida more than anything else on his Philippine tour. He had spent much time in China, and the Chinese had no cause to love the Japanese. Either they were less unfriendly or more clever at hiding their feelings, for Fuchida had never noticed any particular hostility from them. Here in the Philippines the people made no effort at concealment. "Anyone could see it in their eyes, their gestures, their facial expressions," said Fuchida.

Gradually he came to realize that the Philippines was a proud, fierce nation, an irreconcilable enemy of any nation threatening its freedom.

From Batangas Fuchida flew to Legaspi on the southeastern side of Luzon. There Japan already had a naval air base with a number of fighter planes to help protect Manila, about two hundred miles to the northwest. Legaspi was a small town, but here too all the natives were hostile. Fuchida often smiled at anyone he passed on the street, especially in small communities. Here no one smiled back. Soon he discovered this region to be a main guerrilla stronghold, along with mid-Luzon, Cebu, and Mindanao. He recommended bases in those areas so that the naval air arm might help fight the guerrillas as well as enemy ships.

After earmarking two sites near Legaspi, he flew to the city of Cebu on

Cebu Island. Although highly developed, with a fine network of roads, Cebu housed an active and well-organized guerrilla force. Japanese troops had almost destroyed the city in May 1942 in reprisal for the guerrillas' activities. But the guerrillas continued to operate as boldly and cleverly as ever.[23]

Japan had no naval forces in this area, just an army unit, and the base where Fuchida landed had been abandoned. The major in charge of the local army post arranged protection for him and his plane. He also provided Fuchida with excellent accommodations—a large, old-fashioned, American-style house that now served as a Japanese guest house. Fuchida, his pilot, and radio operator stayed there two nights. Japanese lived in all the surrounding dwellings, so Fuchida was thunderstruck to find, on a table in a study just off the living room, several copies of a booklet entitled "I Shall Return." The cover showed a portrait of General Douglas MacArthur. The latest issue was dated May 1943, the earliest December 1942.

Fuchida riffled through several issues. The booklets contained pictures and analyses of the war, telling how and where the Japanese were being pushed back step by step, exhorting the Filipinos to keep up their spirits, and promising that MacArthur would return soon. "Now I understood much more clearly the open hostility of the local population," said Fuchida. "Such literature as this gave them hope and encouragement, assuring them that their allies had neither forgotten them nor written them off as expendable."

From the look of the booklets and their contents, he decided that they must have come from the Philippines or, more probably, somewhere near MacArthur's headquarters. If the first case were true, the Filipino guerrillas had a most efficient information agency. If the second, copies were being smuggled into the Philippines, probably by American submarines. As he stood there with those little magazines in his hands, a disconcerting thought struck him: If the United States could smuggle these into the Philippines, it could also bring in munitions, supplies, and agents.

"I began to realize just what we had let ourselves in for," he reminisced. "How widespread our conquests were, and how very difficult the future would be. I was getting an education on that trip."[24]

Japan had dangerously overextended its empire. Fuchida recognized the difficulty of holding the Philippines or any other area that chose to resist. Since Midway, he had known that in the U.S. Navy Japan faced an aggressive, clever foe, determined to control the eastern and central Pacific. But somehow he had not visualized Japan's running into the same sort of resistance in the Greater East Asia Co-Prosperity Sphere. It came as a distinct jolt to find MacArthur's handsome countenance, with all his cool, well-bred arrogance, staring right into the face of the Japanese army.

Fuchida gathered up some of the copies and took them back to Mikawa's headquarters, believing this would be a valuable eye-opener for the admiral. Mikawa took the incident rather lightly. "I know all about the publication," he said.

Fuchida didn't try to argue the point. Instead, he recommended that Mikawa reactivate two abandoned bases near Cebu for the First Air Fleet's use. He also suggested that they take over the base where Filipino guerrillas boldly left their literature in the middle of a Japanese army post. They might be less impudent if they had to deal with Japan's navy.[25]

Mikawa more or less brushed Fuchida off. One can understand why. Japan had placed such a heavy burden on his shoulders that he could not bother with additional evidence of Filipino antagonism and American ingenuity. Moreover, the navy was stuck with Japan's national policy. As an operational staff officer, Fuchida's problems were tactical; to Mikawa and the rest of Japan's top admirals fell the gnawing headaches of high command and the terrible loneliness of the conqueror. They all rode the tiger and none could dismount at will.

13

"A Little White Monkey"

FROM CEBU FUCHIDA continued his survey, heading for Davao in southern Mindanao. His flight passed over the Mindanao Sea and the city of Cagayan de Oro in the north. He noted the striking beauty of the region and its relative seclusion. A clearing at the foot of a mountain spread out like a mammoth fan a few miles beyond the bay. It looked like an excellent prospect for a secret base.

Fuchida put up at the Navy Officers' Club in Davao and arranged a meeting with the admiral in charge. During their discussion, Fuchida asked that a third base be built in addition to the one already in use and the second, then under construction. To this the admiral agreed.[1]

After three days in Davao, Fuchida decided to fly back to the Cagayan area to see whether the spot he had discovered lived up to its promise. Accordingly, at about 1100 he, his pilot, and his radio operator climbed back into their combat-scarred type-97 bomber, like Fuchida a Pearl Harbor veteran. By noon they were circling over the area, which lay some 100 miles north and slightly west of Davao.

Below them rolled a large plain some several miles back of Cagayan Bay. Fuchida saw that at least three or four runways could be built on the spot without difficulty. So far as he could determine from the air, no villages or habitations broke the dense forest crowding to the edge of the clearing. They landed, took pictures, checked the terrain for smoothness, and measured it for possible construction sites. The area was so extensive that they had to take off and land four times to cover it.

99

Absorbed in their work, they lost track of time until lengthening shadows warned Fuchida that evening had come. So they stowed their gear in the plane preparatory to returning to Davao. The pilot was taxiing into position for takeoff when he pointed toward the woods. "Commander, there's a house in the distance."

Following the pilot's finger, Fuchida spotted a large white house almost hidden in the shade of a big tree. This could be a bit of luck. If they stayed in the house overnight, it would save a trip to and from Davao and they could begin their next day's survey in the cool of the morning.

"Taxi up to the house and let's size up the situation," Fuchida directed.

The plane rumbled to a halt within 100 yards of the house, and they climbed out cautiously. The building appeared to be empty, but Fuchida took no chances. Their long navy pistols drawn, they approached the silent house.[2]

Suddenly an elderly Filipino woman emerged. Fuchida judged her to be a servant, for she was poorly dressed and barefoot. As soon as she saw the three men, she stopped and let out a shrill, piercing scream of sheer panic. No doubt Fuchida and his associates looked menacing—three sweat-stained Japanese with large pistols in their hands.

Before Fuchida could say a word or make a reassuring gesture, a Filipino man, evidently the woman's husband, burst through the door. Like her he was barefoot and appeared to be over sixty years of age. He too screamed. Then they both began to shout in a language strange to Fuchida. He decided it must be Spanish.[3]

He felt disconcerted, slightly at a loss to find himself an object of such terror. At the same time, he had to consider the possibility that the two servants might be calling out a warning to guerrillas in the house or lurking in the nearby forest. So he and the others kept their pistols ready.

The cries produced nothing more alarming than a second woman and a young girl. The former looked to be in her early forties, of medium height and lovely figure. As soon as she saw the Japanese, she became hysterical. Not even the fright distorting her features could conceal rich beauty of heavy black hair and expressive brown eyes. She is a Filipino, Spanish style, Fuchida thought appreciatively. The child, obviously the woman's daughter, was about twelve, wiry, and round-eyed with interest. She put up her slim arms in imitation of her mother's quick gesture of surrender, and the two servants followed suit. Eventually they ceased screaming, as the Japanese made no move.[4]

Fuchida realized that with the possible exception of the little girl, they expected immediate rape, torture, murder, or all three. He was embarrassed. It was a sad commentary on the reputation a certain type of Japanese had earned. Fuchida made no pretensions to sainthood, but he had never been wantonly cruel. Certainly he entertained no sinister intentions toward the little group looking at him as if he had horns and a forked tail.

He broke the constrained silence. "How many occupants are there in the house?" he asked in broken English, lacking Spanish.

"Four," the young woman replied in English and to be sure that Fuchida understood her, she lifted four fingers of one hand.

"Is that all?"

"Yes."[5]

Convinced that she was telling the truth, if only because she was too frightened to do otherwise, Fuchida smiled reassuringly. "Don't worry, we won't harm you." He signaled to his colleagues that all was well. They thrust their pistols back in their holsters, and the atmosphere lightened perceptibly.

"We want to have our accommodation tonight under a roof. Would you mind letting us have some room in your house? We don't need any food or any blankets from you."

The woman nodded to indicate she understood and even managed a shaky smile. Mutual apprehensions thus dispelled, Fuchida sent his crew back to the plane for their gear and entered the house with the others. The large dwelling had obviously seen better days but was filled with an atmosphere of old-fashioned friendliness. Although the woman seemed to be the head of the household, the rooms did not appear feminine or frilly. A pair each of buffalo and deer horns hung from the walls. This was at one time the house of a Spanish landlord. Perhaps it was the country home of a rich man, Fuchida surmised.[6]

If his hostess still felt fear or tension, she concealed the fact by the time his associates brought in their equipment and food, including Fuchida's indispensible bag containing his notes, figures, and material on proposed airfield sites. As they settled their gear, he asked for some water. The woman brought three cups, which they drank eagerly. Then they began to bring out their food. The woman interrupted them. "Wait!" she said. "We are preparing some food for you."

"That isn't necessary," Fuchida assured her. "We have our own rations."

"But we wish to prepare dinner for you."

As Fuchida had already guessed, she was a Filipino of Spanish ancestry, married to an American. It would be difficult to find a combination of blood and culture with a more compelling tradition of hospitality. For the moment these Japanese were her guests, and one could not sit down to a real meal while one's guests ate field rations. Touched by the gesture, Fuchida and his crew gratefully accepted.

This entailed a wait of about an hour. Fuchida directed the radio operator to go to the plane and send a message to Davao informing the naval authorities that they were remaining overnight at Cagayan. Then he opened his bag and began work on his air base report.[7]

In due course the hostess, her daughter, Fuchida, and his crew sat down to eat at the kitchen table. The two Filipinos served a plentiful repast. Soup preceded the main course of meat, potatoes, carrots, and beans. The lady of the house apologized for her inability to serve wine.

"Don't worry about that," Fuchida smiled. "We haven't come to drink wine. We appreciate this food."

He suspected that most of their stock of supplies had been sacrificed on the altar of hospitality. She admitted that this was the last of their meat, and that their rice supply had already been exhausted. So he sent the radio operator for their rations, which contained a generous number of rice balls. Thus they contributed to the feast. The Filipinos cautiously tasted the Japanese tidbits.[8]

After dinner the woman talked with Fuchida freely, seeming to welcome the opportunity to chat with someone from the outside world. Her name was Osborne, and she had lived previously in Davao where her husband, an American, worked as a contractor. Just before the outbreak of war, Mr. Osborne either enlisted or was drafted—Fuchida was not clear on this point—in the U.S. Army. Ms. Osborne and the child remained in Davao while the husband went off to war. When the Japanese invaded the Philippines, she lost touch with him. After a long time, she discovered that he had been taken prisoner.

When the Japanese reached Davao, she and her daughter fled with their servants to this isolated corner of Mindanao. Much to Fuchida's surprise, she told him that the house was not hers; it belonged to the old couple. He reflected that an interesting story must lie behind this fact, but he politely did not ask questions.

After further conversation on general subjects, Ms. Osborne rose and said, "You are welcome to occupy the downstairs," whereupon she, the child, and the servants retired to the upper quarters.

The house had no electric light, so Fuchida and his colleagues lighted candles to work by. But they were tired and soon abandoned the work for sleep. Because of the humid heat, they left the doors open, deciding a good night's sleep justified the security risk. Fuchida saw that his men were established comfortably in one room. Then he stretched out on a couch in the living room and fell asleep almost instantly.[9]

He awoke early much refreshed. The still air and hum of insects promised another hot day. A welcome fragrance told him that breakfast was being made. During the meal, he talked with the little girl and her mother, then went with his crew to load the plane.

He lingered to say goodbye to the four people whose lives had so briefly touched his own. "We appreciate your hospitality," he told Ms. Osborne. Then he climbed into the plane, and the pilot taxied away from the house.

As they sized up the terrain, taking off here and landing there, Fuchida decided that this area of Mindanao would be a good spot from which to repel American forces. The air bases would be designed not primarily to protect the Philippines but as centers of operation for the First Air Fleet. By 1500 the men had finished their survey. Before flying off they circled over the house in farewell. The four occupants ran out and waved goodbye.

Fuchida and his crew spent the evening and night at the officers' club in Davao. Early the next morning they got under way again to the second navy air base. This was being constructed under the direction of a young lieutenant of the Navy Engineer Corps. During the forenoon, Fuchida recounted the previous day's findings at Cagayan. The lieutenant, enthusiastic about his work, wanted to take off right away to see the fine new site for himself. After some discussion, Fuchida agreed to fly him to Cagayan that afternoon.

The lieutenant had a fairly large job considering his junior rank, for he directed a labor force of some eight hundred men. Of these, roughly five hundred were Japanese, two hundred Filipinos, and the rest Americans captured at Bataan and Corregidor. The lieutenant introduced Fuchida to his assistant, and while they chatted one of the American prisoners came up to ask a question of the assistant. The latter introduced the prisoner to Fuchida as Osborne.[10]

"I heard your name yesterday from a lady near Cagayan," Fuchida told the American. "Are you the contractor who lived in Davao?" Osborne nodded. "Is your wife a native Filipino and do you have a young daughter of twelve years old?"

Osborne's weather-beaten face came alive. "Yes, sir."

"Do you know where your family is living and how they are getting along?"

Osborne said no. A shadow passed over his eyes.

Convinced that this was indeed Ms. Osborne's husband, Fuchida smiled broadly and abandoned his semi-official style of questioning. "I saw them yesterday near Cagayan. They are living in their servants' house and getting along fine."

The prisoner thanked Fuchida for his welcome news. "I'm flying back to Cagayan this afternoon. I could bring your letter to them," Fuchida suggested. Rummaging in his pockets, he pulled out a piece of paper and a pen and handed them to the prisoner. "Write a brief letter."

Standing on the spot, Osborne scribbled a note to his wife telling her that he was a prisoner in Davao but in good health. Fuchida accepted the letter, reiterated his promise to deliver it, and charged the lieutenant with bringing back a reply. With his emotions aroused Osborne became inarticulate, but his face showed the depth of feeling behind his simple thanks. He seemed moved to receive such kindness from an enemy officer. The Japanese were not famous for consideration toward American prisoners of war.[11]

Fuchida flew back to Davao with the lieutenant. As his first act there he called on the quartermaster. "I need food for a crew of three for one month," he announced. "Please see that suitable rations are delivered to my aircraft immediately." That afternoon he and his associates loaded these supplies into the plane and flew off to Cagayan with Fuchida at the controls, leaving the pilot in Davao.

As soon as he saw the white house in the trees, he swept low and circled the area, gunning the engine several times to announce his arrival. The four familiar figures came out and waved a welcome. Fuchida taxied the plane near the house, where they disembarked. After introducing the lieutenant to Ms. Osborne, he said, "I've seen your husband in Davao. He's fine."

Ms. Osborne's pleasure was so mixed with astonishment that he pulled out Osborne's note and thrust it toward her as evidence. "Look at this!" he said triumphantly. "This is your husband's letter for you."

She took the precious piece of paper and devoured its contents. Tears welled up in her eyes as she finished. After she had composed herself, Fuchida asked, "Can we have two overnights in your house?" She gladly agreed.

They then unloaded rations that Fuchida had unblushingly stolen from the Japanese navy. "This is our food. You may cook from it," he said.

Knowing that she wanted to be alone to savor her husband's first letter in so many long, unhappy months, he led the men back to the plane to begin their survey. Thinking the little girl might like to fly with them, he looked around for her. At first he couldn't find her. Then a rustling in the tree sheltering the house attracted his attention. High up, the child swung through the branches with the unstudied grace of a small jungle creature. Surprised and amused by her agility, Fuchida called up to her, "Oh, you're a little white monkey!" She was so obviously enjoying herself that he abandoned the idea of taking her along and set off to work.[12]

For two days they surveyed the area. Fuchida was glad the young lieutenant had come along, for he was skilled in such matters. On both days Ms. Osborne served a substantial dinner and breakfast from the rations, and the men enjoyed two evenings in the congenial atmosphere of the old Spanish house.

As the second evening dwindled into night, Fuchida said to Ms. Osborne, "Tomorrow we must return to Davao. If you'd like to write your husband a letter, I'll deliver it for you." Eagerly she penned one, as did her daughter and the two faithful servants who had sheltered them in their hour of need.

When the time came to part after breakfast the next morning, Fuchida told Ms. Osborne that the remaining rations were for her. "We will leave this food for you in thanks." With that, they took off and again circled the house a few times in farewell. The four people on the ground waved until Fuchida lost sight of them in the distance.[13]

The Osborne episode, a curiously idyllic interlude of peace amid the tumult of war, was impressed indelibly on Fuchida's mind. It had been an entirely new experience. He had known many kinds of joy—the warm, homely pleasures of a husband and father, the dedication and comradeship that came of serving his country. At Cagayan, he felt the quiet glow of bringing happiness to distressed fellow creatures.

Many years later he encountered the "little white monkey" again and learned that in her family the name of Mitsuo Fuchida had been gratefully honored.

14

"Kakuta Was Crazy!"

Hᴉs ᴡᴏʀᴋ at Davao completed, Fuchida and his two colleagues flew almost due east to the Palau Islands where, after his usual investigation, he ordered three runways remodeled at Peleliu. From there he moved northwest to Yap, that perennial bone of Japanese-American contention.

The next step on his swing was Saipan. There he ran into Nagumo. The admiral was winding up a brief tour of duty as commander of Kure Naval Base, and early in the spring would become commander concurrently of the Middle Pacific Area Fleet and of the Fourteenth Air Fleet.[1] Thus he would be responsible for Japan's naval forces in the Marianas and Carolines, as well as for the defense of these islands. They represented the last line in the Pacific before the homeland itself, a fact of which Nagumo was acutely aware.

Fuchida had not seen Nagumo since the sad voyage back from Midway. The admiral was his old kindly self, but worry shadowed his mind. He had every reason for concern.

"My Central Pacific forces will be inadequate for their task, being mostly antisubmarine craft with a sprinkling of combat planes," he told Fuchida. "I've been promised troop transfers from Manchuria, but they won't be under my command. How can I defend all these islands with the forces at my disposal? I want the First Air Fleet placed under me as a strong force I can depend upon."

Fuchida tried to explain the current organization, mission, and command channels of the new First Air Fleet. "In case of necessity, the fleet will come to the Marianas or anywhere else that it is needed," he concluded.

But Nagumo had trouble with this concept. "He was too stupid to understand the new situation," Fuchida snapped later, with a brutality born of impatience.[2]

No doubt the admiral had an uneasy feeling that somewhere along the line he would be left holding the bag. This new mobile organization couldn't be in more than once place at a time. Suppose Nagumo needed it at the same moment another commander wanted it somewhere else? What assurance had he that his would be the heeded call? He had a solid precedent to mull over—the way the high echelon had mishandled the old main body under Yamamoto, hoarding it for some nebulous future emergency when real emergency was already upon the navy.

After his talk with Nagumo, Fuchida moved on to Tinian and Guam. As a result of this survey, he asked Nagumo to build a total of ten air bases on the islands of Saipan, Tinian, Guam, and Rota. This completed his work in the Marianas. Fuchida returned to Yokosuka, feeling that he had left behind him a sorely unhappy man.

After settling his gear at Yokosuka, he went to General Staff Headquarters in Tokyo to report to Genda. With him Fuchida found another friend whose career had paralleled his since Eta Jima—Commander Eijiro Suzuki, now in charge of air maintenance on the Naval General Staff. Both men carefully evaluated Fuchida's lengthy report and approved his recommendations, which totaled fifteen new air bases in the Philippines and ten in the Marianas.

Fuchida subsided into routine duties at Kanoya. The autumn and winter of 1943 were busy months for the navy, but he was not directly concerned with any of the action at sea. He remained tied up training the men of the First Air Fleet to be worthy successors of the original force.[3] As fate would have it, they saw action considerably sooner than he expected or desired.

On 20 November, U.S. forces invaded the Gilberts and after savage fighting took over Tarawa and Makin atolls. Having an essential base for air support, and using fast-carrier strikes against the Marshalls, the Americans next occupied Kwajalein and Majuro beginning on 31 January, 1944. Kwajalein had been Japan's main naval base in the area. No Japanese were on Majuro, but it became an exceedingly useful base for the Americans. By these quick, powerful thrusts, the United States secured communications with the south and southwest and began a series of amphibious operations aimed ultimately at the invasion of Japan itself.[4] From this time forth, Admiral Chester W. Nimitz held the strategic initiative to which the Japanese navy had to respond.

The American drive into the Marshalls, and a reconnaissance aircraft hovering inquisitively over Truk in the heart of the Carolines, convinced Koga that this area was no longer a safe haven, if indeed it had ever been. He decided to get his major ships out of there while the getting was good. He dispatched Ozawa with his carriers to Singapore and Kurita's Second Fleet to Palau. Then on 4 February, Koga sailed his flagship *Musashi* to Tokyo for a conference on top-level strategy. There he urged the Naval General Staff that Japan must establish the last defense line in the Marianas and the western Carolines.[5]

If Koga believed his own precepts as expounded to his chief of staff, Fukudome, he had reached that conclusion before February 1944. Like Yamamoto, he thought that the Combined Fleet must fight a decisive battle with the U.S. Pacific Fleet. Koga had little carrier strength left, but he hoped that such an engagement might take place near the Marshalls, where he could count upon Japan's land-based air strength. If the battle did not take place in 1943, it would no longer be possible to fight on the Marshalls line. In that event, Japanese forces would continually be forced back.

Nimitz failed to oblige Koga with the statutory great all-out battle. Moreover, the U.S. Pacific Fleet, plus army and marine units, were methodically penetrating the Marshalls. Hence late 1943 was for the Japanese what Fukudome gloomily called "a transition period in which operations were changed to suicide warfare without a chance of success."[6]

At first the Naval General Staff balked at turning the First Air Fleet over to Koga, being reluctant to commit the force before it was fully trained. But while Koga was thus conferring in Tokyo, Vice Admiral Raymond A. Spruance's carriers, under Rear Admiral Marc A. Mitscher, hit Truk on 17 and 18 February, 1944. The severity of these attacks underlined Koga's arguments more thoroughly than any line of reasoning could have done, and persuaded Tokyo to let him have the First Air Fleet. The invasion of the Marshalls and the raid on Truk also convinced the high command that Koga was right, that they could expect the full force of an all-out American offensive. They had to hold the Marianas and Carolines.[7]

Koga sailed the *Musashi* from Tokyo to Palau, about 1,200 miles west of Truk, where he established Combined Fleet headquarters. As Koga plunged through the Pacific to join Vice Admiral Takeo Kurita, he hoped that the Americans would have to pause and consolidate their gains. In case they didn't, Koga had an alternate plan: If they struck shortly against the Marianas, Koga would move his headquarters to Saipan; if they hit in the south, he would move to Davao and command from there.

Fuchida heard about the Truk raid while busy with his training tasks at

Kanoya. He didn't know the full extent of the damage, but he learned enough to reach a swift conclusion: Nimitz would invade the Marianas much sooner than the Japanese expected. Thus it behooved the navy to lose no time in preparing for the forthcoming trial of strength. In particular, they must redouble their efforts to perfect the First Air Fleet.

Fuchida was dumbfounded to learn of Koga's success in securing that organization. He understood why Koga wanted it, and didn't accuse him of stupidity as he had Nagumo. Fukudome negotiated the transfer. However, in Yamamoto's time the General Staff had established the dangerous precedent of knuckling under to the commander in chief of the Combined Fleet. They wouldn't have given in to Koga had they understood the reasoning behind the present organization of the air fleet, Fuchida thought. He recalled vividly his post–Pearl Harbor encounter with Fukudome about breaking up the Nagumo task force.[8]

News of the impending transfer sent Fuchida posthaste to Kakuta to protest. "Our training mission has been seriously delayed by lack of planes," he reminded his chief. "We need at least two more months of intensive training before the First Air Fleet will be ready for action. This move is premature. Just a few more months and we can send it out as a devastating weapon. I fear we're committing the force in a plan which will dribble away its strength."

"I'm no happier over the decision than you, Fuchida," replied Kakuta. "However, I had no choice but to obey. I already have my orders."

So on 20 February Kakuta ordered the First Air Fleet to the Marianas, headquarters at Tinian. Fuchida went with his flock, not the proud combat leader of a honed fighting instrument, as he had hoped and anticipated, but a seriously troubled man. He couldn't avoid the brutal fact that the Naval General Staff lacked the judgment and the courage to hold the line and buy time until the First Air Fleet could go into action at maximum efficiency. Spruance of Midway had won another major victory over Japanese naval air power without even knowing it.

Fuchida had to make the best of a bad situation, and bad it was, for the air bases he had requested remained unfinished. He had expected that three on Saipan, three on Tinian, three on Guam, and one on Rota would be ready for use. Instead, there were only two incomplete bases on Tinian. The same situation existed on Saipan. Swift American advances were preventing construction from keeping pace with Japan's needs. Where would Fuchida's aircraft fit in? This was an immediate, unexpected problem.

The bombers flew from Kyushu to Iwo Jima, thence to the Marianas. Stormy weather in the homeland held up arrival of the fighters at Kisarazu in east central Honshu. From there they flew to Iwo Jima. On the last stop, a typhoon delayed them again. As a result, the fighters arrived a week late, on 30 February. This seriously weakened the First Air Fleet in its initial days of action.[9]

In the meantime, Kakuta and Fuchida acted promptly. On the morning of the twenty-second, the latter ordered reconnaissance aircraft on a search arc 300 miles to the east and south of Tinian. At about 1530, the admiral and Fuchida set out to investigate the second air base under construction on the island. While they surveyed the work and encouraged the engineers to speed it up, a car from headquarters swung up with a screech of brakes. The driver handed over a message from the scout plane: "Enemy sighted. Force includes carriers."

Kakuta and Fuchida hastened back to headquarters. On the way, they discussed what to do about the sighting. "The enemy will probably attack soon," said Kakuta.

"Yes, most likely tomorrow," Fuchida agreed. It was their only point of agreement in this crisis.

Kakuta wanted to strike at once. Fuchida admired him as a man of exceptional courage, but saw that prudence didn't temper his valor. Proud of his gallant war record, Kakuta thought only in terms of the attack. He was a "wild pig warrior," as Fuchida would say. Fuchida himself had no illusions about the folly of sending half-ready bombers minus fighter escort against the deadly Spruance-Mitscher team.[10]

"Don't risk our forces unnecessarily," he entreated. "Fly all the aircraft back to Japan at once, while they can still escape. Without fighters, the bombers have no cover. The bombers themselves have only just touched down from their long flight. Their crews aren't sufficiently rested to be thrown into battle. We can't face an all-out fight with the American task force."

Kakuta didn't agree. To him, caution was cowardice. Each of these old friends felt a little disappointed in the other. Kakuta believed Fuchida was afraid to go out and fight unless the odds were in his favor; Fuchida thought Kakuta lacked the common sense to order restraint in a situation where judgment should govern ardor.

That night, under Kakuta's orders, about twenty-seven torpedo planes took off under the lead of Furukawa, accompanied by nine night reconnaissance aircraft that sped ahead to find the U.S. carrier force and lead the bombers to it.

Back on Tinian, Kakuta and Fuchida waited anxiously for word. Finally over the radio they heard the attack signal: *"To, To, To!"* Then silence. A few scout planes straggled back to report smoke and fire on the sea, but not one of the bombers returned. There was no way to confirm the result of the attack.[11]

At dawn the next day, 23 February, more reconnaissance planes flew out in search of the Americans. Without waiting to receive any preliminary report, Kakuta insisted that Fuchida send off about fifty-four dive-bombers, still lacking fighter cover. With grave misgivings, Fuchida obeyed orders. Every plane and man in this group was lost, some in attacking the American ships, the rest while attempting to return to Tinian. The U.S. Navy completely controlled the air over the Marianas. Some three hundred planes covered Mitscher's big push of 23 February, and they destroyed not only Tinian's planes but storage depots, houses, and other buildings around the installation.

In spite of the fearful punishment, Kakuta wanted to order Iwo Jima to send him as many of the First Air Fleet's fighters as had reached that point—sheer madness in the circumstances. "Kakuta was crazy!" said Fuchida indignantly. This time Fuchida jettisoned both military decorum and his personal affection for Kakuta. "It's absolutely stupid to bring the fighters down from Iwo," he told him vigorously. "They'll come into the Marianas after a long flight, short on fuel and with their crews exhausted. And as only twenty-seven fighters are on Iwo, they'll be no match for the Americans. The rest of the fighters haven't yet left the mainland."

Kakuta admitted that Fuchida was right, but he was furious at the beating he had taken. He wanted the rest of the First Air Fleet's planes still in Japan, about two-thirds of the whole force, to take off immediately for the Marianas and engage the enemy.[12]

The Mitscher raid was a humiliating defeat for Japan and a deadly punch to the already shaky First Air Fleet. Fuchida mourned the deaths of the men for whom he, under Kakuta, was responsible. The loss of Furukawa was a particular blow. Since before Pearl Harbor Fuchida had relied heavily on his advice, expertise, and cooperation. Now he needed such men to pass on their experience to the green pilots being sent to the First Air Fleet. Like any officer in wartime, Fuchida was prepared to buy results with men, but to lose them for nothing crushed his spirit. And he knew that the raid was only a token of more to come.

Fuchida was not surprised when Koga personally ordered the remainder of the First Air Fleet to Saipan. Under the circumstances, this was the only sensible thing to do. The fleet had lost a third of its force. Additional training and aircraft were needed. Although Kakuta kept reconnaissance planes in the air all day to watch for an enemy fleet, Tinian was vulnerable because it had no radar. Nor could the Japanese launch night scouts. As a commander, Kakuta was a danger if left to himself on Tinian.

"Kakuta would have been A-1 in the place of Nagumo at Pearl Harbor, or in place of Kurita at Leyte Gulf," was Fuchida's judgment. "But he was out of place in the Marianas in February 1944. That situation required a commander who was capable of retreat and flexible thinking."[13]

15

"God Is Testing the Imperial Navy"

Following the Mitscher raids, Fuchida gave Kakuta his estimate of the situation. "This is the first sign that the enemy will invade the Marianas in full force, and soon," he said. "The Americans will probably hit the Marianas another time or two to soften the defenses further, then invade. But before that, they'll raid the Palaus."

This made sense to Kakuta. The Palaus cut across one of Japan's routes to the Philippines or toward the Marianas. And Koga's having stationed his flagship *Musashi* there with important fleet units made the area a natural target.

Fuchida sent extensive searches in that direction every day thenceforth. In the early evening of 28 March, one of the scouts reported three large groups of enemy ships proceeding toward Palau, including eight carriers escorted by battleships and destroyers. As Fuchida read this report, he was doubtful. Not too long ago he would have questioned such news as exaggerated, but not now. Now he thought there might well be ten or twelve carriers in this force, not just eight.[1]

Fuchida was correct. The three-pronged American force consisted of three carrier groups totaling eleven flattops and a strong escort including the new battleship *New Jersey*, with Spruance aboard.[2]

Upon receiving an intelligence report, Koga moved his headquarters and staff ashore, ordering the *Musashi* to Kure and her escort ships to the north. It was none too soon. On 30 and 31 March, Spruance's fleet struck Palau like a typhoon. Then Yap, then Woleai, on 1 April. Palau in particular provided a lesson in what it meant to be on the receiving end of a Spruance attack. Japan's naval air commander at Palau, Rear Admiral Munetako Sakamaki, a rated pilot and no mean opponent, reeled helplessly before the onslaught. Fuchida estimated that Spruance sent in six hundred planes the first day of the attack. "It was a powerful force," Fuchida explained, "almost twice as many as we had in the Pearl Harbor attack. It showed how strongly the United States had developed its air arm."

The Americans destroyed some twenty small ships, played havoc with the shore installations, and sowed mines that tied up the harbor and channel for twenty days. Fuchida estimated that the Japanese lost approximately 160 planes, virtually all they had in the Palau area at the time, against about ten enemy aircraft. Postwar American figures cited 150 Japanese aircraft destroyed, twenty-five American, so Fuchida's guess was not too far out of line. The raids neutralized the western Carolines, protected MacArthur's flank in New Guinea, left Palau an easy prey, and weakened Japan's naval air arm. "This is really a licking," Ugaki, now commanding the First Battleship Division, wrote in his diary.[3]

Koga decided to pull his headquarters out and reestablish it at Davao. It couldn't be moved on either the thirtieth or thirty-first because of the heavy American encirclement, so Koga cabled Davao for some four-engine Kawanishis to pick up just him and his staff.

Around midnight on the thirty-first, two flying boats—all Davao could spare—arrived and took off again with Koga and his staff. As Yamamoto had done, Koga divided his official family between the two aircraft to give him and his chief of staff, Fukudome, a double chance of getting through.

The flight from Palau to Davao was normally three hours. An hour after takeoff, however, the two flying boats ran into a local typhoon with heavy rains.

Fukudome's pilot changed course, avoided the storm, and struggled as far as Cebu, where his aircraft crashed about two and a half miles offshore. Fukudome and several others survived the mishap. But guerrillas captured the party and hustled them off into the mountains. On 12 April, the Third Expeditionary Fleet said that nine survivors, including Fukudome, had been rescued.[4]

The fate of Koga's aircraft remains a mystery to this day. The plane and all on board disappeared as completely as if they had flown out of the solar system. Fuchida and his fellow airmen thought it probable that Koga's pilot, an Eta Jima graduate noted for his personal courage, had pressed his luck too far by trying to ride out the typhoon. In any event, after a thorough search the Combined Fleet had to accept the loss of another commander in chief.

"What rotten luck at a critical time like this!" lamented Ugaki. "It looks as if God is testing the Imperial Navy."[5]

The government kept Koga's death a secret from the public until 5 May, 1944—slightly more than a month after the fact. In the meantime, his loss was admitted to a select group of navy officers, together with the information that Vice Admiral Shiro Takasu had taken his place temporarily. Fuchida heard the sad truth fairly soon. In fact, he had the unpleasant task of breaking it to Kakuta.

Koga's loss didn't deal either Japan or the navy such a paralyzing blow as Yamamoto's had, but it was one in a series of shocks to be credited to Spruance. The parallel with the death of Yamamoto impressed itself on Fuchida. Here was history repeated in uncanny detail—the two aircraft, the divided staff, the loss of the commander in chief, the grave but not fatal downing of his chief of staff.

And it brought personal grief to Fuchida. One of his closest friends had disappeared with Koga, Commander Takeshi Naito, the admiral's air operations officer. Naito and Fuchida had been together in the same class at Kasumigaura. Later, at the Naval Staff College, Naito formed one of the little group so ardently espousing air power. During the early part of the European war, he served as assistant naval attaché in Berlin. In October 1941, when Fuchida was training his airmen in preparation for Pearl Harbor, Naito briefed him about the British aerial torpedo raid on the Italian ships at Taranto. Now he, too, was gone, like their friend and staff college classmate Muroi, who had perished at Ugaki's side on the day of Yamamoto's death.

Fuchida wondered whether the parallel extended further. If Koga's cable to Davao had been intercepted and decoded, American aircraft could have been lurking in wait as they had been on 18 April 1943, when they shot down Yamamoto.[6] However, no American accounts credit any U.S. unit with downing Koga's aircraft. Either they leave the disaster unexplained, or indicate that an accident took place. Thus no conclusive evidence one way or the other has ever been forthcoming.

By this time Fuchida had developed definite ideas about U.S. strategy. He fully realized that the Americans were moving in on Japan from two lines of approach—the MacArthur drive through New Guinea toward the Philippines and the Nimitz offensive through the Marianas. "But of the two, Nimitz was by far the more dangerous," recalled Fuchida. "Because if he soon attacked the Marianas and captured them, the B-29 would come. It would strike at the heart of Japan and then everything would be over. Of course, we wanted to protect both the Marianas and the Philippines, but Japan simply did not have the forces to protect both fronts at once, and of the two, the Marianas were far more important."[7]

Many key Japanese airmen knew about the new big bomber. However, not everyone in authority shared Fuchida's opinion. The Japanese couldn't leave MacArthur entirely to his own devices. Takasu came to the post of temporary commander in chief from the Southwest Area Fleet. Accustomed to thinking in terms of local problems, he continued to concentrate on MacArthur moving along the New Guinea coast. He estimated that the general's next target would be Biak Island, a strategic entry to the southern area that Japan could not afford to see cut off. So the admiral ordered most of the First Air Fleet transferred to Halmahera Island in the East Indies, under his own command, to bolster that area's defense. He pulled about a hundred fighters and bombers out of Nimitz's path and sent them to the back street of nowhere.

This development infuriated Fuchida. Japan urgently needed those forces and many more to counteract the expected Nimitz offensive against the Marianas. But he could only swallow his disapproval and comply with the transfer order. His fears turned out to be doubly justified. While waiting for MacArthur's strike against Humboldt Bay on the north central coast of New Guinea, which came on 22 April, many of the pilots at Halmahera contracted malaria. They had to be pulled out of the running before the race even started.[8]

Fuchida was not yet ready to concede total defeat, but his insistence upon the importance of the Marianas reveals the direction of his thoughts. Japan's objective had been the riches of Southeast Asia, and for a little while it held them. Every day these acquisitions were looking more and more expendable, and the homeland—without oil, tin, rubber, or any of the commodities the Japanese had thought essential for their survival—began to appear more and more precious.

Once more 18 April rolled around. Again it proved a red-letter day in Fuchida's life, although he didn't know it at the time. That evening he had dinner and a discussion on Tinian with Kakuta and others of the First Air Fleet staff. Vice Admiral Seiichi Ito, vice chief of the Naval General Staff, and the indefatigable Genda joined them. The two officers from Tokyo had recently been discussing the progress of the war with Nagumo, who in March arrived on Saipan as commander in chief of the central Pacific and of the Fourteenth Air Force. Nagumo was never one to look on the bright side; now he really had something to be pessimistic about. They wanted to hear Kakuta's and Fuchida's opinion to get a rounded picture.[9]

"The immediate trouble is at the very top," Fuchida declared without hesitation. "A permanent commander in chief of the Combined Fleet must be appointed without delay, otherwise our naval leadership will deteriorate. And Takasu's headquarters is too removed from the heart of events, which isn't very far from Japan."

"Something must be done along those lines," agreed Genda, with a swift glance at Ito. "The next commander in chief may be Admiral Soemu Toyoda."

Genda knew of another projected transfer that he didn't discuss with Fuchida. That very evening, Ito requested Kakuta to release Fuchida for duty as Toyoda's air operations officer. No one said anything to Fuchida about this until the appointment could be confirmed. They didn't want him to be let down in case it wasn't.

Two days later the message came from Tokyo: "Fuchida appointed air operations officer of the Combined Fleet." The order directed him at once to Tokyo to discuss matters with his successor. So the next day, 21 April, he thumbed a hop on a land bomber to begin what was to be his final wartime duty assignment. At the Navy Ministry he reported to the senior staff officer of the personnel section, who passed him along to the air department's senior staff officer. After being briefed, Fuchida was free to look around Tokyo.[10]

Wartime had dropped a depressing curtain over the city's usual brisk vitality. The propaganda line of the day called for austerity at the home front. Respectable women wore a cheap garment called a *mompei*. Stores offered little for sale. The geisha houses were shuttered up.[11] Although economic conditions had worsened, thus far Fuchida's family had been relatively fortunate, for Haruko could shop at the naval commissary.

Fuchida was able to snatch a few visits with his family. "Sometimes he came home with navy friends of his," Miyako remembered. "Then they had a lot of sake and sang the warship march vigorously."

During one of Fuchida's visits, Haruko developed a mysterious illness. Overnight one of her legs swelled to twice its normal size. Fuchida and the doctors feared that amputation would be necessary. At this prospect Haruko balked. Rejecting surgery, she insisted upon injections with penicillin, then still in the experimental stage in Japan, and emerged from the ordeal with two healthy legs.[12]

In general, the navy greeted Toyoda's appointment with approval. He had been commander of Yokosuka Naval Base, in itself an excellent preparation. "Toyoda was a quiet type of man, but a man of strong character," Fuchida later described his chief. "Perhaps he didn't have too much confidence in himself. He understood air operations reasonably well but he didn't know how to lead them."[13] Fuchida had put his finger on Toyoda's main weakness—he didn't know how to lead. Indeed, Toyoda was quite reluctant to become commander in chief. He believed that Koga's logical successor was Nagumo.[14]

Fuchida never ceased to lament that Japan had no admiral to match Halsey. As a good officer will, Fuchida studied the enemy's top leaders, analyzing their mentality and character, and he conceived a sincere respect for this admiral. "If the Japanese navy had had a half-dozen Halseys through-out the war and just one at Pearl Harbor, the story of the war in the Pacific would have been entirely different," he reminisced. "But no such man existed in the Japanese navy.

"Defeat is not only a matter of economics and matériel; it is a question of aggressive leadership. This would have saved the situation for us many times during the war. What we needed was a Halsey."[15]

What they got was a specialist in administration and logistics who had not one hour's combat experience in the current conflict. Fuchida didn't hold this against Toyoda, for he realized that Japan had almost reached the end of its resources; naval operations now had to be planned on the basis of what was available. Toyoda knew every base and its capability, what the navy could supply and build, and what it could not. With this background, Toyoda saw with painful clarity that Japan stood on the threshold of its destiny. Loss of the Marianas would mean the beginning of the end. And because as a logistician he understood the comparable industrial capacities of the United States and Japan, he had no confidence whatsoever that he could carry out his mission. But he was a courageous man and would do his best.

Toyoda selected Kusaka as his chief of staff, so once more Fuchida had the privilege of serving under this fine gentleman.[16] In a world of change, Kusaka remained as nearly unaltered and unalterable as the human condition permits. Through his Zen Buddhist discipline, he merged his will with the divine will. He faced life equally without passion and without reproach, accepting whatever came his way with courteous detachment.[17]

Fuchida discovered that in some respects his job as air officer was the key one of the staff. For all intents and purposes, the only really effective unit at sea was the Mobile Carrier Force under Ozawa. Any staff work Fuchida completed would be significant for the fate of the navy and ultimately of the homeland. He assumed, however, that his efforts would follow the chain of command. He would submit his work to the senior staff officer, who would buck it to the vice chief, then to Kusaka, and ultimately to Toyoda. By the time Toyoda received a plan or suggestion from Fuchida, it would embody the recommendations of several senior officers.

This didn't prove to be the case. His papers went almost directly through Kusaka to Toyoda, virtually without change or amplification, and Toyoda, no airman, invariably accepted his ideas. While flattering to Fuchida, this situation placed a tremendous responsibility on the shoulders of a mere commander. It also reflected the supreme importance that had finally been attached to naval aviation—now that it was virtually too late to matter.[18]

Certainly it was too late for Fuchida to savor what should have been the climax of his career. At that time, the post of air operations officer of the Combined Fleet was the most prestigious staff assignment open to a naval aviator. In anything like normal times, he would have taken pride and pleasure in his selection. Under the circumstances, however, he held the position without the means to use it constructively. It was like finding a million yen notes on a desert island. What could a man do with them except light fires?

16

"God Is Not on Our Side"

A VISITOR strolling into a Japanese officers' club early in 1944 might have seen a little knot of naval brass lifting glasses with a ringing *"Kampei!"*—the equivalent of "Bottoms up!" In this manner the men saluted each oil tanker from Southeast Asia that had run the gauntlet of American submarines to reach the oil center at Yokoyama, near the western end of the Inland Sea. The steel sharks sank so many tankers that any oiler coming safely through the Straits of Shimonoseki richly earned the toast.

If the surface fleet had remained in home waters, it would have been canceled out as an effective force before ever meeting the enemy. As the oil could not come to the ships, the ships had to go to the oil. So in February Toyoda sent most of them to Lingga Roads at Singapore. For once Fuchida did not object to moving the vessels so far from the Nimitz line. Conventional forces, however formidable, would be worthless without command of the air.[1]

Toyoda remained in his headquarters in Tokyo's Akasaka Palace or occasionally in the light cruiser *Oyoda* in the Inland Sea or Tokyo Bay. His staff officers stayed at his side. In some respects the Combined Fleet organization now resembled its American counterpart. Toyoda was comparable to Nimitz, Admiral Shigetaro Shimada, chief of the Naval General Staff, to Admiral Ernest J. King. Ozawa, who had been in command of the carriers and their screen, took over practically all surface ships. His nearest American equivalent at the time was Spruance. Of the nine carriers remaining to Japan, only three—the *Shokaku* and *Zuikaku*, both the worse for wear and having under-

gone extensive repairs, and the new *Taiho,* completed on 7 March 1944—
really deserved the name of carrier.

The painful shortage of skilled pilots continued. Most of the veteran flight
personnel had perished. About this time, five hundred pilots and a like
number of radio operators emerged from Kasumigaura, candidates for carrier
assignments. These fledglings of eighteen to twenty years old normally would
have received further training in the home islands. But scarcely any gas
remained for training purposes, so they and their instructors had to go directly
to the Third Fleet and train at sea under Ozawa.[2]

Through no fault of his own, Ozawa was unable to give them the on-the-
spot training they needed. The fleet had moved to Tawi Tawi, westernmost
of the Sulu Islands. Not only were Tawi Tawi's airfields still incomplete, but,
in the words of Captain Toshikazu Ohmae, senior staff officer of the First
Mobile Fleet, "it was practically impossible for carriers to go out of the
anchorage for the training of the airmen because of the threat of enemy
submarines."[3]

Fuchida arranged for the immediate return of the First Air Fleet's planes
from Halmahera to the Marianas. It was the only thing the Japanese could
do. A mere handful of the more than one hundred pilots remained fit for duty.
The rest had malaria and would be out of action for months. For Fuchida,
this particular misfortune was almost the last straw. Japan's other disasters of
the past year—the loss of Yamamoto, then Koga; steady American progress
through the Pacific islands; the resurgence of MacArthur; and the attrition
of Japan's shipping—were the fortunes of war. A malaria bug canceling out
so many fine airmen fell into the category lawyers call acts of God. With the
grim statistics in his hands, Fuchida began to see an almost mystical thread
of fatality running through the dark tapestry of Japan's misfortunes. "God
is not on our side," he thought bleakly.[4]

But he wouldn't shirk his job. If only his airmen could catch the American
carriers before they reached the Marianas! Where would Spruance go following his April raids? He estimated that the admiral would take his fleet to the
huge harbor of Majuro Island in the Marshalls. A surprise attack there might
pay off. Sinking eight or ten American flattops would put a serious dent in
Nimitz's plan to invade the Marianas.

To that end, all through May Fuchida worked on a plan he named *Tan
Sakusen* (Red Heart Operation). He determined to head the attack force
himself. Toyoda and Kusaka agreed to this reluctantly. Both admirals valued
him as a colleague, and an attack with such limping naval air forces as were
at his disposal virtually guaranteed his death. But he insisted on his duty and
right to lead his men, and they could not deny the logic.[5]

Toward the end of May events diverted their attention. On Saturday the twenty-seventh, MacArthur's forces landed on Biak in the Schouten Islands off New Guinea. Biak was important to Japan. If the Americans built airstrips there, it would be difficult for the Japanese to maintain their own on the western end of New Guinea. Palau would be within American striking range, so, Ugaki estimated, "movements of the Task Force east of Mindanao will be impossible. Finally, Operation 'A' [i.e., the naval Armageddon] will be made impracticable."[6]

Toyoda and Kusaka inclined toward Ugaki's serious view. In fact, they wondered if the Biak invasion heralded the principal American thrust against Japan. Fuchida thought not. "The main invasion will come in the Marianas," he said, "because Nimitz has the bulk of U.S. sea and air power, and these two factors will dictate his major advance."

Neither Toyoda nor Kusaka agreed completely. They rather expected Nimitz to order his fleet to Biak in support of MacArthur. Fuchida remained positive that every available Japanese naval force should concentrate in the Marianas to prepare for Operation A, and kept hammering away at that point. They should forget MacArthur, and acknowledge that they couldn't hold Biak or indeed most of the outlying points. They should abandon them without wasting time, fuel, and men. If Nimitz breached their defenses in the Marianas, he would cut their lifeline and they would lose their outposts anyway, whether MacArthur invaded them or not.[7]

Japanese troops on Biak put up a fierce resistance. Toyoda decided to bombard the enemy's footholds and to help the army by transporting about twenty-five hundred troops from Zamboanga in the Philippines to Biak. This the Japanese named Operation *Kon*.

After two false starts using destroyers, Toyoda called in his first team, the monster battleships *Yamato* and *Musashi*, to sortie from the anchorage at Tawi Tawi and bomb Biak at night. On 10 June the battlewagons and their escorts set out under Ugaki's command. Because these ships had no carrier cover, the navy sent up what planes remained in the Halmahera area to provide air support.

When the ships had steamed to within 200 miles of Biak, a United States reconnaissance plane spotted them, and Ugaki's air cover saw the American scout. When this news reached headquarters, Toyoda's senior staff officer, Captain Fugita, recommended that since Japan had lost surprise, they should call off the expedition. Toyoda agreed. On 13 June he sent the word to Ugaki, who pulled back accordingly.[8]

This development aroused mixed feelings in Fuchida, who had opposed Operation *Kon* from the start. "I never wanted any of the fleet sent to Biak," he later explained. "I wanted to bring all available forces to the Marianas when the time came and there fight the great all-out battle. However, once we launched *Kon* and the battleships reached within 200 miles of the target, I believed they might as well go through with it and inflict what damage they could on MacArthur's troops, rather than waste the trip." So he fumed when Toyoda and Fugita got cold feet. In this opinion he was one with Genda in general headquarters, who knew about the scheme and was sorely displeased that it fizzled out so ignobly.[9]

While *Kon* was under way, the Allies began the invasion of Normandy. There was a general realization in the Japanese navy that this was very dangerous for Germany. Like many Japanese, Fuchida had pinned his faith on the Axis partnership. If Germany won in Europe, Japan might well be victorious in Asia. Now no possibility remained of a Nazi victory. Nor did Fuchida harbor hopes of Hitler holding off the Allies. Long, hard fighting awaited the Allies in Europe, but Fuchida felt certain of the end.[10]

About this time Fuchida returned to his own brainchild, Operation *Tan.* Before firming up plans or taking action, the Japanese would have to survey Majuro Harbor, a project Fuchida entrusted to his good friend and veteran reconnaissance expert, Commander Takehiko Chihaya. He directed two scout planes, Japan's newest and best, to take off on 3 June from Tinian, go to Truk for refueling, and thence proceed to the small, isolated island of Nauru where Japan maintained fuel supplies. Chihaya joined these scouts on 4 June.

That night he flew to Majuro, timing himself to arrive on the fifth at dawn, the hour of the proposed attack. Beneath him lay a sight to make any Japanese bombardier lick his chops—at least twelve carriers, four of them quite small, with their escort ships. Chihaya took pictures of this magnificent array, then flew back to Truk to save fuel. Even so, he cut it fine, touching down with a bare minimum of gas. After refueling, he hastened to Tinian to have his photographs developed and sent to Fuchida.

This evidence removed all doubt as to the advisability of *Tan.* Fuchida planned to lead twenty-seven torpedo planes. Egusa would head a like number of dive-bombers. They established an approach route from Kisarazu to Marcus Island, on to Wake, and thence to Majuro. Fuchida arranged for a last-minute reconnaissance. It so happened, however, that an American bombing mission hit the Truk fields on the very date Chihaya was scheduled to make this check. Fuchida postponed the operation for a few days.

Chihaya scouted Majuro again on 9 June, flying from Truk to Majuro, back to Nauru, and home to Truk. On this mission he had no luck at all. Apparently the whole American fleet had sortied. Great was the puzzlement in Combined Fleet headquarters at this news. Where were Spruance's forces? Nobody had any firm answers. That ended Operation Red Heart—a mission that almost surely would have been curtains for Fuchida, among others.[11]

Foiled in this scheme, the Combined Fleet staff returned with renewed vigor to their planning for the defense of the Marianas, the battle plan called *A-Go* which, according to Fuchida, originated with Ohmae. The Japanese would lure the American fleet south of Palau, Yap, and Wolaei and there join battle. Every available warship would participate, including the nine carriers, protected by submarines and land-based planes.

Fuchida worked on the preparations for Operation A with all his customary vigor, but not with any view to victory in the Pacific. A full concentration of Japanese forces in the Marianas might succeed in sinking a good portion of Nimitz's fleet. If this could be done, there would be a good opportunity for a compromise peace with the United States. But if the Japanese couldn't hold off the Americans there, that was the end of Japan. He doubted the plan's chance of success. Ozawa's pilots were still green and the battle plan overextended them. Moreover, fond as Fuchida was of Ozawa, he doubted his leadership qualities.[12]

On 15 June, U.S. forces commenced landing on Saipan, and Toyoda activated *A* with a grandiloquent message: "The Combined Fleet will destroy the enemy task force which has come to the Marianas area, then annihilate its invasion force."[13]

That is not the way matters turned out. The Japanese plan called for close cooperation between Ozawa's carriers and Kakuta's First Air Fleet covering the Marianas, Carolines, Iwo Jima, and Truk. But Ozawa held off sortie until the last possible moment and had to refuel, which cost him precious time. As he moved toward the scene of action, installations in the Marianas took a terrific beating from aerial strikes and battleship bombardment. By the time Ozawa reached a position to do battle, the First Air Fleet had been knocked out as a force in being.

With Japan's plan for coordinated air effort shot to pieces, Spruance could face Ozawa undistracted. Possessed of his customary cool prudence, he held off attack until he had the chance to clear the air. Ozawa sent a full-scale strike against the American carriers, only to run into a hornet's nest of Hellcats and antiaircraft fire. In these first attacks, he lost most of his aircraft and inflicted little damage on the Americans.

Just when the crews of Ozawa's carriers were congratulating themselves that the Americans either had not discovered them or dared not attack, disaster struck from below. The submarine *Albacore* slammed a torpedo into the brand-new flagship *Taiho*. The actual hit had little effect on the sturdy carrier, but gas vapors began seeping through the ship, so Ozawa transferred his flag to the cruiser *Naguro*. Less than two hours later, a terrible explosion shattered the *Taiho*. She sank at 1640. Within two hours, the submarine

Cavalla sent four torpedoes into the *Shikaku,* which blew up later the same day.

Ill fortune continued to dog Ozawa on the morrow, commencing with a night attack. Spruance took the air offensive, sinking the *Hiyo* and two tankers full of precious fuel. Heavy damage was inflicted on the *Zuikaku, Junyo, Ryujo,* and *Chiyoda,* on the battleship *Haruna,* and on yet another tanker.[14]

The Americans called the air action of 19 June 1944 the Marianas Turkey Shoot, an inelegant but accurate title. By the night of 20 June, when the Battle of the Philippine Sea ended, Ozawa had lost 395 of his 430 carrier aircraft. One fact may best summarize Japan's frustration: In the Battle of the Philippine Sea, the United States lost more aircraft in launching accidents than by Japanese action.[15]

Back on the flagship, listening to the inexorable score of Japanese losses, Fuchida heard the drums of defeat beating in his ears. He was not unduly dejected, for he had expected some such result. On the personal front, however, he had to face a series of stunning griefs. They made the Marianas campaign, particularly the action on and around Saipan, the most tragic days of his life since Midway.

Among those who perished in defense of Saipan were two of his closest Eta Jima shipmates, Taketora Uyoda and Terujiro Urata. They had been members of that the small coterie that included Fuchida, Genda, and Suzuki. Chihaya, too—peerless scout and observer—met his fate over Saipan. Fuchida had worked long and harmoniously with Chihaya; the loss made him feel as though he had lost some of his sight. Worst of all—if one such bereavement can be more cruel than another—was the loss of Egusa, Fuchida's closest Pearl Harbor comrade. He remembered their jailbreak from Yokosuka Hospital after Midway, the steadfast, stalwart Egusa carrying him out on his back. And in that same terrible July, Fuchida lost another Pearl Harbor veteran. In death, as in life, Itaya was different. He fell in the Kuriles, a victim of Japanese antiaircraft gunners who mistook his plane for an enemy's. Fuchida and Itaya had never been cronies, but the fighter ace's death shook him. Of that select group who led the major segments of the Pearl Harbor air strike, only Fuchida and Shimazaki remained.

Also lost were two commanders under whose flags Fuchida had served long and well. Nagumo perished on Saipan, committing suicide when he saw defeat staring him in the face. On Tinian, Kakuta perished with every member of the First Air Fleet staff, whether by suicide or enemy action is not known. Had Fuchida still been with Kakuta, he would have been in the forefront of the action and possibly one of the first to die.[16]

Others more highly placed than Fuchida shared his belief that the summer of 1944, in particular the Saipan campaign, marked a turning point in Japan's fortunes. "The loss of Saipan made a profound change in the prospect of the war situation," recalled General Shigeru Hasunuma, chief aide-de-camp to the emperor. "It seemed to me that at the time many of the intelligent Japanese felt that efforts should be made to terminate the war rather than continue a struggle which held no hope of victory."[17]

In a democracy such opinions would have surfaced rapidly and found spokesmen. No such development was possible in Japan. Suggestions for peace had to be whispered, exchanged by the most subtle of hints between the most trusted of friends. Marquis Koichi Kido, lord keeper of the privy seal, testified that as early as autumn 1943 four of the elder statesmen (former premiers of Japan)—Reijiro Wakatsuki, Admiral Keisuke Okada, Kiichiro Hiranuma, and Prince Fumimaro Konoye—began to discuss ways to terminate the war. Kido was in touch with this group and occasionally expressed his opinions.

Around May of 1944, Okada called on Premier Tojo to "attempt to convey to him the views of the elder statesmen. However, the premier accused these men of plotting the overthrow of the Cabinet, and the interview was broken off abruptly. . . ." At the time Tojo "was in a highly nervous condition and made extensive use of the military police for political purposes." The *kempeitai* constantly tailed Konoye and had Kido's official and personal residences under surveillance. And so the men working for an end to the war "mutually exercised the highest degree of caution, since any mention of peace would automatically mean the collapse of the peace movement."[18]

But the Tojo regime couldn't survive the disasters that followed one upon the other in the summer of 1944. The emperor summoned General Kuniaki Koiso from Korea to replace Tojo. Koiso was not happy, but as a loyal subject he had no choice.

Hirohito received Koiso in joint audience with Admiral Mitsumasa Yonai, and charged them: "The two of you, in cooperation with each other, will form a Cabinet, and will particularly put forth efforts to attain the objective of the Great East Asian War. Further, you must be careful not to irritate the Soviet Union." Koiso interpreted this "as an order to destroy the United States and Great Britain, and to accomplish our objective—to construct a Great East Asia."[19] Yet the presence beside him of Yonai, with orders to form a coalition cabinet with him,[20] should have conveyed its own message. A former premier, the friend and sponsor of Yamamoto, Yonai ranked as a moderate politically. During his tenure he had firmly opposed trouble with the United States. Marquis Yasumasa Matsudaira, chief secretary to Kido, had no doubt of the admiral's significance: "Admiral Yonai was chosen because he had the trust of the Emperor and also because the Emperor knew that he entertained thoughts of peace."[21]

Few in Japan understood the nature and extent of the crisis. The armed forces had fed the government-controlled press a diet of boastful misinformation that was duly served up to the public. Most people didn't realize that Japan was losing the war. Not even Koiso and his high-ranking colleagues in Korea knew that the armed forces were incurring heavy losses. The government believed that if it sued for peace, internal disorders would shake the country. After all, when the Treaty of Portsmouth ended the Russo-Japanese war, indignant citizens had set fire to the Diet Building.[22]

Hunched over his desk, heartsore, disturbed, confused, Fuchida presented a microcosm of the national dichotomy. His common sense told him that the only thing to do was sue for peace before the full fury of war fell on the homeland. On the other hand, Japanese fighting men were conditioned from earliest manhood not to surrender. Fuchida's brain said, "Make peace!" His instinct countered, "Never! Fight to the end!"

When he thought of the fierce resistance the Japanese put up in the islands, he was proud. But when he remembered his dead comrades, he grieved that his nation persisted in continuing a hopeless conflict that would demand the sacrifice of many more valuable lives. It was well for his sanity that his job kept him too busy to brood.[23]

17

"Kill, Kill, Kill!"

WITH THE CLOSE of the Marianas campaign, the Japanese entered a new stage of the conflict. They had enjoyed a brief fling on the offensive, then began a long period of gradual pullback. Now the navy embarked upon a strategy of desperation exemplified in two major projects—Operation *Sho,* and the "special attack" concept of suicide weapons.

Fuchida's introduction to the latter came early in July 1944. At that time, Captain Eichiro Jo submitted a petition to his commander, Ozawa, who endorsed it and sent it up to Toyoda, who in turn passed it down for Fuchida's comments. Jo called for a force of suicide pilots to be sent on missions that would strike a telling blow for the empire.

Fuchida knew Jo well. He had served as assistant naval attaché in Washington, and at the time of Pearl Harbor was an aide to the emperor. When he submitted his petition to Ozawa, he skippered the small carrier *Chiyoda.* Jo had a gentle, warm personality. Fuchida liked him immensely. Jo also had a good record in naval aviation as pilot, student, and teacher. And his devotion to the throne touched Fuchida. "He was so loyal to the Emperor," said Fuchida, "that he wanted to lead the first special attack personally."

But Fuchida didn't care much for Jo's idea. Such a special attack force would of necessity be small, hence not overly effective. Further, he didn't believe that Japan's young pilots were yet capable of executing specialized strikes successfully. Not that he doubted their courage. Japanese navy pilots were not afraid. They would die willingly, but if they were to die, it could not be in vain. Ready to spend men but not to throw them away, Fuchida temporarily pigeonholed the idea.[1]

Jo was not the only Japanese naval officer thinking in terms of suicide attacks. Credit for originating what would be the *oka* ("cherry blossom") bomb is generally given to Ensign Shoichi Ota of the Naval Air Technical Depot, who "began to work on the idea of making himself a human bomb around the summer of 1944, when the Marianas campaign had taken a turn extremely unfavorable" to the Japanese.[2]

Fuchida next heard of the special attack concept early in August, when he received a personal letter from veteran fighter pilot Captain Motoharu Okamura, a friend of long standing. He had preceded Fuchida by three classes at Eta Jima, and they often pulled duty together aboard carriers before Pearl Harbor. The start of the war found Okamura instructing the Yokosuka Air Corps. "He was a lot like Murata—a friendly, easygoing type who liked fun," recalled Fuchida. "He had a great sense of humor, was always laughing and cracking jokes."

Okamura wrote from Katori Air Base, where he commanded a fighter group under Vice Admiral Kimpei Teraoka. His letter didn't go into detail about the organization or formation of a special attack force. He simply proposed the establishment of what he called a Hornet Corps *(Mitsubachi Butai)*, which he wanted to command. He explained that when the hornet attacks, he dies, but so does his enemy.

His mind already fertilized by Jo's suggestion, Fuchida decided that Okamura's idea had merit. He took the letter to Toyoda and Kusaka. "What are your opinions?" he asked.

Neither expressed a thought in words. They looked, first at each other, then at Fuchida, and slowly nodded their heads—a less than enthusiastic response, but one he took for approval. Letter in hand, he set out for imperial headquarters to consult with Genda and Suzuki. Both agreed that Okamura had a good idea. The navy should put it into practice.[3]

The *oka* bomb went into production in September 1944. It was a small rocket glider with tiny wings and a cockpit, and was attached to the bottom of a land-based bomber. The glider pilot rode with the mother plane crew until near the target area, then climbed down into the bomb. At the appointed time, the bomber released the missile. Its pilot steered it to his objective and to his own death.

The glider had a cruising range of about eleven nautical miles, and its bombload of some twenty-six hundred pounds could sink a ship if directly on target. The trick to its effective use lay in the mother ship's evading enemy defenses to move in close to the target. The entire weapon—glider, bomb, and pilot—was named *oka*, because the cherry blossom, which falls at the height of loveliness, has always been linked in Japanese symbology with the young warrior slain in battle.

When general headquarters decided to accept Okamura's idea, they appointed him commander of Katori Air Base. There he trained the pilots and crews in the use of the bomb. He also had under his wing the bombers to transport it and the fighter escorts. He fervently believed in his Corps of Divine Thunder *(Jinrai Butai)* and tackled the job with a passion. But because of his value to Japan's war effort, the navy couldn't permit him to lead a mission. Shortly after the end of the war, Okamura shot himself in the head. Having sent so many young men to certain death, he felt that he must give his own life in final salute and atonement.

The Japanese might have put the *oka* into combat months before they actually did—on 21 March 1945—had the Americans not bagged fifty of them at one blow without knowing they had done so. The huge carrier *Shinano*, converted from a *Yamato*-type battleship, came down the ways on 19 November 1944. Ten days later, on her maiden voyage out of Yokosuka with fifty *oka* bombs aboard, she ran afoul of the American submarine *Archerfish*, which slammed six torpedoes into her. She sank within a few hours.[4]

Oddly enough, the first organized utilization of special attack air tactics in the Japanese navy arose, not as a result of Project *Marudai*, the naval research effort to develop a suitable suicide bomb, but in the Philippines at the instigation of Vice Admiral Takijiro Onishi, who assumed command of the Fifth Base Air Force on 20 October 1944.[5] Onishi was another long-time associate of Fuchida's, a pioneer in naval aviation, and exactly the type of man to sponsor a tactic that depended for success more upon physical courage and self-sacrifice than upon skill or training. An ardent patriot, he believed that nothing was impossible to anyone who brought to his task sufficient spiritual determination.[6]

The day he arrived at Clark Field near Manila, 19 October, he proposed mass-suicide tactics to his Zero pilots. With their tradition of honorable suicide, and fully understanding the urgencies of the situation, the pilots unanimously agreed. Thus was born the group Onishi named the *Kamikaze Tokubetsu Kogekitai* (the Divine Wind Special-Attack Squad), after the typhoon that destroyed the Mongol invasion force in 1570.[7]

The first group of twenty-three petty-officer pilots was under the command of Lieutenant Yukio Seki, a graduate of Eta Jima. Their aim was to obtain a hit with every attack. Fuchida explained the methodology:

The Special Attack planes would approach the target from various altitudes, through gaps in the enemy patrol network. At times flights would be made at high altitudes of about 6,000 meters, or this would be changed to altitudes from 500 to 1,000 meters, and at times, extremely low altitudes close to the surface of the water. However, in any case the suicide plane would break through enemy fighters and defensive fire, approach its target at high speed and at an angle as steep as possible, crash and explode on its deck, or if this was impossible, into its side.[8]

Japanese propaganda boasted that every kamikaze sank a ship. This was wildly exaggerated, yet Onishi's men were successful enough to cause the U.S. Navy serious concern. About one in four inflicted damage; one in thirty-three sank its target. The United States clamped a tight lid of censorship on the subject lest the Japanese discover just how much damage the kamikazes were doing. It appeared that Japan had, in Admiral Morison's words, "sprung a tactical surprise that might prolong the war another year."[9]

Meanwhile, in the summer of 1944, the big question confronting Combined Fleet headquarters was where the Americans would strike next. To meet the threat as best they could, headquarters devised a plan called Operation *Sho*. The plan was divided into four parts, each basically the same, differing principally in possible invasion locales: the Philippines, Taiwan-Nansei-Shoto-southern Kyushu, Kyushu-Shokaku-Honshu, and Nokkaido.

Sho means "to conquer," but as Fuchida remarked, "the plan might well have been called Operation Killer." For the objective was not victory. The strategy behind *Sho* was to exact such a high price from the United States that it would end the war by a compromise. The navy planned to concentrate on troop transports, thus obtaining the highest ratio of loss of enemy life per round of Japanese ammunition. The hope was that some one-hundred thousand U.S. troops would be killed when their transports were hit and sunk. If this happened at one or more invasion points, the Japanese believed that public opinion in the United States might well pressure the government into stopping the sacrifice.[10]

The naval air tactics Fuchida worked out were founded on a refusal to commit aircraft in a hopeless duel with American carrier forces at sea. Instead, planes would concentrate on American transports offshore, while they were still crammed with troops. "An empty ship was no target," Fuchida later observed. "We wanted each one full of soldiers so we could kill them all and make the United States feel the pain."[11]

Ugaki received a copy of *Sho* on 17 August. He confided to his diary, "Whether the plan is adequate or not needs further study, but at the time

when we have been driven to the last ditch we have no other choice. . . ."
Five days later he remarked that fleet headquarters seemed to be "taking
things too easy," for no operational plan had been completed.[12]

Toyoda's staff was far from idle. They worked on the navy's own portion
of *Sho* and coordinated with the army, which would bear the brunt of ground
combat against American landing forces. As Colonel Takushiro Hattori,
former chief of the army department operations section of general headquarters, stated, "The point particularly borne in mind, in drawing up plans for
the operations, was how to destroy the enemy landing forces. The first scheme
was the use of air force to destroy enemy convoys, and the second was ground
combat against landing forces."[13]

An imperial conference was held at the palace on 19 August to arrange
for political backing of *Sho*. The policy that emerged had nothing whatsoever
to say about forcing the Americans to the conference table. Instead, it
proclaimed:

> a. By marshaling her existing fighting power and potential national strength
> which can be turned into fighting power by the end of this year, the Empire of
> JAPAN will defeat the enemy, and crush his plan to continue the war.
> b. Regardless of the success or failure of the plan stated above, and no matter
> how the international situation may change, the Empire of JAPAN intends to
> carry the war to a successful conclusion with her 100 million people firmly united
> in unshakable confidence in her ultimate victory and protecting the Imperial
> Land.[14]

This represented the diehard, unrealistic army line, which the navy had
somehow to counter. Its most potent weapon was Yonai, who wore two hats
as vice premier and navy minister. Around the first part of September,
Toyoda and top members of his staff, including Fuchida, consulted with
Yonai. After listening carefully to their proposal, he replied in effect, "If your
Sho Operation works well during the first American attempt at invasion, I
can bring pressure to bear on the army for a compromise peace, and will not
hesitate to do so."

Thus encouraged, Combined Fleet headquarters immediately arranged
for war games in the Naval Staff College to acquaint all officers concerned
with the new strategy and review in detail how to carry it out. Toyoda held
the chair as supreme umpire. Those in attendance included Toyoda's staff
and certain members of general headquarters who acted the part of the
American invaders. Among these representatives were Suzuki, whose path
had crossed Fuchida's so often since their days together at Eta Jima, and
Commander Yoshimore Terai, one of his good friends from Naval Staff

College days. He came in place of Genda, whom he was scheduled to replace as air operations officer in the near future.[15]

Most of the air fleet commanders attended the war games, along with their staffs. Among them was Ozawa, who still commanded the carriers. Only one, the *Zuikaku*, was a major flattop. Of the others—the *Chitose*, *Chiyoda*, and *Zuiho*—only the *Chiyoda* began life as a carrier, the other two being remodeled submarine tenders. Following the Marianas disaster, these four returned to Japan to be moored and camouflaged in the Inland Sea. Each anchored separately near a small island thickly wooded with pine trees. Scrub pine and other shrubbery concealed their flight decks. Two new sister carriers, the *Unryu* and *Amagi*, took to the seas early in August, but no naval pilots remained to man them.

In opening the war games, Yonai spoke briefly on the problem of compromise peace and Operation *Sho*. His presence underlined the significance of the exercises. Although the Philippines were considered the most likely invasion target, the war games used Taiwan as the guinea pig. It was assumed that before this invasion, twelve American carriers would attack Kyushu, Honshu, Shikoku, and the Philippines.

Among other things, the attendees threshed out the problem of how to save land-based planes from enemy carrier strikes. They decided that the navy should move as many as possible to Korea and Shikoku, there to hide them in the woods and caves. They would also send a number to the Tokyo area. If the Americans raided the capital in force, these aircraft would shift to Hokkaido. Otherwise, the Japanese preferred not to send planes to Hokkaido, so remote from the center of operations.[16]

The war games assumed, too, that an attempted American invasion would follow hard upon the heels of the carrier strikes. This posed a problem: despite the navy's hope of sinking American troop transports offshore, some enemy forces would inevitably be able to land. They agreed, therefore, that the army must be reinforced to stop or at least delay American landing parties while the naval air arm completed its destruction.

"Here, too," Fuchida remarked, "the basic aim was to kill, kill, kill . . ." He didn't fool himself into thinking that only American blood would flow. As he recalled, "We Japanese, too, had to be prepared not only to be bloodthirsty killers—we all had to be ready to be killed. This not only meant the pilots who flew the planes but all of the officers and men aboard all of the ships. Yes, even the ships themselves must become instruments of suicide attacks in order to exact the heaviest possible toll from the enemy."[17]

No doubt Yonai was sincere when he promised to put pressure on the army for a compromise peace if *Sho* initially succeeded. But he didn't have the chance to make his word good. Indeed, the autumn of 1944 provided the Japanese navy with a convincing demonstration of Murphy's Law—if anything can go wrong, it will.

Periodically the Pacific Fleet switched command and title between Spruance (Fifth Fleet) and Halsey (Third Fleet), although the fleets were structurally the same body. Halsey was in command when his carrier forces engaged the Japanese in what the latter termed *Taiwan Oki Kokusen* ("Off Taiwan Air Operation").

On his way home from Manila, Fuchida, along with Toyoda and his assistant chief of staff, Rear Admiral Toshitane Takada, stopped on Taiwan for an inspection tour.[18] He was deeply disturbed when the Japanese elected to give battle instead of dispatching their planes to Kyushu, in accordance with the war games.[19] Reports of ensuing Japanese aircraft losses vary from five hundred planes (Morison) to 143 (Ohmae).[20] Fuchida's estimate of 312 strikes the proverbial happy medium and exactly coincides with the official announcement. In any case, results were bad enough that Fuchida was in no position to celebrate, as he normally would have, when a promotion list of 15 October raised him and Genda to the rank of captain.[21]

Undeterred by facts, the Japanese press proclaimed another great victory. On 19 October the *Asahi* newspaper published its list of alleged enemy losses: sunk, eleven carriers, two battleships, three cruisers, and one destroyer; damaged, eight carriers, two battleships, four cruisers, and thirteen unidentified ships. The nation at large reveled in the news, and the emperor expressed his satisfaction.[22] But knowledgeable navy men, such as Ozawa, victim of Spruance's Turkey Shoot, and Vice Admiral Takeo Kurita, commander in chief, Second Fleet, were skeptical.[23]

Back in Tokyo with Toyoda, Fuchida received material submitted by an officer of the force involved. He studied and discussed this with Suzuki at general headquarters and with the Combined Fleet's intelligence officer. He admitted, ". . . Even the most generous interpretation of the conclusion . . . indicated that bomb damages were inflicted on just four aircraft carriers." After checking later radio intelligence, it appeared "rather unlikely that any of them were sunk. Therefore, it was estimated that the enemy still had ten effective aircraft carriers."

The Naval General Staff agreed, so when the first part of *Sho* went into effect on 17 October with the American landings on Suluan Island, the Combined Fleet "warned subordinate air force units . . . that the enemy task force was estimated to contain 10 aircraft carriers in operating condition."[24]

Altogether, for the Japanese this was an inauspicious prelude to the major battle that they called the Second Battle of the Philippine Sea, and which the Americans knew as the Battle of Leyte Gulf. Convinced that the enemy planned to invade the Philippines by way of Leyte, Toyoda activated *Sho* on 18 October. Roughly, participating Japanese naval forces were divided into three principal groups. Kurita headed the First Striking Force, which in turn was divided into the Center Force under Kurita and the Southern Force under Vice Admiral S. Nishimura. The plan called for these two bodies to catch U.S. amphibians in Leyte Gulf in a pincers movement. Meanwhile, the Mobile Force under Ozawa would sortie from home waters and lure Halsey's carriers north of the main scene of action.[25]

The idea of this decoy operation originated with Fuchida, who felt quite certain that Halsey could no more resist charging after four Japanese flattops than a bull could ignore a matador's cape. Fuchida had difficulty selling the idea to Toyoda and Kusaka, but Captain Shigenori Kami, the new senior staff officer, backed him up. Later Ozawa, the prospective cheese in this mouse-trap, agreed with the concept.[26]

Despite his formidable First Strike Force, which included the *Yamato*, *Musashi*, five old battleships, eleven heavy cruisers, two light cruisers, and nineteen destroyers, Kurita was pessimistic. Remembering Guadalcanal, he believed that

the enemy transports would have to be destroyed completely. However, . . . my opinion at that time was that, in view of the difference in air strength of the opposing forces, our chance for a victory after the sortie would be about fifty-fifty. I had also thought then that the aerial support would fall short of our expectations.[27]

Kurita's fears were well founded. Leyte Gulf did for Japan's surface forces what the Battle of the Philippine Sea had done for the air arm. As it happened, Ozawa's decoy operation was fairly successful. Precisely as the Japanese hoped, Halsey thundered after Ozawa, whose carriers *Zuikaku*, *Zuiho*, *Chitose*, and *Chiyoda* had only 116 aircraft among them. The hybrid *Ise* and *Hyuga*, battleships partially modified as carriers, had no planes aboard. Ozawa's force, without the strength to challenge the U.S. carrier force effectively, suffered heavy losses—the four carriers, one light cruiser, three destroyers, an oiler, and all but twenty-nine of his aircraft.[28]

He had done well to keep American fleet carriers away from the main action. Unfortunately for the Japanese, it was a wasted effort. Not realizing Kurita was facing Rear Admiral T. L. Sprague's famous "Taffy" escort carriers instead of Halsey's mighty flattops, he feared that to enter Leyte Gulf "long after the scheduled time would mean rushing into the enemy, who had completed its defense, and would only result in our becoming easy victims." So he reversed course, greatly to the relief of the Americans, for despite the beating he had potent firepower left. Forces under his command lost three battleships, including the *Musashi*, six heavy cruisers, three light cruisers, nine destroyers, a destroyer transport, and four submarines.[29]

Fuchida didn't speak about what the loss of Ozawa's four carriers meant to him, but of course their sacrifice was implicit in the mission. One suspects that, as a naval airman, he preferred to have them sunk by a worthy foe in a valiant effort rather than hide ignominiously in the Inland Sea.

18

"The Situation Was Bad"

I N THE LAST MONTHS of 1944, the elements themselves seemed to choose sides. On 7 December, the southern coast of central Japan shuddered in the grip of an earthquake that threw the Mitsubishi and Aichi airframe plants in Nagoya out of production for almost a month. They never fully recovered. The quake also flung down the railroad bridge of the Tokaido Line over the Tenryu River, severing one of Japan's key transportation arteries.[1]

Ten days later a ferocious typhoon struck Halsey's Third Fleet. It tossed his flagship, the battleship *New Jersey*, "as if she had been a canoe." Planes aboard the light carrier *Monterey* broke loose and caught fire.[2] Her assistant navigator, Lieutenant Gerald R. Ford, slid across her deck and saved his life by clutching the deck lip and dropping down to a catapult below.[3] Total casualties were three destroyers capsized, a number of others badly damaged, almost eight hundred officers and men lost.[4]

The year 1945 was only nine days old when Fuchida suffered another personal loss. His old comrade Shimazaki perished in the skies between Formosa and the Philippines.[5] His death left Fuchida the last surviving Pearl Harbor air-attack leader.

Another long-time association ended, although more happily, when on 14 January Genda took command of the 343rd Air Corps. This crack outfit flew the new *Shiden* fighter plane, an excellent aircraft, well armed and capable of four hundred miles per hour at the maximum—a very respectable speed for the time. To the 343rd at Matsuyama Air Base on Shikoku came the cream of Japan's remaining fighter pilots. Fuchida's friend Commander Masatake Okumiya, holding down the unenviable position of home air defense officer at the Imperial General Staff, considered this the strongest fighter unit in the army or navy.[6] For the first time since the Pearl Harbor planning, Genda and Fuchida would not be working together, either in the same organization or in the same chain of command.

Immediately after the failure of the first part of Operation *Sho*, the defense of the Philippines, Imperial General Headquarters realized that the next major American operation would be the invasion of the Japanese homeland. Joint defense planning began in November 1944, the first time since the beginning of the war that a single plan of operation was formulated for both army and navy. Colonel Hiroshi Hosoda drafted the plan and conducted liaison with the naval authorities.[7] It called for a series of perimeter defense zones around the home islands, with the main effort in the Ryukyus. Preparations in these zones would be completed during February and March.

One sentence in this plan revealed its pessimism: "When the enemy penetrates the defense zone, a campaign of attrition will be initiated . . ." On 6 February, the army section of the Imperial General Headquarters published an implementing directive, "Outline of Air Operations in the East China Sea Area." This became known as *Ten-go* Operational Plan.[8] It was generally agreed that the East China Sea, lying between the China coast and the Ryukyus, would be the main area, so *Ten* number 1 covered Okinawa, *Ten* number 2 Formosa, *Ten* number 3 the southeast China coast, and *Ten* number 4 Hainan Island. The navy viewed Okinawa as primary and completely ignored *Ten* numbers 2 and 4.[9]

The navy had a very slim stock of air power to embark upon *Ten*. Only about 550 planes of all types were available for offensive operations. The Third Air Fleet under Vice Admiral Kimpei Teraoka and the Fifth Air Fleet (to be established on 10 February under Ugaki) were expected to be "barely ready for use by the end of March." So the navy anticipated that army air units would "carry out the special attacks during the initial stages of *Ten* air operations."[10]

The surface navy was in even worse shape. Of the battleships that survived Leyte Gulf, the *Kongo* had been torpedoed on the way home to Japan. The *Yamato* had been severely damaged in the Leyte engagement. She and the old battlewagons *Nagato* and *Haruna* were laid up in the Hiroshima-Kure area. These three battleships, along with the carriers *Amagi*, *Katsuragi*, *Ryuko*, and *Junyo*, the cruiser *Yahagi*, and ten destroyers, comprised the Second Fleet under Vice Admiral Seiichi Ito.[11] Pitting Japan's remaining ships and naval aircraft against the U.S. forces, once more transformed into the Fifth Fleet under Spruance, would have been like a Pekingese challenging a mastiff.

On 16 February Spruance's carrier aircraft attacked "vast areas" in the Tokyo region. This attack, and those of the succeeding few days, destroyed 150 army and navy planes on the ground. Some 100 fighters rose to the defense, and about 40 were shot down.[12]

Through the latter part of February and early March attention centered on Iwo Jima. Ugaki was worried and disgusted by the apparent ease of the landings. All very well to let the invaders land, then lure them inward. But that army plan "had never succeeded. It had to be regarded as nothing but an excuse for being unable to beat the enemy at the seashore."[13]

The Japanese navy had little to do with the defense of Iwo Jima, and its only air opposition of any note was put up on 21 February. Fifty planes hit Task Force 58, and four kamikazes and two bombs damaged the *Saratoga* sufficiently to send her back to Eniwetok for repairs. Kamikazes also sank the small carrier *Bismarck Sea* and slightly damaged the escort carrier *Lunga Point.*[14]

The navy did have a spectacular action on the drawing boards, another Operation *Tan.* This would deliver "a crushing blow" to the U.S. task force after it had returned to its anchorage at Ulithi in the Carolines. It aimed not at defending Iwo Jima but in delaying the anticipated action at Okinawa. If *Tan* succeeded, the navy would use the time thus gained to rebuild its air strength.[15]

The navy established *Tan* on 17 February, calling for a one-way attack with twenty-four land bombers. Hearing of a large concentration of U.S. ships in Ulithi, the Combined Fleet ordered execution for 10 March.

This was the sort of suicidal action that Ugaki loved, and he sent his men off with a ringing exhortation "to carry out a dauntless attack. . . ." Toyoda also sent a message urging them "to defend our sacred land . . . by ramming yourself upon the enemy." These heroics were wasted. A reconnaissance flight over Ulithi on 12 March disclosed that more U.S. carriers were there than before the mission, and there was no evidence of sunken ships. *Tan* had been a complete failure.[16]

Meanwhile, the United States had visited upon the Japanese homeland its single most disastrous bombing of the war, not excluding the atomic bombs. On the night of 9–10 March, Major General Curtis LeMay's B-29s used incendiary bombs to set mile after mile of Tokyo burning. The results, in the words of MacArthur's reports, were "indescribably horrifying. Well over 250,000 houses were destroyed, rendering more than a million persons homeless, and 83,798 were burned to death." From that day forth, strategic bombing against the homeland ceased to be a dangerous nuisance and became a real threat to the nation's entire economy.[17]

Over a period of days in mid-March an air engagement occurred of which Fuchida thoroughly disapproved, but about which he could do nothing save express his opinion. On 17 March the Combined Fleet received word that an American task force had left Ulithi on the fourteenth, and was steaming north. Ugaki promptly began to prepare his Fifth Air Fleet. Combined Fleet headquarters at Hiyoshi discussed how best to cope with this threat, "failing to reach an early conclusion. But the general trend seemed to be in favor of preserving our strength against them," Ugaki noted.[18]

This was in accordance with the agreed-upon strategy—waste no aircraft against Mitscher's carriers; save them for troop transports. However, such restraint was not in Ugaki's nature. "He was a bit like Kakuta," Fuchida reflected. "He was an attacking type, one who would take up the enemy's challenge no matter what the circumstances might be, and fight back. He was constitutionally and emotionally unable to hold his planes back and wait."[19]

Ugaki protested so vigorously that both the Naval General Staff and the Combined Fleet bent to his will and, as Tomioka stated, "adopted the improper policy of leaving the matter entirely to the discretion of the Commander of the Fifth Air Fleet."[20]

The result was predictable. Ugaki was no fool; he knew that in neither skill nor readiness were his forces fit to challenge a task force of the Spruance-Mitscher type. For one thing, the Fifth Air Fleet's planes had almost completely dispersed in northern Kyushu and Shikoku, so most of them had to make night flights to reach their operational bases. Nevertheless, Ugaki told himself that, in the face of the anticipated massive attack, "we would not be able to preserve our strength even if we tried to do so. I could not stand to see them destroyed on the ground."[21]

On 21 March, two groups of U.S. carriers having been sighted, Ugaki decided that this provided the opportunity to test the usefulness of the *oka*. Of fifty-five scheduled escort Zeros, only thirty were available. Okamura and his staff protested that these were insufficient to break through the American screen of Hellcats. But Ugaki ordered off eighteen land-based bombers, sixteen of them carrying *okas*. Then he retired to his underground operations to await results. All too soon he had a tragic report. A swarm of Hellcats had shot down every *oka* and fifteen Zeros within ten minutes.[22]

Survivors of the four-day battle reported that the Japanese had sunk five carriers, two battleships, one heavy cruiser, two light cruisers and one unidentified ship. Ugaki had sent out 246 planes, including reconnaissance, and lost 161—83 percent of his combat craft. Undismayed by this stunning statistic,

Ugaki believed "we gained a good mark in the operation. . . . I was glad I did my duty."[23]

For a short time, the Naval General Staff and the Combined Fleet "believed without a doubt that the Fifth Air Fleet had sunk half of the enemy aircraft carriers." Then, Fuchida explained, doubts set in because of the loss of the *okas* and the fact that U.S. radio "showed no indication of confusion caused by continuous losses. . . ." So the Combined Fleet cut the estimate to four American ships sunk. Tomioka added, "Although the Naval General Staff made a still more conservative estimate, and estimated about two ships sunk, it did not go so far as to believe that none had been sunk."[24]

That, however, was the case, although the Americans did suffer damage. Kamikazes hit the carriers *Intrepid* and *Wasp,* while conventional bombs struck the *Enterprise, Franklin,* and new *Yorktown.* The *Franklin* suffered the worst damage, and only superb seamanship saved her.[25]

Ugaki's ill-considered action seriously hamstrung the navy when, shortly thereafter, the Americans commenced the invasion of Okinawa.[26] Indeed, Fuchida's friend Suzuki declared that the navy would not be able to participate until May. However, others favored a decisive air battle at Okinawa. At first, the army and navy concurred in all-out air operations at Okinawa. Then the army "decided to reserve a certain amount of air strength to defend the homeland." The navy preferred to concentrate on stopping the enemy at Okinawa.[27]

With the first American bombing to soften up Okinawa, Toyoda dispatched Fuchida posthaste to Kanoya to direct general headquarters air operations, and incidentally to keep a close eye on Ugaki lest he break out again. Fuchida had Toyoda's authority to speak in his name. From Kanoya he maintained direct telephone connections with both Toyoda and Kusaka. This time, therefore, when air attacks came from American carriers, conventional aircraft in the Kyushu area would be hoarded for use against transports.

The main force to resist the Okinawa invasion consisted of the Third Air Fleet under Teraoka, Ugaki's kamikazes, and the army's Sixth Air Division. The Japanese also had the First and Second Air Fleets under Fukudome and Onishi respectively, but these were on Taiwan and very weak.

If Fuchida needed anything to convince him that Japan had lost the favor of heaven, the opening of the Okinawa campaign would have done so. At the very beginning, just as the Americans prepared to disembark, two events effectively canceled the navy's plan to destroy American troop transports in shallow water.

First, the initial landings took place at Kerama Retto, a small island group nearby, instead of on the western side of Okinawa. Reports of the actual landing points arrived in Japan late. By the time the kamikazes reached the scene, the invaders had stormed ashore almost unopposed. Many suicide pilots wasted themselves against empty ships.

Secondly, Lieutenant General Mitsuru Ushijima, commander of the Thirty-Second Army on Okinawa, failed to follow the joint army-navy defense agreement. According to this, the army was to pen up the invaders on the beachheads to give the navy time to slaughter them. Instead, Ushijima abandoned the coastal area and retired to the mountainous interior to dig in, which meant that the navy could not carry out the kamikaze plan.[28]

Although the Japanese had nowhere near the forty-five hundred aircraft the plan had specified, those available inflicted considerable damage to American ships.[29] However, it was not the type of damage the navy hoped for. As one army officer observed, "The plan to sink [the] main portion of the enemy's transports before the enemy could land troops ended in a long-term attrition operation against enemy ships off Okinawa after the landings had been made."[30]

On 5 April, the navy decided on a last-ditch surface action, *Kaijo Tokkotai* ("Surface-Sea Special Attack Unit"). The name told its own story, "special attack unit" being the official designation for any suicide group. In brief, this unit, under the Second Fleet's commander in chief, Vice Admiral Seiichi Ito, would consist of the *Yamato*, the cruiser *Yahagi*, and eight destroyers. As planned, the superbattleship and her escorts would sail to the troop landing area at Okinawa and there run aground. From this unsinkable position Ito would turn his flagship into a steel fortress that, with her huge guns and those of the other vessels, would blast American troop ships.[31]

This operation was the brainchild of Captain Kami, the Combined Fleet's senior staff officer, who sold it to Toyoda. Kusaka disapproved of the idea, and, in Fuchida's words, "the Fifth Air Fleet also was extremely inconvenienced by it." The Naval General Staff took a stand against the project, but gave in "because of the extensive authority with regard to operations" Toyoda exercised. Four years later, Rear Admiral Sadatoshi Tomioka, former chief of the operations section, Naval General Staff, was still angry about it.[32]

Before setting out, the ships refueled at Tokuyama, taking aboard only enough to reach Okinawa. Kami asked Fuchida to set up fighter escort. The air arm could spare only thirty-six planes for the job. These had to accompany the ships in increments of nine, going no further out to sea than 100 miles, so they worked in relays—nine fighters for one hour, then another nine. This meager token did not represent a real escort. Ugaki supplied them at Fuchida's request as a gesture of courtesy and homage to his old friend Ito, the officers, and crewmen.[33]

They never reached Okinawa. Mitscher had been expecting the move and took all possible precautions. His aircraft appeared over the group around noon on 7 April. Messages from the sorely beset *Yamato* came to Fuchida at Kanoya, where he was directing the air operation, but he could do nothing to help. The *Yamato* died hard, taking five 1,000-pound bombs and nine torpedoes before she sank. Despite heroic rescue efforts by the remaining destroyers, 2,498 men went down with her, 446 with the *Yahagi,* and 721 on the stricken destroyers. Fuchida could not regret that the *Yamato* met her fate as she did, with guns blazing, in visible token of the Japanese fighting heart.[34]

On the very day she went down, Japan installed a new cabinet under the premiership of Baron Kantaro Suzuki, president of the Privy Council. Retired Admiral Suzuki was at the helm, and Yonai was retained as navy minister. Ugaki remarked to his diary with grim humor that now that the navy was without ships, it was going to fight by means of a cabinet.[35]

That was not quite the idea. Suzuki, seventy-seven years old, somewhat deaf and vacillating, had been chosen because he fulfilled several basic, though not necessarily compatible, requirements. He must have the absolute trust of the emperor. This Suzuki did, having served for seven years as grand chamberlain. "To Suzuki, I could pour my heart out," His Majesty confided.[36] The new premier must not be associated with any extremist group; on the other hand, he could have no visible ties with the underground peace faction.

After Suzuki's selection, Kido told him, "The emperor is very deeply concerned over the war trends and desires the attainment of peace at the earliest possible moment. I desire your firm determination on this point and hope that you will make your cabinet the final war cabinet." Suzuki declared that he was "in complete accord" with the emperor's views. That would be his duty if he were to head the government.[37] Unfortunately, Kido did not specify that the "attainment of peace" meant surrender, if necessary.

As the price of its cooperation the army presented three demands. The first of these was "prosecution of the war to the bitter end." Suzuki replied that he was "in complete agreement with the first part. . . ."[38] He had little choice. If any suggestion of ending the war leaked out, no one, not even the prime minister, would last in office one day. Yonai "was racking his brains" to find a way to persuade the army to consider peace on any but its own terms.[39]

Exactly one month later, Japan had an excellent opportunity to make peace, for on 7 May 1945 Germany surrendered. Tokyo could have salved national pride by pointing out that Japan and Germany had mutually agreed never to seek a separate peace. Even the army had given serious consideration to what the defeat of Germany could mean to Japan. In the spring of 1944, a group of army officers wrote a thesis entitled "Measures for the Termination of the Greater East Asia War." Copies of this document, classified as state secrets, were distributed to certain key personnel, among them Fuchida's Eta Jima classmate, Prince Takamatsu. The war would be ended "when Germany is destroyed."[40]

Instead of seizing the opportunity, Suzuki issued a statement that "the dire change in the European situation will not cause the slightest change here."[41] He had little understanding of the situation. When he offered the portfolio of foreign minister to Shigenori Togo, he "agreed that the situation was bad, but said he thought we could keep on fighting two or three years longer."[42]

Far down the chain of command, Fuchida had no such illusions. "When the Okinawa battle was over," he observed sadly, "that was the end of our naval air forces and actually the end of our naval resistance. We paid all—all we had. We fought as best we could with everything we had and we were proud of our record. . . . Of course, it was sad and tragic and with Okinawa the Japanese navy was at an end."

Japan was reduced to making military fuel from sweet potatoes and tree roots. Under the circumstances, Fuchida told Toyoda and Kusaka, they might as well disband the Combined Fleet; there were no forces left to command. Instead, a top personnel shuffle took place. Ozawa became commander in chief. Toyoda moved up to chief of the Naval General Staff. Rear Admiral Shikazo Yano replaced Kusaka as the fleet's chief of staff, the latter having already departed for supreme naval headquarters as its chief of staff. Captain Mineo Yamaoka became the fleet's senior staff officer, while Fuchida remained as air officer, partly because the army requested it.[43]

He had become close friends with Lieutenant Colonel Ryuzo Sejima, the army liaison officer with the Combined Fleet. So when the reorganization got under way Sejima asked that the Personnel Bureau not remove Fuchida who, Sejima said, was the officer best able to maintain smooth relations with the army. An expert on Russia, Sejima was later stationed in Manchuria, where the Soviets captured him. They took him to Moscow and kept him there for eleven years as the unwilling guest of the Soviet Union.

Fuchida didn't want to remain with the Combined Fleet, piloting a desk in an Alice-in-Wonderland force of a few ships too damaged to sail, aircraft forbidden to fly, and a waning trickle of kamikazes, the whole running on a combination of vodka and wood alcohol. He had another idea up his sleeve— an attack against the B-29 bases in the Marianas, which he wanted to lead himself.[44]

In this bitter period, Fuchida had one cause for thanksgiving. His family remained untouched. They were isolated enough to escape the major attacks, but close enough to the metropolitan area to see some of the results. "Every night we could see the red sky of Tokyo," Miyako remembered. During one bombing, Yoshiya became separated from his mother and sister, who were frantic until he showed up none the worse. "I hated the war!" declared Miyako vehemently. "It was so terrible!"[45]

At Kanoya, U.S. Army planes were so ubiquitous that, as Ugaki wrote, "Unless we slept in shelters, we could no longer have a sound sleep. We shall have to get back to the primitive life of cavemen."[46] One incident demonstrated how completely the Americans dominated Japan's skies. On 2 June a Martin flying boat, accompanied by over ten Grumman fighters, flew over Kagoshima Bay, coolly landed on the water, and picked up the crew of a plane shot down that morning.[47]

The Japanese army was by no means ready to surrender. It remained a powerful force with enough gas and oil stashed away to put up a good fight against an American invasion. According to Fuchida's estimate, General Gen Sugiyama in Tokyo commanded about two million men, and there was a like number in Kyushu under General Shunroku Hata, who established his headquarters at Hiroshima. And they had the First General Air Force, with headquarters in Osaka and units spread all over the homeland.[48]

Acknowledging that the next American move would be an invasion of Japan proper, the armed forces activated Operation *Ketsu* (Final or Decisive), which had been planned since 8 April 1945. Like *Sho* and *Ten,* it was divided into several parts depending on probable landing areas. Primary emphasis was on *Ketsu* number 6 (Kyushu) and *Ketsu* number 3 (the Kanto plain around Tokyo). In general, the plan estimated that Kyushu would be the initial target. If this proved to be the case, some army officers were

> . . . absolutely sure of victory. It was the first and only battle in which the main strength of the air, land and sea forces were to be joined. The geographical advantages of the homeland were to be utilized to the highest degree, the enemy was to be crushed, and we were confident that the battle would prove to be a turning point in political maneuvering.[49]

Others were not so sure. In the words of Lieutenant General Torashiro Kawabe, "We never anticipated that the homeland decisive battle would lead to victory; it was a step Japan and the Japanese armed forces had to take in order to maintain their prestige."[50]

To this end the army was prepared to see the whole nation go down in flames. Army leaders adopted the slogan "One hundred million die for the country *(Ichioku Gyukusai)*" and called up every able-bodied man. The army also wanted control of the tattered remains of the navy. As of 1 July, the navy had approximately five thousand planes of all types, of which some thirty-five hundred were operational. Of this figure, only six hundred or so were flyable fighters. Moreover, the ersatz fuel held down speed. With the slightly macabre humor the fighting man can summon in the most unlikely situations, the navy called *Ketsu "okatonbe sakusen,"* after a slow-crawling red insect. The only real use headquarters still had for Fuchida was to pick his brains for the best way to utilize the remaining aircraft.[51]

The army maintained its general headquarters slightly south of Osaka, so for greater ease of communication with his opposite number, Ozawa moved Combined Fleet headquarters from Tokyo to Yamato, near Osaka and only ten miles from the border of Nara, Fuchida's own province. Some even suggested that the emperor and the government move to this area if the enemy invaded Tokyo.

Ozawa ordered all sailors to marine status, issued them rifles and bayonets, and put them under army command. Commander Masataka Chihaya joined Ozawa's staff to help organize them. A fine officer, full of courage and good sense, Chihaya was the brother of Fuchida's Pearl Harbor friend lost in the Marianas. These instant marines had no choice but to go along with the proposition, but their hearts weren't in it. Like their superior officers, they were fed up with the army. As Fuchida saw it, the navy had carried most of the load in the Pacific war. Now the army, with its unspent resources and manpower in the homeland, wanted to squeeze the last drop out of the exhausted navy.

Along with *Ketsu,* and an essential part of it, went *Sei Sakusen* (Control Operation), which the army conducted from Osaka to command the skies over the homeland. Fuchida had no confidence in *Sei.* He couldn't visualize any possible way Japan's fighters would halt the B-29s, not to mention American carrier aircraft, once they reached the main islands. In his opinion, the only way to stop enemy bombers effectively was to hit them before they started.

This was the idea behind Operation *Ken*, which Fuchida worked on in secret lest his army colleagues find out about it and mess it up. *Ken* called for aircraft to land on the B-29 strips in the Marianas. There men of a special landing force would jump out, run to the nearest B-29, attach a special short-fused bomb to its wing, and try to race away before the bomb exploded. Of course, the mission meant almost certain death for all the air commandos.[52]

How had an otherwise sane naval officer with a reputation for down-to-earth thinking come to consider such an idea? To our knowledge, though Fuchida didn't mention the fact, there was a precedent. On the night of 24–25 May eleven army bombers, each carrying eleven men of the *gi retsu,* a special attack unit, left Kumamoto. Only one succeeded in landing at

Okinawa. Its men erupted from the plane, tossing phosphorescent bombs and hand grenades. They managed to destroy or damage a number of planes, blow up fuel pumps, and kill a few of the defenders before the latter emerged from the confusion to kill every one of the Japanese.[53]

Whether or not inspired by this example, Ozawa approved Fuchida's plan. Training for *Ken* began at air bases in Hokkaido with a force of forty Douglas transports and four hundred men.[54]

These figures of Fuchida's don't coincide with those of his colleague, Commander Yoshimori Terai, who recalled *Ken* as requiring twenty-five "medium attack planes" and 250 men of the Special Naval Landing Force. He agreed, however, that the object was to land on the B-29 bases in the Marianas and destroy the planes.

> It was to be a night attack during the moonlight period after the middle of July. Misawa Airfield in Northern Honshu was to be used as the base for this attack. However, an American task force attacked this base of departure on 14 and 15 July, and the bombers which were to be used in Operation *Ken* were lost on the 14th. Thus, the plan for the Mariana attack had to be abandoned.[55]

It is possible that more than one *Ken* was planned, for according to Admiral Morison, on 31 July Halsey, once more in command with his Third Fleet, ordered Task Force 38 to the waters off northern Honshu to wipe out Japanese aircraft. This was a concentration of two hundred bombers scheduled to crash-land at B-29 bases with two thousand suicide troops.[56]

As late as the beginning of August, Fuchida had not abandoned his pet project, the nature of which spoke volumes for the desperation of Japan's defenders.[57]

19

"This Must Be the Atomic Bomb"

"**T**ELEPHONE for you, sir!"

Fuchida seized the instrument thankfully, glad of any break in the boredom of the past few days in Hiroshima.

"Urgent business has come up between the army and navy in connection with the army's base at Kashiwara." It was Admiral Yano, the navy's chief of staff. "Ozawa is coming to Yamato soon in anticipation of Operation *Ketsu*, and arrangements are under way to consolidate Kashiwara Army Base and Yamato Navy Base. Unless you are urgently needed at Hiroshima, both the engineering men and I want you back at Yamato."

Fuchida glanced at his watch. The hands touched 1400, plenty of time to fly to Yamato before nightfall. "I'll leave as soon as possible," he answered. "I am not at all important here. I have lost interest in this army operation."

He was one of a dozen navy officers the army had invited to Hiroshima in the latter part of July as observers of a planning conference in preparation for Operation *Sei*. Despite the urgency of the subject, Fuchida couldn't work up an interest in the conference. His mind occupied with his own problems, he had little thought to spare for the *Sei* discussions, which were quite technical, particularly in the field of communications. As most of the other navy observers were experts in that area, they didn't need his assistance. He was restless. He itched to return to work on *Ken*, still hoping to realize his scheme of destroying B-29s at their bases in the Marianas. Coming as it did on the heels of an unproductive luncheon meeting, Yano's phone call was welcome.

As soon as he hung up, he paid a courtesy farewell call at General Hata's headquarters, gathered his gear from the Yamato hotel, which housed most of the navy delegation, and headed for the Hiroshima airfield. At about 1700 he climbed into a navy three-seater and flew alone to Yamato, arriving at 1900. The day was Sunday, 5 August 1945.[1]

At about 0800 the next morning, a train from Kure ground to a halt at the Hiroshima station. Lieutenant Hashimoto, a communications officer who had been commuting between the conference and his home in Kure some twelve miles to the south, swung leisurely down the train steps and made his way to the underground restroom. He had just begun freshening up when he felt a violent shock and shaking as of a major earthquake. He hurried back to the surface to see what had happened.

He emerged from the station in what he later described as "another world, strange and weird." As far as his eye could see, Hiroshima sprawled in a ghastly expanse of smoking ruins and blackened corpses. The shock of this break between his normal routine and the nightmarish sight was too much for Hashimoto to bear. With a protesting whimper, he turned and fled down the railroad tracks in mindless flight from this city of the dead. As he stumbled down the tracks, his body absorbed radiation at every step.[2]

At the Yamato Hotel, six navy officers enjoying an early breakfast were blasted into infinity. Two others still in bed, partially protected by their *futons*, escaped the blast but not the radiation. They lived a miserable six months before death released them at Kure Naval Hospital. General Hata, who with a number of army officers lived in an underground bomb shelter, survived the bombing uninjured.

Hashimoto ran for a mile and a half before his reason returned. He came to his senses in a small suburb called Kaidichi. Panting convulsively, he stopped at the station and tried to arrange his thoughts. Conscience-stricken at having run away, he hurried to the nearest telephone booth and called the Kure naval station. "All Hiroshima is destroyed by a new powerful bomb," he announced. "Everyone is dead." This was the dramatic story he later told to Fuchida in the navy hospital.

As the Kure base had a double telephone hookup with general headquarters in Tokyo and with Ozawa in Hiyoshi, both received word at the same time when Kure relayed Hashimoto's message. Yano telephoned Fuchida at his office at the Yamato base. "Hiroshima has been completely destroyed by a powerful new bomb," he said, his voice heavy with the weight of his message. "All are dead."[3]

Fuchida sat and stared blankly at the telephone receiver. The bustling city he had left only the previous afternoon completely destroyed? The men with whom he had lunched that day all dead? And with them the population of the city? For a moment his mind refused to accept what his ears had heard. He sat in a state of shock.

Meanwhile Yano's voice continued to pour out of the phone, giving a detailed description of the extent and type of damage. As best he could determine, in an instant, a single explosion had blasted Hiroshima and most if not all of its people. "What do you think of this new bomb?" Yano asked, as if from an infinite distance.

"This must be the atomic bomb," Fuchida answered mechanically.

"Yes, I guess so."

Fuchida thought hard and fast. Japan had no time to waste in lamentation; it must seize from this frightful event whatever it could turn to advantage. In flattening Hiroshima, the United States had given Japan the opportunity to acknowledge defeat with dignity. It had also taken upon itself the responsibility to end the war promptly.

"Japan should sue for peace at once," Fuchida told Yano. "Please go straight to the Naval General Staff and pressure them to act!" As he hung up, he thought to himself dully, "The war is over."[4]

Not everyone jumped as rapidly as Fuchida to the conclusion that the Americans had dropped an atomic bomb. Both the navy and army had been studying the possibility of such a weapon for several years. The army's effort centered on the Physical and Chemical Research Institute under Dr. Yoshio Nishina. Lieutenant General Torashiro Kawabe, then chief of the army aeronautical department, had assigned several of his young technical officers to research atomic energy with Nishina. In late 1944, when Kawabe visited the institute, he "received the impression that the research work was still in an embryo stage." On that occasion someone—he didn't remember who—told him "that in America research on atomic energy seemed to be in an advanced stage." Then in June 1945, after he had become assistant chief of the Army General Staff, he learned that research into atomic energy would be postponed because "the very critical war situation made it necessary that we concentrate all endeavors on the imminent decisive battle for the homeland. . . ."[5]

Nishina blamed Japan's failure to develop atomic energy on such factors as the small number of scientists qualified in that area and lack of industrial power to follow up theoretical findings. Even if Japan could have overcome those handicaps, it lacked uranium ore. An air raid on 13 April 1945 razed his laboratory, a major setback. The constant air raids forced the army's aeronautical department to move out of Tokyo, so close liaison was no longer possible. However, he received no definite order to suspend his research.[6]

As mentioned, not everyone agreed that what had exploded over Hiroshima was an atomic bomb. Immediately after that event, the "Atomic Bomb Countermeasure Committee" was formed in Suzuki's cabinet. Sumihisa Ikeda, chief of the cabinet planning board, was chairman. Members included representatives of the war, navy, and home ministries and the Technical Board. The committee held its first meeting on 7 August, at which time the Technical Board representatives strongly insisted that the bomb was not an atomic bomb. They reasoned, "No matter how advanced American technique may be, it is quite impossible for the Americans to bring such unstable weapons as atomic devices to Japan, across the Pacific. We do not know what will happen in the future, but to date American technique is not that highly developed."

"In America, the President has announced that it was an atomic bomb," Ikeda rejoined. "I can hardly imagine that Americans would broadcast such a lie. If it is not an atomic bomb, what is it?"

The reply came somewhat lamely: "It must be a new type bomb with special equipment, but its content is unknown."

This difference of opinion was why the first official announcement didn't contain the word *atomic*.[7] When Lieutenant General Shuichi Miyazaki, chief of the operations division, Army Department of the Imperial General Staff, received instructions on the phraseology to be used in the announcement, they included an explanation that ran somewhat like this: "Although it appears to be an *atomic bomb,* it is too premature to formally decide. . . . Therefore, we will announce it as a *special bomb* and wait for a final finding of the field investigation" (italics in original).[8]

Nishina encountered the same resistance at Tokorazawa on his way to investigate Hiroshima on the spot. Although information was still "fragmentary and scanty," from the accounts he had received the scientist had little doubt what had happened. "However, the general opinion in the military circles held that Truman's announcement that the bomb was an atomic weapon was probably a [sic] propaganda to scare the Japanese."[9]

Grass-roots instinct, however, outran official caution. "The government announced only a powerful bomb, but people already knew the atomic bomb had come," Fuchida recalled. "People always know things like that."[10]

Fuchida had distinguished support for his assessment that Japan should sue for peace and lose no time about it. The emperor "was overwhelmed with grief," and commanded Kido, "under these circumstances, we must bow to the inevitable. No matter what happens to my safety, we must put an end to this war as speedily as possible so that this tragedy will not be repeated."[11]

Others were neither so sensitive nor so realistic. Ugaki admitted in his diary that the bomb was "a real wonder, making the outcome of the war more gloomy." But he added, "We must think of some countermeasures against it immediately, and at the same time I wish we could create the same bomb."[12]

Fuchida didn't have long to muse over the situation. The navy hastily gathered a group to go to Hiroshima and investigate the bombing. Fuchida would meet the others at Hata's headquarters about noon the next day. The other nine officers set out by transport plane from Atsugi near Tokyo.

The officer in charge of the group turned out to be Captain Yasui Yasukado, with whom Fuchida had gone to middle school in Nara Prefecture. The rest of the investigators were engineers, not Eta Jima men; Fuchida was not acquainted with any of them. Yasukado was a bacteriologist as well as an expert on poison gas. He and his engineers had some idea of the hazards of radiation, but Fuchida knew nothing at all concerning the subject. None took precautions; they walked into Hiroshima the day after the atomic bomb exploded with nothing more on their backs than uniforms.

Their mission was to estimate the extent of the damage and to figure out details about the flight that had dropped the bomb, the altitude at which the bomb had exploded, and so forth. They walked around the city; there was no transportation of any kind.

The destruction was dreadful beyond imagination and telling. People wandered about in a daze, some badly burned, others half out of their minds, others poking in the ashes as if seeking something, however hopelessly. "It was like an evil nightmare," Fuchida summed it up. Along the rivers and canals that traversed the city, "bodies were piled six and seven feet high." Most people not killed instantly sought water to ease their excruciatingly painful burns. But the water itself was hot, and multitudes died either in the canals, in the rivers, or along their banks.

Not a speck of cool green remained. Every tree had burned in fires that still smoked and flared. To add to the misery, a fearsome black rain began to fall. Black raindrops formed black pools and stained black every stone—nature spreading a funeral pall over the stricken city. Survivors to whom Fuchida talked were bitterly angry and shocked that the United States would resort to such measures.[13]

Fuchida himself felt no hatred or resentment. Nor in the future would he have any patience with those who tried to saddle the United States with guilt. "That was war," he explained simply. His professional training had taught him that in war any kind of destruction should be expected. He added honestly, "If Japan had had the atomic bomb we would have dropped it on the United States." What is more, Fuchida, as air operations officer of the Combined Fleet, would have been responsible for dropping it in the Marianas, in the Philippines, or even against the continental United States if he had been able to reach it. He would have been willing, even proud, to strike such a devastating blow for his country.[14]

He spent the night in General Hata's underground shelter. The next day he heard a rumor that another atomic bomb had been dropped, landing near the city without exploding. This called for immediate investigation. His group scoured the outskirts of Hiroshima. Somewhat north of the city they saw a strange object in a field. Fuchida and Yasukado, looking it over from a distance through their binoculars, couldn't identify it. Finally they summoned up courage to approach it. They discovered the mysterious bundle to be the parachute that had carried the Hiroshima bomb. It still contained a radio, which Fuchida thought might have been a timing device.[15]

In Hiroshima a day or two later, with an army investigation team headed by Lieutenant General Seizo Arisue, chief of the Second Bureau (intelligence) of the Army General Staff, Nishina learned that three more parachutes had come down near Hiroshima and that a navy group had checked them out. They were carrying "a sort of barometer . . . fitted with an electric wave transmitter." He believed that Americans at distant bases were able to pick up these electric waves, thus calculating "the changes in atmospheric pressure caused by the explosion."[16]

Writing his report by candlelight at the Ujima Shipping Command outside the danger zone, Arisue included this note: "Rumor has it that the same kind of bomb will be dropped on Tokyo on 12 August."[17] But the next bomb did not fall on Tokyo, and it fell before the twelfth. The victim was Nagasaki. Unfortunately for it, the primary target had been Kokura. But smoke so hid that city that the attackers abandoned the attempt and headed for Nagasaki, the secondary target.[18]

As with Hiroshima, Fuchida heard about the Nagasaki bombing from Yano. Again he urged the utmost speed in appealing to the United States for peace and to world opinion to end the holocaust. He asked and obtained permission to hurry to Tokyo, for he feared a third atomic bomb, this time on the capital. He wanted to rush his report in person to the Navy Ministry and make them understand exactly the sort of danger Japan was up against.

Again, he didn't blame the United States, but he did resent the timing of this second bomb. An interval of only three days between the Hiroshima and Nagasaki bombings was unrealistic. "The Japanese government should have been given at least a week after the first atomic bomb to negotiate for the surrender of Japan," Fuchida judged. "Three days were not enough."[19] In fact, doubt lingered as to the nature of the weapon. On 10 August some members of Nishina's group still insisted that the bombs were not atomic. One of these men, an instructor at the Naval Academy, "maintained that it was an application of liquid air." By that time, however, this was a minority view.[20]

Once again, Fuchida hoped for quick action in high places to take advantage of the opportunity for peace. He had noted how President Roosevelt, immediately following Pearl Harbor, shrewdly seized upon that name as a potent emotional symbol of treachery and dastardliness. He wrung every last drop out of the situation to rally the American people behind the war effort and to muster international opinion on the side of the United States. All of which was fair enough, Fuchida conceded.

Now it was Japan's turn. The United States had given Japan a similar chance for propaganda and a means of appealing to the conscience of humanity. The atomic bombs weren't unmitigated disasters if they cut short further senseless slaughter.

Not all of Fuchida's reasoning was military and political. Beneath the uniform was a human being who suffered for the misery of his countrymen. An affectionate father, he writhed at the thought of the dead and maimed children.[21]

Logic points out that the victims of the Tokyo fire bombings of 9–10 March were no less dead than those of Hiroshima and Nagasaki. And citizens of Manila and Shanghai, for example, could have had something to say on the subject of inhuman warfare. But from the beginning, something about the atomic bomb transcended logic. U.S. Secretary of War Henry L. Stimson recognized this as early as 5 March 1945, when the United States government was

> up against some very big decisions. . . . Our thoughts went right down to the bottom facts of human nature, morals and government, and it is by far the most searching and important thing that I have had to do since I have been here in the office of the Secretary of War because it touches matters which are deeper even than the principles of the present government.[22]

What roused Fuchida to absolute anger and resentment was the Soviet declaration of war against Japan on 9 August (although Soviet forces had attacked in Asia two days earlier). This action infuriated him as the whole savagely fought war with the United States had not. "Russia had been waiting for the best opportunity," Fuchida said with disgust. "She was ready but never moved until the atomic bomb. The Russians knew that Japan would have to surrender. Everybody was angry with Russia for doing such a cowardly thing."

Fuchida's hostility toward communism was born that day. Throughout the long hard years of the occupation, it saved him from the blandishments of Japan's native communists.[23]

Therefore he was in a receptive mood the next day, 10 August 1945, when his old friend of post-Midway days at Yokosuka, Rear Admiral Yokoi, now Ugaki's chief of staff, telephoned him from Kanoya. "I favor surrendering to the United States, but not to the Soviet Union," Yokoi told Fuchida, his voice tight with passion. "I suggest we gather all our remaining air forces and send them against Vladivostok or wherever we can find enough Russians. This mission will be without any hope of victory. It will demonstrate to the whole world in behalf of our people their hatred and disgust at Russia's perfidy."

"That is exactly my idea, too," Fuchida replied. "We need no more forces against the United States. We should turn all our remaining strength against the Russians. I will immediately draft an order to attack Vladivostok and take it to Ozawa for signature."

Thus Fuchida abandoned Operation *Ken.* Hurriedly he prepared an order for all naval air forces to attack Vladivostok. But in putting this through channels to Ozawa, he ran into an unexpected snag. Yano firmly put his foot down.

"No more active operations!" he declared. And added, "Please come back to headquarters immediately."[24]

So it happened that in the space of a few days, Fuchida had no less than four escapes from death. First, Yano pulled him out of Hiroshima on the eve of the atomic explosion. Then the Russian move canceled his suicidal Operation *Ken.* Next, Yano ruled out the protest strike on Vladivostok, which undoubtedly would have been fatal for the participants. The fourth was, in Fuchida's eyes, the most miraculous of all.

Shortly after his investigating team left Hiroshima, they began, one by one, to sicken and die. When the pattern became apparent, the navy ordered Fuchida hospitalized for a thorough examination. This revealed that, despite three days of walking over and rooting through the radioactive rubble of Hiroshima, he was completely normal. The doctors had no time to seek a reason why Fuchida should be immune when his teammates were not. They were too concerned with those who needed help. They merely said, "There is nothing wrong with you," and turned him loose.

Fuchida estimated that some seventy men, in addition to him, were involved in the various investigations at Hiroshima. He was under the impression that all of them had died as the result.[25] This was not exactly the case.

For example, his friend from China days, Masatake Okumiya, emerged from the investigations hale and hearty.[26]

Nevertheless, enough of Fuchida's colleagues did perish, of what the Japanese came to call *genbaku sho* (atom bomb disease), that he considered his survival nothing less than miraculous.[27]

20

"The Game Is Up"

HIS HOPES of blasting Soviet territory squelched, Fuchida flew back to Atsugi Air Base late that afternoon, 10 August. There Captain Yasuna Kozono, who had preceded him by one year at Eta Jima, lay in wait. After the briefest of greetings, he burst out, "In no case will I accept any order to lay down my arms. I will kill you if you agree to surrender, because two thousand kamikaze pilots are already dead from serving under your plan. How can you justify living with this knowledge?"

This hysterical outburst took Fuchida completely aback. He replied stiffly, "You may do as you please about this matter, but I shall also do as I please." Then he smiled and clapped Kozono on the shoulder. "Take good care of my plane, and kindly arrange for a car to take me to Tokyo." This matter-of-fact manner seemed to soothe Kozono. He called the motor pool and sent Fuchida off to navy headquarters at Hiyoshi, a two-hour trip. Upon his arrival, Yano informed him that the Supreme War Council was at that very moment "considering the problem of surrender."[1]

The "problem of surrender" had been under discussion for some time in a dramatic series of high-level meetings.* To backtrack, early in the morning of 27 July, Japanese monitoring stations had picked up a broadcast from San Francisco giving the text of the Potsdam Declaration, which specified Allied terms of surrender. Japanese sovereignty would be limited

---

*A brief account of these events is necessary to an understanding of Fuchida's actions and reactions during this period.

to the home islands; Japan would be demilitarized; certain "points in Japanese territory" should be occupied; "stern justice" should be meted out to war criminals; and the government should "remove all obstacles to the revival and strengthening of democratic tendencies among the Japanese people."

To the officials in the Japanese Foreign Office carefully analyzing the document, two items were highly significant: First, the Soviet Union was not a signatory, and had thereby maintained legal neutrality. Tokyo was attempting to persuade Moscow to act as a peace intermediary, and the declaration did not close the door. Second, whereas the Cairo Declaration had demanded the unconditional surrender of Japan, the Potsdam Declaration called for "the unconditional surrender of all the Japanese armed forces."[2]

From the Japanese standpoint, the worst thing about the declaration was its failure to specify the continuation of the imperial dynasty. However, Foreign Minister Shigenori Togo thought that the terms were the best Japan could hope for. But it would be inadvisable to accept them immediately without trying to interpret them to Japan's best advantage. Therefore he wanted to withhold action pending the results of the Japanese approaches to Moscow.[3]

Predictably, Toyoda, General Yoshijiro Umezu, chief of the Army General Staff, and War Minister General Korechika Anami urged prompt rejection. Finally all decided on a compromise: The declaration would be published with no official comment. Even so, the military insisted upon deletion of such humane terminology as the promise that the demilitarized troops would be "permitted to return to their homes with the opportunity to lead peaceful and productive lives.

"We do not intend that the Japanese shall be enslaved as a race or destroyed as a nation. . . ."

Even the military's toughened version seemed to many war-weary Japanese to be unexpectedly lenient. A number of citizens urged Togo to have the government accept immediately.[4]

Meanwhile, the Navy Ministry sent out an instruction to its forces "because it had to check the effects of the proclamation on front-line morale."[5] This aroused Ugaki to a comment all too typical of the armed forces' blind arrogance: "The Navy Minister issued a statement in which he urged the whole Navy to do its best without being bothered by such a thing. He had better not issue such a weak instruction, but instead send a recommendation asking those three countries for an unconditional surrender."[6]

Unfortunately for Japan, on 28 July, under pressure from the high command, Suzuki issued an official statement that the proclamation would be ignored and the nation would continue to wage war. In the delicate phraseology of diplomacy, there was a vast difference between deciding to ignore something and announcing officially that one is ignoring it. To all intents and purposes, by indirection the army and navy had secured the rejection they wanted.[7] Washington so interpreted Suzuki's remarks, and the result was the horror of Hiroshima.

Following that, early in the morning of 9 August, Domei intercepted the Tass announcement of the Soviet declaration of war. This effectively killed any hope of Russian mediation. Suzuki phoned the chairman of the Cabinet Planning Bureau, Sumihisa Ikeda, who had been in Manchuria until that July. "Is the Kwantung army capable of repulsing the Soviet army?" he inquired.

"The Kwantung army is hopeless," replied Ikeda bluntly.

"Is the Kwantung army that weak?" asked Suzuki with a sigh. "Then the game is up."[8]

At 1030, Suzuki met at the palace with the "Big Six"—the Supreme War Direction Council. Togo urged immediate acceptance of the Potsdam Declaration. He reminded his colleagues of the emperor's words after the Hiroshima bomb: "Continuation of the war had become impossible." Soviet Union entry into the war against Japan compounded this truth. They must secure a guarantee of the welfare of the imperial family, but should propose no additional conditions lest the Allies refuse to negotiate further.

Everyone agreed that "the position of the imperial family and the structure of the state" must be guaranteed. That was the only point of unanimity. Yonai supported Togo, but Toyoda, Anami, and Umezu wanted to keep on fighting. Spouting the standard clichés—one more campaign, repulse the invaders before they land, we could destroy the major part of an invading army—they insisted upon three additional conditions: that the Allies either "eliminate the security occupation of the main Japanese islands entirely" or limit it severely; that Japan alone disarm its troops; and that Japanese tribunals try war criminals. After three hours, the council was deadlocked: Togo, Yonai, and—wavering—Suzuki, versus Anami, Umezu, and Toyoda.[9]

Sometime in the course of this session the conferees received word of the Nagasaki bombing. There is no evidence that this event entered into their discussions one way or the other. Perhaps they shared Toyoda's feeling that after Hiroshima, the United States had shot its atomic bolt. He believed "that all the radium-like elements in the world would not have amounted to much." This factor would greatly restrict the number of atomic bombs the United States could use over a given period. He also "wondered whether the world would permit the United States to continue such an inhuman atrocity." Perhaps the American people would turn away from it. In retrospect, Toyoda considered that the Soviet declaration of war did more to hasten Japan's surrender than the atomic bombings.[10]

Fuchida believed that Toyoda was under the influence of Onishi, founder of the kamikazes, "a fire-eating diehard," now vice chief of the Naval General Staff.[11] Onishi claimed "that there were still ample chances of victory." Recalled Vice Admiral Zenshiro Hoshina, chief of the Navy Ministry's Bureau of Naval Affairs, "It looked as if his vigorous pressure had dominating effects even on the chief of the Naval General Staff, to speak nothing of his subordinates."[12]

A cabinet meeting held on 9 August shortly after the War Council adjourned proved to be, in Togo's words, "a repeat performance" of the morning's meeting. This time a majority supported the foreign minister, but the decision required unanimity. At 2230 Suzuki recessed the weary conferees and with Togo sought audience with the emperor. After Togo gave His Majesty a rundown of the situation, Suzuki asked and received permission to convene the Supreme War Direction Council that night in the presence of the emperor.[13]

The clock lacked but half an hour of midnight when the council met with a few augmentations, including ex–Premier Baron Kiichiro Hiranuma, president of the Privy Council, in the sweltering imperial air-raid shelter. This was another replay, if anything more eloquent than the preceding one, for now the speakers had to convince not only their colleagues but also their emperor.[14] The generals were especially forceful. Anami pleaded that the nation "proceed resolutely . . . If all the people go into the final battle resolved to display the utmost patriotism and fight to the last, I believe we can avoid this crisis." Umezu claimed, "Preparations for the decisive battle of the homeland are already completed, and we are confident of victory."[15]

Once more Togo repeated his arguments; once more the lines were drawn: Togo, Yonai, and Hiranuma on one side, Anami, Umezu, and Toyoda on the other. It was past 0200 on 10 August when Suzuki rose and, amid the shocked gasps of those present, approached the throne. Respectfully he asked that Hirohito express his opinion. He implored his colleagues to accept the imperial decision as final.[16]

His Majesty did have an opinion, which he expressed with emotion and no hesitation:

Heretofore the plans of the Army and Navy authorities have always been erroneous and inopportune. . . . I do not want to see the people continue to suffer any longer. Also, I do not desire any further destruction of culture, nor any additional misfortune for the people of the world. On this occasion, we have to bear the unbearable. I do not have the heart to disarm the loyal Military, nor to let my faithful subordinates become war criminals. However, it cannot be helped, for the sake of the country. . . .[17]

One step remained. Suzuki, armed with the imperial decision, reconvened the recessed cabinet. This time he secured unanimous agreement.[18]

Acceptance of the Potsdam Declaration with its provision concerning the imperial family went out early on the tenth. This pleased U.S. War Secretary Stimson, who had wanted the guarantee included in the first place. He told Truman that in his opinion,

> even if the question hadn't been raised by the Japanese we would have to continue the Emperor ourselves under our command and supervision in order to get into surrender the many scattered armies of the Japanese who would own no other authority and that something like this use of the Emperor must be made in order to save us from a score of bloody Iwo Jimas and Okinawas all over China and the New Netherlands [*sic*].[19]

Nothing could be done on the diplomatic front until Tokyo received the Allies' reply. Meanwhile, the government faced a task monumental in its scope, hair-trigger in its delicacy: how to condition the nation to accept the idea of surrender after having been exhorted for so long to fight to the death. This was a special problem for the armed forces. Ground into the consciousness of the Japanese fighting man was that elemental order: Die, but never surrender.

Sensing restlessness in the navy, particularly among Naval General Staff officers, Toyoda ordered them "not to make any hasty move or take independent action."[20] At the War Ministry Anami summoned all officers of the rank of lieutenant colonel and above to tell them of the government's decision. He stressed the importance of unity and order and warned against disregarding the decision.

Among those present was Anami's brother-in-law, Lieutenant Colonel Masahiko Takeshita. "The news of the imperial decision grilled our brain severely," he remembered. ". . . Since such a unique national polity as we enjoyed was beyond the understanding of foreign nations, there was little doubt that the occupation forces would eventually compel us to transform it as they wished. . . . It would be useless for the people to survive the war if the structure of the State itself was to be destroyed."[21]

Unfortunately, the government sent out mixed signals. The cabinet issued an announcement that Japan's fortunes were "now at their lowest ebb." The government would "do its utmost to defend the national polity and the honor of the nation." And it expected the Japanese people "to overcome all difficulties to uphold our national polity." Cheek by jowl with this statement, newspapers printed the army's "Instructions to Officers and Men," which called upon them "to fight to the end in this holy war for the defense of our divine land."[22]

Japan's field commanders had not been taken into the headquarters' confidence. Ugaki first heard that Japan had sued for peace on 11 August, when his chief intelligence officer, "a look of horror on his face," brought him "the most hateful news" after hearing a San Francisco broadcast. At first Ugaki took this for enemy propaganda, but a telephone call from Hiyoshi disabused him of the notion. He refused to admit that the navy didn't have enough strength left to continue the conflict. And what about the "large army forces still in China and in Japan proper?" Ugaki insisted in his diary,

> Even though it became impossible for us to continue an organized resistance after expending strength, we must continue a guerrilla warfare under the Emperor and never give up the war. When this resolution was made firmly, we could not be defeated. Instead, we could make the enemy finally give up the war after making it bitterly taste a prolonged war.[23]

In this spirit, on 12 August Lieutenant Colonel Yoshida, the army liaison officer who had replaced Sejima at Combined Fleet headquarters, approached Fuchida with a proposition. The two men occupied adjoining desks and had become friendly. Both knew that a number of die-hards in the naval air arm were eager to continue fighting. This group comprised in the main junior officers stationed at Kisarazu, on Kyushu, and at such bases near Tokyo as Yokosuka and Atsugi. The latter two bases contained the most vociferous opponents, particularly Atsugi. There not only the reckless airmen were involved; the base commander himself, Fuchida's volatile friend Kozono, was their ringleader. These men demonstrated under the slogan, Surrender is not the will of the emperor. They swore to ignore any such order Ozawa might issue and to fight to the last man.

Yoshida sounded Fuchida out. "What do you think about surrender?" he asked.

Impulsively Fuchida shouted, "No, never surrender!"[24]

This reaction was at total variance with his considered estimate of the situation. He was sick of the war. The roll call of his departed comrades drummed in his ears, the ghosts of Japan's burned-out cities haunted his dreams. Moreover, the concept of a coup d'état was the sort of melodrama from which he usually shrank in suspicious distaste. But he agreed. Like so many of his countrymen in this period, he wasn't thinking; he was a prey to emotion.

If, against Japanese tradition, the government was going to surrender, the emperor's loyal subjects had to remove the government. Such was the rationale of Fuchida and Yoshida. A coup d'état needed support and weapons. To estimate the possibility of acquiring these, Yoshida went to army headquarters and Fuchida hurried over to talk with Onishi at Naval General Staff headquarters.[25]

He could have chosen no flag officer more likely to pour fuel rather than cold water over the proposal. Onishi was too far gone in his fanatical determination to remember the loyalty he owed his superiors. On 9 August he had entered the council meeting and, ignoring Yonai and Toyoda, called Anami out of the room to tell him that the navy minister was weak-kneed and of no use. "Please insist strongly on the continuation of the war," he pleaded. When Yonai found this out, he summoned Onishi and Toyoda and administered such a chewing out that Toyoda "stood at attention, stiffened as though he was frozen," and Onishi "hung his head low with tears rolling down his face."[26]

Fuchida had no difficulty getting in to see Onishi. "What does the situation look like at the Naval General Staff level?" he asked. The admiral gave him a brief summary and was more than willing to support a coup. Assured of Onishi's approval, Fuchida flew to Yokosuka. There the chief flight officer was his Eta Jima classmate, Captain Hiroshi Kogure. Then he went to Atsugi to see Kozono. He told both men that in case of a coup, they must prepare." Both promised they would be ready when and if called upon. Then he returned to Combined Fleet headquarters to await developments.[27]

They were not long in coming. Throughout that day, 12 August, debates began on whether or not to accept the Allied reply. The Americans had widely varied ideas about the imperial dynasty, and the reply didn't contain the reassurance for which the Japanese hoped. The U.S. position was this: "From the moment of surrender the authority of the Emperor and the Japanese Government to rule the State shall be subject to the Supreme Commander of the Allied Powers. . . ." This left considerable leeway for interpretation. So did the statement, "The ultimate form of Government of Japan shall, in accordance with the Potsdam Declaration, be established by the freely expressed will of the Japanese people."[28]

Togo felt that this in effect guaranteed the survival of the emperor system. "Those who knew the Japanese people" could have no doubt that they would wish to retain the ancient dynasty.[29] This interpretation and his assurance of Hirohito's support were the twin sources of strength enabling Togo to endure the next two days. He had to fight off even more determined resistance than before, if that were possible. This time Hiranuma ranged himself with the opposition, and Suzuki came perilously near to submitting to army pressure. It took Kido's intervention to bring him back into the fold.[30]

Anami ranged far out of the channels of protocol in a desperate attempt to secure imperial support for his position. He visited Prince Mikasa, the emperor's third brother, an army officer, "to ask him to change the emperor's mind so as to continue the war." His Highness told him off: "Since the Manchurian Incident, the Army has not once acted in accordance with the Imperial wish. It is most improper that you should still want to continue the war when things have come to this stage."[31]

Umezu tried higher. He and Toyoda had an audience with the emperor to beg him to reject the Allied reply. This earned Toyoda another stern reprimand from Yonai for daring to take such a step without consulting him.[32]

The afternoon of 13 August found Fuchida hastening off to plan with Onishi the seizure of the palace and the government, along with army and navy headquarters. According to the tentative plan, a general would be the new premier and power would rest largely in army hands.

In a hallway of Naval General Staff headquarters, Fuchida encountered Prince Takamatsu. "Just a minute," the prince said abruptly, and motioned him into a nearby small room. He followed reluctantly. "I was in a hurry to meet Onishi," he recalled, "and the coup d'état was so near." But one could not brush off an imperial prince, especially if he happened to be a superior officer and Eta Jima classmate.

With his high broad cheekbones, pointed chin, and taut features, Prince Takamatsu resembled a fine Siamese cat, and he had that feline's disconcerting gaze. Under the spell of those dark eyes, Fuchida began to feel uncomfortable. Suddenly he was sure that the prince knew about the plan and Fuchida's part in it. His words left no doubt: "I have just returned from the palace, where I spoke with His Imperial Majesty personally. The emperor most earnestly desires to surrender immediately and thus secure peace for the nation."

For Fuchida, those few words changed everything. Little remained to give his life meaning but fulfilling the imperial will. "All right," he replied. "The coup d'état will be canceled."

The two men discussed the matter a few minutes longer. "The will of the emperor is the key to an orderly transition from war to peace," Fuchida observed. "May I request that all members of the royal family in the military service go to the various fronts as imperial messengers? They can perform a national service by convincing our military leaders that surrender is indeed His Imperial Majesty's sincere wish."[33]

Whether or not as a result of Fuchida's suggestion, a few days later three princes of the imperial family did go to the fronts as emissaries to insure obedience—Prince Yasuhiko Asaka to China, Prince Haruhito Kanin to the south, and Prince Tsunenisa Takeda to the Kwantung army and Korea. Princes Mikasa, Kuni, Takeda, and Takamatsu were scheduled to visit various army and naval air units later. By the planned departure date, however, matters had settled down and their trips were unnecessary.[34]

As soon as Fuchida left Prince Takamatsu, he telephoned the air bases at Yokosuka and Atsugi. Kogure was willing to call off the coup. Kozono wasn't, being much too bitter to listen to reason. Next Fuchida tried to find Yoshida, but he had left navy headquarters to join his army group. Fuchida never saw him again.

Then in furious haste he started writing a brief pamphlet, "We Believe This," for distribution to all naval aviators. In five pages he laid down his point of view: The navy had fought its best for four years and had nothing with which to reproach itself. Surrender was the will of the emperor. For this statement he had the authority and word of His Majesty's brother, the navy's own Prince Takamatsu. "So," he wrote, "I believe this is the truth."

Without troubling about literary flourishes, Fuchida hurried it off for immediate publication and distribution as his small contribution to law and order. His airmen might listen to him, whereas the words of high command or government would go in one ear and out the other.[35]

Fuchida had promised Prince Takamatsu more than he could deliver. On the night of 13 August, Onishi came to the premier's official residence where Togo was meeting with Umezu and Toyoda, and asked to speak to them. Togo related the incident:

> He contended that the problem in question was not that the Allied reply was unsatisfactory; the need, he felt, was rather for the military to formulate a plan for certain victory, submit it to the Emperor, and then proceed to carry it through. He strongly urged the two chiefs of staff to adopt this course, arguing that we would never be defeated if we were prepared to sacrifice 20,000,000 Japanese lives in a 'special attack' effort.[36]

This horrifying suggestion did not recommend itself to Togo, and the last series of arguments continued through the next day, 14 August. By this time, the only cabinet holdout was Anami. He had a potent weapon at his disposal, resignation, which would have brought down the Suzuki cabinet. To his credit, he didn't resign. Out of office he would no longer have access to the emperor, whom he not only revered as a sovereign but also liked as an individual.[37]

The final conference on the subject of surrender was held on the morning of 14 August, again in the imperial air-raid shelter in the presence of the emperor. After one more plea on the part of Anami, Umezu, and Toyoda, Hirohito delivered his verdict in a voice shaking with emotion: The war must cease now before the nation suffered extermination. Weeping attendants withdrew to prepare an imperial rescript announcing the decision. That night, at about 2250, the emperor recorded a speech to be delivered to the nation at noon the next day. Japan would surrender, effective 2300, 14 August, 1945.[38]

The recording became the focal point of what remained of the rebellious faction. They would steal it before the broadcast. That night a number of army officers descended on the palace. When the commander of the palace guards refused to join them, they killed him and his aide. By means of a forged order they convinced the rest of the guards to let them search the premises. The guards joined them and sealed off the palace. A blackout being in force, they rummaged by flashlight, to no avail. They couldn't find the recording.

A telephone line leading to navy headquarters remained open, and through it an appeal for help reached the outside. The searchers were still combing the palace early on 15 August when Lieutenant General Shizuichi Tanaka, commanding the Eastern District and Twelfth Area Armies, drove into the grounds and restored order. That day and night saw the beginning of a steady stream of suicides, among them Onishi and Anami.[39]

Yoshida killed himself at army headquarters. Had Fuchida continued to be caught up with the rebels, honor and custom would have demanded his own self-destruction. He owed a debt of gratitude to Prince Takamatsu for taking him into his confidence and thus indirectly saving his life.

Shortly before noon on 15 August, Ozawa gathered all the officers and men of Combined Fleet headquarters on the grounds behind the building. There he lined them up in parade review to hear the imperial broadcast. The citizens of Japan didn't know they would hear the emperor's voice. The press release only notified everyone to listen to a broadcast at 1200.

A few seconds before noon, Ozawa called them to attention. The announcer revealed that the speaker would be His Imperial Majesty. At the first sound of the emperor's voice, each of the officers at navy headquarters saluted smartly, remaining at attention until the end of the broadcast, at which time they saluted again.

Underneath their rigid military bearing, every man present grieved for his emperor, placed in such a humiliating position. Fuchida found himself wondering if the outcome of the war would have been different had he fought harder.

Fuchida listened with more than ceremonial attention. One point disturbed him. About halfway through the speech a phrase was spoken that would play over and over in his thoughts: "to pave the way for a grand peace for all generations to come. . . ." Fuchida didn't understand the concept. How could human beings establish a permanent peace? The idea flew in the face of history. Man could not achieve perfection, hence there would always be wars. At that moment he wanted peace so that Japan could rebuild. When the time was ripe, the nation could wage war again, shining with imperial radiance.

With such thoughts in mind, he couldn't help wondering if this phrase represented the emperor's conviction or whether he wasn't, as the Japanese expression has it, "a man who brings to his execution a sweet-sounding gong."[40]

During the ceremony Fuchida observed Ozawa closely. The admiral's stoic face usually kept its secrets, but so disheartened did he appear that Fuchida worried lest he be tempted to suicide. He decided to stick close by Ozawa.

After the broadcast, when Ozawa and his officers had tea together, Fuchida's fears were allayed. They discussed Ugaki's suicide. He had taken off that day from Kyushu with a volunteer crew on the last kamikaze mission. Some present declared that Ugaki had fulfilled his responsibility as an admiral, having sent so many to their deaths under his orders. Fuchida took exception to this idea. "If Ugaki wanted to kill himself, that was his business," he said firmly. "But he had no right to ask for volunteers to go along with him. Furthermore, it was his duty to listen to His Majesty's broadcast and to obey whatever wishes he expressed."

Then he drove home another point: "We fought the war according to the will of the emperor. I have killed and been injured following the imperial policy. Now I will accept surrender in the same spirit of loyalty. We must carry out the surrender in good faith and to the letter. We must withhold nothing—not one sword, not one gun, not one dagger."

Watching Ozawa, he was satisfied that the admiral would live, facing the future like a man. Fuchida himself never considered suicide. Professionally his conscience was clear. He recognized his momentary doubt during the emperor's broadcast for what it was—an emotional reflex response to a dramatic moment. He had carried out his duty to the best of his ability, and had asked no man to do what he did not stand ready to do himself. He had been scrupulously loyal to superiors and subordinates alike.

Very much a son of his nation and his time, Fuchida believed that in certain circumstances suicide was honorable. But under the present conditions, Japan had corpses enough and to spare. Fuchida wanted to live on for his country, his emperor, and his family.[41]

21

"More Trouble Is Coming!"

T HE DAY FOLLOWING the emperor's broadcast, Ozawa and Fuchida closed Combined Fleet headquarters at Hiyoshi and removed it to the Meguro War College in Tokyo. Those who still had a work program mapped out were fortunate—it tided them over the first shock of defeat. Fuchida's main concern was that he and his fellow officers get through the distasteful business of surrender with their dignity unimpaired. In his opinion, they could only do this by preparing for occupation with the same thoroughness they had given the war effort.

Many of his associates couldn't be so detached, particularly those of lesser rank who had nothing left to do. Deprived overnight of their way of life and reason for living, many panicked when they realized that Japan had indeed lost the war, and that occupation forces would take over in a matter of days. Some stole aircraft and flew to remote locations; others commandeered trucks and raced away in aimless flight from unbearable reality. Rumors floated about that the Allies would behead all Japanese officers. In a number of places, demoralized men set fire to navy buildings. Hungry townspeople surged into some of the almost deserted navy bases to loot. "The situation was just like revolution," Fuchida recalled—a nasty preview of what conditions might become when the armed forces were turned loose without employment.

While Ozawa and Fuchida settled into the Naval War College, the institution's press turned out a thousand copies of Fuchida's pamphlet, "We Believe This." The college rushed distribution to all naval bases inside and outside Japan to clarify the situation for young officers and to enlist their cooperation. Fortunately, the tract enjoyed immediate success, helping many to accept the inevitable. But stubborn pockets of opposition remained.[1]

After the abortive coup, troops from outside the Tokyo area were rushed in to replace the palace guard, which could no longer be considered reliable. A replacement platoon from Ibaraki Prefecture revolted and seized Ueno Hill, but shortly was persuaded to disperse. The young officers who had led the revolt committed suicide. Another group occupied Atagi Hill; soon thereafter the entire group blew themselves up with hand grenades.[2]

Fuchida realized the extent and nature of the resistance when he made arrangements for the flight of Japan's peace delegates to Manila. MacArthur had stipulated that the delegates fly from Haneda to Kisarazu, thence to Okinawa in two planes painted white and marked with a green cross on the wings and body. At Okinawa the delegates would transfer to U.S. aircraft. Ozawa authorized Fuchida to secure a Douglas DC from Yokosuka for the first leg. But when Fuchida phoned the order to Captain Kogure, he refused to comply. "The Yokosuka antisurrender group has agreed to work with Kozono at Atsugi in establishing a picket line in the air across Japan between the two bases to shoot down any surrender plane that tries to fly to Okinawa," he said.[3]

Fuchida sizzled with wrath at Kogure and Kozono, both old enough to know better. But he felt sorry for the rebel pilots. He understood how difficult it was for youth to accept defeat. These young men sincerely believed that venal politicians had coerced the emperor into surrender, and that they alone followed the wishes of his heart.

Kozono was the key to the problem, which surprised Fuchida not at all. This thin-faced, determined man was dedicated to the proposition that the average man is a fool and the majority always wrong. Even at Eta Jima he was convinced that he knew all the answers. "He always insisted on his own way," reminisced Fuchida. "Oh, the trouble he caused sometimes!" No one could question his bravery, for he was a fearless fighter pilot. Withal he could be a delightful companion, in token of which his friends nicknamed him Anchon ("Good Guy").[4]

Refusing to accept surrender, Kozono sent his Atsugi aircraft buzzing over Yokosuka, possibly as a hint to Kogure to toe the line. He also had his fliers dropping bills all over Tokyo fulminating against capitulation. "Don't surrender! Don't believe the imperial rescript! It is a false document." He went on the Atsugi radio and broadcasted messages protesting the surrender. Neither he nor his officers, he proclaimed, would obey any order from the Supreme Command to lay down their arms. He added that nothing could convince him that surrender was the emperor's will.[5]

The situation at Atsugi was so potentially dangerous that the emperor "was greatly worried that Japan would lose the faith of the world if something should go wrong when the occupation forces arrived."[6] A good three million men were armed in the home islands and at least that many overseas.[7] Ozawa feared that the popular firebrand Kozono would ignite the entire service.

Vice Admiral Biritaro Totsuka, the commander at Yokosuka, was understandably nervous about Kozono's aircraft circling over his base. He telephoned Ozawa to ask if he could send a detachment of marines to Atsugi and put Kozono under arrest. Ozawa held the phone and relayed the request to Fuchida. "What about it?" he whispered.

Fuchida shook his head vigorously. "It could mean civil war."

Ozawa nodded agreement. "Let's hold off for a while," he advised Totsuka.

While the two admirals talked, Fuchida thought the matter over. This looked like his problem. Kozono was a close personal friend, and Atsugi a naval air base. "As air officer of the Combined Fleet, I will go to Atsugi and talk to Kozono," he declared.

With Ozawa's permission, Fuchida ordered a staff car and, alone save for his enlisted driver, set out for Atsugi, taking with him his sword and a loaded pistol. On the way, he reviewed his strategy. First, he would try to get it through Kozono's obstinate head that the emperor wanted Japan to surrender. If Kozono remained unconvinced—which was all too probable—Fuchida would have to resort to his sword. Fuchida liked Kozono and didn't relish the prospect of killing him, but his revolt could spark nationwide rebellion. "Of course," he told himself, "Kozono will be armed also and will stab back at me with equal good will!"[8]

From Kozono's point of view, he had reason to be upset with Fuchida. One day the latter had stood by him, the next he had made a 180 degree turn and authored a tract saying that surrender was the imperial will. Kozono might well be thinking that Fuchida was vacillating, or shirking his higher duty.

As Fuchida's car came within sight of Atsugi's main gate, he blinked in surprise. Machine guns ringed the base and sailors wearing combat helmets stood guard with fixed bayonets at the closed gates. Evidently Kozono, having heard rumors about a contemplated marine attack, was prepared to go down fighting.

Fuchida instructed his driver to stop, left the car, and approached the gate, calling for the chief of the guard. To this man, a petty officer, he introduced himself. "I am the air operations officer of the Combined Fleet, Captain Mitsuo Fuchida."

The chief snapped to salute and replied, "Yes, sir, I know you."

"I've come to meet with the commanding officer, Captain Yasuna Kozono. But before you tell him I'm here, open the gates and let me drive to his headquarters." Fuchida feared that if Kozono learned of his arrival, he might refuse him entrance. The fact that the guard knew him by sight and reputation was a piece of luck. Without further ado, the petty officer signaled his men to open the gate.[9]

Thankfully, Fuchida reentered the car for the five-minute drive to Kozono's headquarters. There he met another acquaintance of former years, Lieutenant Commander Toshio Hashizumi, the base air operations officer and Kozono's second in command. Hashizumi recognized Fuchida at once, for they had seen considerable prewar service together. He saluted. "What can I do for you, sir?"

"I've come to see Captain Kozono," Fuchida replied. "What are the prospects?"

Hashizumi's face clouded over. "Kozono has been drinking heavily," he admitted. "I'm afraid that he's losing his mind."

Fuchida was relieved. Up to that moment he hadn't known exactly how to go about his mission, for it appeared that his friend was doomed no matter what course he took. If he refused to give up his rebellion, Fuchida would have to kill him. But if he surrendered, he faced court-martial and perhaps a firing squad. With Hashizumi's words, Fuchida saw a pattern of action that would save all faces and lives. It required Hashizumi's cooperation. Looking the unhappy officer squarely in the eye, Fuchida said, "Under the circumstances, are you with me or are you against me?"

Hashizumi didn't flinch. "I'm with you," he replied.

Fuchida nodded his satisfaction. "What I have in mind," he explained, "is to overpower Kozono and get him to a hospital. If the doctors declare him insane, the navy cannot hold him responsible for his conduct. And if the rest of your officers and men understand that their commander is mentally ill, they can lay down their arms honorably with no feeling of disloyalty or disobedience. Order an ambulance to report at once in front of headquarters."

Hashizumi did so, then together he and Fuchida hastened to Kozono's private quarters, an office and a bedroom on the second floor near the main entrance. Fuchida burst in through the bedroom door and beheld Kozono in full uniform, sitting beside a table methodically drinking sake. Although well under the influence, he recognized his visitor at once. Oddly enough, he had been reading Fuchida's pamphlet.

With a roar, he leaped to his feet. Kozono had always had difficulty speaking, pulling his words out like olives from a bottle. "Fuchida, you have betrayed us!" he spluttered. "And *surrender* is not a word in the dictionary of our country!" He snatched up the booklet from the table and ripped it in two under Fuchida's nose, yelling furiously, "This is only your opinion. It is not the will of the emperor! You must be killed!" And he clapped his hand to his sword hilt.

As Kozono struggled in his drunken mist to pull the sword from its scabbard, Fuchida grabbed him by the elbows. "Help me!" he shouted to Hashizumi.

Whereupon that man rushed forward, seized Kozono around the legs, and with Fuchida wrestled him to the floor. Kozono struggled and screamed as four sailors from the ambulance arrived. They forced him into a straitjacket and bore him, stretched stiff as a plank and howling at the top of his lungs, to the waiting ambulance. Then the vehicle sped off for the hospital at Yokosuka.[10]

Fuchida telephoned Yano to give him a quick account of events. "Please get in touch with Admiral Totsuka immediately," he said, "and have Kozono committed to the psycho ward at Yokosuka. May I suggest that I be made temporary commander at Atsugi? That will give me authority to restore the base to normal."

Within two hours he received the necessary orders. At 1300 he summoned all officers and men of Atsugi to report in front of the headquarters building for a general assembly. Over one hundred officers and three thousand enlisted men had gathered when Hashizumi climbed onto a platform and introduced the new commander. Fuchida stepped forward and announced that he was taking over command of the base. Then he issued his first order: "All preparations for fighting must cease. All machine guns must be removed, all propellers taken off all airplanes, all weapons turned in."[11]

Much grumbling ensued. Most of the young men had been enjoying the atmosphere of drama. But in the end they obeyed, except for eighteen fighter pilots, all inexperienced and little more than boys. A day or so later they climbed into their planes, took off, and headed for army air bases in Saitama Prefecture, where they hoped to find support. It was not forthcoming, and they surrendered on 25 August.[12]

By way of postscript, the pilots were tried for their mutiny and received from two to four years in prison. Kozono recovered his sanity quite soon. A civil court tried him for disobedience to military law and handed down a sentence of thirteen years' imprisonment, which Fuchida considered a severe penalty imposed to placate the occupation. Kozono went free after serving seven years. He bore Fuchida no grudge for clapping him into a straitjacket; however, he remained convinced that Japan should have resorted to guerrilla resistance and retained his political views, which were somewhat to the right of the late dowager empress of China.[13]

As soon as Atsugi was secured, Fuchida was relieved as commander. But he was present on the afternoon of 30 August when MacArthur landed there. Commander Terai, a member of the surrender delegation to Manila, had informed Fuchida that MacArthur chose Atsugi as his landing site against his, Terai's, advice and that of Captain Ohmae. Terai informed certain of MacArthur's officers that Atsugi was dangerous. This was an honest attempt to avoid trouble, but poor psychology in dealing with MacArthur.

Though Fuchida didn't serve on the welcoming committee, he got a good look at MacArthur. He admitted to prejudice against the general, sight unseen, not because he came as Japan's conqueror but because he had abandoned his men on Bataan. "No Japanese supreme commander ever fled, leaving his troops and officers. This is not the Japanese tradition," explained Fuchida. " 'I shall return!' That was okay. But not leaving his troops. I didn't like that. . . ."

His first sight reinforced his bias. Fuchida described the scene: "MacArthur walked proudly, his head high. He shook hands with a U.S. general [Lieutenant General Robert L. Eichelberger, commanding the Eighth Army] on the ground—I don't know who. His hat was on one side and he wore sunglasses. He smoked a big pipe. But he paid no attention to the Japanese delegation, standing straight and saluting him. I thought to myself, Much too proud!"[14]

Almost immediately Fuchida returned to headquarters at Tokyo. At last he could turn his attention to burning classified materials. The senior staff officer, Captain Yamaoka, had ordered this at Ozawa's direction on 14 August. The items to be burned consisted of all the navy's top-secret, secret, and confidential documents, a monumental task that consumed three entire days and nights. The papers, stored at Yokosuka, had to be trucked to Combined Fleet headquarters for destruction.

Fuchida didn't openly object to this procedure, but it did seem like wanton destruction to him. Japan had no more secrets to keep. Why should Ozawa and Yamaoka insist upon the letter of security? Some day this information would be important. Future historians had the right to be able to say to their generations, "This is how it was."

Impelled by instincts he could scarcely recognize or define, he set about securing one copy of each important document pertaining to the war, especially those dealing with Pearl Harbor and Midway. Later he put this collection into six large aluminum containers and buried them in an underground shelter in his garden at Kashiwara.[15]

Soon Combined Fleet headquarters began to receive orders for representatives to report to MacArthur's temporary headquarters in Yokosuka. There they would receive instructions concerning the forthcoming surrender ceremonies aboard the battleship *Missouri.* One of these problems was arranging for a Japanese pilot to bring the *Missouri* in safely. With Tokyo Bay heavily mined, only an experienced bay pilot could thread through the channel.[16]

MacArthur ordered the air bases around Tokyo cleared out and prepared for occupation forces. Fuchida made the two-hour train trip to Tateyama, some seventy miles south of Tokyo at the tip of the Boso peninsula, to remove military personnel from the base there. Likewise he prepared and inventoried all weapons and aircraft for turnover. By the time he finished the base was secure, with only twenty or thirty administrative personnel remaining.

He waited at the pier on Tateyama Bay to greet the new American commanding officer and turn the base over. He expected the ships to pull up at the pier and unload their troops as at any commercial port. Instead, they dropped anchor some distance out and disgorged about twenty-four small boats full of grim-looking, combat-ready marines. The boats ran up on shore, then the marines jumped into the bay and waded to land with rifles ready. They're getting all wet, Fuchida thought in amazement, and it isn't necessary.

Evidently the Americans felt they might have to fight their way in. When the marines discovered they had no enemy to contend with, they subsided, slightly deflated, and gazed curiously about. Then their commanding officer appeared walking down the pier from the land side. He had jumped into water up to his chest and was practically wrapped up in grenades. Fuchida swallowed his amusement and addressed him in halting English: "Is this your maneuver?"

"No," the colonel replied, "this is a genuine operation."

Saying no more, Fuchida accompanied him and the Japanese base commander to the headquarters building for private surrender ceremonies. As soon as he decently could he slipped away. Despite his amusement at their full-scale landing operation against a score of clerks, he was sorry for the drenched troops. They were squelching about in their heavy combat boots and shivering from the chilly waters. Tateyama boasted a huge bathhouse that could accommodate a hundred men at a time. Fuchida suggested they have hot baths while their clothes dried. The men appreciated the gesture and soon recovered in steaming, relaxed comfort.[17]

These preliminaries led up to the climax on the morning of 2 September, the formal surrender aboard the *Missouri*. Fuchida prepared transportation for the Japanese delegation, but the launches he secured proved unnecessary. An American destroyer carried the official party to the battleship. Several liaison officers, army and navy, went out in a "big, beautiful launch" assigned to the Yokosuka commander. Fuchida was among them. These men ranked too far down the echelon to rate a position on the surrender deck, but he could see the ceremony clearly from an upper deck.[18]

By this time Fuchida had been through so much—four years in the thick of a fiercely fought war, seeing his dearest friends whirled away one by one into the vortex of death, enduring the slow, inexorable approach of defeat, treading the blasted streets of Hiroshima, assisting in the mechanics of capitulation—such excitement, such tension, such horror, such grief, that by now he had attained a curious sort of detachment. He surveyed the scene with intense interest. An almost mystical sensation of witnessing a historical turning point enveloped him.[19]

The ceremony itself wasn't unduly humiliating. Fuchida was honest enough to admit that if the Japanese had won, they would have made a big production out of the surrender. He found one aspect ironic. "At the time I believed Japan had been beaten by the U.S. Navy, not the U.S. Army," he explained. "It was the same with Japan—our army never fought much against the U.S. Army. The Pacific war was mostly a naval war. But at the end of the war all the political matters were handled by the two armies, Japanese and American."[20]

Still, the surrender arrangement had a certain grim justice. The army had been the prime mover in Japan's drive for the conquest of Asia, constantly beating the drums of military glory and racial supremacy. The army had controlled one government after another, moving ever nearer all-out war with the Allies. Perhaps it was only right that it should endure the major ceremonial shame.

Fuchida observed MacArthur with special interest, impressed by the atmosphere of a show well stage-managed. This was MacArthur's moment of moments, and he dominated the proceedings with the chill glitter of a diamond. "Frankly," remarked Fuchida, "MacArthur was stiff and yet so proud and full of dignity. I respected him as a brilliant soldier, but I had no feeling for him. He was too cold and distant. A man like Eisenhower I could feel some warmth for, but not MacArthur."[21]

Fuchida looked behind MacArthur, seeking the man who in his opinion had really beaten the Japanese. Yes, there he was: Admiral Nimitz in his summer khakis. He looked serious, as befitted the occasion, but lines of good humor and kindness were etched on his face. "I was greatly impressed by Admiral Nimitz," said Fuchida.

Mamoru Shigemitsu, Japan's new foreign minister and head of the Japanese delegation, came forward to sign the surrender document. He had a wooden leg and used a cane. Prolonged standing or moving about pained him, and he seemed to grope for his place. Nimitz's face softened with sympathy for the crippled statesman. Fuchida saw this. Such a big man and yet so humble, he thought approvingly.

Umezu, who had fought surrender to the last ditch, signed for both the

Japanese armed forces. As he did so one of the Chinese delegates hissed loudly and triumphantly. "The U.S. delegates didn't like this impolite gesture, from the expression on their faces," Fuchida recalled.[22]

Next the Allies came forward. At 0908 MacArthur, "the Supreme Commander for the Allied Powers, signed for all nations."[23] General Arthur Percival of Singapore and Lieutenant General Jonathan Wainwright of Bataan stood beside him. MacArthur signed his name in sections, using several pens. He gave one to Wainwright, one to Percival, and reserved a few.

When Admiral Nimitz stepped to the table, accompanied by his war plans officer, Rear Admiral Forrest P. Sherman, and the redoubtable Halsey, he made no such theatrical gesture. He took his own pen out of his pocket and carefully wiped it with a piece of paper so as not to blot the historic document. A great gentleman! Fuchida thought. If Japan had won the war and if I were signing that document for Japan against the United States, I would sign like Nimitz.

Before signing, MacArthur had delivered a brief speech. Throughout the ceremony Fuchida reflected on his words. An eloquent if somewhat baroque speaker—even with his limited English, Fuchida could recognize this—he talked of the restoration of peace and a world of "freedom, tolerance, and justice." Whose justice? Fuchida wondered. The Japanese thought they had justice on their side, too. Japanese justice collided with American justice and neither of them won—superior power won.[24]

MacArthur ended the ceremony with these words: "Let us pray that peace be now restored to the world and that God will preserve it always. These proceedings are now closed."[25]

Fuchida listened skeptically. He had doubted his own emperor when he spoke of everlasting peace, and he didn't believe the general now. No, he thought, you are wrong, MacArthur. Peace isn't coming to the world. More trouble is coming.[26]

22

"Sad and Demoralizing"

FOR JAPANESE ex-officers it was a time of trial and tribulation. Defeat and unconditional surrender came as traumatic shocks. A sense of individual responsibility gnawed at many. Moreover, their personal dislocation was abrupt and complete. Before and during the war, their lives had been mapped out for them—a routine of hard work, strict discipline, and serious responsibility, but also security, dedication, and companionship. Now events turned them loose. The economy was broken. They had neither jobs nor prospects. Small wonder many resorted to irrational activity, things they would never consider under normal circumstances, from black-marketing to murder.[1]

Some followed the Pied Piper of Moscow. Fuchida heard Japanese communist agitators for the first time in late September or early October, while passing Hibiya Park in Tokyo. They screamed that the war had never touched Hirohito, yet Japanese died for him. "Down with the emperor!" they yelled.[2]

Early in the occupation, MacArthur emptied Japan's jails of political prisoners. Many had been imprisoned for speaking out against the government's expansionist policy, in the belief that along that path lay ruin. But many others were active communists. As soon as the prison gates swung open, swarms descended on the palace to demonstrate. Among other things, they demanded to know who fed the emperor, when the whole country was poverty-stricken and food scarce. Fuchida had no use for the Soviet Union after its belated entry into the Pacific conflict. To hear His Imperial Majesty insulted convinced him that the homegrown communists deserved the same contempt as their Russian masters.[3]

A month or so after the surrender ceremonies, Genda came to Tokyo to discuss with Fuchida the matter of the imperial family's safety. He had organized a number of officers to protect the imperial family with their lives. "We want to protect the entire imperial family if possible," he explained, "but if not we should at least protect Princess Suganomiya. She's only three years old, and we could hide her for ten or even fifteen years until the danger is over. Then we'll bring her out of hiding and restore the royal blood line."

"I don't believe the family's in any danger," Fuchida replied. "But it's a good idea to have your organization around in case we ever need it."

Then Genda showed Fuchida the membership list, which became known as *Genda Kikan* (Genda's Organization). Fuchida didn't add his name, but he assured his friend of support if the need arose.[4]

Shortly before this encounter, Fuchida received orders to report to Kure Hospital for examination in connection with his experience at Hiroshima. At least fifty officers in the hospital were suffering from radiation. Most of them had investigated the disaster. Three of the patients had been in Hiroshima when the bomb exploded, the two partially protected by their beds in the Yamato hotel, and Lieutenant Hashimoto. The latter recounted to Fuchida his experience on that ghastly morning.

All three expected to die soon. Everyone knew they were doomed. "But it was a terrible thing," recalled Fuchida, "to hear it from the lips of the victims." They had no appetite. Only injections kept them alive. They had begun to lose their hair—it stuck to their fingers whenever they touched their heads. Tumors had started to grow on their faces and bodies. "These men were human relics by then, no more than that," Fuchida said somberly. "They had lost all their energy, and they could barely speak. They were pathetic. There is no other expression for it."

He had been pondering the emperor's words about eternal peace. But until this moment, he couldn't imagine a world where mankind had improved to the point where everlasting accord was possible. Death as such he could regard with oriental unconcern. It came to all sooner or later. But the slow agony of his three friends? That was a different matter. It was better to have been killed at once than to die a miserable death from radioactivity. Of that Fuchida had no doubt. Whether or not everlasting peace was possible, the atomic bomb left mankind no choice but to try and achieve it. Looking down at the living remains of his three fellow officers, he said to himself, No more Pearl Harbors! The atomic bomb must never be used again! No more Hiroshimas! No more Nagasakis!

The Kure hospital kept Fuchida for a month of intensive tests. By the time he left, two of the investigating engineers had died and the rest were slowly perishing. The doctors released Fuchida and his friend Yasukado together. Neither of them showed any symptoms of exposure to radiation. As they walked out Yasukado remarked, "We're so lucky!" But in his case the effects were merely delayed; he died within a year.[5]

Fuchida had landed on his feet. He had survived the war in perfect health, and unlike so many of his fellow officers, he had a job. As soon as he came out of the hospital, he joined the navy's historical group on war documentation. The chief of this office was Rear Admiral Sadatoshi Tomioka, who had been the senior naval representative at the surrender ceremonies. The staff included Tomioka's immediate assistant, Captain Mineo Yamaoka, Ozawa's former senior staff officer; Captain Toshikazu Ohmae, an expert on Japanese naval history; Commander Masataka Chihaya, who had worked with Fuchida for a few months toward the end of the war; and Commander Yoshimore Terai, a war college classmate who had been a member of the peace delegation to Manila.[6]

In this office, Fuchida had work for which he was well qualified and association with some of the best minds in the Japanese navy. But instead of making the most of the opportunity, he plunged into hot water. He had known Tomioka slightly for years, but they had never worked closely together. A shrewd man, courtly, urbane, he was a baron by birth and an aristocrat to the tips of his fingers. He had everything to recommend him, yet Fuchida harbored an irrational dislike.[7]

The two men crossed swords over a policy problem. When occupation headquarters requested that Japan's military forces turn over their official documents, the Japanese told the Americans that these had been burned. So MacArthur's headquarters asked that Japanese military personnel be thoroughly interrogated and documentation submitted on the basis of their recollections. Former officials of the army, navy, and civilian government agreed that in preparing these "memory documents," as Fuchida called them, they must protect the emperor and not mention his name in connection with military activities. According to Fuchida, Tomioka supported this policy and worked hard to protect Hirohito.

Fuchida yielded to no man in devotion to the emperor, but he believed that the facts should be divulged. Hirohito had known all about the war planning, including Pearl Harbor. "This, of course, did not make him responsible," Fuchida emphasized. "Knowledge and responsibility are not the same. The responsibility rested with the military." That being the case, Fuchida didn't see how imperial dignity could suffer from the truth.

This issue came to a head between him and Tomioka almost at once. Fuchida cautioned his chief to be careful in juggling the facts. "There might be documents someplace in the world," he said, referring obliquely to his own collection of which Tomioka knew nothing. Oddly enough, shortly thereafter American investigators discovered a rich store of documents when they raised the bombed and sunken Japanese cruiser *Nachi* in Manila Bay. This unexpected turn of events did nothing to endear Fuchida to Tomioka.[8] A prophet in his own country can be highly irritating.

Soon the U.S. Strategic Bombing Survey came to Japan. Fuchida found these men easy to work with, unconcerned with touchy questions of right and wrong. Nevertheless, as Fuchida saw it, they were obsessed with the B-29. They seemed more bent on confirming their preconceived ideas of the big bomber's power and accuracy than in objectively assessing the overall strategic bombing picture. "Your carrier forces played an important role in Japan's defeat," Fuchida insisted, but they didn't seem to believe him.

Rear Admiral Ralph A. Oftsie, head of the team, was one who did give a good deal of weight to Fuchida's testimony, particularly after scrutiny of the *Nachi* papers confirmed many of his statements. When the survey team gave him a subject to review, Fuchida would search through his private files and come back with detailed facts. "The Americans were impressed with my memory," he reminisced with a grin. Many of the *Nachi* documents duplicated those in his possession.

The disagreement between Tomioka and Fuchida split the office, Yamaoka siding with Fuchida, Ohmae with Tomioka. In the past, Fuchida had often worked harmoniously with his colleagues despite differences. But he was no longer under military discipline, and he had a stubborn streak.

In this immediate postwar period of raw nerves, bruised pride, and thin skins, tempers flared at the slightest touch. Fuchida lost support when early in 1946 Yamaoka died of the flu. By March Tomioka so strongly wished Fuchida elsewhere that he felt he had no choice but to leave. As luck would have it, his Eta Jima classmate Eijiro Suzuki came in as his replacement. "He was a charming fellow with a fine fighting spirit," Fuchida described him. Basically he shared Fuchida's attitude regarding policy, and moreover had a fierce temper. He wasn't much of an improvement over Fuchida in Tomioka's eyes. Terai constantly acted as mediator.[9]

Another event in Fuchida's life may have had something to do with his parting of the ways with the war documentation office. In the months after the surrender a young woman, Kimi Matsumoto (a pseudonym), frequently came to Naval General Staff headquarters bringing rice cakes and other tidbits. Creamy-skinned, doe-eyed, and soft of voice, she moved like a shadowy lady of legend through the dreary ruins. She became a general favorite. In her house certain officers hid papers they wanted to keep under cover, and there they met one another in an atmosphere of dreamy intrigue.

Kimi was unofficially engaged to a fine ex-officer whom Fuchida knew well—unofficially because he was married. His wife was terminally ill, and it was understood that he and Kimi were a twosome who would marry a discreet period after his wife's inevitable death.

Fuchida fell in love with Kimi and besieged her with such ardor and determination that they became lovers.[10] This in itself was not remarkable; many ex-officers were turning from their wives to other women, as if trying to bury the tarnished past. Fuchida, however, had deliberately pursued and stolen the bethrothed of a brother officer. For this many of his comrades never forgave him.[11]

When Fuchida left his job, he automatically lost his civilian status with the Japanese government and the occupation forces. For the first time in his adult life, he was unemployed—a middle-aged man of purely military experience in a country with no military tasks left to be performed. MacArthur had disbanded the Japanese armed forces.

Fuchida considered this move most unrealistic. He believed that Japan should have been allowed to keep a hundred thousand men under arms, as the Allies had permitted Germany after World War I. "Japan needed a national defense force for security purposes," he insisted.[12]

To Fuchida, the entire occupation policy toward Japan's former fighting men was misguided. MacArthur established arbitrary limits on the jobs available to former military men, especially officers. Civilian employers could hire only a small percentage of their work force from the ranks of the ex-military. Nor could former soldiers and sailors take jobs in the government, run for office, teach school—the very positions for which they were best qualified. This prohibition worked hardships on individuals and deprived the struggling economy of a sorely needed reservoir of vigor and experience.

Jobs of any kind being so scarce, many settled for any honest labor they could find—bootblacks, ditch diggers, and so on. Many had to beg their bread. The more fortunate started life over as farmers or small merchants. Even those who enjoyed good health found life hard and frustrating. For the sick and wounded, it was plain hell.

Sometimes Fuchida came across old companions, both officers and enlisted men, begging on the streets. "It was a sad and demoralizing sight." They had nowhere to go, for the occupation had closed all military hospitals. Fuchida couldn't escape the heartrending sight of these men sleeping in doorways and in railroad stations, shivering with cold as they pulled the rags of old uniforms around them. "By building or subsidizing a few hospitals for these men," Fuchida declared, "MacArthur would have won the respect of all Japan and erected a real monument to his name."[13]

Had the occupation confined its restrictions to Japan's active-duty military personnel, Fuchida could have understood, even if he didn't like it. The United States had just won a long, cruel war that had cost millions of American and Allied lives. No sensible Japanese could expect the imperial army and navy to remain intact. But—and this was Fuchida's principal grievance—the occupation abolished all pensions, even those of generals and admirals retired for years before World War II broke out. A number were over eighty-five years of age. Some of these retirees committed suicide when they lost their only means of support. And MacArthur cut off the pensions of war widows. Such needless brutality horrified Fuchida.[14]

He identified far too closely with his former comrades to evaluate the occupation objectively. Japan's fate could have been much worse. The Allies didn't impose direct military government as in Germany. Tokyo had not been split in two, like Berlin. Shrines and imperial property were strictly off-limits; art objects and religious monuments were respected.

When the Japanese occupied a territory, they lived off the land. If there was not enough food for occupation troops and natives, it was too bad for the natives. The Japanese fully expected the Americans to treat them to a dose of their own medicine, and the prospect terrified them. To feed its own millions stretched Japan's resources to the breaking point. How could its agriculture possibly absorb the requirements of thousands of GIs with voracious Western appetites? So the relief and astonishment of the Japanese were immense when they learned that the Americans would not only supply their own provisions but also help feed the populace.[15]

While Fuchida prowled dispiritedly about Tokyo seeking employment, heartsick for his country and his friends, Kimi issued an ultimatum: He must divorce his wife and marry her, or their relationship would end.[16] In the romantic, sensual world she inhabited, it was that simple: Haruko would accept a divorce without protest; she and the children would vanish without trace; Kimi and Fuchida would marry and live happily ever after. It was Fuchida's self-inflicted misfortune that he had chosen a woman who couldn't see their relationship for what it was—two people seeking solace in a time of unhappiness, who would part with mutual tenderness and without regret when the crisis had passed.

An officer who knew them both bluntly characterized Kimi as "a psychotic lunatic."[17] Certainly she was a woman of impulse, living on her emotions, and she saw Fuchida as the fulfillment of her dreams. She was hysterically jealous of Haruko and couldn't admit that his wife had first claim on his loyalty.

But she was a beautiful woman of much charm, and Fuchida was in love with her. He didn't have the courage to take her at her word and make a clean break then and there. Nor did Kimi have the resolution to stick to her ultimatum.

Haruko had never given Fuchida the slightest cause for divorce. On the contrary, she had given him a serene home and two fine children whom he loved dearly and had no intention of losing. Torn between his infatuation for Kimi and his duty, he turned tail and fled like a wounded animal to the hills of Nara Prefecture, his native soil.[18]

23

"Under the Grace of God"

AFTER FUCHIDA left the dismal rubble of Tokyo behind, he entered upon a short interlude that he never mentioned. Years later, his son remarked briefly, "My Dad went downhill. He was very unhappy."[1] According to Kimi, Fuchida holed up in a sort of hermitage in the forest. During his self-imposed exile he let his hair and beard grow and his body go unwashed.

The war crimes tribunal was being set up and the authorities wanted him as a witness. They sent him one telegram after another, which fearful, well-meaning Haruko tore up as fast as they arrived. Finally Yoshiya got his hands on one. He realized that ignoring the messages could get his father in worse trouble than answering them. So he brought him the telegram, which Fuchida had brains enough to heed. Looking and smelling like a Neanderthal man, he took the train to Tokyo, where he went to Kimi's house.

At the sight of this apparition Kimi gave a horrified squeak, set about drawing a bath, and began to mend his clothes. She summoned a barber, who took one incredulous look at his beard and demanded three times the normal fee before he would begin hacking away.[2]

Once more neat, clean, and shaved, Fuchida came to himself and soon returned to Nara to put the shattered pieces of his life into some sort of order. But it was not the last time he would see Kimi.

He and his family had a good temporary home. Haruko's sister and brother-in-law took in the Fuchidas. The couple owned a prosperous drugstore in Tawaramoto, "a small merchant town," as Miyako described it, located in the center of Nara Prefecture, not too far from Kashiwara.[3]

Outside aid came from an unexpected source. A large Shinto organization with headquarters in Tenri City near Nara gave him a monthly grant of ten thousand yen. The money came with no obligation, a token of his service to Japan. Fuchida didn't want to accept it unless he could do something in exchange; the organization had nothing available except the presidency of its library, a sinecure. Fuchida couldn't afford to devote his time to a purely honorary position. So he swallowed his pride and accepted the yen. The grant continued for about a year, after which Fuchida was able to take care of his family without it.[4]

After the money was offered, Fuchida had determined that the only course open to him was to become a small farmer. He had saved from his salary a nest egg sufficient to purchase a four-*tan* (about one acre) tract from his father-in-law. Mr. Kitaoka's original holdings had totaled some one hundred *tan*, which he farmed out to neighboring tenants. At harvest time they paid 60 percent to him, keeping 40 percent for their work. This was the customary rate under that system.

But it so happened that the occupation's agricultural reform program had recently begun. No one could possess more land than he himself could till, and landlords had to put any holdings over ten *tan* up for sale at what Fuchida considered a ridiculous price. With such cheap land on the market it moved quickly, leaving the former owners with neither land nor adequate recompense.

Fuchida had no quarrel with land reform as such, for he realized that the old semifeudal system had long needed overhauling. But he had a twofold objection to the manner in which the occupation instituted it. "First, MacArthur didn't do it in the democratic way, as a democracy like the United States would," Fuchida commented. "He did it like a communist dictator." In the second place, the occupation should have insured that the government bought the land for a reasonable compensation, offering it for sale directly to the poor tenants at a cost they could afford.[5]

Legally, Fuchida could have bought the land for the proverbial song, but he insisted that Mr. Kitaoka accept what the farm would bring in the normal real-estate market of the day—the equivalent of about $12,500.

With inflation soaring, the purchase nearly cleaned Fuchida out. He started his new life from scratch, and he knew nothing about farming. Moreover, his family needed a home. Unable to afford labor, he had to build it himself, and he had never constructed so much as a doghouse. Then, too, he had to plant crops and devise some means of livelihood to carry the household through until the farm began to produce. He and his family faced months of poverty.

The adjustment from Fuchida's former status as a famous navy captain to that of a poor, obscure farmer was difficult.[6] He had almost no experience of the struggles and aspirations of daily family life. Nor had he ever come in contact with the harsh demands of the land. A gregarious soul, there had been no room in his days for true reflection and contemplation, the fruits of solitude.

Soon he realized that such solitude would be his portion. "Whereas my Dad was a hero during the war . . . after the war, he was looked on as a war criminal by his own people," Yoshiya wrote.[7] His father agreed: "My own people treated us cruelly." He suspected that the good folk of Kashiwara feared to be seen befriending him lest they incur the wrath of the occupation. They avoided him, and no one ever visited him on the farm.[8] It is also possible that, along with the desire for self-preservation, they saw in Fuchida a personification of the militarism that had brought down the nation.

He couldn't help recalling other days, such as the occasion in December 1941 when he described the Pearl Harbor attack to a packed house in the Kashiwara auditorium. That audience applauded him loudly; now they would scarcely give him the time of day. Indeed, they fully expected him to be tried and hanged for his part in the Pearl Harbor operation.[9] Even the children suffered. At school Yoshiya's fellow students jeered at him, "Your father lost the war."[10]

Fuchida withdrew into a sullen shell of resentment, hungering for companionship. He had confidence in his abilities and decided to ask help of no one. For a rank beginner to feed and house himself, a wife, and two children from such a small farm would require much study and hard work. At night he pored over books and pamphlets on carpentry, chicken raising, and gardening. In the daytime he took the train from Tawaramoto to Kashiwara, a twenty-minute ride, and worked on the land putting his knowledge to use.[11]

He divided the holding roughly in quarters, sowing half with alternating strips of rice and wheat. On the third quarter he planted vegetables and fruit trees. Because they would live off the produce rather than market it, he could afford to plant a variety. He put in a few fruit trees, and he tossed in three grape vines. To put meat and eggs on the table, he bought a few rabbits and ducks.[12]

The last part he reserved for the house and for a hundred Leghorn chickens, the VIPs of the establishment. He built their house before his own, taking such pains with it that the neighbors thought it was to be the family dwelling. They gaped in surprise when he moved in the Leghorns. He learned the poultry business from the ground up, mostly from books, with occasional tips from the neighbors when they discovered they could speak to him safely. He coddled those chickens like a mother her babies. In winter he kept them warm by the Korean method of heating from below, and in summer kept them scrupulously clean and free of insects. The hens became good layers and a source of steady income.[13]

With the chickens sheltered and crops planted, Fuchida turned his attention to a house for the family. This project had its ironic aspects. Like many people whose careers rule out a permanent home, he had dreamed for years of retiring to the perfect dwelling constructed to his specifications. Often in the evenings during his brief home leaves, he would make sketch after sketch of floor plans. Sometimes he would become so absorbed that he didn't stop until dawn streaked the windows. "My father was really a frustrated architect," Yoshiya commented years later.[14]

So, while he had no practical experience of architecture or carpentry, he had some ideas. The books on house construction he had read told him that the edifice should face 15 degrees southeast for maximum sun in winter and protection from direct rays in summer. He had no compass, but many times he had stood on the deck of a carrier and used a sextant to shoot Polaris. One clear evening he took Yoshiya and Miyako to the spot where he wished to build. There he gave Yoshiya a long pole and lined him up with the North Star, with Miyako some distance behind him. Using them as a sextant, Fuchida located north and marked off the angle of his home site.

He had never been spiritual, although by no means was he a pugnacious atheist. He simply had accepted the universe of which he was a part without wondering what made it tick. Now as he looked into the bright night sky and saw the North Star, "so steady, so beautiful, and so useful," he began to see the workings of a supreme intelligence. "That night, there on my farm, God began to come into my heart," Fuchida said reverently.

As he continued building and farming, he thought seriously about God's intervention in his war career. God protected my life during the war, he mused. Why? He must have a mission for him. Fuchida couldn't tell what it would be, but surely whoever created the glory of the skies did nothing without a purpose. Such thoughts wove in and out of Fuchida's mind as he went about his work between farm and forest.[15]

For building material, Fuchida turned to two acres of timberland which Haruko had received as part of her marriage dowry. MacArthur's agricultural reform did not include forests, so this still belonged to her. The plot consisted of timber that Haruko's great-grandfather planted in mountainous terrain about three miles from the farm. Each day Haruko packed a large lunch and the whole family marched off. Fuchida selected and cut down a tree or two, then Yoshiya and he trimmed them, loaded them on a cart and pulled them to a sawmill about halfway between the timber site and the farm. The mill owner, a man named Yamaga, at one time had been a guard for Kitaoka's timberland. Whenever he could spare the time he helped the Fuchidas fell trees and haul them to his mill.

Fuchida selected the wood for the house with all possible care for the good of the forest. He cut only twenty trees, choosing crowded ones which should be thinned so that the rest could grow better. As he cut them, he thanked his wife's ancestors for having bought the land and planted it against a day of need. Fuchida could have made ready cash by selling any of the trees, and from time to time Haruko suggested that they do so. Building lumber and firewood were in heavy demand. But Fuchida resisted the temptation. For one thing, the land belonged to Haruko; it was a reserve source of income for her if anything happened to him. As long as possible, he would support his family. Furthermore, he respected tradition and loved beauty; Haruko's great-grandfather had planted the majestic trees, and Fuchida wouldn't cut any unless no other course remained.[16]

He worked hard and well to rebuild the family fortunes, but, whether or not he realized it, the rock upon which he built was Haruko. Because of her, land was available for the buying, trees for the cutting. She couldn't compete with Kimi on the score of beauty or allure; she looked like what she was—a solid countrywoman, wife, and mother, who knew how to conceal her thoughts and emotions. Haruko had brought to her marriage many beautiful, expensive kimonos and pieces of jewelry. The latter she had contributed to the government during the war. Now she traded many of her kimonos to farmers in exchange for sweet potatoes, slipping out before daybreak so that no one should see the Fuchidas reduced to such straits. With considerable originality, she cooked anything she could pick or catch—dandelion greens, chickweed, frogs, rabbits—even Miyako's pet chicken. "I think my father is a great man," said Miyako almost twenty years later, "but my mother is a great woman, too."[17]

This period of labor, sacrifice, worry, and isolation, so difficult for Fuchida and Haruko, was a time of pleasure for the children. They reveled in having a full-time father and pitched into their tasks with a will. More important, day by day they experienced one of life's great satisfactions—that of being necessary, working members of a family team.

Participating in the construction of a house was Yoshiya's idea of earthly bliss. Many of his friends and relatives had assumed that he would become an officer like his father. But this experience inspired a lifelong passion for architecture.[18] As for Miyako, "Many of my pleasant . . . recollections came from this period," she said. She trudged happily to the forest to watch her father and brother cut down trees, and lent her small strength to pushing the cart. She delighted in feeding the chickens, hunting for eggs, and gardening, but viewed the kitchen askance. There she performed her chores with obedience but no pleasure. Her greatest joy was painting inside the house.[19]

In the beginning, the shelter was a long way from the beautiful, functional home of Fuchida's dream. Yoshiya remembered it as a shack.[20] Fuchida dug a well and the family moved in, unrolling their *futons* wherever they found a few feet of space. Meanwhile, they added on to the dwelling. Much of the construction was a difficult business of trial and error. But Fuchida kept at his books and went to a carpentry class at the local high school. Soon he discovered that the secret of good carpentry was good tools, so he bought the best he could afford. He asked no help from the neighbors. As the house took shape over the years, the townspeople thought he had hired a professional builder. When they learned that the home was a do-it-yourself project, they were surprised and respectful. From that time on they called Fuchida *Sensei* (teacher), a term of honor. At last, he had achieved full acceptance in his village. Basking in the admiration of family and neighbors, he grew smug.[21]

But as his work with the crops continued, he grew less dependent on his fellows, more pensive and contemplative. He felt burgeoning within him a sense of responsibility for the Japanese people, whom he now understood so much better than before. He often reflected upon the war and his part in it. When it ended, he had had no doubt that he had done his best and could face his countrymen with a clear conscience. Now he asked himself, Where did I go wrong? Where did I make mistakes? He had held important posts in the Combined Fleet. Had Japan lost the war through some sin of omission or commission on his part?[22]

These were the first halting thoughts of a man unaccustomed to self-questioning, slowly realizing he was a part of mankind. Fuchida couldn't understand why he should be on his little farm, with his devoted family, in health and slowly increasing prosperity, when so many others, surely as worthy or more so than he, were either dead or in the direst need.

Again he thought of how God had protected him during the war.[23] The slow recurrence of the seasons, the plants springing to life, the birth of the baby chicks, all the complex workings of creation wove themselves into the fabric of his consciousness. He came to love each task on the soil, particularly the hardest work of all—planting rice in the water and weeding it by hand. He worked in the paddies barefoot, delighting in the feel of earth and water oozing between his toes. And he liked to tend the green vegetables, to plant seeds, to see the first shoots push slowly through the soil, grow in the warm sun, and finally reach maturity.

As one season passed into another, from "the miracle of spring" to "the patience of winter," he experienced a revelation: "I began to realize slowly that all things were dependent upon a divine Creator, and that I was living under the grace of God. I could sow the seeds; I could plant the saplings; I could draw water with my hands. But they all came from the benevolence of a kind and far-seeing Creator."[24]

He became ashamed of his brash confidence in his own abilities and his strict dependence on himself. He began to understand that he, like the plants, lived and grew through the Creator, and that he owed to God whatever abilities he possessed. As he worked on the farm he reflected, Ah, the Creator, He is so wonderful![25]

24

"In the Name of Justice"

As TIME PASSED in the quiet village, Fuchida's native optimism and adaptability asserted themselves:

> This was the hardest time of my life, because I was so poor. . . . But it was so peaceful working on the land and I had no great responsibilities as I had in the war. . . . I didn't have to worry about a major naval operation, the life and death of those under me, the fate of my staff, or the destiny of my country. Everything was now reduced to simple terms—earning a meager existence from the soil for my wife and my son and daughter.[1]

The Fuchidas were living what an environmentalist might consider an ideal existence: tension-free work outdoors, eating fresh fruit and vegetables with an occasional chicken or rabbit raised under humane, natural conditions. But all was not sweetness and light. Fuchida still had spells of black depression and bitter regret over the lost war, moments when his temper flared and he took out his frustrations on Haruko and the children.[2] He nursed hostility toward the occupation, which pervaded every phase of life. Closely he followed MacArthur's shogunate in the newspapers and magazines and on the radio. In his more logical moments he tried to be, if not objective, at least realistic.

After the townspeople opened up to him, they called on him to make a number of speeches. "I hated occupation policies, but I couldn't speak against them because it was prohibited," he explained. He could and did counsel patience. "Wait, wait, wait!" he urged audiences in Kashiwara. "Don't be discouraged under these circumstances. The world situation will change. Japan can be prosperous again, and real friendship can come between Japan and the United States. So please work diligently and hard and calmly."[3]

To advise patience was easier than to live it. To Fuchida, the supreme commander seemed to be pursuing a course composed half of woolly-headed idealism, half of petty vindictiveness. He read MacArthur's New Year's message for 1947 with sardonic interest. In essence, the message averred that although Japan had lost the conflict, it had gained a precious heritage—peace for the future. By renouncing war as an instrument of national policy, Japan had set an example all the world could follow.

Oh, no, it will not be that simple, Fuchida told himself as he folded the newspaper. The present world is not that much of a Utopia. Nor did he believe that MacArthur was sincere; he thought the general was propagandizing as part of a sinister plot. The truth, he felt, was that Allied policy wanted to weaken Japan but Allied policy hid its aims behind the idea of peace.

The average Japanese, however, enjoyed his newly assigned role as model world citizen and thoroughly approved article 9, the peace clause of the new constitution.[4] He had patiently borne the burden of war and an enormous military structure; now he was grateful for the prospect of peace with security. Fuchida was inclined to blame the occupation for anything and everything he didn't like about Japanese conditions of the day, whereas much of the nation's troubles sprang from war and subsequent defeat, and would have been much the same had no single Allied soldier ever set foot on the home islands.

MacArthur's policy offered the Japanese a way to regain face. Although defeated militarily, Japan could be a leader, the first nation to embrace disarmament officially. Most of Fuchida's war-weary countrymen wholeheartedly bought the appealing idea that armaments make war, ergo, no arms, no war. "But this was false," Fuchida reflected. "War is made by the human heart."

Fuchida also believed MacArthur's tranquilizing of the Japanese tiger to be shortsighted. When the United States disarmed Japan, the Americans had assumed responsibility for protecting it. Obviously this situation couldn't last forever. Fuchida foresaw that in the not-too-distant future the Peace Clause would embarrass Washington. He was so sure of this that when asked for his opinion of it during the war crimes trials, he answered frankly, "In ten years I will wear my navy uniform again." In less than a decade many of his former colleagues, if not he, once more donned uniforms.[5]

In the larger sense, MacArthur's and Fuchida's aims were not incompatible. Ever since his talks with Hiroshima victims at the Kure hospital, Fuchida had firmly believed that for mankind to survive, it must renounce war. As his contribution to the good cause, he commenced writing a book tentatively entitled *No More Pearl Harbor.* But the deeper he dug into the subject, the more baffled he became. He didn't see how true peace could come about just from fear of atomic warfare. The people of the world must genuinely want and demand peace, not only for themselves but for each other. Unilateral disarmament such as the Allies had forced on Japan was not the answer as long as the rest of the world remained armed to the teeth.

Fuchida knew well that the concept of peace through mutual caring would require a thorough change of human nature. All over Japan, large rallies were passing high-sounding resolutions in favor of the peace clause, opposing rearmament, and calling for the cessation of atomic bomb tests. Fuchida attended some as an interested, troubled spectator. The participants cried out for peace and disarmament in voices shrill with hatred. They signed petitions, their hands quivering with resentment. What sort of peace could Japan or any other nation build on such sandy foundations?

Somehow, mankind must escape from this cycle of hatred generating hatred, of resentment breeding resentment. Writing his manuscript, he came to realize that only transmuting destructive emotions into brotherly love could save humanity from itself. He flung down his brush in despair. How could such a miracle come about? Who could show the way?[6]

Japan's native communists proclaimed that they could lead the nation to the promised land. "Occupation policy opened the door to communism," Fuchida stated. "Communist leaders came back from China and the Soviet Union just like victorious generals, you know. Many leaders came out of jail." These ex-prisoners were vigorous propagandists and part of an active underground working to build its own secret military forces and eventually overthrow the government. To this end, the Soviet Union sent weapons to Japan via the Japan Sea near Niigata. Rumors ran rife that Japanese troops captured in Manchuria were being communized and trained in Siberia to take over Japan. Fuchida talked over this menace with a number of his friends, including Genda.

Genda thought it possible that these troops might invade the homeland at Russia's behest, in which case Japan would have a civil war on its hands. For the government, with no forces in being, the prospects would be grim. Genda feared that MacArthur might even have to leave Japan as he had the Philippines. Undoubtedly he would return, but in the meantime the country might be overrun and the emperor killed. A communist attempt to take over would mean a showdown between the United States and the Soviet Union with Japan as a battleground. Meanwhile the occupation prohibited capable, patriotic Japanese from running for office because they had served in the armed forces. Native communists were permitted to be politically active.

"Some communists were elected. It was ridiculous!" exclaimed Fuchida, disgusted at the incongruity.[7]

Although sounded out occasionally, Fuchida was never tempted to join the brethren of the hammer and sickle. The communists who thrived on dissention couldn't supply the answers he sought. They were "beasts without hearts, human decency, or sympathy," he felt. Moreover, he despised the Soviet Union politically. He cited the situation in North Korea. At the end of the war, many Japanese of both high and low degree lived there. When the Russians came in, they roused the lower elements against their countrymen. These new communists held public kangaroo courts and in the name of the people convicted upperclass Japanese of any crime they could think up. "Many a Japanese woman came back from Korea a widow because the Japanese themselves . . . had killed their husbands," Fuchida related.[8]

The Japanese had little to do directly with the Soviet Union during the occupation, because it kept only a token force in Tokyo. They did have indirect contact because of prisoners of war. Rumors placed the number of Japanese taken to Siberia from Manchuria and Korea at well over one million. This figure included civilians as well as military personnel. Only some two hundred thousand ever returned to Japan.[9]

In 1946 repatriation began. It soon became apparent that Moscow was first releasing those too feeble or too old to contribute to the communist cause. The majority of those returned had no use whatsoever for the Russians. From 1947 through 1949, Moscow exported an entirely different breed. Seduced by the improvement in the Soviet economy and subjected to ceaseless indoctrination, these people had become communist guided missiles.

"Are these men or beasts the Soviets are sending back to Japan from their prison camps?" asked the *Nippon Times* in anguish on 5 August 1949. They were neither one nor the other—they were zombies. They came back to Japan waving red flags and singing the "Internationale." Some resisted landing on their native shores. Their homes and families meant nothing to them; they were uneasy and alienated apart from their fellows, and packs of them roamed through the countryside. In returning the men in this condition, Moscow overreached itself. The Japanese people reacted with grief and horror and asked themselves what sort of system could thus dehumanize fellow human beings.[10]

According to Fuchida, the Australians were a close second in being hated by the Japanese. Most of them worked in the British zone at Kure. "They would take rides in taxis and not pay the driver," declared Fuchida. "Not only that, they would often rob the driver. They would go into restaurants, buy beer, and refuse to pay for it." Of course, Fuchida added, there were exceptions, but in his opinion "the Australians never represented Australia like the GIs represented the United States."[11]

Before the GIs arrived, the Japanese had braced themselves as if for an invasion of Goths and Vandals. Press and radio implored women to keep indoors as much as possible. When venturing out, they must make themselves unattractive—as if anything could be less fetching than the *mompei,* that monstrosity guaranteed to demagnetize an Elizabeth Taylor.[12] After the horrendous buildup the populace was pleasantly surprised to find GI Joe a rather simple soul, friendly and kindly, especially toward children. His drinking and womanizing didn't scandalize the Japanese. They regarded these as part of life, nothing to make a fuss about.

Inevitably, there were a few nasty incidents. Any group as numerous as the American occupation force was bound to include undesirables. And the Americans carried their race problem to Japan, because their armed forces had not yet integrated. The Japanese, who had never seen black troops before, at first treated black and white alike. But soon they caught on that a distinction was made, and restaurant and hotel owners began discriminating against blacks. This sparked some ugly incidents, such as the burning down of a brothel. But aside from isolated occurrences, relations between conqueror and conquered were reasonably friendly. "The individual Japanese came to like and in some cases even to love the American," Fuchida remembered. He considered this personal contact one of the best features of the occupation.

Inevitably, fraternization led to marriage. Fuchida objected to these unions, not on nationalist or racist grounds but because young Americans had little opportunity to meet Japanese girls of good family. Many of the brides were bar girls. He feared for the reputation of his country and its women when these brides accompanied their husbands to the United States. Whenever an American did marry a girl of reputable family, he was pleased.[13]

Fuchida established excellent commercial ties with an American artillery camp not far from his farm. These troops had landed at Wakayama in the autumn of 1945 and en route to the camp site passed through Kashiwara. There some hungry youngsters stole food from the supply train. In scurrying off, a boy caught his hand in a car door and hurt himself painfully. Half-amused soldiers caught several of the children, including the injured one, and brought them to the colonel in command. Instead of scolding them, he personally treated the boy's bleeding hand. When he finished wrapping the bandage, he gathered the children around him and told them kindly, "Don't steal from us. If you're hungry, ask us for food and we'll give it to you." Soon the story of the American colonel's kindness spread through Nara. Fuchida heard it when he returned to Kashiwara.

When his hens began laying, he went to the camp and asked to see this officer. He introduced himself as a former navy captain, and the colonel received him cordially as a fellow officer of equal rank. "I'm now a poor man and need help," Fuchida said honestly. "Would it be possible for you to buy eggs from me for your officers' club?"

The colonel looked at him keenly and must have been satisfied with what he saw, for he shot out his hand, shook Fuchida's warmly, and without asking to see one agreed to buy eggs from him on a daily basis. "If the eggs are good and fresh," he added, "I'll be willing to pay you two yen higher than the going market price."

Fuchida immediately contracted to supply the officers' club needs, then went out and doubled his flock of white Leghorns. For the next four years, rain or shine, he delivered the eggs each day. If his own hens didn't lay enough, he bought from his neighbors to make up the total. Each morning he left home at 0500, went to the local Densha depot, rode the train to the station nearest the camp, then walked to the club. "So they had fresh eggs for breakfast each morning," he said. His customers knew they could depend on him, and he never had a single complaint. This arrangement lasted until the outbreak of the Korean War, when the artillery unit transferred to Korea. By that time Fuchida had too many irons in the fire to handle the chicken business, so he closed it.[14]

Fuchida had much less pleasant experience with the Americans as a witness in the war crimes trials. He testified at Ichigaya in behalf of Admirals Nagano and Shimada, principally about the Pearl Harbor attack. The prosecution insisted that the Japanese had planned the attack for years, but both Genda and Fuchida held firmly to their testimony that it had been on the boards for less than a year before.[15]

In April 1949 Fuchida witnessed for Toyoda. The admiral had suffered a nervous breakdown and his mind no longer functioned clearly. The charge against him was a kamikaze attack at Okinawa that sank two hospital ships with all their sick and wounded, a violation of international law. The prosecution charged that the Combined Fleet kamikazes under Toyoda's command made regular targets of American hospital ships.

On the witness stand, Fuchida came under fire from the prosecuting attorney after questioning brought out that he had led the Pearl Harbor air attack. Attempting to discredit Fuchida as a witness, he shouted, "You must be guilty yourself!" and began to hurl questions at him about Pearl Harbor. But the judge cut off this line quickly. "You need not answer these questions," he instructed Fuchida. "They are irrelevant to the case being heard." This surprised Fuchida. He accorded the judge a rather grudging respect.[16]

In the two and a half days he was on the stand, Fuchida testified that the

Combined Fleet's targets had been carriers, battleships, cruisers, and destroyers. The fleet issued orders against hitting hospital ships. However, he pointed out, such vessels, even if marked in accordance with international law, often couldn't be recognized from the air, "because modern planes fly at such high altitude and such fast speeds."[17]

Fuchida took it for granted that Toyoda's verdict was a foregone conclusion, that anyone called before the court would be found guilty. He was astonished and impressed when the judge declared the admiral innocent.

Another series of trials covered prosecutions of enlisted men and certain officers charged with inhumane acts against prisoners of war. Fuchida disapproved of these trials and was astounded at the severe sentences. He sincerely believed that Japanese imprisoned by the Americans must have been just as badly treated as American captives of the Japanese.

These trials reminded Fuchida of the festivals of primitive tribes when the heads and scalps of enemies are displayed after a victory. He told friends exactly what he thought: "Such savagery in the name of justice and civilization is a mockery."

"Keep quiet or your turn will come next!" they begged him.

Fuchida testified three times in Yokohama, once in Manila and once in Ambon in the Netherlands East Indies. He was scheduled to go to Rabaul, but Chihaya deputized for him. The Ambon trial in particular pained Fuchida. The officer in the dock was Rear Admiral Tameji Okada, like Fuchida a native of Nara Prefecture and a veteran of Pearl Harbor, where as a captain he had commanded the heavy cruiser *Tone.* The Australians who conducted his trial accused Okada of overworking prisoners of war until they died and similar atrocities. They sentenced him to be hanged and executed the sentence promptly. "I was very bitter," Fuchida remembered.

With the war crimes trials he began to think a lot about justice. He didn't question their legality, based as they were on the Potsdam Declaration that Tokyo had accepted. But how could moral responsibility be adjudged in this manner? Each combatant nation in World War II believed itself justified. "But after the war, the victors who had won their decision on the basis of their strength and the power of their swords, judged the defeated in the name of humanity and righteousness." This made no sense to Fuchida.[18]

He didn't pause to consider that for the conquerors to bear down on the conquered was neither a new development nor exclusively Western. Victorious imperial forces had exiled his own grandfather as a war criminal. He understood, however, that because both the Japanese and Americans had fought in the name of what they saw as right, neither could judge the other objectively. To render a just judgment, all the facts must be known and weighed dispassionately. Who knew all the facts, and who would be able to assess them without bias? True justice could only come from a source above the heat of battle, above human weakness, from an omniscient superior being.

This thought led Fuchida to reflect on the nature of God. He had come to know God the creator through the majestic ebb and flow of plant and animal life. In the orderly procession of the constellations he recognized a guiding intelligence, a sort of divine commander in chief. Brooding over the war crimes trials and the complex ethical and historical problems they raised, he began to recognize that God must also be the arbiter of the universe, the judge of the nations.[19]

25

"Where Does This Great Love Come From?"

FUCHIDA participated in the war crimes trials for several years. Long before they were over, he resolved to back up his beliefs with action. He didn't understand such concepts as courtesy and mercy toward a fallen foe, and assumed that Japanese in American prison camps must have suffered atrocities equal to those for which Japanese were being tried and convicted. He made up his mind to collect evidence proving his contention. He would attend the next session of the tribunal and fling his documented charges into the judges' faces. "See, this is what you have done!" he would cry triumphantly. "You also have mistreated prisoners. You too should be tried."

While Fuchida brooded, in the spring of 1947 he read that 150 prisoners of war would soon return to Japan from the United States. He determined to visit them and find out from their own lips just what they had suffered. So he made his way to the receiving camp at Uraga Harbor near Yokosuka, where the released captives would disembark from American naval transports. The first proved to be the sick or injured. So, although he observed them closely as they disembarked, he couldn't tell whether they had been mistreated or not.[1]

Suddenly among them he spotted a good-looking young man rather taller than the rest. It was Sublieutenant Kazuo Kanegasaki, who had served with him through the Indian Ocean campaigns. He had been assistant engineering officer on the carrier *Hiryu,* and everyone in Japan believed that he had been killed at Midway. Why should Kanegasaki be here at Uraga instead of on the bottom of the Pacific? And why, being alive, had he not been reported as a prisoner?

"Everyone thought you were dead," Fuchida told him. "A tombstone has been erected in your honor in Aoyama Cemetery in Tokyo."

This idea amused his friend, as well it might. Not every man has the opportunity to inspect his own tombstone.[2] Kanegasaki explained that, ashamed at being captured, he had given the American authorities a false name. The Swiss, who acted as go-between for the United States during the war, couldn't report him to Japan as a prisoner. He was delighted to see Fuchida and readily poured out the story of his escape from the *Hiryu* and subsequent capture.

Fuchida listened with intense interest, meanwhile wondering how he would tell Kanegasaki about his wife. Shortly after the Indian Ocean campaign, Kanegasaki had consulted Fuchida about getting married. Despite the latter's advice that he wait until after the war, the young man went ahead and married his sweetheart in Tokyo. They set up housekeeping in Hiroshima, where they had a few idyllic weeks together before he had to return to the *Hiryu*. Then came Midway and his disappearance. Despite official notification of his loss, his wife clung to the thought that by some miracle her husband might have escaped. Only after four years did she abandon hope and take another husband. Knowing how deeply Kanegasaki loved her, how he must have hungered for her in his years of absence, Fuchida wondered how he would react to the news of her second marriage.[3]

Kanegasaki continued his narrative. Fuchida knew about the last hours of the *Hiryu*, but found it poignant and gripping to hear the story from an insider. When the American dive-bombers set the ship ablaze, flames trapped Kanegasaki and a number of others below decks. With communication ruptured between the bridge and engine room, the Japanese gave up these men for lost. When Nagumo realized that the flattop was beyond salvage, he ordered the destroyer *Makigumo* to sink her.[4]

The *Hiryu* didn't sink immediately. Kanegasaki and his superior officer, along with some of their men, managed to scramble topside and break out on deck. They saw no other survivors. As the carrier foundered, it seemed that they had escaped death below only to meet it under the open sky. Then, about two hours after the torpedo struck, they saw a Japanese reconnaissance plane hovering overhead. They whooped and hollered vociferously. Evidently the pilot saw them, for he circled over the carrier before winging off.

This scout radioed the *Yamato* that the *Hiryu* was still afloat with a number of survivors. Yamamoto ordered the destroyer *Tanikaze* to return to the spot, rescue the survivors, and sink the carrier. An attack on this destroyer by American carrier-based dive-bombers delayed the mission. When the

Tanikaze did reach the *Hiryu*'s reported position, she found no trace of either carrier or survivors, although she combed the area until nightfall.[5]

According to Kanegasaki, the *Hiryu* sank at about 0900 on 5 June 1942 Midway time. The survivors dived overboard just as she settled for the final plunge. They swam to a nearby lifeboat, fortunately stocked with emergency rations, water, and beer. The boat drifted for thirteen days, during which time four of the thirty-nine men died.

On 18 June an American patrol plane sighted them. Sometime thereafter the U.S. seaplane tender *Ballard* scooped up all the survivors. On the voyage to Midway another man died; the group now numbered thirty-four. After a brief interrogation at Midway, the Americans flew the prisoners to Pearl Harbor.[6]

From Hawaii they were transferred stateside. During their captivity most tried several times to commit suicide. In San Diego, Kanegasaki attempted to kill himself by starvation. The authorities kept him alive by injections of vitamins and food concentrates. After some twenty days of this routine, his captors requested a Japanese pastor, Hiroshi Sakai of Los Angeles, to visit the prison camp and persuade Kanegasaki to eat.

By a twist of fate, several years later Fuchida became acquainted with Sakai and heard the same story from him. The pastor spoke to Kanegasaki for two hours in his native language, telling him that he had done his best and had nothing to be ashamed of. Circumstances alone made him a prisoner. He was still young; he had his life ahead of him after the war. Then he could serve his country some other way.

Kanegasaki didn't utter a word; he just shot cold glances at his visitor. Finally, discouraged, Sakai departed.[7]

After the pastor returned to his own internment camp, a group of Japanese women heard the story. They requested and received permission to visit Kanegasaki. They understood that a man who has not tasted food for twenty days is in no frame of mind to listen to abstract exhortations. Here was a man hungry, therefore a man sulky and unreasonable. These ladies touched his heart. He listened to their pleas that he should return to Japan and lead a happy, useful life. Having thawed him out, the women presented a basket of food, coaxing him to take just a bite. By happy inspiration they had included in the contents some morsels of *magure no morimaki*—tuna in rice wrapped in seaweed and dipped in soy sauce, Kanegasaki's favorite. Telling himself that he would eat only out of courtesy, he tasted the tuna. That did it! Kanegasaki fell upon the meal with the hunger of youth. His eyes filled with the charm of Japanese womanhood, his stomach full of tuna and seaweed, Kanegasaki decided that life was worth living. He let his new friends talk him into abandoning his fast permanently.

From San Diego the prisoners were moved to a prison camp-cum-hospital. Some had become nervous wrecks from their combat experiences and suicide attempts. The camp lay in the magnificent area where Colorado borders Utah. Kanegasaki spoke with enthusiasm about the pure air, the stream that flowed nearby, the natural hot spring where patients swam, the blazing landscape, so different from Japan but with a savage beauty all its own.[8]

Fuchida told Kanegasaki why he had come to Uraga. He told him about the war crimes trials and how unfair he thought they were. Hadn't Japanese prisoners been treated cruelly in the United States?

"Prisoner-of-war camps are much the same the world over," his friend replied. "They aren't nice hotels, there is no liberty, and the guards exercise all-mighty power. At best they're gloomy places. But I never experienced nor saw atrocities in American camps. No, I wasn't always treated kindly. But most of my suffering was mental and spiritual."[9] Then he smiled. "Something happened at my camp which made it possible for all of us interned there to stop nursing our resentment and to return to Japan with lightened hearts."

And he told the following story: Shortly after the end of the war, an American girl about eighteen years old came to the camp as a volunteer social worker. She ministered to the Japanese with tireless energy and kindness. Her name was Margaret Covell. The men called her Peggy, as did her American friends. She spoke no Japanese, but the prisoners had picked up enough English to communicate with her. "If you're uncomfortable or need anything, let me know," she would say. "I'll do anything I can to help."

With her conscientious care she touched the prisoners. She also puzzled them. Some three weeks after her first visit, one of the men asked her curiously, "Why are you so kind to us?"

"Because Japanese soldiers killed my parents," she answered.

As the prisoners stared at her in astonishment, she explained that her parents were missionaries who before the war had taught at the mission school in Yokohama. Shortly before the outbreak of hostilities, the Covells moved to Manila where they thought they would be safe. When the Japanese captured that city, they fled to Baguio and the mountains of the north. There they remained until the Americans chased the Japanese out of Manila, and it was the latter's turn to flee to the hills. There they discovered the missionaries and found in their possession a small portable radio that they mistook for a secret communications apparatus. They tried the couple as spies, convicted, and beheaded them.

Peggy, who had been living in the United States, didn't learn of her parents' fate until the end of the war. At first she choked with hatred for the Japanese. Then she began to meditate on her parents' selfless service to them. Slowly she became convinced that her parents had forgiven their executioners before death. Could she do less? So she volunteered to work with Japanese prisoners of war. Her example of charity and gentleness greatly impressed the men, and they loved her with a pure tenderness.[10]

Fuchida was thunderstruck. "This beautiful story overwhelmed me and made me ashamed," he reflected. He had come to Uraga with hate in his heart. What he found was goodness that he could scarcely comprehend.[11]

Then Kanegasaki asked the dreaded question: "How is my wife?"

Fuchida stalled. "If you go to your home, you'll find out about her," he mumbled. At this, Kanegasaki's face clouded over. Fuchida didn't have the heart to tell him the truth.

To complete the sad story of this Japanese Enoch Arden, when he finally did discover that his beloved wife had married again, he lost his mind. In August 1947 he thrust himself head down into a well. He wedged himself in so tightly that wouldbe rescuers couldn't pull him out in time. His death always preyed on Fuchida's mind. "If I had been a Christian at the time, I would have saved him," he declared.[12]

Fuchida made a point of talking to all the ex-prisoners who had known Peggy Covell. He asked no more questions about treatment in American prison camps; he had lost interest in that project. Perhaps, as Kanegasaki said, if he searched long and hard enough he would have found instances of brutality. But how could they outweigh the goodness of Peggy Covell? Fuchida asked only for details about the woman and for confirmation of Kanegasaki's story.[13]

For a long time he made this search. Through Filipino sources he heard about their last moments. They had been blindfolded, their hands bound behind their backs, and forced to their knees as Japanese soldiers stood behind them with drawn swords. All the while husband and wife united in prayer. When Fuchida heard this, he asked himself over and over, "What did Mr. and Mrs. Covell pray as they were about to be beheaded? That was my long, long wondering."

The story puzzled him. The Japanese considered revenge a beautiful moral. A man captured and awaiting death never forgave his captors. He prayed to be born again seven times, and to exact revenge in each life. And his sons and daughters lived to avenge him. The Japanese word for revenge, *katakiuchi,* means literally "attack enemy." Steeped in Japanese history and culture, Fuchida fervently believed in the principle of *katakiuchi.* Now he heard a story of unjust suffering and death, and a daughter left to continue the bloodline. But the tale featured no vow of vengeance from either the dying or the survivor.[14]

Many of Fuchida's countrymen would have seen Peggy Covell as contemptibly weak and lacking in filial respect. At best they might conclude that she had gone mad. And a certain type of psychoanalyst would pigeonhole her as a masochist.

Fuchida entertained no such thoughts. Not only did the Covell story cure him of his spite, it also dovetailed perfectly with his thoughts about eternal peace. Who or what could free mankind from the shackles of hatred and suspicion? A teenaged American girl had given him the answer. Now he saw clearly that the roadblock was *katakiuchi*, or whatever it was called in other languages. As surely as the sun would rise, *katakiuchi* was wrong and Peggy Covell was right. She had stopped one wheel of hatred. The prisoners who knew her would tell her story to their children and grandchildren, and thus the world would be a little brighter and cleaner.

He also learned that such towering goodness had not a human but a supernatural source. Where did this great love come from—this love that could forgive enemies their cruelest deeds? What was the prayer of Mr. and Mrs. Covell at the moment of death?[15]

26

"The Knowledge of Christ"

FUCHIDA saw nothing incongruous in the fact that, at the very time he was seeking a formula for universal peace, in his personal life he was heading down a path bound to lead to dissension, even tragedy, for those concerned.

On the home front, he had no cause for complaint. His little farm was beginning to sustain his family's needs. He had a faithful, hardworking wife, solid as the earth. He had a son he would not have exchanged for Crown Prince Akihito, and a daughter in whom he took ever-increasing delight. His neighbors respected him and even looked to him as a leader. What reasonable man could ask for more? But Fuchida wasn't reasonable. He continued his affair with Kimi, whenever his rather frequent trips to Tokyo permitted.

Evidently he couldn't see that Haruko had cause for grievance as long as he supported her and the children. Nor did he understand how this self-indulgence in any way conflicted with his spiritual gropings. He lived a dual identity. As soon as he set out for Tokyo, Fuchida the farmer, husband, and father faded away. So sharp was this sense of dislocation that, according to Kimi, the pair actually considered themselves as man and wife. Fuchida assured her that as soon as he had made a suitable home for Haruko, he would seek a divorce. He spoke to Haruko tentatively about ending the marriage, but she took an adamant stand in the matter. From Kimi's brief account, there emerges the picture of a battling wife, a wishful-thinking mistress, and a weak man.[1]

To our knowledge, Haruko never spoke to anyone about her position. No doubt, as any good mother in similar circumstances, she saw the children's security threatened and fought like a tigress defending her cubs. It is also possible that she considered her husband to be suffering from a virulent if nonfatal disease, and resolved to save him from himself until he sweated out the fever.

If so, she was more than half right. So unrealistic and self-centered were Kimi and Fuchida that they conceived a child, not in a moment of uncontrollable passion but by choice. They told each other that they should start a family while still able to do so, even though marriage lay in the future. Their daughter, Yoko (a pseudonym), was born on 4 May 1948. She grew up with Fuchida's features strongly marked on her face, a bright, nice child, as quick and elusive as a fox.[2]

During these years Fuchida spent much time in Tokyo with Prange, who was working in the G-2 historical section in MacArthur's headquarters. On Fuchida's way to Prange's home in Washington Heights he emerged from the Shibuya station in Tokyo. There he always noticed a bronze statue in memory of a loyal dog, Hashiko. The little fellow had belonged to an official who commuted each day to downtown Tokyo on the Shibuya train. Hashiko would see him off each morning and meet him each night. One day the master perished in an accident, but the dog continued his daily vigil until he died. The people of Shibuya erected a small statue in his honor.[3]

One day in early October 1948, an American stood beside this statue passing out leaflets. He handed one to Fuchida, who glanced at it carelessly before the title caught his attention: *Watakushi Wa Nippon No Horyo Deshita* (I Was a Prisoner of Japan). With the subject of prisoners of war so much on his mind, he read the pamphlet on the spot. The story started with Pearl Harbor and went on to tell how an American sergeant named Jacob DeShazer had become a Christian while in a Japanese prison camp. The pamphlet was only four pages, just enough to whet Fuchida's appetite for more.

When he boarded the tram to Washington Heights, he saw among the many advertisements one with the same title as the pamphlet, publicizing a book which DeShazer had written and which was available in Japanese. When Fuchida got off at Yoyogi he found a nearby bookstore and bought the volume. During the week or so that he stayed with Prange, he finished the book. What follows is the essence of DeShazer's story.

When he heard about the attack on Pearl Harbor, he burned with hatred for the Japanese. About a month later a call came for volunteers to go on a dangerous secret mission. DeShazer jumped at the chance, and entered intensive bombardier training. Not until his crew boarded the carrier *Hornet* did he discover what his mission was—the Doolittle Raid.[4]

DeShazer's aircraft, number 16, seemed jinxed from the outset. On the flight to Japan, a hole in its nose reduced speed and forced the plane to consume extra gas. At last the plane swung over Nagoya. He released the bombs and his pilot headed for China as planned. As the bomber sped toward the ocean DeShazer, in an upsurge of vindictiveness, loosed a machine-gun burst at a fisherman's boat. Fortunately he missed. Having lost so much time because of the damage to the nose, the plane couldn't reach the designated friendly field. The crew had to bail out in occupied China. The Japanese captured the men and sent them to Tokyo for questioning, after which they were sent to Shanghai to stand trial.[5]

Eventually most of the Americans were sentenced to life imprisonment; however, three officers were executed. DeShazer spent most of his prison years in various camps in China. During that time, his captors beat and otherwise tormented him and his fellow prisoners. They were kept on near-starvation rations and suffered severely from malnutrition and disease. De-Shazer's hatred for the Japanese grew into an obsession and almost drove him out of his mind.[6]

Gradually, however, he began to wonder why so much hatred existed in the world, especially between Japanese and Americans. Within him a memory stirred of the teachings he learned from his Christian mother and stepfather. After two years in prison, DeShazer's troubled, homesick spirit hungered for a Bible. He knew that one was circulating through the camp, but, being the only enlisted man among the war prisoners, he had to wait until last. Finally he received the Bible. It was his for three weeks. With this time limit hanging over him, DeShazer read swiftly but thoroughly, memorizing many of the passages. As he read, he found Christ.[7]

The DeShazer who handed back the Bible was not the same man as before. His conversion was thorough. He promised God that if he got out of prison alive, he would return to Japan as a missionary. At the end of the war he was alive and repatriated to the United States. He enrolled in a theological college to become a missionary. After he received his degree, he sailed with his wife and baby son for Japan and settled in Osaka.[8]

Fuchida read this remarkable story with intense interest. The parallel between DeShazer's experience and that of Peggy Covell was not exact, but it was there. This second example of love overcoming hatred hit him with even greater impact, DeShazer having been a tough airman. Fuchida knew the breed well and could identify with him. He determined to read the Bible and find out what this was all about.

He had no intention of investigating Christianity as such; he simply wanted to understand DeShazer. In fact, he later conceded that he probably wouldn't have pursued the matter had DeShazer been just any American prisoner; what secured his interest was DeShazer's being one of the Doolittle Raiders. Their exploits had excited his admiration.[9]

Prange did not have a Bible in Japanese, and Fuchida didn't read English well enough to tackle the King James version. He determined that on his way back to Kashiwara he would purchase a Japanese-language Bible. As he strolled toward the Shibuya bookstore, he stopped near the statue of the dog in the hope of seeing the young American who had given him the pamphlet. Instead, he saw a Japanese man about thirty years of age dressed in a black suit. He stood beside several boxes piled high with books. "Man shall not live by bread alone [Luke 4:4]!" he shouted. "Get your Bible—food for your soul!" Struck by the coincidence, Fuchida bought one. It cost only forty yen. "I was surprised," Fuchida said later, "because everything else in Japan was so high at the time."

As the train sped back to Kashiwara he leafed through the book. He did not realize it then, but he had bought a New Testament only. It looked like hard sledding, not at all the sort of thing to dip into on a train ride. He slipped it into his suitcase, deciding that he would wait until he reached home. It lay untouched for nine months.

One morning in June 1949 something in the newspaper caught Fuchida's eye, a column entitled *Tensei Jingo*. This translates loosely as "Heaven Voice Human Voice Told." On this particular day, Hakucho Masamune, a famous novelist and a Christian, wrote the feature. He devoted his column to the Bible. He wrote that no book in the world could compare with it. If a Western man was sentenced to an isolated island and could take with him only one book, that man would choose the Bible. Masamune begged every Japanese to read it for himself. "Please read only thirty pages anywhere in the Bible," he urged, "and undoubtedly you will find something that will touch your heart."

Fuchida digested this column with his breakfast. Surely this *is* the voice of heaven, he thought. Normally he glanced at the headlines; yet on this particular morning he had read the newspaper thoroughly and thus come across Masamune's article. He accepted this as a warning from God to stop putting off reading the Bible.

Thus motivated, he sought out the neglected New Testament. He read two or three chapters each day and pondered them by the hour. As if evaluating a battle plan, he tested the message of Christ as he went along, proving and clearing up one point before going on to the next.[10]

Fuchida did much of his Bible reading outdoors. The garden was his favorite spot, cool and shady, and usually had a steady breeze blowing through it. Every once in a while a terrific racket interrupted his reading. He had bought an instrument with five or six keys. This was used to call the family

Fuchida's mother, Shika, and father, Yazo. Nagao, Nara Prefecture, ca. 1910.

Fuchida (second from left) in February 1919 as a 17-year-old student at the Unebi Middle School. Although uniforms were mandatory, it was not a military school.

Flight school at Kasumigaura, which Fuchida attended for a year from December 1927. He is the serious one on the right.

Vice Admiral Chuichi Nagumo, commander of the First Air Fleet.

Commander Minoru Genda, air staff officer of the First Air Fleet, and chief planner of the attack on Pearl Harbor.

Commander Fuchida leading the training for the Pearl Harbor attack. October 1941, Kagoshima Air Base.

he farewell meeting in the wardroom of the carrier *Agaki* just before setting off for
awaii, November 25, 1941. Fuchida is fourth from the left, in the rear. The ship's
pper, Captain Kiichi Hasegawa, is second.

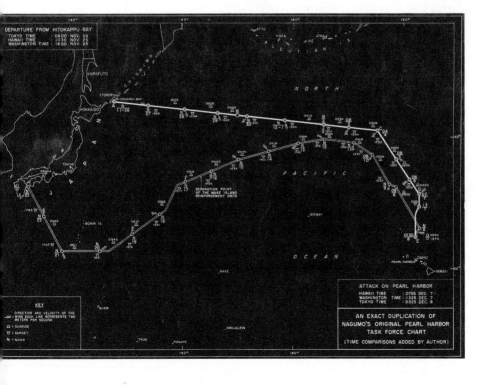

December 1941. On the flight deck of the carrier *Agaki* en route to Hawaii.

Fuchida, in center wearing white cap, chats with his fellow pilots the day before the attack.

A Zero of the second wave races down *Shokaku*'s flight deck.

Under the watchful eyes of an officer, the aircrews are stirred by an exhortation written on a chalkboard above the flight deck: "Japanese Imperial Fleet! You have to obey and die for your country, Japan! Win or lose, you will fight and die for your country!"

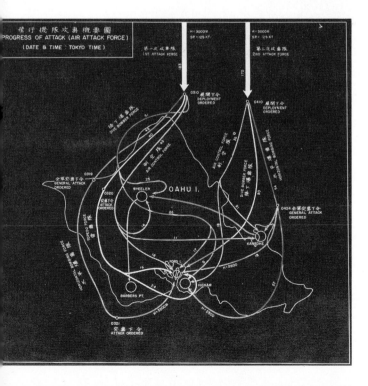

Pearl Harbor as it appeared to Fuchida on the morning of December 7, 1941. Captured Japanese photographs. (U.S. NAVY)

海軍省許可濟第三八七號

Battleship row under attack. Left to right: *Nevada, Vestal* alongside *Arizona, West Virginia* alongside *Tennessee, Oklahoma* alongside *Maryland, Neosho, California.* Note the *West Virginia* listing to port immediately after a torpedo hit. Torpedo tracks and shock waves are visible. (U.S. NAVY)

Planes and hangers burn at Wheeler Army Air Field just after being attacked, as seen from a Japanese plane. (U.S. NAVY)

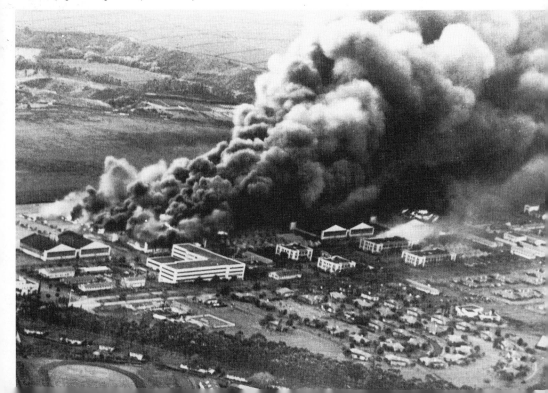

The forward magazine of the *Shaw* explodes. At the right is the *Nevada*. Photographed from Ford Island. (U.S. NAVY)

Sailors of the submarines *Dolphin* (left) and *Narwhal* battle back against the second attack wave. (NATIONAL ARCHIVES)

The parade ground of the Marine Barracks between 9:00 and 10:00 A.M.

One of approximately 29 Japanese aircraft downed during the battle.

June 1943, at Kanoya. Fuchida, now a commander and the senior operations officer on the staff of the First Air Force, is seated at the right.

Fuchida had risen to captain by war's end.

After the surrender, a dejected Fuchida returned home and took up farming. He soon found peace in Christianity.

Distributing scriptures in Hokkaido with American missionary Reverend George Vorsheim (left).

With Reverend Billy Graham in November 1952. Their paths crossed several times, and they became good friends.

With daughter Miyako, wife Haruko, and son Yoshiya (Joe).

Mitsuo Fuchida, the man who led the air attack on Pearl Harbor. Photo taken around 1964 in the garden of his home.

together for meals or domestic emergencies. The summons resounded in every corner of the farm, and not only the family but the animals got the message. Lity, the German shepherd, would come running to the door and bark. The four goats would stop in their tracks and trot bleating up to the house. And the chickens would cackle in unison. It sounded like mess call in Noah's ark.

At Fuchida's first reading, it was the New Testament's moral message that attracted him most. The Sermon on the Mount struck a responsive chord. The miracles he found difficult to understand. First, there was the virgin birth of Christ; second, Jesus walked on the sea; third, he fed the multitude of five thousand with only a few loaves and a few fish; fourth, he healed the sick; and fifth, he even raised the dead from the grave. Still, Fuchida determined to keep an open mind and finish the book.

In later years, Fuchida became convinced that miracles were the bedrock of Christianity, the touchstone for faith. He found that many people attracted by the Bible's philosophy were suspicious of the unscientific events it relates. This sidetracked their religious life, he felt. Important as the moral aspect of Christianity was, what set it apart was the incarnation, resurrection, and redemption. Those who persevered in reading and meditating on the Bible, as he did, would come to recognize that what at first repelled them was its core.[11]

One day early in September 1949 Fuchida came upon the Gospel of St. Luke, chapter 23. For the first time he read the story of the crucifixion. He knew in a vague way that Jesus had been nailed to a cross, but he didn't know the details. The calvary scene pierced Fuchida's spirit. It all came alive in St. Luke's starkly beautiful prose. In the midst of the horror Christ said, "Father, forgive them, for they know not what they do [Luke 23:24]."

Surely these words were the source of the love that DeShazer and Peggy Covell had shown. It came to Fuchida that, as they knelt to die, Peggy's parents had prayed just such words: "Father, forgive them, for they know not what they do." Tears sprang to Fuchida's eyes; he had reached the end of his "long, long wondering."

As Jesus hung there on the cross He prayed not only for His persecutors but for all humanity. That meant that He had prayed and died for Fuchida, a Japanese man living in the twentieth century.[12]

By the time he finished St. Luke, Fuchida recognized Christ as his personal savior. The more he read, the more he became sure that he could accept the entire New Testament, miracles and all. He discussed his Bible reading with no one—neither wife, children, nor friends. "I had no Christian friends, so I had to think and study by myself," he explained. "There was no one to tell about my new experience. I was always alone."

So he read in quiet contemplation. "As I labored on the farm I thought of God, creation, the miracles of the seasons, the growing plants. These things never failed to awe me," he recounted reverently. "And now this new element enriched my life—the knowledge of Christ."[13]

27

"You Must Bear Witness"

FUCHIDA was afraid to openly declare himself a Christian. His Shinto friends, he felt, would say he had renounced the faith of his fathers. In any case he experienced no real break with Shinto; he had merely moved onto a broader road. "It was like having the sun come up," he described it.[1]

To complicate the picture, Christianity was the religion of Japan's former enemies and of the occupation. MacArthur helped Christian missionaries with their work in Japan, and many Japanese regarded this policy as an insidious attempt to weaken their national identity.

Quite aside from the nationalistic angle, many Japanese men found Christianity difficult to understand, let alone accept. The philosophy of loving and forgiving one's enemies was too alien. To those for whom face was everything, the idea of God executed as a criminal could only be revolting and unnatural.

Traitor, opportunist, coward—Fuchida could expect all of these epithets if he openly became a Christian. Of all possible accusations, he dreaded these the most. For a long time he didn't even tell his family.[2]

But he did confide in Kimi. From her he feared no criticism, for she believed everything he said or did to be perfection. Kimi considered herself a Christian. Though she had never been baptized, she had prayed in the Christian manner since childhood and read the Bible regularly. She encouraged Fuchida to go the entire way.[3] Perhaps she saw this mutual attachment to an unusual faith as a further bond between them.

Fuchida still saw nothing wrong with their relationship. He had no idea what was expected of him as a follower of Christ. He believed Jesus had died for his, Fuchida's, sins, but just what those sins might be he didn't know. He hadn't yet discovered the Old Testament, hence knew nothing of the Ten Commandments, the background of the law, and the moral code Jesus said He came not to destroy but to fulfill [Matthew 5:17].

By this time convinced that he wanted to become a Christian, he wondered how to go about it. Then he remembered that a name and address had been stamped on the back of the little tract about DeShazer. He rummaged among his papers until he found it. There on the cover was the Tokyo address of one Timothy Pietsch. Late in 1949 Fuchida wrote to Pietsch, explaining his circumstances and asking what he must do to become a Christian officially.

Months passed with no reply. He feared he would never hear, but continued his daily program of Bible reading, contemplation, and prayer. Finally in the spring of 1950 a letter came in Japanese. Pietsch apologized for the delay, explaining that he conducted an evangelical radio program and received mountains of mail. He belonged to the Pocket Testament League, currently holding meetings in Osaka. He asked Fuchida to come to that city and talk with him at his hotel.[4]

On 14 April 1950, a date he would never forget, Fuchida set out for Osaka. Immediately after lunch he met Pietsch in his hotel. The latter had with him Glenn Wagner, chief representative in Japan of the Pocket Testament League. They brought along two interpreters, much to Fuchida's relief. In one of these interpreters he recognized the man from whom he bought the New Testament at the Shibuya railroad station. Pietsch introduced him as Kiniji Sato. The other was Yokane Fukuda, who worked for the league. The five men distributed themselves on chairs and sofas in the Western-style lobby.

Wagner opened a Bible and spoke to Fuchida at some length concerning salvation. "Do you accept Christ, and do you repent of your sins?" he asked.

"I accepted Christ as my savior in September 1949 when I finished reading the Bible at my home," Fuchida replied with a touch of impatience. "At that time I repented of my sins. I'm here today to find out how to become a Christian."

Wagner bowed his head in brief prayer, asking God's blessing on the new convert. Then he addressed Fuchida: "You must do three things. First, you must read the Bible every day. This is the food for your spiritual growth. God speaks to you through the Bible, and you, too, should speak to God. You do this by prayer. This leads me to the second point—you must pray every day in communion with God."

"I do these things already," Fuchida interrupted. "In fact, I've been doing them since last September. I understand the importance of reading the Bible and of prayer."

Next Wagner said what Fuchida had been dreading. "You must bear witness. Like a child who takes in food, but also needs exercise for growth, so also you, Mr. Fuchida, need exercise for spiritual growth. Thus you must go out among the people and bear witness to your rebirth in Christ."

"This will be very difficult," Fuchida admitted, and explained the situation. "I'll continue my prayer and Bible reading in private, but I won't give testimony."

"Very well, I understand your feelings," Wagner answered, undismayed, "and I don't want to force you to bear witness. Just continue your life in Christ. Pray and read the Bible." Then he smiled. "Eventually you'll bear witness on your own—that is, if your faith continues to grow."[5]

Even as Wagner spoke, Fuchida saw that his desire to practice his faith in secret was a cowardly evasion. Surely God had spoken through Wagner's lips. "I realized that I was born again, and that I was no longer the old Captain Fuchida of the Imperial Japanese Navy. I was still that man in a way, but I was a new man as well." Physically and mentally he remained the same, of course, but he felt that spiritually Christ had renovated and relaunched him.

"You're right," Fuchida told Wagner. "I'm prepared to bear witness in the name of Jesus."

Pleased, his new friends took him to preach with them that very day. As they walked out of the lobby, they explained to Fuchida the league's purpose in Japan, which was to distribute pocket-sized New Testaments printed in Japanese. Right now they were handing out only the Gospel of St. John. If the response proved encouraging, they would follow with the rest of the New Testament.[6]

It seems strange that neither Wagner nor any of his associates suggested that Fuchida be baptized. On the other hand, one can understand that these people had a certain sense of urgency. They had spread their net at random, caught a tiger, and were not about to let him slip away. Here, out of the blue, had come the answer to their prayers—someone to whom the Japanese public would listen, a well-known, respected figure with a fine war record.

The group drove to the business section of Osaka and parked at the foot of a bridge over the Yodogawa River. There they set up two sound trucks,

1949 Chevrolets equipped with public-address systems and platforms on top. Men from the trucks began to distribute the Gospel of St. John to passersby. Wagner and Pietsch, along with Reverend Leyman W. Ketcham, a pastor from Baltimore, Maryland, preached from the platform with Fukuda interpreting. Pedestrians would stop for a moment or two, then go about their business. Not more than thirty-five listened at any one time.

After about an hour of this discouraging response, Ketcham beckoned to Fuchida. Now that the time had come, he felt neither hesitation nor fear. He seized the microphone and began: "I am Mitsuo Fuchida, a former navy captain who commanded the air attacking forces against Pearl Harbor on 8 December 1941. But now I'm a Christian, and I want to let you know how I became one. All Japanese want peace, I'm sure of that. No one wants war again, no one less than I who engaged in war as a naval officer for almost four years. I know the brutality and the cruelties of war better than many people. Now I want to work for peace. But how can mankind achieve a lasting peace? True peace of heart, mind, and soul can only come through Jesus Christ."[7]

Fuchida was feeling his way, uncertain of the reaction he would get. Instead of passing on people began stopping. He could see the deep interest in their eyes. While he spoke, the small group grew. At first dozens, then scores, gathered around the truck, staring up at him with keen attention. They knew who Fuchida was, and were obviously amazed to hear him deliver such a message.

With the crowd swelling, he lost all diffidence. Not only did he testify from conviction, but he also enjoyed himself. He was pleased to discover that he could still grip and hold an audience.

Enthusiastically, he told about his conversion. He outlined his war career and explained his feelings upon hearing the emperor's broadcast with its plea for future generations. The crowd continued to grow until it blocked the bridge and the adjacent street. Special policemen came to the scene to direct traffic, but they, too, stopped to listen. Fuchida's first testimony, delivered to such an unexpectedly large audience, gave him an emotional lift and launched his career as an evangelist in a blaze of glory.[8]

Instead of disbanding when Fuchida finished, the crowd hung around the sound truck as if reluctant to leave. So the group gave a second performance. Once more the crowd listened intently. The meeting went on until nearly 1800.

His new partners congratulated Fuchida heartily, and with reason. To have stopped traffic in downtown Osaka during the homeward rush was no mean feat. No doubt part of the audience had listened out of curiosity, but many were genuinely interested. This relieved him of his fear about being cut off from his countrymen. And he had the satisfaction of knowing that he hadn't failed Christ at the initial challenge.[9]

He had planned to go home to Kashiwara immediately, but Wagner invited him to dine at the hotel. He wanted to discuss matters at greater length with Fuchida and the rest of the group. Following the meal, Wagner told Fuchida something of the history of the Pocket Testament League. Early in 1949, they had sounded out MacArthur about a campaign in Japan and received his approval. Originally they had planned on a million copies of the St. John Gospel, but in a personal interview MacArthur said, "Make it ten million! The opportunity to win a nation only comes once in the history of that nation."

From its headquarters in New York City the league went on the air with an appeal for financial support to meet MacArthur's goal. The response brought in enough to procure the ten million booklets and to arrange for evangelical mass meetings in Japan. Wagner admitted to being discouraged; attendance had been poor.

Now he saw light breaking. "A great multitude gathered today to hear your testimony. We are convinced that you may be a special instrument whom God has chosen for these times. Because of your sincerity, spirit, message, and prestige, you will be a valuable asset to the Pocket Testament League. Will you join in this work?"[10]

Fuchida agreed to assist the league team while they remained in Japan. Delighted, Wagner promptly decided on a grand rally in the Central Public Hall in Osaka. This would be scheduled for 14 May 1950. During the interim, the two trucks would advertise throughout Osaka that Captain Mitsuo Fuchida, leader of the Pearl Harbor aerial striking force, would speak on the fourteenth on the subject of war and peace.

The group disbanded with bows and handshakes. Fuchida returned to Kashiwara where he had the delicate task of telling Haruko that he had become a Christian and would be working with the Pocket Testament League in Osaka. She had already noted his constant reading of the Bible. Her only outward reaction was to nod her head. Fuchida hoped she would follow him, but he knew that the move would be much more difficult for her than it had been for him. His only barriers had been worldly ones; hers would be spiritual. He put no pressure on her. He wanted her to come to Christ from conviction, not just to please or obey him.

For the next few weeks Fuchida commuted between Kashiwara and Osaka in preparation for the rally. Occasionally he remained overnight in Pietsch's hotel. During this period, he helped distribute copies of the St. John Gospel. But for the most part he and the other league workers directed their energies toward the rally.[11]

Meanwhile Fuchida asked to meet DeShazer. So Wagner, with Fukuda as interpreter, took him to the home where DeShazer lived with his wife Florence and little son Paul. DeShazer roomed with a Japanese family to improve his knowledge of the language, which he spoke only haltingly. It was a high point in the life of each man when the Pearl Harbor commander clasped the hand of the Doolittle Raider.

DeShazer told Fuchida that although he had preached all over the country, people weren't too interested in his message. He had become quite discouraged. Moreover, he was dismayed by the situation in Korea, on the verge of war, and by the inroads communism seemed to be making in Japan. He had decided that a miracle was needed to win Japan for Christ. To this end, he had gone on a strict forty-day fast. During that period he took no food at all and drank nothing but water.[12]

Thus Fuchida faced a man haggard from fasting and unremitting labor. But DeShazer gave no impression of weakness. His body seemed almost irrelevant, a mere accessory to his dauntless soul. From a thin face, with "something wild" about it, keen blue eyes looked directly into Fuchida's. "His eyes were piercing, somewhat like Genda's," Fuchida remembered.[13]

While he admired DeShazer's faith, he didn't know what to make of the fasting. It struck him as totally unnecessary. "Christ made complete atonement for mankind on the cross," Fuchida explained, "so there was no room for us to make an effort like DeShazer's, which was like the Buddhist way. We should do only one thing—fully rely on Christ. That's all.[14]

DeShazer, however, found his fast rewarding. His willingness to suffer on their behalf touched many Japanese. And he pointed to Fuchida's conversion as a sign that God had heard his prayers for Japan.[15] Here was a mediator, someone to whom the Japanese would listen and who understood them.

Fuchida and DeShazer talked to one another briefly through Fukuda, then knelt together in prayer. When Fuchida, Wagner, and Fukuda left, they took with them DeShazer's promise to speak at the Osaka rally.

By 1300 on the appointed day, the big auditorium was packed. People jammed into the aisles. Outside more pushed to get in. The crush generated such confusion that the league had to ask the police for help. The chief of police himself answered the call with about forty patrolmen. They brought the crowd under control and helped set up an improvised outdoor public-address system. These unexpected developments delayed the meeting half an hour.[16]

Wagner presided with Fukuda as interpreter, and he spoke briefly about the league. After this introduction, helpers distributed copies of the St. John Gospel. Then the Reverend Ichijiro Saito led the assembly in singing, in

Japanese, "What a Friend We Have in Jesus." At first the audience responded haltingly and self-consciously, but under Saito's skillful leadership the simple melody soon caught on and everyone joined in. Fuchida liked this idea, new to him, of singing hymns. "It prepared the people for the word of God," he said.

Next DeShazer testified, with Reverend Mikio Oda as interpreter. Like DeShazer, Oda was a graduate of Seattle Pacific College. He was the only really effective translator for DeShazer's picturesque English.[17] DeShazer told the crowd about his war and prison experiences, his reading of the Bible, and his acceptance of Jesus. His quick smile breaking over his lean face, he declared, "Now I love you as a brother in Christ! Come to know Christ, now, this afternoon!"

The audience listened intently, and when he finished they gave him a long ovation. Then Saito conducted the group in another old hymn, "Washed in the Blood of the Lamb." With this song the audience grew even more receptive. Then Wagner introduced Fuchida. "This is Captain Mitsuo Fuchida, your national hero, who once led the attack on Pearl Harbor. Have you ever heard of him?" Wild applause. "He is not only the hero of the war, he is the hero of the peace. So please listen to his testimony."[18]

"I rose with great pride and spirit to bear witness in the name of the Lord," Fuchida recounted. Briefly he sketched his personal history, starting with his attendance at the naval academy as a young man. "Fifteen years passed, and I became one of the aces of the Japanese naval air force. During this time I logged thousands of hours of flight time. Then I was chosen to lead the Pearl Harbor attack. I felt very proud to lead this strike as a loyal soldier of my motherland. I did my utmost for my beloved country." Fuchida stopped while the audience roared its approval.

"But four years later," he continued, "Japan was defeated. In my discouragement, when the war ended, I hated the United States as our former enemy and I hated the war crimes trials. But I want to tell you a beautiful story." Then he talked about Peggy Covell. "Revenge has always been a major motif in Japanese thought," he concluded. "But I am here to say to you that forgiveness is a far greater moral than revenge."

He went on with the story of his own conversion, then appealed to the audience's war weariness. "I know how you long for peace—personal peace as well as world peace. And real peace comes only through Jesus Christ."

When he sat down the audience surged out of their seats and broke into a thunderous burst of applause. Then Wagner took over again and invited all who wanted to accept Jesus to come to the front of the auditorium. About five hundred answered the call.[19]

News of the great rally sped through Japan's small Christian community. For the Pocket Testament League, it meant a new lease on life; for DeShazer, it was another proof that his Master blessed his work. As for Fuchida, he was relieved that it was over and had been so successful.

28

"A Real Soldier of Christ"

BEFORE LEAVING Osaka, Fuchida and his colleagues tentatively planned a second rally, this time at Kyoto, to follow a two-week relaxation period after the strenuous efforts at Osaka. But thinking matters over, he suggested that in the meantime they hold a meeting in his hometown.[1]

He had two reasons for this suggestion. First, he knew that after the Osaka rally there no longer could be any question of keeping his conversion a secret from his neighbors, even had he wished to do so. Nearly every major newspaper in Japan reported the event. He wanted to be straightforward and go before his townspeople himself. Moreover, what Wagner predicted had come about—giving testimony had strengthened his resolution and zeal to the point where he had shed all hesitation about it.[2]

In the second place, Kashiwara occupied a unique position in Japan's spiritual life. Two major shrines, one Shinto, one Buddhist, were located there. According to legend, the first emperor, Jimmu Tenno, who lived several hundred years before Christ, founded the first of these shrines. Many years later Crown Prince Shotokutaishi imported Buddhism and in Kashiwara established the first Buddhist temple in Japan. Kashiwara was something of a holy city for both faiths. Fuchida planned to raise the standard of the cross in the very stronghold of the old religions.

Wagner conducted the rally, with Fukuda standing by to translate. Fuchida spoke for almost an hour, centering his speech around the ancient

Shinto concepts of *hakko ichiu* (all the world under one roof) and *shikei doho* (all nations are brothers).

"These slogans were twisted for propaganda purposes before and during the war, but essentially they are noble concepts and we shouldn't abandon them," he told his audience. "All the world is indeed under one roof—heaven—and all nations, all peoples regardless of race or color, should be brothers, for are we not all God's children?

"The biggest mistake we Japanese made in the past was to consider the emperor as God and the whole world as destined to come under the imperial roof. This was wrong! God is above everyone, including the emperor. It is God's world and all in it must be brothers. This is the eternal truth.

"God sent His only begotten Son into the world to save that which was lost," he emphasized. "God wants everyone to come back to Him through Jesus Christ. We all love our emperor, yes, but he is human, so he too lives under the grace of God. He too must receive Christ to be born again. And when this takes place, the slogans of our ancestors, 'All the world under one roof' and 'All nations are brothers,' will really come true. So you people here now—come to God through Christ! This is salvation for you and the world.

"There is no compromise in my own belief," he concluded. "Henceforth I shall devote the remaining years of my life to serving Christ."

As he took his seat amid cordial applause, his head swam with the exhilaration that comes with crossing a personal Rubicon. He felt clear and cleansed, sure and determined. Now I am a real soldier of Christ, he thought.[3]

If he had expected swarms of his neighbors to convert, turning Kashiwara into the Japanese Jerusalem, sacred to three great faiths, he was unrealistic. The result came as something of a letdown. After Fuchida's testimony Wagner asked the audience, "Who among you knows Captain Fuchida?" Every hand shot up. Then he asked, "Who among you will follow in his footsteps?" Only a few raised their hands.

Fuchida was downcast over this response, and regretted that the audience reacted with more astonishment than enthusiasm to the news that he had embraced Christianity. He had fallen victim to the prophet-in-his-own-country syndrome. Osaka saw him as a glamorous figure standing on the pedestal of his wartime reputation; in Kashiwara he was just a neighbor, a struggling farmer.

As soon as his countrymen had time to digest the various headlines about his adoption of Christianity, letters began to pour in. Many were friendly and heartwarming; some reproached him harshly for embracing the religion of Japan's former enemy. These said in effect: "We know you very well. You can't believe in Christianity, because you were a typical soldier of Japan in the past. This must be some scheme. When we think of your sincere and wholehearted devotion to the cause, we feel very sorry for you."[4]

Among those who sent congratulations was the Catholic bishop of Osaka. He wrote courteously, in English, saying that he had mailed Fuchida a book in Japanese entitled *The Origin of Truth.* He asked that he come to his church to discuss some important matters. As Fuchida had to go to Osaka the next day on business anyway, he decided to call on the bishop at once. In Osaka he went to the Catholic church, not difficult to find because it was one of Japan's largest Christian houses of worship. The bishop had spent more than thirty years in Japan and spoke the language fluently. "He was a five-star general," said Fuchida, smiling at the memory. The bishop expressed genuine happiness to hear of his conversion, and suggested that he become a Catholic.

He gave Fuchida a copy of a book written by Kazuo Sakamaki, *I Attacked Pearl Harbor.* The English version[5] had been published in the United States under the auspices of the Young Men's Christian Association and enjoyed much success. According to the bishop, Sakamaki had already received a million yen in royalties. He suggested that Fuchida write the story of the Pearl Harbor attack under Catholic sponsorship. He assured him that he would receive at least the same remuneration as Sakamaki, perhaps double that sum.[6] The prospect of earning two million yen by honest means didn't pain Fuchida; he still wasn't very well off. So he examined Sakamaki's slim volume curiously.

He saw immediately that he was in a position to write a book at least as good, probably better; however, the suggestion that he do so under Catholic patronage, coming hard on the heels of an invitation to join that church, bothered him. While he thought the matter over, the bishop conducted him through the church. The huge building with its ornate decorations and large sanctuary impressed Fuchida unfavorably. This is all very beautiful and impressive, he thought, but this type of religion is just like big business. It is no different from the Higashi Hongangi in Kyoto and the other great Buddhist temples.

When he took leave of the bishop he said he would let him know his decision soon. But he had already made it. That very night, after returning to his farm, he wrote the bishop that he didn't wish to become a Catholic. The church he had seen that afternoon, he explained, didn't seem to have anything of the spirit of Christ in it. Not wanting to offend a good man, he softened the impact: "Of course, I know little about Catholicism, so I can't make a considered judgment."

On two other occasions Catholic delegates came to his home to talk to him about joining them. He told them there was too much ceremony, ritual, and decoration in the Catholic church for his taste.

Fuchida consulted with Wagner about these proposals. This was näive of him, as Wagner was a Protestant, but at the time he knew nothing about Christian denominations. Naturally, Wagner advised him against acceptance.[7]

A number of communists also wrote Fuchida urging him to become one of them. They used a stockpile of pet words and clichés, for instance, *jimmin* for "people" in the sense of "human beings." The word is the closest in the Japanese language to the Marxist word *masses*. Most Japanese used either *shimmin* (subject of the emperor) or *kokumin* (native) when referring to their countrymen. So Fuchida could always identify communist correspondents by looking for the ideograph denoting *jimmin*.

One such letter came from the party leader in Osaka. Another interesting one reached Fuchida from a coal miner in Kyushu, a former grammar-school teacher and army lieutenant. Taken to Siberia as a prisoner near the end of the war, he had been clever enough to yell "Comrade!" at appropriate times. So the communists sent him to a training school in Siberia and afterwards assigned him inspector of Japanese prisoners in Siberia. They also rewarded him with return to Japan after only four years of imprisonment. Once back at home, he went to work in the mining area of Hokkaido, spreading the communist word among workers there.[8]

Fuchida's correspondent didn't introduce himself in precisely those terms. Politely he pointed out the error of Fuchida's ways and offered to become his guide, philosopher, and friend in the true faith:

> I surmise that this is your first contact with the Bible, which also may be true of Lenin-Marxism. Therefore, I advise you to give the same persistence and fervor you are devoting to the Bible also to Lenin-Marxism. If you will allow me, I shall undertake to guide you to knowledge of the doctrine of Lenin-Marxism.

Courtesy demanded that Fuchida answer:

> I acknowledge your most cordial letter. As you have surmised, this is my first step in searching the Bible. In my forty-seven years of life, I have learned that a dose of hydrocyanic acid, if taken internally, will lead to death, yet I have never seen this poison. Therefore, I have not the faintest idea of its form, color, or odor. But if someone should hand me this deadly poison, it would be ridiculous for me to experiment by taking it just to see if it was poison or not! To me Lenin-Marxism is like hydrocyanic acid. Thank you.

Not surprisingly, he never heard from the correspondent again.[9]

A postcard Fuchida read with much interest and regret came from a former colleague, Captain Kita (a pseudonym), a brave, intelligent man well-known in the navy. "I have learned from the newspapers that you, Fuchida, have become a Christian," he wrote. "But don't be deceived by MacArthur! He wants to destroy Shinto and replace it with Christianity. This occupation policy is American imperialism. *Hakko ichiu* is the truth, and you should proceed to the people on the basis of this slogan."

Fuchida grinned ruefully. The "people," "imperialism". So Kita had become a communist. The postcard concluded, "You are a war hero and you have much influence with the people, and you must stand with the people."

Fuchida put the card aside with a sigh. Later he checked up on Kita's activities since the end of the war. With the coming of peace, Kita had fled Japan for China, where he became active in the communist underground. Then he returned to Japan and became a key man in the Japanese communist structure. Fuchida believed the communists had slated him to be commander in chief of their troops if they took over Japan. So Kita's zeal was not entirely disinterested—he had a few feathers to pluck for his own future nest.[10]

Many strange callers began to stop at Fuchida's little farm, among them a young man with one leg who swung himself on crutches up to the house. He introduced himself as Noboru Nakamura, a former second lieutenant in the navy. According to his story, he had lost his leg when his suicide torpedo boat blew up in an attack against Okinawa. There U.S. marines took him prisoner and sent him to the Philippines. Repatriated to Japan after the war, he couldn't secure work and became a mendicant.

He was president of an organization of disabled veterans, almost all of them reduced to begging. Understandably, he was bitter. He regarded MacArthur as the source of all his woes, and anything to do with the United States was anathema to him. That included Christianity. It's "only the camouflage of the wicked occupation policy of MacArthur," he said.[11]

He knew Fuchida well by reputation. "I always respected and admired you as a brave and brilliant officer. When I read of your conversion I couldn't believe it, and I've come to ask if the story is true, and if so, what made you change your mind."

When Nakamura heard from Fuchida's own lips that he had indeed turned Christian, he shouted incoherently, "You have changed! You have become a Christian! You will betray the emperor and the people! Reconsider your action. You were so brave during the war, you planned operations, thousands of suicide pilots went to their deaths because of you. How after killing so many loyal Japanese men, how can you become a Christian?"

With that, he pulled out and flourished a dagger, which Fuchida recognized as the type Toyoda had presented to kamikazes in token of his respect.[12] If his answer didn't satisfy Nakamura, the man would try to stab him.

Fuchida, far from pleased to be lectured on patriotism by a young ex-second lieutenant, nonetheless understood that much of Nakamura's hostility rose out of disillusioned hero worship. He would have to convince Nakamura that Christianity wasn't something MacArthur dreamed up to support the occupation.

"Have you ever heard anything about Jesus Christ?"

"No, never," Nakamura replied, eyeing him cagily.

Fuchida began an earnest effort to dig the man's thinking out of the nationalistic rut. They talked for three hours. Toward the end, he said, "You admired me, the former Captain Fuchida, as a patriot of the Japanese nation. When I became a Christian, I remained a patriot of Japan. I still love my country and my people.

"When the war ended, the main point of the imperial rescript was permanent peace for coming generations. Who can bring peace to the world forever? Only Jesus Christ! You should not confuse the righteousness of the victor MacArthur with the righteousness of God. The latter will come to us only when Christ conquers.

"I'm not an opportunist," Fuchida went on, "even though you think so. This call to Christ is the greatest call of my life. And I will devote the rest of my life to Him. No persecutions, threats, or dangers will cause me to change my mind."

Then he laid his hand on the man's shoulder. "In fact, Nakamura-san," he said, "God is calling you right now. If you want to stab me, I can give you my life. But remember God is calling you, too."[13]

Slowly Nakamura returned his dagger to its sheath and bowed his head. "I apologize to you, Fuchida-san," he said, "for my hostility and for having spoken against Christianity when actually I am ignorant of Christ."

Fuchida made deprecating noises, and Nakamura dragged himself out of his chair and adjusted his crutches. "Perhaps some day I myself might find the way to Christ," he observed.

As he moved down the path, Fuchida looked after him with a slight smile. This one, at least, was a patriot—not one of the *jimmin* boys! Five years later, Fuchida preached at Amagasaki, located between Osaka and Kobe. There he saw Nakamura in the congregation. He had indeed found the way to Christ.[14]

Another, less fruitful encounter took place about the same time as Nakamura's visit. Fuchida testified in the mountain town of Haibara City, not far from Kashiwara. Following the meeting five communists came up and asked to talk with him. He agreed with resigned courtesy, for he recognized their leader as one Kanji Watanabe (a pseudonym). Fuchida respected him because he was an excellent doctor who treated the poor without charge. He served as chief of the Communist Party in the Nara district and as their perennial candidate for the diet. The four with him were poorly educated types in their late teens or early twenties.[15]

Watanabe proceeded to tell Fuchida about the communist movement in Japan. First, he announced the Russians had trained and stationed about a hundred thousand Japanese troops in Siberia for their own purposes. "These troops are under the command of Tokumaro Konoye," he said. The information interested Fuchida exceedingly. He knew that this son of the former premier, a first lieutenant in Japan's Manchurian army, had been taken prisoner and sent to Siberia. Thus far he hadn't returned to Japan. The Russians reported him as dead, though rumors persisted that he was still alive.

The Russians had handpicked these men from the prisoners in Siberia and shipped them to the Kuriles and to Sakhalin, whence they would invade Hokkaido in the near future. "South Korea will soon fall to the North Koreans," Watanabe continued, "and after that our troops will take over Kyushu. Not a Soviet soldier will set foot on Japanese soil! The invasion will be entirely by Japanese, so it will be a civil war. Within one year," he boasted, "Japan will be taken by communists.

"We are well disposed from Hokkaido to Kyushu in strategic places such as coal mines, railroads and other key industries," he informed Fuchida. "The party isn't large in Japan, but it's well organized and determined. We're the spark that will ignite the revolution in Japan—the revolution that will be carried out by the Japanese people who are so poor and so miserable."

At this point, he broke off his lecture to ask Fuchida to become a communist. "You are a war hero and very influential. You are a key man. You could work effectively among former army and navy officers." Without waiting for a reply, he launched into a tirade against MacArthur's policies. Nothing in this was news to Fuchida. His attention began to wander.[16]

Watanabe's cohorts had been punctuating his speech with boasts of the fine jobs they would have after the revolution. All four planned on becoming chiefs of police in nearby towns. These kids aren't enthusiastic about Lenin-Marxist doctrines, Fuchida thought, they're just ambitious. They saw the chance to drive someone else out of office and take over key positions for themselves.

"I'm confident of an eventual communist takeover in Japan," Watanabe was saying, "just as Mao's Red troops took over China against the U.S.-backed Chiang Kai-shek. That's the way the Japanese Red troops from Siberia will do it. Japan has no real means of protection any more. With no Japanese army, navy, or air force, the job won't be too difficult."

Then he returned to the occupation, assuring Fuchida that the troops in Siberia had been told how bad life was for their ex-comrades at home. "With your influence among ex-navy officers," he concluded, "you could induce many of them to follow you, if you join the Communist Party. Don't remain a Christian! Become a communist! If you remain a Christian, MacArthur will use you. But if you become a communist, you'll be working against Allied policy and for the Japanese people. You are the key man for us in all Japan. You could play a most influential role in the party."[17]

For a long time Fuchida had been building up steam about this issue. Now he seized the chance to get certain matters off his chest. He had a pretty good idea that his words would be carried higher up, perhaps to the chief of the Japanese communists, whoever he might be. Watanabe and his four satellites must have come on orders from a top superior. He wouldn't have dared spill so much information had he not been instructed to bring Fuchida into the ranks at any cost.

"Maybe your Red troops will take over just like Mao's took over China," he began. "But I've observed international events carefully since the end of the war. And what do I see? I see East Germans fleeing to West Germany, North Koreans fleeing to South Korea, mainland Chinese fleeing to Formosa and to Hong Kong. I don't see anybody fleeing the other way, into communist territory. So I conclude these communist countries must not be very comfortable places to live.

"I'm also bitter about the Allied occupation policy, because I'm also an ex-navy officer. But I'm much more bitter about communism. It doesn't have a human heart. Japan is far better off occupied by the United States than by the Soviet Union. In this respect, the Japanese people are so fortunate! I'm grateful that Japan hasn't been divided between the Allies and the Soviet Union like Korea and Germany. That would have been a terrible tragedy."

Then Fuchida said, in his loud, clear voice that had once carried over carrier flight decks, "Now you tell me Japanese Red troops are coming to invade Japan! Some Japanese may join them and many may flee Japan. Remember this: When your Red troops come in, I, Captain Mitsuo Fuchida, will stay right here and fight communism in Japan even if I'm the last man left in the country!

"Don't deceive yourselves about these important jobs if the communists take over," he said grimly. "You'll be neither governors, mayors, nor chiefs of police. Moscow will fill these positions, just as in Poland, Czechoslovakia, or North Korea. Moscow will decide things, not you. Your heads will be cut off. If you want to live a long life, you should leave the Communist Party."

On this note the meeting broke up with scant ceremony.[18] As Fuchida strode off, he noted that Watanabe looked fearful. Perhaps he was wondering how to soften this answer into terms suitable for the sensitive ears of his party chiefs.

That the communists planned to take over Japan Fuchida had no doubt.

But whether the Soviets actually had one hundred thousand well-trained Japanese troops poised in Sakhalin and the Kuriles he didn't know. This meeting took place a few weeks before the outbreak of the Korean War; recalling the conversation with Watanabe, Fuchida wondered if that war wasn't part of the communist strategy to take over Japan. Luring American forces into Korea would leave the demilitarized Japanese in no position to resist Red troops. If this idea lay behind the Korean War, Japanese communist bosses must have known it would soon start; certainly Watanabe's remarks hinted as much. Therefore Fuchida's relief was immense as time went by and no Red troops descended on Japan.[19]

29

"The Fellowship of Christood"

G EOGRAPHICALLY, historically, and psychologically, the next logical objective for evangelism was Kyoto, located slightly northwest of Nara City. This capital of old Japan had escaped the worst of the war and then been removed from the list of prospective atomic bomb targets at the insistence of Secretary of War Stimson.[1] Like other world cities with a long history of cultural leadership, Kyoto lived in serene awareness of her own excellence. A suggestion that anything in Kyoto might be improved wouldn't go down well. Fuchida fully expected the city to resist Christianity.

Kyoto's citizens held to Shinto fervently so as to reaffirm their loyalty to the motherland. In view of this situation, Fuchida advised Wagner and other league representatives to soft-pedal the fact that MacArthur had invited them to Japan. But they ignored his suggestion and announced, in advertising the Kyoto rally, that they had come under occupation auspices.

Sure .enough, hecklers disrupted the meetings in Kyoto. Quite a few of the interruptions came from Buddhist priests. They gave Ketcham a particularly hard time when he tried to preach on the doctrines of sin, resurrection, and the hereafter. This was sheer fantasy to Buddhists. "Don't tell us such a fairy tale!" the priests yelled out. "We have a much more sophisticated religion than Christianity."[2]

In Fuchida's opinion, the league should have worked through local Christian churches. But it preferred to operate independently of Japanese Christians, who were members of the United Churches *(Kyodan)*. This organization had been founded during the war under government sponsorship. All Buddhist, Shintoist, and Christian houses of worship formed a united spiritual front. The association, fruitful in promoting mutual understanding, continued after the war. To the Pocket Testament League the United Churches bore the mark of the cloven hoof; they wanted nothing to do with it.

For sheer size, the final meeting in Kyoto was impressive. An estimated ten thousand attended the gathering, held in Maruyama Park on 27 May 1950, a beautiful afternoon. The league had used Fuchida's name freely in advertising, and the large audience consisted primarily of those curious to see and hear a war hero. Few came out of spiritual hunger, for the results were far from spectacular.

Reluctantly Fuchida concluded that the league had failed in Kyoto and would continue to fail because it was attempting to convert people whom it made no effort to understand. The urgent need was for a native Christian evangelist. Fuchida decided that surely this must be the mission for which God had intended him.[3]

For all his lofty and sincere intentions, Fuchida still saw no reason to abide by at least one Christian precept. While he was evangelizing, he kept up his liaison with Kimi. Once more the couple conceived a child, again by choice. This time, however, severe complications developed, and upon her doctor's recommendation Kimi had an abortion in October 1950.[4]

Following Kyoto, Fuchida and his associates spent three weeks in Nagoya. There matters moved along fairly well until they took to the outdoors. One day at 1700 the league set up the sound truck in front of the Nagoya railroad station and commenced preaching. The timing couldn't have been worse— the afternoon rush hour. Then rain began to fall, and the few passersby whom the speakers had attracted ran off to seek shelter in the station. Wagner moved the truck as close as possible to the depot and continued preaching.

The speakers amplified his voice so loudly that railroad employees couldn't make their train announcements heard. The stationmaster came out and asked Wagner to stop, whereupon the latter pulled out a document from MacArthur's headquarters stating that the Pocket Testament League had come to Japan at the general's invitation. The stationmaster was unimpressed. So Wagner produced a permit from the local provost marshal granting him the right to preach anywhere in the city.

At this the official capitulated, but with icy wrath. "By the power of force and superior strength you may preach here," he said contemptuously. And the next day he canceled a league meeting scheduled for the benefit of railroad workers.[5]

This ugly incident upset Fuchida. Not by "force and superior strength" do you lead people to Christ, but by the spirit of God, he thought. A little Christian humility on Wagner's part, a graceful apology for disturbing the railroad men, a request that the stationmaster name a suitable time to preach—these would have saved the rally and won a friend.

Another difficulty was the matter of invitations to accept Christ. At the end of each rally, Wagner asked his audience, "Who will accept Christ? Anyone who does please raise your hand." He believed that any raised hand indicated a new convert and reported to his headquarters on that basis.

Fuchida knew better. Because the league advertised the business about MacArthur's invitation, many Japanese assumed it would be the better part of valor to put up their hands. Still others responded out of oriental courtesy. Then, too, many Japanese were compulsive joiners or simply responded impulsively to an emotional appeal. Thus Fuchida took many conversions with a liberal sprinkling of salt.

Of course, some raised their hands because the message genuinely attracted them. But these by no means accounted for all or even most of the responses,[6] as attested by an incident at Nagoya.

Wagner was eager to evangelize among the police cadets of that city, so the league arranged a special meeting at the police academy. The film "God's Creation" would be shown, Wagner or one of his representatives would preach, Fuchida would testify, then Wagner would issue the invitation. The site of this meeting was a small movie theater seating only 250. The cadets numbering five hundred, the academy divided them into two groups to attend on succeeding days.

On the first day the cadets listened with courteous attention, but when Wagner invited them to come to Christ, none responded. Wagner had an impulsive temperament, easily elated and just as easily deflated. By the end of this day he was discouraged and demoralized.

Shortly before the next day's gathering, the film projectionist fell ill. Fuchida agreed to take over his job, being familiar with the 16-millimeter projector. To set it up, he came to the theater before any of the other league personnel. From the projectionist's box he had a good view when the cadets marched in. They couldn't see him.

After the young men had settled into their seats, the chief of police came on stage and gave them a little lecture. "Yesterday when the missionary asked for a show of hands, no cadet responded," he said. "This missionary came to Japan at MacArthur's invitation. He must be sent back satisfied in order to promote good relations with the United States and to please MacArthur. So today, all of you raise your hands." Fuchida had to strangle his whoop of laughter so as not to be discovered.

That day when Wagner appealed for converts, every hand shot up. "He was beside himself with joy and enthusiasm," Fuchida recounted, chuckling at the memory, "and wrote up a big report on the success of revivalism in Japan." Fuchida never had the heart to tell him that the chief of police was responsible for this mass conversion.[7]

For the final effort at Nagoya the group staged a meeting at Tsurumai Park. Fuchida disapproved of the location, because the U.S. Army had taken it over and the only Japanese who could use it were those working for the occupation. Wagner had to receive special permission from the army to speak there to an open audience. This dispensation seemed to highlight the tie between the Pocket Testament League and the occupation.

Nevertheless, they drew a big crowd. A few days before the rally they advertised that Fuchida would speak on the subject of war and peace. This theme was timely, because the Korean War had broken out just two days before the meeting. About fifteen thousand Nagoyans swallowed their scruples and gathered for the occasion. Of this number, something like seven hundred—a disappointingly small percentage—responded to the call to accept Christ.[8]

When Fuchida had first seen the war headlines, he remembered Watanabe's boasts. But he didn't believe Japanese communists would be able to take over the country. The United States wouldn't permit it. On the contrary, he felt Japan would benefit from the Korean War. In this he was correct. The war put the country on its feet economically and changed the psychology of the nation. So much American and Japanese energy was diverted that occupation policies received only perfunctory attention. Many Japanese who had been in hiding came into the open and reentered national life.[9]

Fuchida's Nagoya period drew to a close and with it Ketcham's tour of duty in Japan. The Reverend H. George Vorsheim, pastor of the Westminster Presbyterian Church in Philadelphia, replaced Ketcham. With this enthusiastic new helper, the group continued its campaign, moving to Hokkaido. They split into two teams and divided the big island, roughly along a line from Ashigawa eastward to Kushiro.

One unit, Wagner with Fukuda as translator, took the southern portion, while the other, comprising Vorsheim, Sato, and Fuchida, covered the northern sector. With half a million copies of the Gospel of St. John among them they set forth, each team in a one-ton Chevrolet truck, four loudspeakers, and a platform on top.

Vorsheim was a dynamo, speaking at least once a day, sometimes as often as four. He distributed the gospel, then preached from it, referring to verses which the people could look up and follow as he spoke. This proved an effective method, judging by the many hands raised when he called for converts. He requested these people to meet with him after the service, at which time he explained their duties as Christians and led them in prayer. Fuchida took advantage of Vorsheim's knowledge and experience to study the Bible with him each day.[10]

They spent a week in Nemuro, the easternmost point in Japan. Separated from Kunashiri Island in the Russian Kuriles by the narrow Strait of Nemuro, the area was a hotbed of communist agitation. Circumstances enabled Fuchida to obtain insight into this problem. One day as he and Vorsheim preached from the truck, Fuchida noticed a fine-looking man about forty-five years of age. Although clad in a simple kimono, he was obviously a person of some consequence. Fuchida felt drawn to him. When Vorsheim asked for converts, he was one of the first to raise his hand.

At the follow-through service he introduced himself. "I'm the chief of police of Nemuro. I believe that what you have to offer is something I need more than anything else in the world." The next night at an indoor rally in the city's largest auditorium the new convert showed up in uniform. He remained outside to help his police keep order, for, according to him, this was the biggest crowd in the city's history. He sent his wife and son to the meeting in his stead.[11]

The conversion of this important official was the high spot of the swing around Hokkaido. Fuchida became well acquainted with him. Among his reasons for becoming a Christian, the chief said, was his belief that this would be an effective way to combat communism. The comrades were making his life miserable. To their usual fulminations against occupation policies they were adding predictions of communist conquest now that the Korean War had commenced. Nemuro's location between the Russian Kuriles and northern Japan would place the town in the direct line of march.

Fuchida feared that in a showdown, the people of Hokkaido could not be depended on to shed their blood for the motherland. At this time, few American troops remained in Hokkaido and Japanese forces were not yet available. If the native Reds bided their time in the Kuriles and Sakhalin, now was their big chance. He worried over "the crisis of Hokkaido," as he and the chief termed the situation. It was in a sober frame of mind that he bade farewell to his new friend and retraced his steps to Sapporo.[12]

There, as arranged, Fuchida and Vorsheim joined Wagner's group and compared results. Originally they had planned to swap territories immediately, but during their stay in Sapporo the first voluntary police reserve force of five thousand men assembled at Chitose Air Base for training by American personnel. Fuchida suggested that they go there and preach to these men. Wagner agreed, so the whole group set out for Chitose, where they spent a week. This was in late August or early September 1950.

Their experience with the police reserve proved to be one of the most disheartening the team ever encountered. Another American missionary was visiting Chitose at the same time. With the best of intentions, he had ruined his own as well as the league's chances of reaping converts. Proud of his war service, he congratulated the assembled reservists on becoming soldiers. "Jesus died for the whole world," he said. "The soldier shares this great love in being prepared to die for his country."

But these police reserves, principally former enlisted men, noncoms, and junior officers, had no idea of being soldiers. The peace clause in Japan's new constitution precluded admitting the Police Reserve to be a military force. These men had joined simply for a job and some income. The missionary's words plunged them into an apathy of sullen resentment from which not even Fuchida could rouse them. They wanted to talk to him about their hopes and plans; they had no interest in hearing the gospel.

Fuchida was discouraged, but couldn't blame them. Instead of becoming members of an elite police force—and an officer of the law enjoyed great respect in Japan—they found themselves slipped into the discredited military. Fuchida attributed this sorry situation to MacArthur's attempt to reestablish a Japanese army while retaining the peace clause.[13]

Once more the team split and returned to the mission field elsewhere in Hokkaido. Wagner and Fuchida joined forces while Vorsheim went with the others. Now Fuchida took another important step. For the first time the league sought the cooperation of the Japanese Christian community, and through this contact Fuchida came to know the Protestant church. Before this he hadn't set foot in a Christian house of worship, except for the Osaka cathedral. He had been evangelizing for Christ unbaptized and had never attended a Christian religious service. The Protestant church was a great discovery. He loved the unassuming eloquence of the sermon, the simple, tuneful hymns, the atmosphere of reverence and peace within the building.[14]

What impressed him most was the fellowship among the churchgoers, particularly the younger people and teenagers. "How kind they were to me and to one another, how pure, honest, and unselfish!" he exclaimed. They were a refreshing antidote to some of Japan's postwar youth, who disgusted him. "It was so bad in some cases it was unbelievable," declared Fuchida.

In Hokkaido it dawned on him that there had been a void in his Christian life. So, when the time came to leave for a two-week vacation, he told Wagner that he had decided not to join them. "I want and need the fellowship of Christ as a member of His church," he explained. "I'm going back to Kashiwara to join the Christian church in Osaka." Wagner heard him out and agreed that it was the right thing to do.[15]

Still, Fuchida left Hokkaido filled with misgivings. The island was woefully weak in both defense and morale. The new police reserve had neither weapons, training, nor spirit. "They were really only a paper force," he recalled. "I was grieved that my homeland, once so strong and secure, should now be so weak, and that it had to depend for its protection and security on the United States. How much better it would have been if the Japanese themselves could have protected Japan!" Shortly after he reached Kashiwara, the information that the United States had sent two divisions into Hokkaido relieved his fears for that island's safety. But it offended his pride and sense of fitness that Americans should risk their lives to protect his homeland.

He pointed out, however, that some Japanese did help in the Korean War effort. To take one example, MacArthur and his admirals needed expert navigational assistance for the Inchon landing because of the treacherous tides in that area. As the Japanese knew these tides well, the Americans asked for a number of pilots and navigators to assist. About fifty of Fuchida's former colleagues participated. After the Inchon landing, many small Japanese boats became transports plying the waters between Japan and Korea. To Fuchida, such incidents were a source of keen gratification. The Japanese-American relationship had moved beyond that of guardian and child into partnership, however one-sided.[16]

Fuchida returned to his farm to face another war, one within himself. He had reached a crossroads. He needed and wanted to be a member of a Christian community such as he had known in Hokkaido. But church membership carried a price: If he became a baptized Christian he must give up Kimi, and that would not be easy.

He worried over little Yoko. What would become of her if her father bowed out of her life? In anguish he took the problem to the only person he knew wise and kind enough to understand—Haruko. She listened silently as he stammered out his story and explained his dilemma. When he had finished, she raised her head and said simply, "I will accept your child. Bring her home."[17]

This would have been the ideal solution. Yoko would have a full family life, the best education Fuchida could afford, the companionship of a brother and sister, and a good mother, too. Haruko would never take out on a child the distress her husband had caused her.

But in Kimi Fuchida was not dealing with a woman capable of assessing what was best for her daughter; emotion ruled her. She considered herself Fuchida's wife and never accepted his decision to break with her. She refused to give up Yoko. She loved her, and no doubt obscurely felt that with her daughter by her side, Fuchida might come back. Yoko grew up knowing that Mitsuo Fuchida was her father, but Kimi never told her that Fuchida had a wife and legitimate children. Hence the girl couldn't understand why her father didn't visit her and her mother, confining his contact to occasional letters and postcards.[18]

Having broken with Kimi, in October 1950 Fuchida joined the Sakai Church in Osaka. Although the nearest Christian church to his home, it was an hour and a half from Kashiwara by electric car. The minister, Reverend Toshio Saito, became one of his best friends and a spiritual father to him. During that fall and winter, Haruko attended services with him every Sunday, although she was still a Buddhist. She sat in the congregation on Easter Sunday morning, 25 March 1951, when Reverend Saito baptized her husband.

His parting with the Pocket Testament League had been friendly, but Fuchida would never have recommended that other new converts plunge immediately into evangelism. An evangelist, he came to believe, should be someone who had had plenty of practice witnessing for Christ by following a good life, and who worked up gradually to intensive public campaigns. Then his testimony to large audiences would be "clear and triumphant."

After his baptism, Fuchida gave personal testimony anywhere people expressed interest in hearing him. These appearances carried him all over Nara and the surrounding prefectures. Haruko often went along and watched him closely, as if judging just how deep this reformation went. Soon it became obvious that he was sincerely trying to lead a better life.[19]

In his navy years and immediately thereafter Fuchida had drunk heavily, while never permitting the habit to get out of hand. Now, and with remarkably little effort, he gave up hard liquor entirely. He didn't abandon beer and wine, which he considered primarily food drinks. Smoking was more of a battle. In those days, the link between smoking and deadly diseases was not generally recognized, so he had no tangible motive for quitting. The Bible didn't speak against tobacco—not discovered until long after Christ—thus no religious conviction supported him. The only motivation he had was an uneasy feeling that this was an unnecessary self-indulgence. But the craving was so strong that even during church activities he would sneak into the men's room and light up. He persisted in his struggle and gradually freed himself.

These efforts were not lost on his family. With joy and relief they saw him change from "a dissatisfied, defeated man" into one at peace with himself and his environment, gentle and affectionate.[20]

But he kept a nostalgic spot in his heart for the days of military glory. To reporters who sought interviews on the tenth anniversary of Pearl Harbor, he said he had "lived his finest hour . . . when he led the surprise air attack. . . ." But now he saw that his "patriotism was a narrow-minded one not to be accepted by the peoples of the world. . . . Today I believe no war could be righteous and prepare the way for peace."

Fuchida observed reflectively, "I might call myself a pacifist. But I must say that I'm not a pacifist to the nth degree as yet.

"If for the defense of Japan my service is needed again, I'm ready to answer the call at any moment.

"This old soldier has not completely faded away."[21]

That month brought the Fuchida family another landmark: Haruko was baptized on Christmas Eve 1951—exactly twenty years after she and Fuchida met for the first time in her parents' home. On Easter Sunday 1952 Yoshiya and Miyako were baptized.[22]

Fuchida's evangelical activities kept him busy well into 1952 and absorbed a large percentage of his income, because he had no source of revenue except the farm. This provided food but brought in no cash. He had closed out his chicken business when the Korean War started, needing time and energy for his lay ministry. During his absences relatives and in-laws tended the farm, which relieved him of anxiety. Still, he needed funds for transportation and expenses. His evangelical work paid him almost nothing. Occasionally audiences would collect an offering of about a thousand yen, a little less than three dollars at the then-current exchange rate. Although he received it gratefully, it didn't go very far.[23]

During these years, people's memories of World War II faded. As the conflict became less a living experience than a historical event, books and articles about various phases of the war proliferated. To catch this rising tide, Fuchida turned author and found a ready if erratic market for his writings. As he was well known and considered knowledgeable about naval matters, the reading public received his articles well. Some appeared in the magazine *Kido Butai*, others in *Bungei Shunju*, *Chuo Koron*, and various newspapers.

He also wrote two books. One, *Task Force*, told the story of the Pacific war from Midway to the end. It proved quite controversial and brought down on his head the wrath of a number of admirals. This was because he took Yamamoto to task for various mistakes Fuchida attributed to his failure to understand air power.

In the West, Fuchida is best known as an author for a book he wrote with his friend Masatake Okumiya, *Midway: The Battle that Doomed Japan*. [24] According to Fuchida, Okumiya did the research and Fuchida did the writing. They were uniquely qualified for this task: Fuchida had witnessed the carrier battle in the Midway area, while Okumiya had been with the diversionary attack against the Aleutians.

The largest sum Fuchida received for an article was four hundred thousand yen, or a little over one thousand dollars at the time. Although his income as a writer provided a welcome and needed supplement, it was neither steady nor dependable. The farm remained his basic resource.[25]

Despite a strict budget, only once during this time did Fuchida seriously think of abandoning evangelism. Temptation presented itself in a most attractive guise. The government offered him a top-level post in the Self-Defense Air Force, soon to be activated. With his experience, and by joining at the outset, he could have looked forward to high rank, a regular income, and public prestige. Equally pleasant was the thought of working once more with friends like Genda and returning to a way of life he had loved. More important was another consideration: Did he have the right to refuse to serve when his country called?

Fuchida considered the problem long and deeply, then turned down the commission. He would be honored to serve the new organization in an advisory capacity, he said. But he believed that he could best serve Japan and humanity by bringing souls to Christ.[26]

30

"My Wonderful Reception"

A s THE PACE of Fuchida's evangelizing stepped up, transportation became an acute problem. Accustomed to flight, he found ground travel maddening. Yet commercial air was too expensive and too limited, for he particularly wanted to reach Japan's rural population, scattered far and wide. Evangelism had neglected the farmers and concentrated on the cities. This could be a perfect mission field—about fifty million good country folk, like Fuchida, tillers of the soil.

Quite aside from convenience, he longed for his own aircraft. He was practical enough to understand that an airborne preacher would strike a dramatic note and attract a large audience. No doubt a little nostalgia for the sky mixed itself with zeal.

He decided a helicopter would suit his purpose best, freeing him from dependence on landing strips. But his finances were such that purchase of a bicycle would have been a strain. A helicopter seemed as far beyond his reach as a private yacht. He nourished the hope, and prayed that some day his dream might come true.[1]

Aviation had fallen upon evil days in Japan, for a general headquarters order prohibited Japanese from piloting planes. "This was another childish act of MacArthur's occupation!" snapped Fuchida. In protest, a number of pilots formed an organization in the Gotanda district of Tokyo. They called it Pilots without Wings and, not to be outdone in silly gestures, ran up a white flag each morning in front of their headquarters to call attention to the enforced surrender of their livelihood. When the Korean War started the occupation policy flew out the window, down came the white flag, and once more Japanese pilots took to the air.[2]

This was a step toward the materialization of Fuchida's dream. If a plane should pop up miraculously, he could fly it legally. The phrase "wings for Christ" flashed across his mind, and he wrote an article using it for the newspaper *Asahi.* In it he explained that the airplane ranked with the very best of scientific achievements. So far, however, men had used this magnificent instrument for supremacy in war. If properly utilized, airplanes could help bring mankind to salvation instead of destruction.[3]

In California, the Reverend Elmer B. Sachs headed the Worldwide Christian Missionary Army of Sky Pilots, an organization he had established on military lines in 1945. Its purpose was to build boys into future leaders of church, home, and community. Sachs wanted to set up a branch in Asia, especially Japan, but had no idea how to go about it.

Through Ketcham, he heard about Fuchida's conversion and the public impact it had had in Japan. He promptly decided that this Mitsuo Fuchida must be the man destined to lead the Sky Pilots in Japan. Through a pilot, Bob Hamilton, who crossed the Pacific every nine days on the Korean airlift, Sachs contacted Fuchida by letter. On a certain day in early 1952, Fuchida found it in his mail. Sachs offered him command of the Japanese branch of the Sky Pilots. "Inasmuch as Japanese boys and men love and enjoy regimentation," he wrote, "we feel that one or two men like you, building an army for the Lord Jesus Christ in Japan such as we are building in North, South, and Central America, will help to do in one generation a better job for Christ than has been done in previous generations."[4]

Fuchida turned back to the envelope and noticed stamped across the top, "Wings for Christ." Struck by the coincidence, he was strongly inclined to accept Sachs's offer, but wanted to know more about the Sky Pilots before committing himself. About two months later he traveled to Tokyo to visit Bob Hamilton at the Shiba Park Hotel. Hamilton told him that the Sky Pilots operated two aircraft from an airport south of San Francisco. He assured Fuchida that God would provide a plane for him, too.[5]

Sachs entered into correspondence with Fuchida and urged him to come to the United States, where Fuchida would be more likely to secure the wherewithal to purchase an aircraft than in Japan. The Sky Pilots would pay his transportation costs and other expenses, and give him a small allowance during his stay. Sachs also suggested that he attend the Tokyo Bible Seminary and there learn conversational English.

In August 1952 Fuchida arranged to stay with Timothy Pietsch while attending the seminary. His career as a seminarian lasted exactly three days. "The study of the Bible there was too liberal, too scientific, and too logical," he explained. It attempted to present the miracles in the light of modern scientific thought and theories. This transgressed Fuchida's concept of faith.

The Sky Pilots fretted over his abrupt departure, because they wanted him to become reasonably proficient in spoken English before he came to the United States. But Fuchida rationalized that he could always use an interpreter, and could give his testimony more convincingly if he didn't have to grope around in a foreign vocabulary.[6]

He arranged to travel with Pietsch aboard a Danish cargo steamer, the *Nicoline Maersk.* He had no written contract, only an informal agreement, and had no idea just what the Sky Pilots had in mind for him once he reached America.

Fuchida and Pietsch embarked at Yokohama on 10 October 1952. After poking around sundry Japanese ports for several days, the ship left Shizuoka on the sixteenth. Ten days later it stopped at Vancouver to reload the cargo, then proceeded to San Francisco, docking at 2000 on 29 October.

Just before leaving Japan, Fuchida had written an article for the Osaka *Asahi* in which he told readers,

> Eleven years ago this November 1952 I headed east across the Pacific aboard *Akagi* to bomb Pearl Harbor. At that time I was a brilliant soldier of the Emperor, and I was very uneasy because of all the responsibilities on my shoulders. Now I am again going east across the Pacific to the United States. This time too I am a soldier, but a soldier of Christ. This time I have a calm, easy and relaxed feeling and the desire to be a good-will ambassador for Christ.[7]

Nevertheless, he had some reservations as the ship sailed into San Francisco Bay. After all, he mused, I am the attacker of Pearl Harbor. Perhaps the Americans will hate me. As he stood on deck and saw the magnificent span of the Golden Gate Bridge and the city climbing the hills, he thought that this, truly, was a great country. He resolved that, if he ran into unpleasant situations, they would not be of his making.

When he left the ship reporters swarmed about him. Sachs, who had come to meet the ship, fended them off with the customary "No comment." But they did take some pictures, and Sachs gave them a brief statement. Obviously he was accustomed to dealing with newspapermen.[8]

The far-off *New York Times* took note of Fuchida's arrival in a small article datelined San Francisco, 30 October 1952:

> Capt. Mitsuo Fuchida . . . began a life of missionary work today. The slight, 50-year-old pilot said his heart was filled with revenge when he led the Dec. 7, 1941, air strike against the United States Navy, but "Christianity has 'opened my eyes' and I hope through Christ to help the young people of Japan learn a great love for America."

After passing through customs, the group proceeded to Sachs's home in San Jose, which was also headquarters of the Sky Pilots. By the time they arrived the clock hands stood at 2300 and Fuchida was glad to retire.[9]

The next morning Sachs handed him a letter from a Mr. Takeji Manabe of Berkeley. This gentleman had learned about Fuchida through the *Kirisuto Taishu Shimbun* (Christian People's News), a monthly printed in Japan and edited by Fuchida's pastor, the Reverend Saito. Manabe wrote that he wanted Fuchida to speak at the Layman Christian Church in Berkeley at some future date. He enclosed a newspaper clipping, an editorial from *Nichi Bei Jiji* (Japanese-American Times) of San Francisco. It breathed nervous fear lest Fuchida rock the boat: "Already eleven years have passed since Pearl Harbor and the relationship between Japan and the United States has progressed remarkably. But don't feel too easy! On Pearl Harbor Day each year in the United States the newspapers write 'Remember Pearl Harbor.'"

The editorial went on to say that evidently Fuchida's work in the United States was of a religious nature. But, after all, he had commanded the Pearl Harbor attack pilots. "Don't touch the old wound!" the writer begged. "Don't recall the old memory!" According to the editor, all Japanese-Americans in California feared Fuchida's coming. He closed by suggesting that the Japanese government be more careful in issuing passports to the United States.

Fuchida read this thoughtfully. His feelings as he approached the United States had been those of a new groom about to enter the stall of a powerful horse, uncertain whether the animal would greet him with a friendly whinny or a good swift kick. Now, after scarcely twenty-four hours in the country, he read this discouraging editorial.

The editor of *Nichi Bei Jiji* had not only written this piece for his own newspaper, he had sent it to Japan in his capacity as American correspondent for *Asahi*. The editorial received wide coverage in Japan and many Japanese wrote to Fuchida about it. Most of them urged him to return at once and accused the American people of being small-minded.[10]

Fuchida had no intention of turning tail and running, nor did he wish to prejudge the United States. Indeed, even as letters from Japan poured in, he made a friend for whom he had the highest respect and affection. After a few days at Sachs's home, Fuchida went to Hollywood to prepare a television program with the famous evangelist Billy Graham. Hearing of Fuchida's arrival in the United States, Graham had asked him to appear on his program "Hour of Decision," to be broadcast on 7 December 1952.

Fuchida took an instant liking to Graham, "a wonderful man, so sincere and encouraging." At this session they were preparing a tape for rerun, hence had no studio audience. Fuchida gave his testimony in Japanese with the

young Nisei pastor of the Evergreen Baptist Church, Reverend Eddie Hashimoto, as translator. Then Graham took over, citing Fuchida as an example
of how Christ can renovate an individual completely.

Fuchida listened in wide-eyed admiration. He himself needed the inter-
play between speaker and audience for his best efforts. Evidently Graham
required no such stimulus. "There was no audience, only the eye of the
camera. But oh how he preached, as though thousands stood before him! His
voice, his gestures, his energy—such power, such conviction! He really was
seeing people, although no people were there."

The warm sincerity of Graham's welcome helped cancel the impact of the
unpleasant editorial. "I was so encouraged and inspired from meeting him,"
Fuchida recounted, his eyes lighting up at the memory. "I took new heart."[11]

Fuchida's first major engagement was at the big Church of the Open
Door, in the heart of Los Angeles' business district. The audience, composed mainly of white Americans, filled every seat in the large auditorium.
Fuchida could not help wondering how they would receive him, but as he
rose he thought only of witnessing. He spoke in his native tongue, with
Hashimoto interpreting. When he finished, the people gave him a standing ovation. Someone began to sing a hymn, and the whole group took it
up. The force of so many voices spontaneously bursting into a song of
praise thrilled Fuchida. This is the token of God's blessing on me and my
work, he thought.

Sachs followed him on the platform and spoke for some thirty minutes
about the Sky Pilots. He explained that Fuchida would become head of the
organization in Japan and needed a helicopter to take him to the rural
districts. A small Hornet cost eight thousand dollars, he said. He asked that
the audience produce this sum on the spot.

Fuchida felt himself go hot all over. He wanted that aircraft badly but
would have preferred striking the financial note a little more subtly. If the
audience resented the appeal they didn't show it, however. They had already
taken up the usual collection; in response to Sach's plea they took up another
for the Sky Pilots.[12]

After the service, the pastor requested Fuchida to stand at the front door
with him and greet the congregation as they filed out. Hundreds shook his
hand with a kind word of thanks and congratulations. "Some even embraced
me and kissed my cheek," he said wonderingly. Among those who shook
hands was an elderly woman with a boy about eleven years old. She asked
Fuchida to accept an envelope from the boy. Smiling his thanks, he pock-
eted it.

When Fuchida and Sachs returned to their hotel, the latter sat down to
count the money from the collection. Fuchida opened the envelope the boy

had given him. Inside he found a check for $25, earmarked for the helicopter. With the check was a letter that told a sad and dramatic story.

The boy's father had been killed during the Pearl Harbor attack. His mother gave birth about a week later but lacked the strength and the will to recover from childbirth. The woman who had spoken to Fuchida so kindly was the grandmother. Her letter told Fuchida that she and her grandson prayed for him and his work. She was not rich, she wrote, but she wanted to contribute, so would Fuchida accept this check in her grandson's name. She added that she thanked God that Christ had entered the heart of the leader of the Pearl Harbor attackers.

Touched, Fuchida prayed silently for the old lady and her grandson. He offered thanks that the Church of the Open Door had received him so openly. Americans must be an open-hearted people with the capacity to forgive, he thought.[13]

Thus his first experience with a large American audience went off better than he had dared hope. He had imagined something like noncommittal courtesy interspersed with heckling and crank mail. He never expected anything like the outpouring of welcome he received at the Church of the Open Door. The day gave him confidence to face future engagements.

When Fuchida rose the next morning, he was troubled. In his heart he had criticized Sachs for his eagerness to take up a special collection, but hadn't he himself, come to the United States with his hand out, hoping to obtain a helicopter?

"My wonderful reception in Los Angeles so inspired and gratified me that I no longer thought in terms of a new helicopter," he recalled soberly. "I thought only of glorifying Christ, praising Him, and serving Him."[14]

He had ample opportunity to do so. All day Sachs's telephone rang with calls requesting that Fuchida appear in various churches in the Los Angeles area. By the time they turned in, Sachs had booked his guest solid for ten straight days. He bubbled about the prospects of their tour. "He saw in me the opportunity of developing his weak Sky Pilot organization and solving his most basic problem—money," said Fuchida realistically.

At one of these gatherings, Fuchida encountered someone else with Pearl Harbor ties. After he had given his testimony a woman rose and asked permission to testify also. She had lost her husband at Pearl Harbor and been almost consumed with hatred of everything Japanese. Now that had all changed. "Praise God," she cried, "for the attacker of Pearl Harbor has come to our country in the name of Christ! Now I can forgive all things in His name."[15]

Another notable incident occurred in Long Beach at a Youth for Christ rally held late in November. At church meetings Fuchida sat with the minister and other speakers on the platform. This time, however, the gathering met in a movie theater, and the director had arranged matters along theatrical lines. Fuchida was to wait in the wings until introduced.

As Fuchida waited for his cue an usher approached him with a folded piece of paper. On the outside was written, "To the Japanese Navy Captain, Pearl Harbor Attacker." Fuchida opened it casually. The message jumped out at him: "Go home, you murderer. You killed over three thousand boys without warning. Get out of this country."

He had just finished reading the note when the director of the rally came to usher him to the podium. Fuchida showed him the message, whereupon he strode back on stage alone. In a grim voice he told the audience about the note and read it. "One of you here in this audience wrote this note," he said. "Now I want to know whether this represents your will."

A vociferous roar of protest indicated that the majority didn't share the writer's sentiments. Gratified, the director started backstage to escort the guest. But at that very moment Fuchida appeared on stage on his own. As he did, the large audience applauded wildly, trying to make him feel doubly welcome—for his own sake, and to make up for the anonymous writer's violation of American hospitality.

After Fuchida testified with Hashimoto translating, Sachs explained the Sky Pilots and collected a large sum at the offering. "This made Sachs very happy," Fuchida commented. He was beginning to take notice of his host's preoccupation with the collection.[16]

After about ten days in the Los Angeles area, he and Sachs returned to San Jose. Using Sky Pilot headquarters as their base, they swung through Berkeley, Oakland, Richmond, and San Francisco. In this area they acquired a new translator, the Reverend Akira Aoki, a Nisei and pastor of a Japanese church in San Jose.

From Oakland, Fuchida and Sachs returned directly to San Jose. At 0300 the telephone rang. Sachs stumbled sleepily toward it. A medical doctor from Oakland was on the line. This man belonged to the Assembly of God and had heard Fuchida speak in his church. "I have just experienced a vision as I slept," he told Sachs. He didn't explain what form the vision took, but it inspired him to give Fuchida a grant of fifty dollars a month. Thenceforth for eighteen months, until the doctor's death, this contribution arrived regularly, a welcome supplement to Fuchida's scanty income.[17]

Fuchida sent Haruko what money he could, but financial conditions at home remained close to the bone. His wife coped with her usual ingenuity. For one thing, she made the children school clothes from her husband's old navy uniforms.[18]

The Sky Pilots' executive committee decided that Fuchida should be the chief Sky Pilot of Japan with the rank of brigadier general. Sachs, as commander for the United States and for the overall international organization, held the rank of four-star general. He explained that this was as high as the earthly echelon went; Jesus Christ, with five stars, was commander in chief. Fuchida remarked rather dryly, "I never saw Jesus in the picture as a five-star general in the Sky Pilots, although I often saw Sachs as a four-star general!"[19]

A high point in his American tour came at the First Baptist Church in San Francisco. This being a Sunday, he and Sachs went together ahead of Dr. Aoki, the translator, who would follow in his car after his own church service. Aoki hadn't appeared by the time the meeting started. The host minister opened the ceremony and the congregation of some four hundred sang a hymn. Still no Aoki. Fuchida grew nervous. How could an American congregation understand him without a translator? He surveyed the audience to see if he could spot a Japanese face, or even, rather wildly, anyone who looked as though he or she could translate Japanese into English. With the help of a dictionary he could read English, albeit with difficulty, and could manage a halting conversation. But to deliver a full-course address in English was something else again. What shall I do? he asked himself in dismay. If I speak in Japanese, they won't understand me and the evening will be wasted. So he gathered up his courage. He would try to speak in his broken English rather than disappoint the audience. He prayed fervently: "Dear God, give me the words I need to speak! Please endow me, your humble servant, with the gift of tongues as in the old days in the Pentecostal meetings described in the scriptures!" His petition finished, he whispered to the agitated Sachs, "Don't worry, I'll go ahead and talk English as best I can."

At that moment the minister introduced him. He waited for the cordial patter of applause to settle, then said, "This is my first English speaking. I have been United States one month only. I will try make you hear my message your language." As the audience realized what he was attempting to do, they broke into a round of clapping by way of encouragement and a vote of confidence.

Fuchida proceeded haltingly but with conviction. Often during his thirty-minute talk he had to grope for words. At the end, the congregation applauded heartily, more in sportsmanlike praise for his effort than for his actual testimony, of which they could have understood little.

Later he stood with the minister to greet his audience. Among those who shook his hand was a charming old lady with white hair and a sweet smile. "I could not understand your English," she confided, speaking slowly so that Fuchida might comprehend. "But I could well understand that you love the Lord Jesus Christ."[20]

31

"The Work of the Lord"

FROM CALIFORNIA, Fuchida and Sachs traveled up the west coast of Oregon, speaking everywhere to overflowing congregations. As he sat on the platform at Klamath Falls, waiting for the meeting to start, he began to look through one of the church bulletins. Since arriving in the United States he had been so busy that he'd lost track of time. The date on the bulletin came as a shock—3 December 1952. "Today is my fiftieth birthday," he whispered to Sachs.

As he waited, the highlights of his life passed before him. Isn't it a true wonder that I of all people should be spending the evening of my fiftieth birthday in a Christian church in the land of my former enemies? he asked himself. Truly, this is the work of the Lord. It can't be explained in any other way.

While he mused, Sachs must have spread the word. When Fuchida rose to speak the congregation jumped to its feet and sang "Happy Birthday."

After the service the pastor invited Fuchida and Sachs to his home, along with some prominent members of the congregation. Someone had hastily rounded up a large cake with fifty candles, and Fuchida found himself the center of an impromptu party. "Sometimes in Japan I celebrated my birthday, and sometimes it was forgotten," he said, smiling. "But these generous and kind American people celebrated for me as never in my life. We were a big family that night, as Christians should be. We were one body in Christ."[1]

His schedule in Oregon carried him to Salem, Jacob DeShazer's home-

246

town. His mother, Ms. H. P. Andrus, and other close relatives of DeShazer's came to the First Methodist Church to hear Fuchida. After the meeting they all got together. Naturally, Ms. Andrus enjoyed talking about her son to a man who admired him so much. She told Fuchida of a curious psychic experience. One night she awakened trembling from a terrible dream about being pulled down into a vast darkness. Later she discovered that at the very moment of her dream, her son was parachuting into China after the Doolittle Raid.[2]

In Portland Fuchida found an unexpected link with the past. On Saturday evening, 6 December 1952, he testified at a Youth for Christ rally held in one of the big high schools. Afterwards, as he sat on the stage, an usher brought him a note reading something like this: "I am sure you are the Captain Fuchida who befriended my mother and me in the Philippines during the war. My mother and stepfather often speak of your kindness and wonder what became of you. You used to call me the Little White Monkey."

Fuchida's mind flew back to that interlude in the midst of war. Eagerly he scanned the audience, but the years had changed his little friend from a child to a woman and he couldn't recognize her. Unfortunately her note didn't contain an address or telephone number, and his schedule was too tight for a thorough search. He rather expected her to come to see him after the service or to call at his hotel, but she didn't. Fuchida marveled that their paths, which had crossed so briefly in the Philippines, should have crossed again in Portland after so many years.[3]

A little flurry of disapproval appeared in the press before Fuchida's scheduled appearance in Spokane, Washington. Colonel Clarence A. Orndorff, retired commander of Spokane's 161st National Guard Infantry regiment, criticized the school board for allowing Fuchida to appear in the auditorium of the Lewis and Clark High School. "Sure, this man has repented and has become a Christian," he conceded. "But are we to glorify him by use of our public auditoriums, forgetting the miles and miles of white crosses at Pearl Harbor?"

Reverend William H. Schaffer of the First Brethren Church, who had arranged for the visit, reminded Colonel Orndorff that Fuchida had been under orders at Pearl Harbor, just like the Americans who dropped the atomic bombs on Hiroshima and Nagasaki. He added pointedly, "We pose as a Christian nation, but have we no sense of forgiveness for a repentant enemy?"[4]

From Spokane, Fuchida and Sachs went to the Bremerton Navy Yard to address a large gathering scheduled for 13 December under the direction of the local navy chaplain. About two thousand attended, mostly petty officers, enlisted men, and their wives and children. During a break in the program, almost at its close, a woman came forward with her eleven-year-old son. She asked the chaplain if he would permit her son to shake hands with Captain Fuchida in full view of the congregation. She wanted to explain why. The chaplain agreed, and the woman turned to the audience. This is the story she told:

Her husband had been a first lieutenant, a gunnery officer aboard the battleship *Arizona*. On the evening of Saturday, 6 December 1941, she lay in the navy hospital at Pearl Harbor expecting her child. Her husband was there when the Japanese attacked the next morning, and all personnel visiting the hospital had to hasten to their battle stations. So he raced back to the *Arizona*. Almost immediately thereafter, the battleship blew up. The labor room shook from the impact just as the baby uttered its first cry. The husband must have died at the very instant his son was born.

"Today," she finished, "in token of Christian brotherhood, I have brought my son to hear Captain Fuchida, and now I want them to shake hands."

This touching story and the woman's noble spirit moved Fuchida deeply. He clasped the sturdy little hand while the audience applauded in sympathy and approval.[5]

Fuchida and Sachs returned to San Jose for Christmas. In January 1953 they took to the road again, this time traveling through the South, then up the East Coast. The route took them through Arizona and New Mexico. From there they drove across Texas to San Antonio, then north to Fort Worth, Dallas, and Houston. As they chugged along mile after mile, Fuchida would ask, "Where are we now?" and Sachs would answer, "Still in Texas." Texas, Fuchida thought to himself, is a great empire in itself.

Texas stood out in his memory as the scene of his first direct contact with blacks. In particular he recalled the Sunday morning he spoke in an all-black Baptist church in Dallas to a congregation of four hundred. His first impression was of "warm and friendly" people. "Above all, they were beautiful singers. It was sing, sing, sing—wonderful deep voices. There was an adult choir and a children's choir, and they could all sing so beautifully."

They took up three collections that morning—first for their church, then for their missionary fund, and finally for the Sky Pilots. "Sachs never went to a church unless there would be a Sky Pilot offering," Fuchida recalled. "He was all business."

On this occasion, Fuchida was surprised to see people making their own change as the basket circulated. They gave what they could afford, without embarrassment and with no false pride or attempt to outdo anyone else.

After the service almost the entire congregation came up to shake Fuchida's hand. "Such good Christians, I loved them," said Fuchida.[6]

After this experience Fuchida had a warm spot in his heart for blacks.

Passing through the South, he became sensitized to the atmosphere of racial conflict. It seemed to him that the Civil War was still going on. Even in the Christian homes he visited as a guest, segregation was an inescapable fact of life.

Being neither white nor black, Fuchida could survey the problem without heat. He held two basic convictions: First, having the same Father, all men are brothers; second, all races should be equal before the law as they are before God. He believed that time was on the side of the blacks, remembering the experience of Japanese on the American West Coast. After a long history of exploitation and prejudice, they had come to be accepted almost everywhere.

He didn't think that interracial harmony would come easily. He had been a racist himself. For years he had accepted as axiomatic that the Japanese were a superior people destined to rule all Asia. It had taken a world war, stunning defeat, and religious conversion to knock racism out of him. So he knew the United States had a problem, but a problem that could be solved, granted time, patience, give and take, and a sense of Christian brotherhood.[7]

Fuchida's first American tour went so rapidly and covered so much territory that he had difficulty sorting out his recollections of the various places. In one eastern town, a police escort accompanied him everywhere. "It was just like the president and the Secret Service," he chuckled. "I didn't know why this was at first. And in the church where I spoke there were policemen everywhere—at the main entrance, at the side door, near the aisle and the pulpit." After the service, the minister told him the reason: Someone in the town had written him demanding that Fuchida's appearance be canceled; otherwise, the church would be blown up while he was speaking. The wouldbe assassin must have had second thoughts, for nothing untoward happened.[8]

Fuchida found New York spectacular and impressive, but a little of it went a long way with him. "New York is too big, too noisy, and too gloomy. I much prefer the quiet countryside to live in." In that city he had a brief meeting with General Doolittle. Fuchida would have relished the opportunity for a personal exchange, but the public nature of the encounter made this impossible. Sachs had arranged it to publicize his Sky Pilots and the news media were very much in evidence. Fuchida remembered how courteous and patient the general was with them. "Doolittle was a fine Christian," he said.[9]

In the Washington, D.C., area Fuchida stayed several days with Prange. During this visit he spoke at the University of Maryland, the Pentagon, the Navy Annex, and the U.S. Naval Academy. The authorities had arranged a room that could hold a few hundred midshipmen, but a good thousand showed up, so the meeting had to adjourn to larger quarters. This time the usual program was followed by a brisk question-and-answer period. Fuchida felt right at home with these navy audiences. He was pleased to discover that the navy's chief of chaplains had been in the carrier *Hornet* at the time of the Doolittle Raid.[10]

While Fuchida and Sachs toured the country hundreds of letters poured in, some addressed to the Sky Pilots or to Sachs, some to Fuchida. Many were gracefully written communications from well-educated people; others were semiliterate scrawls that Fuchida cherished all the more because the money their writers enclosed must have represented a real sacrifice.[11]

Some letters expressed hatred or resentment. These saddened Fuchida rather than angering or discouraging him. The one he most vividly recalled was addressed not to him but to Billy Graham. Graham told Fuchida that after their "Hour of Decision" television tape was broadcast from Hollywood on 7 December, 1952, he received a letter signed "A Mother Who Lost a Son at Pearl Harbor." As she watched the television show she had spit on the screen and cried out, "You beast! You rat!" But Fuchida's favorable letters outran the critical ones by a hundred to one.[12]

Back in California, he took the opportunity to fulfill a personal ambition unconnected with the Sky Pilots or his religious experience. He asked his associates if he might meet Fleet Admiral Nimitz. In Fuchida's opinion Nimitz, not MacArthur, was the real American genius of the Pacific war, and the admiral's impeccable conduct abord the *Missouri* had convinced Fuchida that Nimitz had a heart to match his brain.

Reverend Hiroshi Omi, pastor of the Free Methodist Church in Berkeley, telephoned the admiral to ask if he would see Fuchida. Nimitz told him by all means to bring Fuchida to his home. As the two drove down the admiral's street, Fuchida spotted Nimitz standing in his driveway looking around expectantly. He smiled a welcome and called out, "Here you are!"

He ushered his guests into the living room and gave Fuchida a comfortable chair near a window looking out on the Golden Gate. Ms. Nimitz was as friendly as her husband. A number of her paintings, some of them Japanese scenes, hung on the walls. Fuchida had dabbled in oils and could recognize good work when he saw it. They were so lovely they made him homesick.

Then the admiral showed them his pet project, an authentic Japanese rock garden of pines and strategically placed stones around a little pond. "He made it with his own hands," said Fuchida admiringly. "Lovely! Not big, but just like in Japan."[13]

After dinner they settled down for a long, leisurely exchange of wartime reminiscences. Nimitz asked Fuchida's advice on how to proceed with an action he had been considering. After the surrender, of the Combined Fleet staff had given up their swords to their American opposites. Accordingly,

Nimitz had received Admiral Soemu Toyoda's sword. With the war long over he wanted to restore the weapon to its original owner. He asked Fuchida if this would be the right thing to do, and if so, how he should go about it.

"This would be a most considerate gesture," Fuchida replied. "I suggest that you arrange to return the sword through our embassy in Washington." Here is a great American admiral, Fuchida thought. He is willing to give back Toyoda's sword. Only a big man would do this, a humble gentleman with a good heart. Shortly thereafter Nimitz returned Toyoda's sword, as Fuchida learned through the Japanese press. The action made a favorable impression on the Japanese people.[14]

Nimitz also asked Fuchida to translate a letter he had received from a little town near Fukuoka in Kyushu. It came from a group of schoolchildren, thanking him for restoring their church bell. Fuchida was sure there must be a story behind this, and Nimitz obliged with the details.

During a speaking tour of the United States shortly after the war, he addressed an audience at a certain university. This institution boasted a considerable collection of Japanese items, one of them a large chime bell, which Nimitz recognized as being of religious provenance. He told the university authorities that this item was not a legitimate war souvenir and should be returned.

Eventually they traced it to a church in the village of Zasahonokuma, a seaside suburb of Fukuoka. During the war the village children wanted a bell for their church, but the government had forbidden bell casting because of the scarcity of metal. A kind blacksmith told the youngsters, however, that if they collected enough scrap he would cast one. The children rounded up enough odds and ends of suitable metal. They were very proud of themselves and of their bell.

Then came the occupation, complete with souvenir-hunting GIs apt to "liberate" anything not nailed down and quite a bit that was. The bell was sent to the States. The people of Zasahonokuma gave it up as hopelessly lost. So all of them, especially the children, were grateful to have it restored so unexpectedly.[15]

One more visit remained to round out Fuchida's American experience, and that would be the acid test—Hawaii. In a newspaper photograph taken after landing in Honolulu early on 1 July 1953, he looked like a well-pleased baby elephant, all ears, nose, and happy smile.[16]

He was not as confident as he looked. Sachs, who with his wife accompanied Fuchida to Honolulu, had in mind the making of a movie about him and planned some Hawaiian scenes, among them a shot of Fuchida placing a wreath on the *Arizona*. Fuchida was not at all enthusiastic. It would look

artificial and self-conscious and could well give the impression of a hypocriti-
cal publicity hound. But Fuchida couldn't claim to be an expert on American
psychology and public opinion; presumably Sachs understood his countrymen. And so Fuchida went along with the plan.

His estimate of the situation turned out to be correct. A sounding out of
the plan in the Honolulu press revealed that such an act would be unpopular,
to put it mildly. After about two weeks Sachs officially withdrew the request,
much to Fuchida's relief.[17]

This action elicited general approval, expressed in divergent ways. The
anti-Fuchida camp was well represented by a letter to the editor of the
Honolulu *Star-Bulletin:* "It is gratifying to note our shrine at Pearl Harbor
will not be blemished. . . . It is mockery to our Christian way of life when
this convert, with blood of thousands shed in his greatest hour of triumph,
should now seek forgiveness. . . ." The same newspaper printed a well-
balanced editorial the same day that expressed Fuchida's own sentiments:

> The [Fuchida] visit, and the publicity given it, have roused some bitter
> resentment. To some . . . his visit to the United States and particularly to Hawaii,
> was an affront.
> The other point of view is that Fuchida personally was no more to blame for
> the attack on Pearl Harbor than the Japanese emperor. . . .
> True, Fuchida directed the great air raid on Oahu December 7, 1941. But
> he did so under orders. . . .
> These two points of view are irreconcilable—at this time. . . . So it is wise
> that the request . . . has been withdrawn.[18]

While this problem was being thrashed out, Fuchida participated in an
all-Japanese television program—another mistake in judgment, for it gave the
impression that he spoke as a Japanese to Japanese, instead of as a Christian
to all Hawaiians. Evidently, too, some people got the idea that in some
obscure way he was being honored for attacking Pearl Harbor. The studio
received many letters of protest.[19] Fuchida came in for a thorough panning
in the press. A representative letter appeared on 8 July:

> I would like to ask the owners . . . of KGMB-TV just what the purpose was
> of having, as a guest, the Japanese who led the attack on Pearl Harbor? . . .
> Perhaps the people on the Japanese program would like to bestow upon him
> the Congressional Medal of Honor? . . . In my opinion he took a very active part
> on [sic] a program of Mass-Murder.[20]

Fortunately for Fuchida, the virulence of such letters aroused the American sense of fair play. Many hurried into print to protest the protesters. One
writer cited the case of St. Paul. "No one today harbors any resentment

against Paul or has not forgiven him for his actions prior to becoming a Christian. Can't everyone do likewise for Mr. Fuchida?"[21]

None of the publicity, favorable or unfavorable, deterred Fuchida from his purpose of evangelizing in Hawaii, and he covered most of the main islands. The schedule was much too full. On Molokai, during a meeting with a Chinese group, he fainted from exhaustion. A Japanese doctor invited him to recuperate at Kona, on the "Big Island" of Hawaii. He stayed in that beautiful spot for two weeks, until once more able to take the road.

Fuchida could have done no better for his cause than to be stricken in the line of duty. When the press reported this, public opinion swung in his favor. Hawaiians of all national and racial extractions wrote letters wishing him good luck and a speedy recovery. These considerably lightened his convalescence and his morale. When he boarded the *President Cleveland* on 12 August to return to Japan, a friendly group came to the pier to wish him Godspeed.[22]

In one respect, Fuchida's trip to the United States had been a failure. He had come to find the means of buying a helicopter, and no aircraft had materialized. But very early recognizing that this desire was selfish, he had put it behind him.

In Japan, the Pocket Testament League had exploited him. This he accepted because it rose from an excess of zeal. He had cooperated gladly, knowing that their aims were identical, and he never lost his respect for his league associates. But Sachs had proved to be a different type; he wanted Fuchida, not to stimulate conversions, but to get the Sky Pilots off the ground. Once Fuchida had burst out, "It seems just like I'm a monkey. And you're the master with a trumpet to make the monkey play to bring in money. I don't like the Sky Pilots anymore. I'll be a monkey for Christ, but not for you and the Sky Pilots!"

Yet he would continue the association for several more years, believing that the idea behind the Sky Pilots was sound. The Boy Scouts stood as witness that boys enjoyed group activities, wearing a uniform, striving for ideals of social and moral excellence. Add to that the young people's enthusiasm for aviation—it seemed that the Sky Pilots was a sure winner. When Fuchida had reached the United States membership stood at around three hundred; when he left, it had risen to three thousand. No one could complain that he hadn't pulled his weight. Yet the organization would never realize its potential. Fuchida believed that Sachs lacked leadership, being so obsessed with finances.[23]

From a personal standpoint, Fuchida had profited by his tour. To a degree unusual for a foreigner, indeed for many Americans, he penetrated the culture below decks. Visiting mainly small cities and towns, he met the Americans who never made the headlines. He grew more tolerant and appreciative not only of Americans but of all Westerners. By the same token, in Fuchida hundreds of Americans met a real Japanese for the first time, and had direct experience of their common humanity. Thus in a small way he had contributed to better relations between two nations.

32

"Be with Me Today"

ALMOST IMMEDIATELY after Fuchida's return to Japan in early September 1953, invitations began to pile up. He never had to solicit speaking engagements; his problem was how to fit them all in.[1]

During September, he stuck close to home in Nara Prefecture, holding fifteen meetings with an estimated total attendance of five thousand. Soon he branched out. In October, traveling principally in Fukuoka and Shimane prefectures, he addressed thirty-three audiences and reached over twelve thousand listeners. Over the next three years he would travel all over Japan.[2]

It is possible that, caught up in the happy excitement of evangelism, Fuchida did not give his wife due credit for her sacrifice in behalf of his new career. Yoshiya believed that during his father's navy years, his preoccupation with a dream house was a great comfort to Haruko, because it seemed to promise a shared future of domestic contentment.[3] Instead, Fuchida's life changed direction rather than style. As a navy officer he had traveled far and wide for his emperor; now he traveled for Christ.

Newspapers covered his activities, and each speaking engagement led to another. Although he feared a breakdown such as he had experienced on Molokai, he turned down few requests, leaving his health in God's hands. He spoke in all sorts of institutions to anyone who wanted to hear him. He thought that the willingness of Shintoists and Buddhists to open their shrines and temples to him spoke well for their broadmindedness. He feared that few if any Christian churches would do the same.[4]

Soon he discovered that his triumph in the United States lessened his popularity in certain Japanese quarters. Those of his own generation enjoyed hearing him and flocked to his lectures. To them, he was still the Pearl Harbor leader who personified their hour of victory. But many of the younger set, in particular leftist university students, eyed him askance. They twisted his appreciation of the American people's hospitality into hopeless pro-Americanism. Fuchida found himself a somewhat controversial figure, although nothing could have been further from his mind than propagandizing for the United States or any other country.

He vividly recalled an occasion when he spoke at the University of Kyoto. Elated at securing a prominent speaker, the Bible class there advertised the meeting all over the campus—at that time Japan's number one communist academic stronghold. The result could have been expected. No sooner had he mounted the platform than he knew he couldn't deliver his prepared address. The local cell had turned out in full force, and no voice of authority rose to quell them. Hysterical shouts whizzed around him: "You are pro-American!" "You are a spy from the U.S. government!" "You are in favor of rearmament!" "We are against U.S. atomic bomb testing!"[5]

An assembly whipping itself into a frenzy is an ugly sight, but Fuchida felt neither fear nor anger. He looked into their faces with a mixture of impatience and compassion. It was difficult for him to understand what possible appeal communism could have for a Japanese; however, at the moment he faced a challenge to his leadership. He stepped to the edge of the platform and summoned his flight deck voice.

"Do the majority of the students assembled here wish to continue this meeting?" he roared. His voice cut through the clamor and a great calm ensued. "If you don't," he continued, "then the meeting should be dismissed. But if you want to hold it, then listen to me."[6]

The students indicated that they wished him to continue. Obviously, however, they were in no mood to hear a spiritual message. He gave up his prepared lecture and spoke in a calm, businesslike manner: "Very well, if you have questions I'll try to answer them. After that, I'll continue with my talk."

Questions rolled at him right and left. If they were callow, at least they were honest and deserved honest answers. One student asked, "Are you pro-American?" "I'm not pro-American and I'm not pro–Soviet Russia," Fuchida replied. "I'm a citizen of heaven. I'm pro-Christ, and my main topic today is my Christian work in the United States."

It was difficult for them to understand spiritual motives. Obsessed with politics, they could think in no other terms. "Is America imperialist?" they persisted. "Won't the United States use Japan as a catspaw?"

"The United States wants Japan to be in a position to protect herself," he said. "It's infinitely better to have U.S. forces in Japan than to have the Soviets here or to have the Japanese communists take over our country. If the communists controlled Japan, in all probability there would be two million young men under arms, and you would be among them."

He spoke of the unhappy condition of the nations under communist domination: "This is the worst kind of imperialism. You shout 'Youth should not shoulder a rifle' and you cry 'Yankee, go home!' Suppose the Yankees *do* go home! Suppose the United States withdraws its military forces from Japan before we're ready to protect ourselves? What would happen then?

"I'll tell you! The communists would take over. Soviet Russia would see to that. Red forces would conquer Japan, a Japanese communist government would rule from Tokyo. Once that puppet government came to power, Japan would become a communist armed camp. And you would serve in that camp! You who shout 'Don't shoulder a rifle' would shoulder a communist rifle because you would be forced to do so."[7]

As he spoke, the students quieted and listened with keen attention. They still asked questions, but in an entirely new spirit. A heckling mob had turned into a discussion session.

"How about the United States and the atomic tests in the Marshall islands?"

"I don't like atomic tests either," Fuchida responded. "But it is much better that the United States publicly announces to the world that it is carrying on these tests rather than conducting such tests in secret as Soviet Russia does."

The Soviet experiments were news to his audience. Some of them asked in shocked dismay, "Is what you are telling us about Soviet Russia true?"

"Yes, it is true," he answered, "and some day you will know the whole truth."

"What do you think of the use of the atomic bomb against Hiroshima and Nagasaki?"

"Those bombs were used in wartime," Fuchida pointed out. "War is always unfortunate and evil, but once it breaks out the only way to fight it is all-out. That's how both Japan and the United States fought." Now, he emphasized, the war was over, and peace could not come "from an attitude and in an atmosphere of resentment and hatred. In time these things will only bring down other atomic bombs."

"What about the American occupation of Okinawa?"

"Yes, the United States now occupies Okinawa. But have you ever thought about the Soviet record? Do you know what Soviet Russia did to Japan?

"In the first place, Russia broke its treaty with Japan. At the very end of the war Soviet forces attacked our forces in Manchuria. Then they took over all of Sakhalin Island and the Kuriles. They occupy them still. What is more, the Soviet Union captured about two million Japanese in Manchuria and today, after almost ten years of peace, has returned a mere handful. What do you students think of these facts?"

Then Fuchida's contempt swelled. "The truth of the matter is," he thundered, "Soviet Russia was the thief at the fire!"[8]

That expression had a special meaning for Japanese. Their buildings were made of inflammable materials and fire had always been a dreaded catastrophe. Recovery was possible only by mutual assistance and protection. To the Japanese, a looter at a fire who enriched himself at the expense of his suffering neighbors was the lowest of the low. Fuchida had dared to stand before a leftist audience and apply to the communist homeland the ultimate epithet of disgust.

Instinctively, he felt that the moment had come to give them his real message. "You cry 'peace, peace'! But is peace actually in your hearts? You can never have peace while your hearts are full of bitterness, hatred, and revenge. You can only have peace through the spirit of Christ and through forgiveness."

He stressed what Pearl Harbor had meant to Americans, yet he, the Pearl Harbor raider, had been "received in a spirit of forgiveness, in a spirit of Christ Himself." Then he told the students about some of those who had been kind to him even though they had lost loved ones at Pearl Harbor. The young men listened intently until he finished, then gave him a good round of applause. A number of them pushed forward to shake his hand. Students and lecturer had reached a point of mutual respect. They gave Fuchida credit for sincerity and courage, while he recognized that they were not hard-core communists who would knowingly sell out their own country to Moscow. In their muddled way they, too, wanted a Japan of peace and prosperity.

Finally the president of Kyoto University emerged from his inconspicuous spot in the rear and came forward with congratulations. "I have never heard such a brave address," he told Fuchida. And he added a bit wistfully, "You controlled the students so wonderfully!"

"I'm accustomed to high-spirited young men," Fuchida replied, smiling. "At one time I was the Pearl Harbor commander and today I am a soldier of Christ. He has never failed me, and I will try never to fail Him."[9]

Fuchida spoke at many universities. Almost invariably he ran into the same initial hostility, although never again so violent. The meetings fell into a pattern as predictable as an old-time western. A large group of leftist students always attended, apparently with the purpose of heckling Fuchida as a "tool of American capitalism." Knowing that any attempt to talk to them along strictly religious lines would be futile, he spoke to them, as at Kyoto, in a political context.[10]

In Kyoto Fuchida had his first encounter with another, very different audience—convicts imprisoned for nonviolent crimes. Here were thieves, embezzlers, pickpockets, burglars, forgers, confidence men, the whole dismal roll call of man's attempt to secure a livelihood without putting himself to the trouble of working. The city's chief of police had asked Fuchida to address these men. He invited various religious speakers from time to time, and a certain number of convicts always turned out, if only to seize the chance for a break in the deadly boredom of their daily routine.

To the surprise of many, a large audience gathered to hear Fuchida. They took nearly thirty minutes settling into their seats, for they shuffled along with a dispirited gait. Always sensitive to atmosphere, Fuchida sensed unwholesomeness, a mental, physical, and spiritual desert that he could find no adequate words to express. Never before had he faced such an assortment of human flotsam. Somehow he would have to establish a rapport. About all he had in common with them was manhood and nationality.

Fuchida decided to talk about his part in the Pearl Harbor operation, spiced with incidents to arouse or amuse them. Gradually he worked up to the story of his conversion. After finishing he felt that they had received his talk well, but he had no way of proving it because applause was prohibited. He sensed in these men a latent hunger for spiritual food, which had to be served in the right way. They had listened with respect to him; they probably wouldn't have done so with the average priest or minister.[11]

Fuchida's next major prison engagement was in the summer of 1955, when he toured northern Honshu and crossed over to Hokkaido. There he spoke in a number of the island's forty-odd Christian churches. At Abashiri, a town situated in the bleak northeastern part of the island, an American missionary working in the local prison arranged for him to speak to his flock.

Fuchida had seldom seen so gloomy a place. It housed only the most hardened cases. The men, with long records of rioting and jailbreaking, were under heavy guard. Indeed, the prison director permitted only about a hundred to hear Fuchida at one time, fearing larger gatherings. Observing his rough-looking audience Fuchida could understand this reluctance. He gave the men much the same talk as at Kyoto. Once more, he had no way of judging his success or failure. Not until three years later did he learn that on that day at least one man took his first step toward Christ.[12]

In the big prison at Fukuoka in northern Kyushu, an assembly of several hundred gathered to hear the same sort of talk with the same result or lack of visible result. Shortly thereafter, someone in the town of Fukuoka mentioned to Fuchida that the prison housed about twenty convicted murderers who hadn't been permitted to attend the lecture because they were kept in isolation. Immediately Fuchida determined to visit them. One of the local pastors made the necessary arrangements. Fuchida spoke to these doomed men for an hour. This was no occasion for war stories or his personal experiences. He went straight to the point, recounting everything he could recall to illustrate Jesus's concern for sinners, His compassion for the unfortunate. He stressed how He had died for them, crucified between two thieves, and how he had promised the good thief who acknowledged him as Lord, "Today shalt thou be with me in paradise [Luke 23:39–43]."

These men soaked up every word of Fuchida's message. On the spot, every one accepted Christ as his savior and, kneeling, asked His pardon for their sins. Then they banded themselves together in the Calvary Club, for mutual help and consolation.

Later Fuchida received word from the prison director of how these men went to their deaths. "Before, the guards had to drag condemned men to the gallows," he wrote. "But the members of the Calvary Club walked to the gallows like men, upright and straight, praying every step of the way, 'Christ, be with me today in paradise!' "[13]

33

"Preparing the Soil"

URING the mid-1950s Fuchida found many Japanese ambivalent about Christianity. They liked its teachings of love, virtue, and forgiveness, but disliked the insistence that salvation was only possible through Christ. And many missionaries plunged immediately into the gospel without preparing the way. This Fuchida saw as a spiritual and social error.

"When I became a farmer," he explained, "my primary concern was the improvement of the soil so that I would not sow seeds in vain." Accordingly, in his evangelism, he started with subjects that would interest his audiences and concepts that would attract them, slowly and gently working Jesus into the picture. "I am preparing the soil for a later planting, for seeds, no matter how rich, will not grow on barren soil."

Its intolerance was another strike against Christianity. Believing theirs to be the only true religion, Christians made no attempt at a *modus vivendi* with any other. Fuchida wholeheartedly believed that Christianity was the only truth and must not be compromised; however, he also believed that in Japan it would profit by a more cordial relationship with the old, established religions. Such give and take would show Buddhists and Shintoists that Christians were still good Japanese. Openness might well lead to conversions. Fuchida had no doubt that Christ's teachings would win in an unprejudiced comparison with either Buddhism or Shinto.[1]

Since his return from the United States, the evangelist campaigns had been quite successful. At the end of 1955 he added up the score: at over six hundred meetings during which he had spoken to almost two hundred thousand people, slightly under three thousand had converted. Not inclined to count chickens in their shells, before he listed anyone as a convert he waited to hear that a church had issued a certification of baptism. As of the end of December 1955, he received 568 such notifications.

One of his more fruitful campaigns was in Fukuoka, which he had visited in October 1953 and again in February 1954. The pastor of one church in that city wrote Fuchida that his usual Sunday attendance had been no more than fifty, but since Fuchida's talks a congregation of over two hundred had filled his church to capacity.

After he spoke at a rally in Okayama, one of the local pastors later informed him that on the next Sunday sixty new attendees came to his services. All of them were baptized at Pentecost.[2]

Obviously Fuchida was effective as a lay missionary. The Sky Pilot drive, however, gave him his comeuppance. No matter how hard he worked, it wouldn't take root. He envisioned the organization as a leavening element in Japan, which he saw as threatened on the left by communists and on the right by a possible resurgence of imperialism. An organization of half a million boys learning Christian principles could help Japan maintain its balance. He was sure that the project was feasible, granted the necessary funds. A friend of his, a retired rear admiral, had succeeded in recruiting half a million boys into the Sea Scouts.

Cultural and financial factors hindered the Sky Pilots in Japan. Fuchida was aware of these circumstances, but either underestimated them or believed he could overcome them. The average Japanese parents of that day would be no more inclined to permit their sons to sign up for the Sky Pilots than the average Americans would be to allow their children to join a Shinto organization. Moreover, the Japanese wouldn't support any movement with a military flavor. Nor could Japan's tiny Christian community support the Sky Pilots financially.

When 1955 passed without Fuchida's having established a single squadron, Sky Pilot headquarters discontinued the fifty dollars a month they had been sending him as chief Sky Pilot of Japan. He couldn't blame them; nevertheless, the loss was a severe financial blow.[3]

Added to these problems was a serious personal worry. Yoshiya had been attending Waseda University in Tokyo, where he lived alone in a rented room. In 1954, at the age of twenty-one, he contracted tuberculosis. Hemmorhaging rapidly, he came perilously close to death.

Yoshiya's hospital was the National Nara Sanitarium in Nara City, a forty-minute train ride from Kashiwara. There, supported by the loving prayers of family, friends, and congregation, he put up a tremendous fight.

Gradually his wiry strength won back his protesting lungs. After he had been hospitalized for almost seven months, the doctors discharged him with a clean bill of health. They recommended, however, that he recuperate for two years before returning to college. So he remained at home throughout 1955 and 1956.

Yoshiya had joined the church in high school but had maintained a pessimistic attitude toward life. Now, as he realized that death had passed him by, he became convinced that, just as God had spared his father for a particular mission, so He had saved him. Yoshiya developed a fundamental optimism and planned to express his faith through architecture.[4]

In August 1954, while Yoshiya was in the hospital, Fuchida spoke at a number of places on Kyushu, among them Sasebo, where he had served so long ago on the naval base. In the middle of the city, the Catholic church still stood. With mingled remorse and amusement, Fuchida remembered how at one time he would cheerfully have taken a pickax to that building as a potential spy nest. The church had endured, while the naval headquarters had disappeared along with the entire Imperial Japanese Navy.

At the site of the old headquarters building, the U.S. Navy had erected a Protestant chapel. Into this modest edifice Fuchida walked one hot August evening to address an audience of over a hundred U.S. servicemen. He told them about his conversion and about his reaction to seeing the Catholic church again, which amused his listeners. But in the main, Fuchida's mood was serious. "If Jesus had come to Sasebo in 1938 when I was stationed here as a naval officer, and if He had spoken in the Catholic church, no doubt I would have been among those who hated and jeered Him. I might have been chosen to head a squad to arrest Jesus as a dangerous agitator. And in prison He might have been beaten and put to death all over again."[5]

With Fuchida on the road so much and Yoshiya in the hospital, Haruko held down the farm alone during the daytime. Miyako was attending Yasuko Uedo fashion school in Osaka as a day student. Fuchida didn't fear for his wife's safety because, as he wrote, she had "a big shepherd dog as her physical escort as well as her spiritual escort of the Good Shepherd."

At the end of 1955 a mysterious illness laid Fuchida low, probably brought on by physical exhaustion. It wasn't dangerous, but it kept him confined to bed and somehow affected his vocal chords. He could hardly speak. He managed to do some research and writing, among his publications a booklet about Billy Graham. Drawing on his friendship with Graham and material gleaned from American magazines and newspapers, he finished a seventy-page brochure, "Billy Graham, Great Evangelist of Our Day," with some thirty illustrations. As a result, the Graham crusade committee made Fuchida one of their publicity chiefs.[6]

In 1956 Fuchida returned to the United States to preach to Japanese-Americans and seek their support for the "Japan for Christ" crusade. His friend and pastor, Reverend Toshio Saito, was president of this organization, Reverend Totsuma Hiramatsu vice president.

In two respects, this trip differed from his first tour of the United States. Instead of traveling economically in a Danish freighter, he flew Japan Air Lines. And this time he didn't feel uncertain and fearful. "It was like coming back to my second home," he remarked.

Although his swing through the United States was a long one, it was largely routine. He gave many interviews to newspaper reporters. They no longer looked upon him as a novelty, nor did he now find the United States strange and exotic.

He had an amusing little adventure in Spokane.[7] On a certain evening in September 1956 he spoke at an American church in that city. His hotel being only a few blocks away, he walked back, enjoying the brisk early autumn air. As he made his way along the street he noticed two men, one tall and thin, the other short and fat, emerging from a bar near the hotel. They were obviously laborers, clad in working clothes, their faces worn by outdoor exposure. They looked hard-bitten, and while by no means too drunk to navigate, they were having difficulty holding a straight course.

A street lamp illuminated the area directly in front of the bar, and Fuchida walked into this spotlight. The tall man cast a piercing glance at him. "Aren't you Captain Fuchida?" he called out.

"Yes, I'm Captain Fuchida."

At this exchange, the fat man asked his friend, "Hey, do you know this guy?"

"Haven't you seen Captain Fuchida's picture posted on every street?"

"No, I ain't seen it. Who is he?"

His companion thrust a long bony finger under Fuchida's nose and proclaimed, "He's the man who attacked Pearl Harbor."

Whereupon the short one asked the sixty-four-dollar question: "What's Pearl Harbor?"

Fuchida was astounded. In all his travels through the United States, he hadn't encountered a soul to whom that name meant nothing. Everyone remembered it as though it had happened yesterday, and most could recall exactly where they were and what they were doing when Pearl Harbor was attacked. Yet here stood an adult American who had never heard of Pearl Harbor!

This would have been a timely moment for Fuchida to fade into the shadows. But curiosity kept him rooted to the spot. The tall laborer, evidently the moving spirit of the duo, was as flabbergasted as Fuchida at his friend's ignorance. "You don't know about Pearl Harbor?" he inquired. Then, with elaborate sarcasm, "Well, you know about World War II, don't you?"

The fat man acknowledged that he had indeed heard of the war.

"Well," continued his companion, "you know that wars begin one way or another, and the war against Japan began when Captain Fuchida here attacked Pearl Harbor. That started the whole works in the Pacific."

"The hell it did!" exclaimed the short man. "Why, the damn bastard!" Then he rounded on Fuchida and bellowed, "Why in the hell did you bomb Pearl Harbor?" He underlined the query with a ferocious scowl and doubled fists.

Fuchida glanced around. The three men were alone. Seldom had he felt so inadequate. His English wasn't fluent enough to explain why he had attacked Pearl Harbor, especially to a belligerent working man who had been drinking. And even if he had spoken with the tongues of men and angels, this was no moment for a well-reasoned lecture on Japanese-American diplomatic relations.

Fuchida was no physical coward, but two-to-one odds, outreached on one hand and outweighed on the other, didn't appeal to him, particularly as his Christian ethic instructed him to turn the other cheek. Moreover, as a guest in the United States he wanted no unfavorable publicity.

It looked as if the fat man would pounce on him and beat him up. But evidently the other one resented his satellite's seizure of the initiative. "You can't blame him," he said. "He's not responsible. He just carried out orders and did his duty."

"He did, did he?"

"Yes, he did. You know what Captain Fuchida is doing now?"

"No, what's he doing?"

"He is preaching the gospel here in Spokane. He's now a Christian minister."

"Well, I'll be damned!" exclaimed the fat man cordially. "What do you know about that!" His whole attitude turned to one of friendliness, much to Fuchida's relief. "Dear Captain," he beamed, with the overblown courtesy that comes from a bottle, "I didn't realize! Please excuse me!"

"It's okay," Fuchida smiled. His potential opponent shook his hand with a warm "God bless you," and the two faded into the night.

Fuchida told this story with great relish to Japanese friends and in churches throughout his tour as an example of how deeply rooted the Christian tradition is in the United States.[8]

The tour took Fuchida principally to cities with large Japanese-American populations. From California he journeyed up the coast to Portland, Tacoma, and Seattle, thence to Idaho. Quite a few Buddhists as well as Christians came to his talks. For the most part, the Buddhist temples graciously allowed their members to hear Fuchida's testimony. A few were reluctant to expose their charges to his influence. From Idaho he moved through Denver to Chicago, New York, and Philadelphia. Then he swung back west by the southern route through Texas.[9]

While Fuchida traveled and testified, in Kashiwara his son convalesced. By the spring of 1957 Yoshiya felt well enough to continue his studies. Although physically able to return to Waseda University, he didn't believe this would be practical. Instead, in May 1957 he wrote to his father asking permission to study architecture in the United States. He mentioned wistfully that his classmates had all graduated and already found jobs in leading Japanese corporations. He could never catch up with them by picking up where he had left off in Japan. But he was sure he could succeed if given the chance to study in the United States.[10]

Yoshiya wasn't exaggerating his disadvantage. The academic-social-corporate system of which he wrote placed heavy pressure on young Japanese. A frightening number committed suicide when something happened to break the continuity of their program. The whole family agreed that it would be best for Yoshiya to complete his college years in the United States.

Accordingly, Fuchida wrote to his son to come immediately. Then he hustled about finding a sponsor for him. At that time, anyone entering the United States from Japan, even as a tourist, needed a letter of invitation with an affidavit guaranteeing travel and living expenses. Three months elapsed before Yoshiya finally received a six-month visitor's visa. While waiting, he and Miyako attended a class in conversational English three evenings a week at a branch of the YMCA in Osaka. Yoshiya soon dropped out, believing that he wasn't learning enough to justify attendance. He tried to study English on his own, but without much success.[11]

He turned twenty-four on 27 September 1957, and that evening his mother, sister, various relatives, and close friends gave him a combined birthday and farewell party. Two days later he left the family home. Standing straight and serious before Haruko, he said, "Goodbye, Mother, I'll be back if I succeed." Haruko smiled sadly and replied, "Come back as soon as possible, regardless of success." Yoshiya himself knew that he would never return permanently.

He was scheduled to arrive at San Francisco International Airport via Japan Air Lines the morning of 30 September. At the last minute Fuchida decided to fly from Texas to meet him, and reached San Francisco about an hour before his son's plane was due. Yoshiya's face lit up with "great surprise and joy" when he spotted his father. He had been nervous, tired from the thirty-hour flight, and, as he wrote later, worried about all the affairs he would have to handle himself after arriving.

Fuchida gave Yoshiya a guided tour of downtown San Francisco, then treated him to lunch at a good American restaurant. Finally, he took him to a department store and bought him a whole new outfit. "No more 'Made in Japan'!" Fuchida grinned. "Now you are completely American!"

Fuchida had no idea how truly he spoke. Privately Yoshiya had decided to sink his roots in this new soil. For the spring semester of 1958, he attended the University of Colorado at Denver as a special student. That summer, he worked in a Congregational summer camp near Colorado Springs. Then in the fall of that year he entered Pueblo Junior College[12] as a freshman, majoring in pre-architecture.

As if to signal his Americanization Yoshiya took a new name, behind which lies a story. After his baptism, while still in high school, he began reading the Bible. When he reached the Second Book of Chronicles he was surprised to find the name Josiah. Yoshiya is the Japanese phonetic spelling of that name. Delighted with the coincidence, Fuchida often quoted affectionately, "And he [Josiah] did that which was right in the sight of the Lord, and walked in the ways of David his father, and declined neither to the right hand, nor to the left [2 Chronicles 34:2]." When Yoshiya reached the United States, he adopted Joe as his nickname. He came to like it so much that eventually he took it as his legal first name.[13]

To return to Joe's first day in the United States, Fuchida saw that his son was settled with a Japanese family in Berkeley for the remainder of 1957. The next day he returned to Texas to continue his evangelical campaign.[14]

34

"What a Big Difference!"

BY THE END of Fuchida's American tour he had collected about three thousand dollars for his Japanese organization. For the small Japanese and Nisei congregations in the United States, most of whom were in modest circumstances, the money represented a real sacrifice of which Fuchida was proud. His mission completed, he returned to Japan by way of Honolulu. He looked forward to landing there with no such happy anticipation as he had experienced in coming back to the mainland, for his previous visit to the islands had been uncomfortable. He tried to banish the memory and composed himself for sleep. A violent pitching of the aircraft awakened him at about 0230. Vicious gusts of wind buffeted the plane and lightning flashes lit up the cabin. The plane dropped sickeningly, one hundred to two hundred feet at a time, then struggled gallantly upward, only to plummet again. Not in all his years of flying had Fuchida encountered such rough weather. He wondered whether the Pan-American aircraft could stand the stresses.

If an experienced combat pilot was alarmed, one can imagine the panic of the other passengers. Soon airsickness added its distress to the picture. One after another passenger succumbed, as did the three seasoned stewardesses. Fuchida seemed to be the only person impervious. Years of flying in a tiny craft had given him a cast-iron stomach.

He shed his coat, rolled up his sleeves, and pitched in. He disposed of full paper containers and brought clean ones, carried fresh water to rinse sour mouths, kept clean napkins in circulation. The pilot had his plane under control, he assured each passenger—and hoped it was true. He couched his comments in technical terms and delivered them with a knowledgeable air. The travelers decided this Japanese knew what he was talking about and relaxed a bit. The purser followed him around as they staggered down the aisle, helping Fuchida as best he could.

The pilot fought his craft through the storm. Mercifully, it touched down on the runway at Honolulu at about 0700. Fuchida emerged tentatively into a barrage from news cameras as a friendly pack of reporters in full cry closed in on him. Some crew member had radioed ahead to tell of Fuchida's efforts aboard the aircraft. In addition to the Japanese pastors who came to greet him, a fair-sized crowd clustered around to wish him well.

Not knowing who Fuchida was, his fellow passengers wondered why he rated so much attention. When they discovered that their airborne Good Samaritan was the Pearl Harbor raider, now a Christian evangelist, many wanted to be introduced and thank him individually. This cordial welcome to Hawaii relieved and gratified him.[1]

He stayed in the archipelago for a month, visited the main islands, and preached many times. On this swing around the territory he made no controversial moves and therefore aroused no expressions of resentment.

A high-ranking officer of the U.S. Pacific Fleet invited him to dinner in a restaurant situated on a hilltop with a fine view of Pearl Harbor. He also invited several of his navy cronies, active and retired, to meet Fuchida. Thus he sat down to dinner with six American flag officers.

When they had finished their meal the host rose. "This would be an excellent time," he said, "for each of us to deliver a one-minute speech on the subject of where we were and what we were doing at 0800 hours on December 7, 1941. Captain Fuchida, will you start the ball rolling?"

Fuchida announced that in that hour he was leading the Japanese attack over Pearl Harbor. One by one each admiral followed to give a quick flashback. What a big difference from 1941! Fuchida thought. Warmed by good food and drink, surrounded by the soft beauty of the Hawaiian night, swapping yarns with fellow sailors in the age-old comradeship of the sea, Fuchida knew that this would live in his memory as one of the happiest evenings in his life.[2]

With a heart full of warm memories and a neck covered in fragrant leis, Fuchida boarded ship for Yokohama. At home he was back in the full swing of evangelism. A rally in Kobe was particularly noteworthy. Gazing out over the audience in the Sannomiya auditorium, Fuchida was sure that this meeting would be special. The building was generally used for professional wrestling matches. In the last year or so American-style wrestling, such a contrast to the ritualistic *sumo* variety, had become popular. So the auditorium did not come cheap. The offering that night canceled out the advertising expense; only a few dollars were left over.

This rally marked the first time that all of the twenty-three Christian churches in Kobe cooperated for a common purpose. Of the two thousand present, five hundred elected to receive Christ, a remarkable percentage.[3] For Fuchida it was an uplifting experience. It also led to an unexpected encounter. A week or so after the meeting, he received a letter from Kofu City in Yamanashi Prefecture. "Thirty years ago I served aboard the *Ryujo*," the missive began. "I was a sailor second class, and I was your 'boy.'" Fuchida glanced at the signature, Yasuji Saito [a pseudonym]. He remembered him well—excellent at his job, loyal to his friends and officers, but off duty a heavy drinker always in some sort of scrape.

His letter outlined his life since their last meeting, and it made for a depressing tale. His troubles began one day in Osaka when he had been scheduled to board a ship bound for Sasebo. Having spent the night carousing, he overslept and missed his ship. According to Japanese naval law, Saito could be jailed for this offense. He so feared this fate that he lost his head and went AWOL. The navy soon tracked him down and sent him to prison for five years.

After release, his life became one long series of mistakes. He went to jail seven times for various minor offenses. He emerged from the seventh term over fifty years of age, single, without a relative or friend, and as he put it, "at the end of the world."

Saito decided to commit suicide. And he would make a production of it, for something in him revolted at the idea of a death as petty and futile as his life had been. He would go to Kobe, take a ship to Shikoku, and somewhere between the two points throw himself overboard—the farther from shore the better, so no one would ever find his body.

As he stepped off the train in Kobe the first thing he saw was a big sign announcing Fuchida's appearance at the auditorium. Having some time to kill before his ship sailed, Saito decided to go hear him. At the auditorium entrance someone handed him a copy of Fuchida's pamphlet, "From Pearl Harbor to Golgotha," which he slipped into his pocket. The speakers made little impression on him, wrapped as he was in his gloomy thoughts. He hesitated to seek out Fuchida after the meeting, fearing that to recall himself to his former officer would only embarrass both of them.

Saito caught his ship, which sailed that evening on the Inland Sea, and settled down for his last night's sleep on earth. The next morning, lounging in a deck chair and wondering what to do with himself until nightfall, he remembered the pamphlet and read it.

In it Fuchida emphasized that no one had sunk so low as to be beyond the reach of Christ's mercy. Saito knew nothing about Jesus, but he did know Mitsuo Fuchida. With the trust of a good sailor for a straight-shooting officer, he believed quite simply that if Fuchida wrote that Christ wanted to rescue sinners, then it must be so. The more Saito thought the matter over, the less the idea of suicide appealed to him. Here was at least an outside chance to make a clean breast of his dreary little sins and start life anew.

Accordingly, when he landed at Muroto Harbor on Shikoku he went straight to Kochi City. There he gave himself up to the police. They promptly escorted him back to Kofu where he was wanted for forgery. Languishing in prison awaiting trial, Saito wrote to Fuchida. He made only one request—he would like to have a Bible, and Fuchida was the only person he knew to whom he could appeal for one.[4]

Fuchida reread Saito's letter carefully. What a piteous waste! The productive years from twenty to fifty gone with nothing to show for them but a police file! Yet the prospect appeared by no means hopeless. In Saito's record one could find weakness, immaturity, and lack of self-respect, but not violence, malice, or meanness. He didn't rail against fate or blame society for his woes. Then on that voyage to Shikoku he had begun to grow up.

Fuchida picked up a Bible and set off. When he walked into the cell at the Kofu jail Saito beamed with astonished delight. Obviously the years had been unkind to him; his face told its story of struggle and misery. He handed Saito the Bible and asked him what had happened.

"I committed forgery to get thirty thousand yen I needed," he admitted. He made his confession baldly, neither evading the unpleasant truth nor wallowing in self-pitying excuses. Fuchida went to the police office, paid the thirty thousand yen, and asked that the charges be dropped against Saito. About a month and several miles of red tape later, they cleared the record and released Fuchida's old friend.[5]

He kept in touch with Saito, who had problems adjusting to an honest way of life. At one time he fell ill and wrote to Fuchida from a hospital for the indigent in Tokyo. Fuchida felt responsible for the man but realized that a constant diet of handouts would never solve his problem.

And so Fuchida decided on a course of action. He told Saito's story during a sermon delivered at the Fugimicho Church in central Tokyo. One of the largest Protestant churches in Tokyo and a favorite with Fuchida, Fugimicho had an intelligent, cultured congregation from the upper strata of Tokyo society.

After listening to the story of Saito the congregation offered him the position of church custodian. The work helped to build his self-respect, and there was enough of it to keep him out of mischief. In time he established the habit of honest labor and followed a Christian life.[6]

In 1958 Fuchida had another happy experience. A Mr. Sakuramachi invited him to preach at the Holiness Church, located in the Fukushima slum district of Osaka. "I have a special reason for wanting you to talk to my parishioners, Captain Fuchida," he said. "You may remember that one day a few years ago you addressed an audience of convicts at Abashiri Prison." Fuchida did remember the occasion, and how discouraged he had been by the lack of response in that repository of hard cases. "I was one of those convicts," Sakuramachi continued. "Your talk impressed me very much. When I finished my sentence I investigated Christianity and in time converted. So here I am now, a preacher with a church of my own in the Osaka slums."

This example of an ex-convict ministering to the underprivileged was a salutary reminder to Fuchida not to become discouraged by an unresponsive audience. Evidently some conversions required a long, slow growth.[7]

On 15 January 1959 when he returned to the United States, flying into Denver.[8] Elmer Sachs met him there. Apparently Sachs expected Fuchida to encounter some hostility in the United States but not because of his role as the former enemy.

"Our biggest problem is convincing people of Captain Fuchida's sincerity," Sachs told the press. "He turned down the position of chief of staff of the newly revived Japanese air force in 1952 and in 1957 refused the high position of minister of defense. Does this sound like an opportunist who is preaching Christianity for his material gain?"[9]

Sachs whisked his guest off to his home in nearby Aurora, Fuchida's new base of American operations. Sachs, full of grandiose plans, assigned Fuchida no less a task than founding a Sky Pilot academy to train chaplains for all the armed services. This institution he hoped to found in the Denver area, not too far from the U.S. Air Force Academy at Colorado Springs. He also wanted Fuchida to head a drive to raise sixty thousand dollars for a color movie, "From Pearl Harbor to Calvary," telling the story of Fuchida's conversion.[10]

One can understand the doubt that had arisen about Fuchida's sincerity. Phony evangelists have been known to appear where the pickings are good.

What was more troublesome about Fuchida's third American tour was the number of questionable statements, misconceptions, and downright falsehoods about him that appeared in the press. Whether these were reportorial embroidery, misunderstanding of Fuchida's broken English, or plain mistakes is difficult to determine. Among the dubious items was the statement that Fuchida was offered and turned down the positions of chief of staff of the Self-Defense Air Force and of minister of defense. This appeared in a Sky Pilot press release that many newspapers picked up.[11] Certainly Fuchida's record made him a logical candidate for chief of staff, but it is doubtful that he would have been considered for minister of defense.

Less easy to swallow were false statements attributed to Fuchida: at Midway he was "hurled into the sea"; of the Pearl Harbor attack force, only he and twenty enlisted men were still alive in 1959; and before Midway he "was shot down six times." He was also quoted as saying, "I was directed by our war college to organize my Pearl Harbor attack squadron in January 1941. We trained for the raid from that time until the actual attack."[12] A later article observed, "He knew of the attack from August 26, 1941 . . . ," which is much closer to the truth.[13]

His circuit took him through the Rocky Mountain states, Arizona, and the West Coast. During the summer Joe joined him to assist in his evangelical campaign in Idaho, Montana, and eastern Oregon. They made their new headquarters in a small rented house in Nampa, Idaho.[14]

In September Fuchida passed an interesting two weeks in Spokane. Among other events, he enjoyed a tour of Geiger Air Force Base, where he received a thorough briefing on two new fighter planes, the F-104 and F-106, and on the local defense plan. These beautiful aircraft and the workmanlike setup impressed Fuchida. "A surprise attack on America would now be impossible," he told his hosts somewhat optimistically.[15]

The rest of 1959 and early 1960 passed uneventfully. In March he established himself in Berkeley, California, which became his home base for several years.[16] That summer brought a personal highlight: Joe graduated from Pueblo Junior College, where he had been studying for two years and helping support himself by working as a draftsman. In Pueblo he had met a fellow student, pretty Marie Rael. They were married the day after graduation, on 11 June 1960. Then they left Colorado for California, where they met Fuchida in Berkeley a few days later. While Joe completed his schooling, Marie worked for the telephone company. Fuchida was fond of his daughter-in-law. He enjoyed her intelligence, wit, and geniality.[17]

35

"We Must Have Another Reformation"

I N THE LATE summer of 1960, an old dream
came true for Fuchida. He had the opportunity to visit Europe. The Pocket
Testament League sponsored a three-month trip to evangelize in Berlin and
Paris. One group consisted of about ten people with Fuchida's former associate, Glenn Wagner, as leader. They flew from Chicago by way of Canada,
picked up two large sound trucks in Amsterdam, and proceeded to Germany.

They spent a few days at Braunschweig at a league convention.[1] Representatives gathered from the United States, Germany, Holland, Belgium,
Great Britain, and China.[2] Fuchida met these people and spoke at the official
reception. His schedule then called for an address to a group of American GIs
in Helmsted, followed by a visit to Berlin.

At Helmsted, a checkpoint between West and East Germany, Fuchida
saw firsthand the division of Japan's former ally. A dispute over the trucks
held up the little cavalcade. The vehicles carried a load of sound equipment,
copies of the Scripture, and other essentials for the mission. The East German police would have passed them on after a routine check, but behind
them stood two Russian soldiers.

These two were not watching the league people; they were watching the
East Germans, as if fearing that their colleagues might bolt for the West. The
Russians refused entry to the trucks. Fuchida and his colleagues had to wait
two or three hours while American authorities, bored but resigned, negotiated
in their interest. Finally the Russians relented, granting passage on condition
that they not use the trucks in East German territory.[3]

In preparation for their stay in Berlin, the league had prepared 250,000 copies of the St. John Gospel and scheduled meetings in various locations. "Already West Berlin was a new city," Fuchida remembered. In some places they saw the remains of wartime destruction, but overall the city seemed to be growing prosperous.

Fuchida had decided not to sightsee in West Berlin until later. The group would be there for over two months, so they had plenty of time. First he wanted to see the Eastern sector and verify or disprove for himself all that he had heard about it. What immediately struck Fuchida, accustomed to the heavy traffic of Tokyo, Osaka, and the bustling American cities, was the scarcity of cars. Most people walked or pedaled along on bicycles.

The shop windows seemed to display plenty of merchandise. He went into stores to check the volume of sales and the prices, which hovered in the stratosphere. Few in East Berlin had that kind of money; any cash they accumulated went for necessities. Fuchida could easily spot bakeries and vegetable stands by the long lines of people waiting, stolidly patient, for their turn to buy.

Men in uniform abounded. Perhaps this was one reason East Germany was so poor, he reflected. Most of their money went to maintain the military. He had trouble distinguishing policemen from soldiers; East Germany almost seemed to be under martial law.

He felt no sense of personal danger. The people to whom he spoke responded in a friendly way, and his heart went out to them in troubled sympathy. Twice he visited East Berlin—on 7 September and 1 October—and each time returned to West Berlin with a grateful prayer of thanksgiving for his liberty.[4]

Wagner had been naïvely eager to testify and distribute the gospel in East Berlin, but the authorities denied permission. West Berlin, however, kept them busy. In Fuchida's opinion the Berliners needed a spiritual shaking up. He had a particularly disconcerting experience speaking to a large church which, according to its bishop, had a membership of thousands. Fuchida climbed four steps to reach the pulpit, placed high so that the minister would be visible and audible through the vast nave. Between the size of the church and its official membership, he expected a teeming congregation. So when he peered over the lectern he was astonished to face a sea of empty benches with a scant crowd clustered around the base of the pulpit like shipwrecked mariners on a coral islet. Later he found that many in the congregation came to church only four times—to be baptized, confirmed, married, and buried.

Reformation Day, 31 October, a significant holiday for all Protestants, came and went in a jangle of bells. Children flocked to the churches, which pleased Fuchida until he saw that they came for free cakes and cookies. The next day, All Saints' Day, found the Catholic churches full of youngsters clutching free goodies. Fuchida talked the matter over with an old German who shook his massive grey head thoughtfully and said, "We must have another Reformation."[5]

Upon reflection, Fuchida attributed the problem to West Germany's state church. All sects enjoyed freedom of worship, but the government supported the Lutheran church, to which a large majority of West Berliners nominally belonged. All Lutherans paid a church tax. The government paid the pastors' salaries and maintained the buildings. "Just like Buddhism in Japan," Fuchida said regretfully. "As a result, the churches were beautiful but the people were sleeping. There was no spirit or heart in their Christianity."

Obviously his task was clear-cut—to recall to these people that they needed Christ and He wanted them. Testifying again and again throughout the city, he discovered that the Germans enjoyed his message. Beneath their big-city sophistication they seemed ready and eager to recharge their spiritual batteries.

Fuchida spoke at many schools, and to the American, French, and British military as well as to the West Germans. He even ran into a group of about two hundred Japanese students who carried him off for a picnic. The league's largest rally drew several thousands in the hall of Siemen's Electric Works, the biggest factory in West Berlin. "The director was a widow, a fine Christian," Fuchida remarked. She made sure the workers would be paid for the time they attended the rally.[6]

All this time Billy Graham was in West Berlin, speaking in a large hall packed to capacity every night. Once he invited Fuchida to share his platform. The Graham crusade drew large numbers from East Germany, although they came under a humiliating condition. The East German authorities allowed them to attend but not their pastors, who were held at the Brandenburger Gate as hostages to insure that the members of their flocks returned. If anyone was missing, the pastor would go to jail.[7]

One night Fuchida and his group happened to drive their sound truck past the biggest movie theater in the city. The film being shown was *Von Pearl Harbor bis Hiroshima.* Fuchida, an ardent fan of the cinema, suggested that this might be worth seeing. His colleagues agreed to take a break. They parked the truck and went into the theater. The movie proved to be a documentary made up of Japanese and American film reports. Fuchida had known that such reels existed somewhere, for his comrade Furukawa had carried a 16-millimeter camera on board *Akagi* and taken pictures on his flight over Pearl Harbor.

Here on a screen in West Berlin he saw the fruit of Furukawa's labors. The movie impressed him tremendously, not only because of the skillful editing of some remarkable shots of Pacific war actions but also for its objectivity. It offered no propaganda, waved no flags, pointed no finger; it simply presented war as it was. "Terrible—the brutality of war!" exclaimed Fuchida. "Anyone who sees this film must want peace."

It so struck him that he took the whole group around to the manager's office to express his appreciation in person. When Fuchida introduced himself to the manager, Fräulein Gisele Paetow, and explained his special interest in the film, she invited him to appear on the platform after the movie for the remainder of the run. This arrangement suited all concerned: The theater received wonderful publicity, and Fuchida had the opportunity to preach. Three days later Fräulein Paetow held a press conference, introduced Fuchida, and announced that he would testify after each showing.

For the next two weeks he spoke three times an evening after the close of each performance. His message itself lasted only six or seven minutes, but the translating extended the time to fifteen. For each performance, Fräulein Paetow sent a car to his hotel to pick him up and take him back. At every show the theater was filled to capacity, and many had to be turned away. The audience always remained seated for Fuchida's talk and always applauded him warmly, on the way out accepting a copy of the Gospel. Many came around to the office to greet him personally.[8]

Next the Pocket Testament League team left West Berlin for Paris. On 3 December they flew to Orly Field. Fuchida stayed in Paris only three days and spent most of his time sightseeing. He found there the same phenomenon he had seen in West Berlin, only worse. In France the majority of the population called themselves Christians. The dominant church was Catholic, which seemed to Fuchida as moribund as Germany's Lutheran church.

He left Europe a sadder and more thoughtful man. He had looked forward to visiting Europe with its tradition of almost two thousand years of Christianity. What he had seen was a civilization losing its spiritual life.

"They had lost Christ," he lamented. "And now, all over Western Europe, I saw how materialism had conquered most of the people, like a false god. This was the reason I wanted to make a second and third trip to Europe. I wanted to reach the heart of Europe through the spirit of Christ, so He wouldn't be lost to Western civilization."[9]

The first three months of 1961 found Fuchida in Florida. There once more he met Billy Graham, who recruited him to speak at an afternoon seminar at the University of Miami. It was an education to watch Graham's deft fielding of arguments hurled in his direction by the cynical students of the sixties. None, however, indulged in the rude heckling to which Fuchida had grown accustomed in Japanese universities.[10]

By mid-April, again with Glenn Wagner, Fuchida was in Michigan, then

Toronto, where he spent two weeks testifying. The usual flock of "sea stories" followed him about: He had been blown off the *Akagi* at Midway;[11] he had personally piloted the plane that took Japan's peace delegation to Manila.[12] One newspaper even recounted that on this occasion Fuchida's legs were still in casts—over three years after Midway.[13]

From Toronto Fuchida and Wagner flew back to Europe. On the way over the aircraft developed engine trouble and made an unscheduled stop in Scotland. The delay lasted a night, long enough for Fuchida to add another country to his collection and chat with a few Scots. "All Scottish people said that Scotland is the best in the world," smiled Fuchida. "They are so proud of their country!"

After this unexpected digression the plane resumed its course, touching down in London on 2 May. Fuchida and Wagner went on to Hamburg, which served as league headquarters for this tour. In all, the party totaled nineteen workers representing nine countries.

The citizens of Hamburg cooperated well with the league, which scheduled almost two hundred meetings in every imaginable place, from hospitals to prisons, from military installations to gypsy camps. And every Saturday and Sunday they held forth in a vacant lot owned by a brewery in the heart of one of the most active vice districts in northern Germany.

They did run into a certain amount of opposition arranging to speak to students. The Hamburg schools had both Protestant and Catholic chaplains, and the latter objected to the league's evangelizing. But by the end of the tour such resistance had melted away; eventually they had more requests to visit schools than they could handle.

In the meantime, Fuchida concentrated on the German military, having been granted official permission to work with them.[14] A surprising number of young soldiers brought along a German translation of his book about Midway. They asked him for his autograph or for clarification of a point that puzzled them.

The German chief of staff introduced Fuchida to the cadets at Kiel Academy. He was a Christian who had been a prisoner of war in Russia for eleven years. After Fuchida testified, he held a question-and-answer session. The cadets were frank. Some were worried about the apparent discrepancy in ethics and loyalty a Christian soldier faced. Wasn't the Christian soldier a contradiction in terms? "Christ tells us to love our enemies," one said, "but if such a doctrine is spread among the military, how can they fight?"

Fuchida was no theologian, and could only answer in the simple words of his belief: "Christianity might weaken a soldier's ardor for battle, but on the other hand, a strong military force without Christianity is the most evil thing in the world. I know this from my own experience in the last war." At the end of the session the chief of staff shook Fuchida's hand and warmly thanked him for his message.[15]

The league completed its mission to Germany around the middle of June. Fuchida returned to Paris for about ten days. He testified in several Protestant churches and twice spoke at rallies held under a tent at Clignancourt. As before, the French capital gave the impression of spiritual malaise. The political picture was equally unpleasant. Every day the streets erupted in violence over the Algerian question.

Fuchida spent three entire days in the Louvre. He was especially interested in the religious art. "But mostly this was Catholic church art," he said. "And many buildings in Paris were Catholic church buildings. . . . I never saw Christ in France."

Nor did the days he spent in London after his visit to Paris inspire him. He couldn't understand what real difference existed between the Anglican and Roman Catholic churches. The pope headed the latter, the ruler of England the former, which seemed to him a rather minor point upon which to place so much emphasis. "Too much ceremony in both churches!" Fuchida exclaimed. "Too much ritual! Too much ceremony and ritual spoil the faith of the heart." He addressed a number of school gatherings, which convinced him that Christianity was divorced from everyday life in London.[16]

The British press, like its American counterpart, published its share of misconceptions about Fuchida. According to one newspaper, he was "the only one of the 360 pilots in the [Pearl Harbor] raid who survived the war."[17] This would have amused those of Fuchida's Pearl Harbor comrades who were very much alive in Japan. Probably the journalist had meant to convey that all the other flight leaders, not all the pilots, had perished in the war.

More distressing was an article titled "Target for the Pearl Harbour Pilot America—to teach them to forgive . . ." One paragraph read, "Yesterday, almost 20 years later, Mr. Fuchida, now 58, was in London—en route to America, where he proposes to 'preach forgiveness' to his former enemies."[18] It is difficult to imagine Fuchida feeling himself called upon to teach the American people how to forgive. In any case, an impression to that effect would have ill become him in view of the friendly hand the United States always extended to him.

In the autumn, Fuchida returned to his new base at Berkeley and decided to bring Haruko and Miyako to the United States for a bit of sightseeing. The American consular official to whom they applied for passports, however, considered them immigrants rather than tourists. He couldn't be convinced that they planned to return to Japan. And so they were not allowed to come to the United States. Haruko was glad that matters turned out as they did;

she was deeply attached to her home and didn't want to visit a strange country.

Miyako, however, longed for broader horizons. She never lost an opportunity for self-improvement. One day in Kashiwara she met an American missionary of the Assembly of God church. She arranged to study conversational English with this woman and to repay her by teaching Japanese to her two daughters. Miyako also worked in her office a few hours a day typing letters, for which she received four thousand yen a month. This small but regular income helped put Miyako through Tesukayama Junior College, where she majored in English literature. Her conversation class was taught by an American, so Miyako obtained a good grasp of English. In fact, when she graduated from junior college she received credentials to teach English at the junior-high-school level.

With this background and her degree from Yasuko Ueda fashion school, Miyako hoped to come to the United States, like Joe, for further education. She knew she could count on her father's support. Where his daughter was concerned, the tiger was a pussycat. Haruko was another matter. She and Miyako had grown very close and were the best of friends. The mother wasn't willing to let her last chick leave the nest. Ever since Joe left Japan Haruko had been looking for a *yooshi*—a husband willing to marry into his wife's family. She introduced Miyako to a number of eligible young men, but nothing came of the overtures. This was no reflection on Miyako. Stated baldly, the problem was this: Fuchida had high honors but no money. Moreover, Haruko had come up against a will as strong as her own. Miyako had set her heart on further education, and she also wanted to be independent for a while. So the two women worked out a compromise—Miyako could go to the United States, but for one year only.[19]

Miyako flew to California in September 1961, landing in San Francisco. There Fuchida, Joe, and Marie met her. She went to Berkeley, where she lived with Fuchida while studying interior decorating at the California College of Arts and Crafts at Oakland. Just as Joe had, Miyako fit right into her new surroundings. The United States struck her as a dynamic country. Fuchida's acquaintances received her cordially, as did her college classmates. She had a little trouble understanding lectures and conversations in English, but she soon made friends of both sexes who helped her with her school work.[20]

She resolved to contribute to the household, and to that end borrowed three hundred dollars from her father to buy a sewing machine. Immediately she started doing alterations and making dresses. Soon the word spread about a Japanese girl who did exquisite sewing at a reasonable price. "She was so very skillful!" Fuchida boasted. Miyako's machine whirred steadily, and within three months she had paid for it.

She made time for her spiritual and social life. She became an active member of the Assembly of God church. Between her church and school affiliations she soon had a host of friends. Fuchida paid her tuition for the first year, and wasn't surprised when she extended her stay to four years by winning three annual scholarships.[21]

The seventh of December 1961 occasioned a blizzard of Pearl Harbor recollections. The Berkeley *Daily Gazette* featured a long interview with Fuchida beginning with a full-page spread on page one. John Raymond, a *Gazette* staff writer, was responsible for this article, remarkable for its accuracy and its faithful reporting of Fuchida's words. This edition of the *Gazette* also printed a large picture of Miyako, paintbrush in hand.

Most treasured of Fuchida's souvenirs of December 1961 was a cordial handwritten letter postmarked Pebble Beach, California. It was from Raymond A. Spruance, victor at Midway, who more than any other of Nimitz's lieutenants had secured the American victory in the war at sea.[22]

36

"A Good Mission Field"

Fuchida spent much of early 1962 in the South, especially Texas, where he was scheduled to speak at various churches and at a Southern Baptist missionary conference held in Dallas.[1] Along with his official commitments, he had a self-appointed mission close to his heart.

A story had received much publicity in the United States, Japan, and Europe about a man named Claude R. Eatherly, a former major in the U.S. Air Force. He had piloted the reconnaissance plane that led the B-29 *Enola Gay* to Hiroshima with the first atomic bomb. Soon after the event, Eatherly became consumed by guilt. Over a fifteen-year period he had been in and out of the psychiatric wards of veterans' hospitals at least ten times. Nothing seemed to help him, and as he could not be labeled insane, the authorities released him periodically. After each release he would wander around aimlessly, driven by the gales of conscience.

This man had been much on Fuchida's mind. "I want to tell him to accept Christ, and he will feel peace in his heart," Fuchida told reporters.

It may appear to have been presumptuous of Fuchida to believe he could succeed where so many competent doctors had failed. But he didn't think of himself as personally able to solve anyone's problem. He merely served as a channel of God's grace. Then, too, as the Pearl Harbor air leader, he considered himself uniquely qualified to talk to Eatherly. DeShazer, the Doolittle Raider, had been instrumental in bringing the light of Christ to Fuchida, and it seemed fitting that he should pass the torch to Eatherly, the Hiroshima scout.

He sought Eatherly in vain. Representatives of the Henderson *Daily News* discovered that he had been in the Veterans' Hospital in Waco for some time in 1961, but he had left several months ago. No one seemed to know his whereabouts.[2] Eatherly knew that Fuchida was seeking him but claimed that he did not want a religious answer to his problem.[3]

February dealt Fuchida a much better hand than January. While he was in Atlanta, Georgia, on the fourteenth, John Mitsuharu Fuchida made his noisy entrance onto the world's stage in Springfield, Oregon. Fuchida was on Cloud Nine, thinking it was fitting that his first grandchild bore the name of the disciple St. John. And with delicate consideration Joe and Marie had given the boy a middle name which combined Mitsuo and Haruko.[4]

Miyako was the next Fuchida to break into the news. Her self-education program included a painstaking daily perusal of each page of the Berkeley *Gazette*, with the aid of her cherished Japanese-English dictionary. In the *Gazette* she read about the sister city program thriving throughout the United States, and Berkeley was considering the offer of a sisterhood to a foreign community. This project of grass-roots international understanding involved correspondence and visits between citizens, exchanges of schoolchildren, and other official and unofficial contacts. In some instances, American cities carried on this relationship with the towns in England or elsewhere for which they had been named. In other cases, they attempted to find a city of comparable population and community interests.

The idea of joining Berkeley and Nara immediately struck Miyako. She wrote her mother long, glowing letters describing the university town in California. She even translated an editorial about the project and mailed it to the *Yamato Times* in Nara. The newspaper picked up the idea and published the editorial, along with a picture of Miyako and some of her letters.

When a *Gazette* reporter asked how she had come to take up the banner, Miyako replied, "When you want to do something, just go ahead and do it. Sometimes you think about it too much and forget to act." She saw many similarities between Nara and Berkeley, she explained. "I love Nara the best in the world, therefore I will suggest this thing. After I finish my studies here in interior design, I will go back and live in Nara my whole life."[5] Her efforts prospered, and shortly thereafter Berkeley and Nara did become sister cities.

That spring the Protestant churches in Warsaw, Poland, invited Fuchida to preach to them under the sponsorship of the Pocket Testament League. Glenn Wagner preceded him to that city. But Fuchida's own hopes of breaking through the iron curtain were doomed. The Polish embassy in Washington refused to grant him a visa. A travel bureau in Atlantic City tried to secure one for him from the Polish consulate in New York, without success.

Late in June, Fuchida flew to Paris to try his luck nearer the scene. He stayed in the home of Mr. John Jessberg, who made the arrangements for the Pocket Testament League's tour. Every day Fuchida presented himself at the Polish embassy to ask for a visa, and every day he met with a polite brush-off. First they were too busy, then the proper official was away. And so on and so on. "Always excuses, excuses, excuses, and wait, wait, wait," fumed Fuchida in retrospect. "Finally I guessed this must be the Polish strategy: Never to refuse me but never to give me a yes. So I decided I would never get a Polish visa. . . . I guess communist Poland didn't want this new Japanese Christian warrior preaching there," he added quizzically. He had more important things to do than play games with communist bureaucrats, so after ten days he gave up and notified Glenn Wagner that he couldn't join him in Warsaw.[6]

From Paris Fuchida flew to Helsinki, where about twenty members of the Pocket Testament League awaited him. He arrived on the Fourth of July with Wagner not far behind. The expedition to Finland was delicate. The Finnish Lutheran churches wanted to hear Fuchida but were not receptive to the idea of swallowing the entire league package. This caused some ruffling of feathers in the league. Fuchida pointed out, "The important thing is to preach Christ both in season and out of season." Whereupon Wagner generously replied, "Okay, Captain Fuchida, go ahead and preach the gospel."[7]

As it turned out, Finland gave them all plenty of work to do. As one young Finn working with the league observed, "Christians in Finland have been praying for many years for a real visitation of the Holy Spirit, and they believe that the Lord has sent our team in answer to their prayers."

He warned that the group might run into trouble. While most of Finland's young people had no use for communism, the few who did were fanatics. To complicate matters, Helsinki would play host to a communist youth festival during the latter part of the month, and the native Reds wanted to demonstrate their enthusiasm. The league's mission could well give these people an opportunity.[8]

Accompanied by Mr. and Mrs. Don McFarland, Fuchida left Helsinki on a three-week trip, first heading north, then east, then west. He discovered Finland to be as solidly Lutheran as a country can be. The sprinkling of Roman Catholics and Greek Orthodox made up around one percent of the population; the rest belonged to the state church. But evangelical missions enjoyed complete freedom, so Fuchida spoke at many open-air meetings and in various Lutheran churches.[9]

Behind each church lay a cemetery full of the graves of young men—the dead of the Russo-Finnish War of 1939–40. As Fuchida stood beside their tombstones he was deeply moved. The brave fight the Finns had put up in the face of fantastic odds kindled his admiration.

He fell in love with them. "The character and personality of the Finnish people are most like the Japanese," he explained. "They have a national feeling which is the same as the Japanese *yamato damashii.* . . . The Finnish people are not only brave in a military way. They also have such sweetness and delicacy in their poetry, music, and art. . . . That is like Japan—brave in battle but sweet and delicate. So I loved this beautiful Finnish people."[10]

He took a quick trip into Lapland. This being July, it looked as if the Biblical pledge "there shall be no night there" (Revelation 21:25) had been fulfilled. It amused Fuchida to see people wandering around at all hours and reading newspapers outdoors at midnight. "The birds . . . went to their nests to sleep," he chuckled. "Wiser than people!"[11]

The primary reason the league visited Helsinki was because the World Youth Festival, which the Kremlin sponsored every four years, was taking place in the Helsinki Olympic Stadium that year. The authorities, expecting trouble, requested the league not to use their public-address system in the street.

The presence in one spot of young people from 101 countries was an opportunity made to order for the league. Now it could communicate with the youth from behind the iron curtain. Realistic people, the team knew they could not hope for spectacular results, but they made a huge effort, bringing to Finland two hundred fifty thousand copies of St. John in Finnish and another ten thousand copies in twenty-seven different languages. Between them the twenty members of the task force could speak seventeen languages. Among others, they had a Chinese and a Korean, a man who spoke five Slavic tongues, and of course Fuchida with his Japanese.[12]

Some members went to the stations and docks to catch the delegates on arrival, before they went to the stadium. Apparently the opposition expected such a move. A number of Finnish communist guards turned up at these entry points and did their best to thwart the league, actually roughing up a few of its members. The league also tried to reach the delegates in their quarters. There, too, Finnish guards shouted abuse and ordered them off the premises.[13]

Fuchida and his colleagues did not direct their efforts exclusively at the youth conference. Fortunately they had the services of a Finnish gentleman named Kärnä, who had been a missionary in Kyoto for seven years and was now pastor of a Baptist church. He spoke excellent Japanese and English and frequently translated for Fuchida.[14] One Sunday afternoon, just before the festival opened, the group held an open-air meeting in a park by the lake under the sponsorship of Kärnä's church. In the audience Fuchida noticed many Japanese. Later he learned they were delegates to the festival. They had emerged from their billet in a high school behind the park upon hearing his voice, curious to see who could be speaking Japanese in the Finnish capital.

Owing to an odd set of circumstances, this delegation was one of the few—probably the only one—at the conference not predominantly communist. This was because the Zengakuren, the powerful Japanese communist student organization, was temporarily languishing in the Soviet doghouse. Normally the Zengakuren toed the party line docilely, but when the Soviet Union exploded its fifty-megaton atomic bomb, the Japanese horror of atomic weapons had overcome these young people. In front of the Soviet embassy in Tokyo they demonstrated angrily against the test. As punishment for such unorthodox behavior, the Soviet Union snubbed the Zengakuren by inviting to the festival some two hundred students from various other organizations. Many of them were not communists. In talking with some, Fuchida formed the impression that they didn't realize Moscow was behind the affair.

The day after the outdoor meeting, he went to the high school housing these young people and took with him two hundred Japanese copies of the Gospel of St. John. He arrived at an opportune moment, just as all the students were finishing their lunch. He greeted them politely, then said, "We've come to give you the scripture, but before we do, please listen to me for ten minutes."[15]

He told them that the Kremlin was sponsoring the festival. His message was simple: "You're all students, and you're looking for the truth through your studies. But the truth had been available for two thousand years. Jesus is the truth! . . . Right now you may not believe this, but you too can reach the truth through studying the scriptures. How many of you would like a copy of the Gospel of St. John?"

All but about twenty of the students raised their hands, and Fuchida gave each one a little pamphlet. Those who refused called out, "We want to hear more concrete and radical answers."

Fuchida smiled ironically at the idea that the truth could be cut and tailored like a suit of clothes. He shrugged and answered simply, "There are no concrete and radical answers. There is only faith in Jesus Christ through the Holy Spirit. His eternal truth is the answer."[16]

On the first day of the conference, Sunday, 29 July 1962, the league distributed gospels to the spectators streaming into the stadium. Most accepted one, although some of the delegates refused with unnecessary rudeness and even violence. The team distributed over eight thousand gospels that day alone.[17]

Thenceforth they held streetcorner meetings at various spots in Helsinki.

Fuchida drew larger crowds than anyone else; no doubt he appeared quite exotic in that setting. He remembered these gatherings as a montage of endless lines of people, some pausing briefly to listen and to accept a pamphlet. A small knot of people would linger, from interest, curiosity, or lack of anything better to do.

Sometimes the ubiquitous festival delegates paused to listen. None of them heckled, but those who accepted a gospel did so only to tear it up, throw it on the ground, and stamp or spit on it. Some added a word of explanation: "We are communists. We do not believe in any God and do not need these scriptures."[18] Soon Fuchida discovered that at least part of this public vulgarity was "for the record." If none of their fellow delegates were around, students would often take the pamphlets.[19]

The friction between some of the local citizens and the delegates broke out in open demonstrations. Some anticommunist youths attended get-togethers in the stadium and hurled soft drink and beer bottles at the delegates. Rioting broke out in the streets and police with tear gas had to disperse demonstrators. Because the situation was so explosive, the Finnish government withdrew the public-address permit.

Only outdoor meetings without amplifiers were authorized. So the league held brief meetings throughout the city—three each morning and three each evening. This schedule kept Fuchida hopping, for he spoke at all of them, his testimony and translations taking about thirty minutes. He often noted that behind the audience little groups from the festival lingered furtively. So the league mobilized more of its translators until at one time all its seventeen languages were being used.

Festival delegates couldn't afford to be seen at the indoor sites. Outside they could always pretend to be passing by if any of their cronies spotted them. For that reason the indoor congregations were almost entirely Finnish. The league required only one translator on those occasions.[20]

During this period Fuchida lived on the third floor of the YMCA. On the fifth floor roomed a group of Russian acrobats from the world-famous Moscow Circus, which the Soviet Union had sent to Helsinki as part of its sponsorship of the festival. Moscow was extremely proud of this circus and eager to demonstrate that it was the best in the world. For once Fuchida could heartily agree with the Russians. "I never saw such a circus!" he exclaimed in admiration.

Discovering that at precisely 1300 all the acrobats piled into a bus in front of the YMCA to be taken to the circus, Fuchida stuffed some Russian copies of St. John into his pocket and stationed himself at the door to pass them out; as he had anticipated, the Russians refused to accept them.

The next morning as he entered the self-service elevator he saw a young man of about eighteen or nineteen, one of the acrobats. Fuchida smiled a greeting which the lad returned rather doubtfully. He eyed Fuchida covertly and opened his mouth to speak once or twice, rather like a child who is unsure whether the dog it is trying to make friends with will wag its tail or bare its fangs. After a few false starts, he mustered enough courage to indicate with a quick gesture that he wanted one of the pamphlets. Fortunately the Russian gospels were still in Fuchida's pocket, and he happily gave the boy one. As they reached the lobby and the elevator door slid open, the boy hastily concealed the pamphlet and disappeared. Fuchida was touched and heartened by this evidence that a Russian wanted to receive the word of God.[21]

That evening the acrobat came to Fuchida's room, where they had a brief, somewhat surrealistic conversation, conducted in a sort of international semaphore and with a few English words they discovered they had in common. His new friend wanted two more gospels, one for his mother and one for his sister back in Moscow. Fuchida gave him the pamphlets with joy and respect, knowing that it took courage for the young man to smuggle the gospel into Russia.

Later that night a soft knock sounded on Fuchida's door. Opening it, he saw another of the Russian acrobats, this time a girl about the same age as the boy in the elevator. She shook her head when Fuchida held the door open invitingly. She held out one hand and with the other made a rapid movement indicating the size and shape of the pamphlet.

Nodding, he hurried to his stockpile and picked up a number of the gospels in Russian. On impulse he added a few in Polish, Czech, and German. "Take all you want," he said in English, with a broad sweep of his hand and a grin of comradeship. The girl nervously sorted through the booklets, took three Russian, two Polish, and two German, smiled her thanks, and stole quickly down the corridor. Fuchida closed the door, pleased and more than a little awed.

When another rap sounded on his door the next morning he knew what he would find before he opened it. Sure enough, a third Russian acrobat, another young man in his late teens, stood on the threshold. This one asked for and received three copies of the gospel in Russian.

Thenceforth until the end of the circus's stay in Helsinki, Fuchida gave pamphlets to the acrobats. Some came to his room; some waited to catch him in the elevator. If they were alone, he would be asked for more gospels; if not, he would be passed with no sign of recognition. Fuchida didn't resent the snubs. "They couldn't trust one another," he said sadly. "One might tell on the other. Then the secret police would arrest them and they would be sent to prison." Fuchida's heart ached for these likeable young people whose talent gave so much pleasure to so many and yet who had to live in fear of each other.[22]

Yet there was a touch of the comic in this situation—young people poring over the Gospel of St. John in secret as if it were blacklisted pornography. Who can say what lay behind their interest? They might well have been directly, consciously hungry for God's word, as Fuchida hoped and believed. They might have been egged on by the lure of the forbidden, or by an intellectual drive to investigate and decide about Christianity for themselves. Or it could have been youthful recklessness and a love of danger for its own sake. Whatever the reason, through the unlikely medium of the Moscow circus, the Gospel of St. John would penetrate the iron curtain.

Fuchida and Wagner decided that the league would have to go underground to reach the communists. They gave away ten thousand gospels printed in the various languages and had to order more.[23]

Toward the end of his stay in Helsinki an unexpected distinction came to Fuchida—a visit to one of the league's meetings by a reporter and television crew from Moscow. The leading spirit was a young woman—"such a nice, charming girl," Fuchida described her.

"May I shoot you?" she asked in excellent English.

Fuchida blinked at this rather ambiguous question, then realized that she wanted to take pictures. "Okay, go ahead," he agreed. She ground away while Fuchida gave his testimony.

But the Russians didn't want his message. They wanted information. After the meeting the girl interviewed him. "What is it that you are doing? What is your purpose?" she inquired curiously.

"I'm evangelizing for Christ, who is our only savior," Fuchida replied. He explained how he had come to Helsinki because Poland wouldn't let him in. "This is a good mission field from which to reach you communists," he continued with relish, "because you sent so many young people to Helsinki for this festival."

The girl's eyes widened. Evidently she had not expected to hear her government thanked for performing valuable spadework for a team of Christian evangelists. "This is a good mission field," Fuchida repeated. "I must take advantage of such a big opportunity for Christ. Don't you think so?"

His interviewer seemed surprised at his answer, but promised that she would relay his reply to Moscow exactly as he gave it. Later he discovered through Japanese sources that the Moscow TV did indeed broadcast the shots of his testimony. The *Okahoto,* the communist party organ in Japan, reported somewhat extensively on his Helsinki mission and the Russian telecast, referring to him as *tekki* (the enemy). Fuchida grinned wryly at the idea of being called an enemy in a Japanese newspaper. But he considered the source and lost no sleep over it.[24]

Toward the end of August, Fuchida and the McFarlands left Finland by truck and headed for a two-week trip through Sweden, Norway, Denmark, and Holland. Their ultimate objective, Essen, would be the league's base of operations for a three-month stay in Germany. They chugged through Scandinavia like carefree gypsies, though neglecting no occasion to witness. Fuchida spoke to congregations in Stockholm. The visit there and to Oslo was uneventful by comparison with Helsinki, but he welcomed the opportunity to ease himself back into a normal routine and do a bit of sightseeing.[25]

From Norway they moved to Copenhagen, where Fuchida spoke at the Danish Christian Fellowship. A ten-day meeting drew members from many countries, including the United States. In this atmosphere Fuchida felt at home, for the fellowship had no formal organization, no constitution, and was not affiliated with any church.

Originally Fuchida was baptized a Presbyterian, but as his devotion to Christ grew so did his dislike of specific doctrines, and he became a *mukyokai* (no church) Christian, the Japanese equivalent of a member of the Danish Christian Fellowship. He even refused to be officially affiliated with the Kyodan Church of Christ, the organization to which eighty percent of Japanese Protestant churches belonged, including that of his pastor, the Reverend Saito. Fuchida's home base in the United States was the nondenominational Berkeley Layman's Church in California, which had no ordained ministers, only lay preachers whose duty it was to help individual members know Christ.[26]

After Denmark, Fuchida and the McFarlands visited the league's Netherlands branch. Then they moved on to Essen, headquarters for another swing around Germany. As before, Fuchida spoke principally to German military personnel. Thus it came about that he was at a large army camp in Hanover when the Cuban missile crisis arose.

His first intimation of trouble came when officials abruptly canceled his speaking engagement, explaining that the German troops were going on maneuvers. Fuchida asked and was given permission to accompany the troops to the maneuver area near East Germany. And so he lived through those tense days alongside West German troops on on the alert. The well-trained, disciplined West German soldiers impressed Fuchida exceedingly. These must be the best troops in Europe, he thought.

Later his engagements took him outside the cities and into the countryside. He approved the thrift and diligence he saw on all sides. Rural Germans worked hard and saved everything, especially food. Fuchida had often been aghast at the amount of food some of his American friends threw out. "All these things belong to God, Who allows us to use them," he explained earnestly, "so we should save everything."

In Essen McFarland asked permission for the league to pass out literature inside the prison. The chaplain refused; Christian groups had bombarded the inmates and they were fed up. But when McFarland mentioned that Captain Mitsuo Fuchida, leader of the Pearl Harbor air attack, belonged to the team, the chaplain changed his mind. Fuchida was proud and a bit smug about so many gates being opened at his name.[27]

37

"Return to Japan"

BACK in the United States, Fuchida took up his familiar round of lectures and testimony. Nineteen sixty-two had been a year of the tiger, the cycle bringing his sixtieth birthday. In many oriental cultures this is the most auspicious birthday of all, but Fuchida's slipped by with little or no notice, as indeed did the balance of 1962 and most of 1963. This was a quiet period of travel and work across the United States.[1]

A newspaper article provided a few examples of the persistence of skepticism about him. It was a good specimen of what one might call interpretive reporting, where the writer rather than confining himself or herself to facts manages to convey personal opinions. The writer, Joy Evans, referred to Fuchida as "a professed convert to Christian mission work," adding that Fuchida's address "is prepared carefully and is given with little deviation from the pamphlets of introductory literature."[2] Fuchida's talk was indeed "prepared carefully." He was delivering a serious address in a language foreign to him. As he had only one message to deliver, and wanted to put it across to as many as possible as clearly as possible, any major "deviation" from the text would be undesirable.

Unfortunately, Mr. Jessberg of the Pocket Testament League, Fuchida's escort on the night Ms. Evans was covering the story, barred newsmen from meeting with him after a speaking engagement and the dinner that followed. This may have antagonized the journalist, who ended her article:

What progress is Christianity making in predominantly Shinto and Buddhist Japan? Would Japan . . . like Germany in the past . . . repeat violence against the West, in his opinion? Regardless of his welcome among church and mission groups, have there been any untoward incidents in connection with Fuchida's appearances in this country? Does he plan to return to Japan soon? If so, will he continue his evangelistic tours, which in the past have drawn large crowds throughout Japan when he lectured on the topic, "From Pearl Harbor to Calvary?" What fees does he receive from his lectures here, if any?

The above questions are among those that remain unanswered when Fuchida's advisors refused to permit him to talk to reporters without advance preparation.[3]

Pearl Harbor Day, which in 1963 followed close upon the assassination of President John F. Kennedy, overtook Fuchida in Washington, D.C. He spoke at several churches there, including the two chapels at Andrews Air Force Base, then hurried back to California. He had a particular reason for being in Berkeley for the holidays: Miyako was to be married on Christmas Day.[4] Her fiancé was a fellow student at the California College of Arts and Crafts, Harrison James Overturf III. His father was headmaster of a primary school in Yosemite, California. Jim had shared a number of Miyako's classes and was one of those who assisted her with her studies. He would go on to study carpentry at Laney College for four years. After graduating, he worked mainly for large construction companies building skyscrapers. He was a reservist in the U.S. Marine Corps, and his shock of sandy hair proclaimed a proud Scottish ancestry.

At her wedding, Miyako wore the traditional white dress and veil of a Western bride. The four hundred or so guests who crowded to the ceremony attested to her popularity.[5] If Fuchida had a regret, it was that Haruko could not be at his side to see her daughter married and to meet a son-in-law of whom she could be proud. Haruko had not seen Joe since September 1957, Miyako since September 1961. But she bore her sacrifice patiently. If her children found their happiness across the Pacific, so be it. Her love for them held no taint of possessiveness.

She kept an unbroken stream of correspondence flowing to them. Those who saw only the impassive face she chose to present to the world, even those who glimpsed her earthly strength and humor, would have been astonished to read those letters. Each was a little masterpiece, recounting the incidents of life on the farm, the growth of the trees and flowers, the adventures of the animals, anything interesting or amusing that crossed her daily path.[6]

In early February 1964, Prange sent a letter to Fuchida with good tidings: a national magazine had agreed to sponsor the story of Fuchida's life. He would give the details to Prange, who would write it. Fuchida was happy with this arrangement. For a long time he had wanted to tell his story in a way that would reach the widest possible audience, but he found the task of writing it in English next to impossible. After fulfilling a few speaking engagements on the West Coast, he flew to Maryland, where he and Prange worked together almost daily. Fuchida returned to the West Coast to testify again. Then he hastened back to Maryland, for more work on the project.

As the next step, the sponsor agreed to send them both to Japan, where they could study the events of Fuchida's life in their proper setting. Throughout June, July, and August, Fuchida traveled across the United States testifying, ending in Oregon. In late August he met Prange in San Francisco, and they made their travel plans. Fuchida preceded Prange to Japan by a few weeks.[7]

He headed straight for Kashiwara to pick up the threads of life with Haruko. If she felt any resentment at his long absence, she kept it to herself. Fuchida slipped easily into the familiar routine of life in his beloved Kashiwara. The little farm had prospered under Haruko's firm hand, and he was proud of her.

Fuchida had a touch of the chameleon in him. He fit quite readily into any surroundings. Thus he had adapted well to the United States and its culture. Now, back on his native soil, he began to be more Japanese than his neighbors who knew no other life. He reacted like a hedgehog to the slightest shadow of criticism about Japan.

This was not an attitude he embraced deliberately or even consciously. Nevertheless, when about mid-September Fuchida and Haruko met Prange in Tokyo, Fuchida had altered somewhat from the man to whom Prange saw off in San Francisco.

They stayed in the Imperial Hotel until the Olympic Games began. Then they started out to cover Japan. Thus commenced an excursion into Fuchida's past, with a few speaking engagements on the side. The trip brought happiness, sadness, and ever-increasing nostalgia on Fuchida's part.[8] They visited Kasumigaura, moved through northern Honshu to Hokkaido, where Fuchida proudly showed off the prosperous city of Sapporo, and then proceeded to bleak Nemuro by way of contrast. Time constraints brought them back to Honshu, where, among other places, they visited Yamamoto's boyhood home.

As their route turned southeastward toward Tokyo, every click of the wheels drove Fuchida deeper into memories, not all of them pleasant. He gazed upon Mt. Akagi as long as it remained in sight. That name unlocked recollections too grand for laughter, too deep for tears.

After an overnight stay in Tokyo, on Sunday October 25 they caught the famous express train to Osaka. Admiral Kusaka met them at the station there. He knew Prange well from occupation days and greeted both travelers as if they were long-lost sons. In the background stood Haruko, reluctant to intrude on this reunion.

They went to a church where Fuchida was to speak. They were half an hour late, but the congregation of some one hundred people had waited patiently. Happy to be back in home territory, Fuchida was at his best, enthusiastic and often witty, and the congregation frequently broke into laughter.

The next day Kusaka entertained Fuchida and Prange at his home. While Kusaka remained a devout Buddhist of the Zen discipline, his wife and eldest daughter, Kazuko, were Christians. The three veterans held a long, wardroom-type session in which Kusaka expounded his views about the Pacific war.

After saying farewell to the Kusakas, Fuchida, Haruko, and Prange moved on to Kashiwara. On 30 October the two men left for Hiroshima. For Fuchida, Hiroshima had changed more than any other city they visited. "Not many people from the old days are left," he explained as they walked to the hotel. "Mostly new people live here now." This struck him as a healthy development.

He remembered that back in 1958 when preaching in Hiroshima to an audience of several thousand, he had urged the citizens to put the past behind them, look ahead, and build a new city and a new life. A minister friend of his, he found, had kept the picture of the ruins of his old church. Fuchida begged him to get rid of it. Fuchida pointed out he had a fine new church that deserved his full attention. Thus on this visit, Fuchida was pleased to see Hiroshima moving forward.

He and Prange proceeded by way of the Shimonoseki Tunnel into Kyushu for a brief stop in Nagasaki. At the time of their visit, the United States was considering sending an atomic submarine to Japan. While the mission was entirely friendly, the idea made Fuchida exceedingly nervous. Like many of his countrymen, he had an antipathy to atomic power in any form.

The large naval base at Sasebo held so many memories of Fuchida's naval career that he almost dreaded returning there. But he showed Prange the house where he had lived when stationed in Sasebo, the spots far out in the harbor where the *Akagi* and *Kaga* had once anchored, the U.S. chapel where he had preached, and the Catholic church of the Sacred Heart, which had excited his suspicions in the old days. Thirty years had passed since Fuchida first came to Sasebo. He kept repeating this as if he couldn't believe it: "Thirty years ago!"

On 4 November he and Prange followed the returns of the U.S. presidential election. "Johnson will win," Fuchida predicted—a fairly safe prognosti-

cation—"but he is no Kennedy; he is weak." Fuchida had his favorites among
American presidents, notably Lincoln, Theodore Roosevelt, and Eisenhower.
And he had been strongly attracted by Kennedy's dynamic personality. He
didn't care for either Johnson or Goldwater, so exhibited only tepid interest
in the election.

That afternoon he and Prange reached Kagoshima, forever associated in
Fuchida's mind with the days spent there training his pilots for Pearl Harbor.
Not all his reflections about the past, however, concerned Operation Hawaii.
In the old days, the women of Kagoshima were famous for their wifely virtues.
These memories made Fuchida think of Haruko. He admitted frankly that
he felt guilty about having neglected her. "She is so loving to the children,"
he said. "For six years I left her alone in Japan, but she thought only of the
children and caring for the home. I appreciate her so much and want to make
up to her for the past."

In a way he was glad to return to Tokyo and settle down to long interviews
with Prange. But the past had not yet loosed its hold. Kimi came to see him
at the hotel, accompanied by her sister. Whenever Fuchida could he had sent
her money to support Yoko, and he had written to his daughter on his travels.
Now Kimi begged him to visit the child. According to her, Yoko hadn't seen
her father since she was ten years old. The girl threatened to commit suicide
if he didn't come.

Kimi's plans went much farther. She want Fuchida to divorce Haruko,
marry her, and legitimize their daughter. Yoko was sixteen and would soon
be of college age; Kimi was sure she wouldn't be eligible for a reputable
college as long as she was illegitimate.[9]

While this proposal was totally unrealistic, on its face Kimi's request that
Fuchida visit their daughter seemed reasonable. But, however keenly Fuchida
sorrowed for Yoko, he dared not open that Pandora's box again. He acknowledged his responsibility and vowed he would do what he could financially, but
for him Kimi represented what the Catholics call an occasion for sin, to be
avoided at all costs. If Fuchida's return to Japan had resolved nothing else
in his life, it had solidified his commitment to Haruko.

38

"Remember Pearl Harbor"

Despite Fuchida's reactivated pride in everything Japanese and his avowed intention to compensate Haruko for his long neglect, he returned to the United States for several more years. He began to think seriously about becoming an American citizen and went so far as to take out his first papers.[1]

A number of factors made this decision a logical one. He seemed most useful in the United States, where he was a lay minister to older Japanese-Americans, many of whom spoke little or no English. Moreover, his unusual background gave him an advantage with American congregations, drawing many who would not bother to turn out for a less exotic evangelist. Above all, his children had made the United States their own.

But what of Haruko? One cannot doubt that to be near her children and grandchildren would have meant much to her. Yet since the proposed trip in 1961 which came to naught, she had resisted all suggestions about visiting the United States.[2] At least twice in a crisis situation, Haruko had laid back her ears and balked, and in both cases she had been right. In the face of expert medical opinion, she had saved her leg by refusing amputation. Years later, she had refused Fuchida's request for a divorce. On that occasion she had known what was best for her husband. Was her instinct equally sure now? There in Kashiwara stood the home the family had built with their own hands, there sprang the trees and flowers, there the grain and vegetables they had planted and tended. As long as Haruko remained in Kashiwara, the home would be there waiting for Fuchida.

Joe was now an American citizen, having received his papers in November 1964 while studying at the University of Oregon in Eugene. Many Japanese on their native soil found it almost impossible to separate nationality from blood. To be Japanese meant to be both a citizen of Japan and a member of the Japanese race. After living in the United States, Joe was able to separate citizenship from ethnic background. He became a citizen because he was attracted to the American way of life, and also because many states required citizenship as a qualification for registration as a professional architect.

Fuchida couldn't attend Joe's citizenship ceremonies. He had visited him in September 1964, staying overnight in Eugene on his way from Vancouver to Berkeley. Two or three days after he reached Berkeley he left for Japan. He was also unavoidably absent when in March 1965 Joe received his B.S. in architecture from the University of Oregon. He had worked long and hard toward that goal. All the family had underestimated the difficulty of studying at college level in a foreign tongue. Despite this handicap, Joe won two scholarships in 1962 and held down part-time jobs as a draftsman and designer to help put himself through school.[3]

Fuchida happened to be lecturing in the eastern United States when Miyako's daughter, Miharu Melinda Overturf, was born. Miyako had been working as a freelance interior decorator in a department store. After the birth she had difficulty keeping up with this job. So some time later she opened a shop for costume design in her own home. Meanwhile Jim worked as a contractor.[4]

Next, on 17 June 1966, in Englewood, New Jersey, Marie gave birth to a daughter, Ellen Harumi. She and Joe had moved east after graduation, where he worked as a designer for a firm of architects in New York City. In the evening he pursued graduate studies at Columbia University. His goal was to have his own architectural business, and he seemed well on his way to achieving it.[5]

At year's end Fuchida was finishing a long journey around the Pacific that had included speaking engagements in the Philippines and Guam.[6] From Guam, he slipped without fanfare into Honolulu on 2 December 1966. He requested no publicity until after the forthcoming ceremonies marking the twenty-fifth anniversary of the attack on Pearl Harbor, and the Fourth Estate respected his wishes. While the Pearl Harbor Survivors Association had indicated that he would be welcome, he didn't wish to be too conspicuous, laying himself open to a charge of courting publicity. Jack Connor, a well-known marimbist and vibra-harpist, accompanied Fuchida. He handled business and professional arrangements while Fuchida addressed a few church gatherings.[7]

One of these was at the Kawaihao Church. The pastor, Reverend Abraham Akaka, introduced Fuchida, in token of welcome placing a lei around guest's neck and kissing his cheek in the ancient Christian gesture of peace. During Fuchida's stay, Akaka more or less took him under his wing.[8]

On the evening of 6 December Fuchida, Akaka, and his wife joined other guests of two retired U.S. Army officers and their wives, Brigadier General and Mrs. Kendall J. Fielder and Colonel and Mrs. George Bicknell. Fielder had been the Hawaiian department's intelligence officer twenty-five years earlier, Bicknell his counterintelligence officer. A few Honolulu citizens with a particular interest in the Pearl Harbor attack joined them. Fuchida spoke briefly about the background of the attack.

"But did Japan really expect to win the war?" asked Katsuro Miho, an attorney.

"We had no confidence in victory over the United States," Fuchida admitted. "But we had confidence we could cripple the fleet, and that we could defend ourselves. Meanwhile, if Germany wins in Europe . . ." His voice trailed off.

"Why didn't the Japanese Army take part in the attack?" asked former Sergeant Hugh O'Reilly. "I mean, invade Hawaii?"

"We had no plans for that," Fuchida replied. "We wanted to cripple the fleet."

"We knew they could not make a landing," Fielder assured the company. Japan did not have the necessary ships and Oahu was too well defended, he said in effect.[9]

"Were you surprised to find the aircraft carriers gone?" Miho inquired. "Didn't you expect to find them in Pearl Harbor?"

"No, we had that intelligence," Fuchida responded. "A man working in our Japanese consulate here, a retired ensign, watched the ships every day. He put reports on the advertising hour of the Honolulu radio. 'Two German shepherd dogs missing.' That meant the aircraft carriers had gone to sea."

"Frankly, I take that with a grain of salt," Fielder observed skeptically.

Bicknell added, "Yes, we had all sorts of reports like that, including reports that there were newspaper ads that had hidden meanings. We checked them all out and we've never found a word of truth in any."

"But, yes," Fuchida insisted. "We had a code, and we knew where every battleship is [sic], the *Arizona,* the *Utah,* when the radio man said, 'Papayas, thirty-three cents, pineapple twenty-nine cents,' we look up the book, and we know the order of the battleships."[10]

The yarn did take a bit of swallowing. Fuchida may well have believed it.[11] The tale might have been circulated among the Pearl Harbor airmen deliberately to protect the actual source of intelligence. Questioned on 9 October 1945 by a special counterintelligence agent, Lieutenant Commander

Yoshio Shiga cited as an example "that if . . . it was broadcast that the German attaché lost one dog, it might mean that a carrier left Pearl Harbor . . ." Shiga added that, after the Task Force returned to Japan, he had received this information from Murata.[12] Murata had a mischievous personality; he might have been pulling a few legs.

In fact, a former naval officer, Takeo Yoshikawa, had been operating as a spy out of the Honolulu consulate, reporting to naval intelligence in Tokyo effectively but prosaically by consular code through the Foreign Ministry. In turn, naval intelligence, using the top secret naval code, kept the Nagumo task force posted as it sped toward Hawaii.[13] Police dogs, papayas, and pineapples made for a much better story.

Akaka tactfully changed the subject. "One thing I've always wondered. Why did one plane land on Niihau?" Fuchida informed him that the Japanese had selected Niihau as a rendezvous for damaged planes. A submarine was stationed off that little island to pick up survivors. But the submarine failed to appear off Niihau and it was never heard from again.

Everyone present was interested in what had happened to Fuchida after Pearl Harbor. Briefly he told them about his adventures, his miraculous escapes, his conversion, and his subsequent career as an evangelist. After the party broke up and Fuchida had left, Bicknell remarked, "He seems like a sincere fellow. He was only doing a job."

"You try to forgive and forget," agreed Fielder. He paused before adding, "I lost a lot of friends that day."[14]

Shortly before 0800 Wednesday 7 December, Fuchida stood with Akaka at the National Memorial Cemetery at Punchbowl Hill. They chose an inconspicuous spot slightly to one side beneath a tree and watched the quiet, reverent crowd of about five thousand gather to honor the fallen and hear an address by Secretary of the Navy Paul Nitze. Members of the Pearl Harbor Survivors Association wore easily distinguishable white overseas caps. No one noticed Fuchida—just one more medium-sized Japanese, no more a curiosity in Honolulu than he would have been in Tokyo.

He glanced at his watch. The ceremony would start at 0755, the exact moment his airmen had begun their attack a quarter of a century before. As the speeches commenced, Fuchida wandered off by himself among the graves. At a certain spot he paused and knelt beside one of the plain white markers, that of Ensign Robert W. Uhlmann, born in Detroit, Michigan, on 16 August 1919, died 7 December 1941.

Suddenly a band broke into "The Star-Spangled Banner" and Fuchida snapped to attention. When the last note died away, he and Akaka entered the latter's car and set out for Aiea Heights with its magnificent view of Pearl

Harbor. There they climbed a water tank towering above the Aiea sugar mill. A scattering of photographers and reporters joined them. At their request, Fuchida and Akaka stood with their arms linked for a photograph. Fuchida pointed out the high spots of the attack.[15]

Later in the day he looked at the local newspapers. One ran a front-page photograph of Minoru Genda and carried an interview with him. From Genda's frank, forceful comments, it appeared that the Liberal Democrat diet member had changed little in essence from the commander of the Pearl Harbor planning boards.[16] Fuchida clipped out the article and added it to his scrapbook. It was fitting that on this anniversary he should be reminded of his old friend.

At last Fuchida felt free to visit the *Arizona*. That afternoon he and his colleague Jack Connor paid their respects. Since its erection, the beautiful memorial had been visited by thousands of tourists, so Fuchida could go without violating good taste. He wanted to meditate there for a few minutes, let Connor's photographers shoot some film, and return to shore well before anyone came to arrange for the afternoon memorial scheduled to start at 1730.

Back in Honolulu, Fuchida and Connor discovered that they had plunged into hot water. From the *Arizona* memorial there was a good view of the installations at Pearl Harbor, and no one was allowed to take pictures there without the express permission of the commandant of the Fourteenth Naval District. But no harm was done. The naval authorities confiscated the film, looked it over, gave it a clean bill of health, and told Fuchida it could be picked up on 10 December.[17]

On the eighth, Fuchida spoke at a breakfast sponsored by the International Christian Leadership. At his side sat Mr. Dan Liu, president of that organization's Honolulu branch and also Honolulu's chief of police. Beyond them sat Billy Graham and Akaka. Graham was visiting Hawaii to rest before going to Vietnam to spend Christmas with the servicemen.[18]

The previous day Fuchida's thoughts had turned to Genda, whose intrepid spirit and devotion to Japan typified the best of Fuchida's old life. It seemed equally significant that on this anniversary his path should cross that of Billy Graham, who symbolized Fuchida's new life. What better place to end Fuchida's story than in Honolulu, where he had bombed Battleship Row and decades later knelt in prayer over the *Arizona?* Honolulu, which had adopted Hiroshima as its sister city?[19]

But of course it was not the end. For almost another decade Fuchida continued his evangelizing. Inevitably, he resolved the dilemma of which country should be his home. Despite his love for the United States and the presence there of his children and grandchildren, the call of his native land could not be denied. There in Kashiwara he passed his remaining years with Haruko, tending the farm and preaching the gospel.

In one respect Fuchida's mission had failed. He had hoped and worked for world peace, but humanity had not evolved to the point where it could totally accept the concepts of peace and forgiveness. He was practical enough to understand that the Japanese must deal with the world as it existed. So he allowed a melancholy realism to temper his idealism. In the words of the *Japan Times* of 31 May 1976, "As president of the Osaka Suikokai, a society of former navy officers, he held the view that Japan should possess its own nuclear weapons because war will never disappear from human world."

On 8 January 1972 Miyako and Jim had another child, a son, "very smart and quick-tempered like his grandfather." In April 1976 Miyako received an urgent summons to Japan. She found her father in a hospital bed, thin and almost blind but happy to see her and her children. After two weeks they returned to California. Miyako never saw her father alive again. He died of diabetes on 30 May 1976, at the age of seventy-three. She returned to attend the funeral and memorial services at the Gokoku Shinto shrine in Osaka, given by his old navy friends and "national followers."[20]

As an evangelist, Fuchida was ahead of his time. A man attempting conversions in his generation had to overcome two powerful forces—machismo and the intellectual dominance of science. The influence of the first is apparent in Fuchida's own story. For all his goodwill and kindliness, he didn't appear to give women the same serious consideration that he gave men. Of the hundreds who accepted Christ at rallies where he spoke, some must have been women. But one would never have known it from him. He took pride and interest in his male converts. In converting them, he felt, he had achieved a real breakthrough. This is understandable, for the average male of Fuchida's generation would have found it easier to confess to being Jack the Ripper than openly to avow a religious experience. Public displays of emotion were not considered masculine.

The infallibility of science, part of the mythology of the day, was also a stumbling block to conversion. Science threatened faith. He who professed a belief in anything that could not be analyzed, weighed, dissected, or reproduced at will in the laboratory was "unscientific" and not to be taken seriously.

Today's more holistic approach to life concedes that the individual consists of something more than a few dollars' worth of chemicals. He who admits to experiences immune to analysis is not necessarily written off as fuzzy-minded or a charlatan. In this atmosphere, Fuchida's gifts as a dynamic evangelist might have made a greater mark.

Undoubtedly, Fuchida would have considered his whole life worthwhile if he had recruited just one soul for Christ. And he counted his converts in the hundreds. He was able to depart this life knowing that, first as an officer, then as an evangelist, he had performed his duties well. Who can ask for more?

APPENDIX:

KEY PERSONNEL

Akaka, Reverend Abraham	Honolulu pastor
Anami, Korechika	War minister, 1945
Chihaya, Masataka	Member, Navy Historical Group
Chihaya, Takehiko	Aerial observer
Covell, Margaret	Daughter of American missionaries
DeShazer, Jacob	Participated in Doolittle Raid; later missionary to Japan
Doolittle, James	Leads aerial raid on Japan, April 1942
Egusa, Takeshige	Dive-bombing leader, second wave, at Pearl Harbor; hospitalized with Fuchida
Fuchida, Haruko Kitaoka	Wife of Mitsuo Fuchida
Fuchida, Marie Rael	Wife of Joe Fuchida
Fuchida, Mitsuo	Japanese naval air officer; later Christian evangelist
Fuchida, Shika	Mitsuo Fuchida's mother
Fuchida, Yazo	Mitsuo Fuchida's father
Fuchida, Yoshiya (later Joe)	Son of Mitsuo and Haruko Fuchida
Fukudome, Shigeru	Chief, First Bureau, Naval General Staff; chief of staff, Combined Fleet

Furukawa, Izumi	Reconnaissance pilot
Genda, Minoru	Friend and colleague of Fuchida who held important positions throughout the Pacific war in the Imperial Navy and afterward in the government
Graham, Billy	American evangelist
Halsey, William F.	American admiral
Hasunuma, Shigeru	Aide to the emperor
Hirohito	Emperor of Japan
Itaya, Shigeru	Led fighter planes at Pearl Harbor
Jessberg, John	Pocket Testament League worker
Kakuta, Kakuji	Japanese admiral; commander, Third Air Squadron, Second Carrier Division and land-based First Air Fleet
Kanegasaki, Kazuo	Assistant engineering officer, *Hiryu;* survivor of Midway; POW in the United States
Ketcham, Leyman W.	Preacher in Japan working with Pocket Testament League
Kido, Koichi	Lord keeper of the privy seal
Koga, Mineichi	Commander in chief of the Combined Fleet after Yamamoto
Koiso, Kuniaki	Premier, 1944–45
Kozono, Yasuna	Commander, Atsugi Air Base
Kusaka, Ryunosuke	Chief of staff, First Air Fleet; chief of staff, Combined Fleet; chief of staff, navy headquarters
MacArthur, Douglas	Supreme Allied Commander, Far East
Matsudaira, Yasumasa	Secretary to Kido
"Matsumoto, Kimi"	Mitsuo Fuchida's lover
McFarland, Don	Missionary-evangelist
Mikawa, Gunichi	Commander in chief, Eighth Fleet
Miwa, Kazuo	Kakuta's chief of staff, First Air Fleet
Murata, Shigeharu	Torpedo ace
Muroi, Suteji	Naval Staff College classmate of Fuchida

Nagano, Osami   Chief, Naval General Staff

Nagumo, Chuichi   Commander in chief, First Air Fleet, Pearl Harbor through Midway; commander, central Pacific; other important wartime positions

Naito, Takeshi   Naval Staff College and Kasumigaura classmate of Fuchida

Nimitz, Chester W.   Commander in chief, U.S. Pacific Fleet

Ohmae, Toshikazu   Expert on Pacific war

Okamura, Motoharu   Originator and trainer of *Oka* pilots

Okumiya, Masatake   Friend and colleague of Fuchida

Onishi, Takijiro   Commander, Second Air Fleet; originator of kamikazes

Overturf, Harrison James, III   Fuchida's son-in-law

Overturf, Miyako Fuchida   Fuchida's daughter

Ozawa, Jisaburo   Commander, Singapore area; commander in chief, Third Fleet; commander in chief, Combined Fleet

Pietsch, Timothy   Missionary in Japan

Prange, Gordon W.   Chief, historical section, G-2, FEC headquarters; friend and associate of Fuchida

Sachs, Elmer B.   Head of Worldwide Christian Missionary Army of Sky Pilots

Saito, Reverend Ichijiro   Son of Reverend Toshio Saito

Saito, Reverend Toshio   Fuchida's pastor in Osaka

Shimada, Shigetaro   Navy minister

Shimazaki, Shigekazu   Leader of second wave, Pearl Harbor

Spruance, Raymond A.   American admiral

Suzuki, Eijiro   Classmate of Fuchida's at Eta Jima and Kasumigaura; air officer, Second Carrier Division; air supply officer, Naval General Staff

Suzuki, Kantaro   Retired admiral; premier 1945

Takahashi, Kakuchi   Dive-bomber ace; colleague of Fuchida

Takamatsu, Prince	Brother of emperor; classmate of Fuchida at Eta Jima; member, operations section, Naval General Staff
Terai, Yoshimori	Classmate of Fuchida at Naval Staff College; member, Navy Historical Group
Togo, Shigenori	Foreign minister, 1945
Tomioka, Sadatoshi	Represents Japanese navy at surrender; chief, Navy Historical Section
Toyoda, Soemu	Commander in chief, Combined Fleet; chief, Naval General Staff
Ueno, Keizo	President, Yokosuka installation
Umezu, Yoshijiro	Chief, Army General Staff, 1945
Vorsheim, Reverend H. George	Pastor preaching in Japan with Pocket Testament League
Wagner, Glenn	Chief representative in Japan of Pocket Testament League
Yamaguchi, Tamon	Commander in chief, Second Carrier Division
Yamamoto, Isoroku	Commander in chief, Combined Fleet
Yano, Shikazo	Chief of staff, Combined Fleet, after Kusaka
Yokoi, Toshiyuke	Chief of instructors, Yokosuka; Ugaki's chief of staff at Kanoya, 1945
Yonai, Mitsumasa	Navy minister, 1945

NOTES

Introduction

1. *Japanese Operations in the Southwest Pacific Area,* vol. 2, part 1, of *Reports of General MacArthur* (Washington, D.C.: U.S. Government Printing Office, 1966), p. 33, n. 14.

2. This clipping appears in Fuchida's 1962 file. Unfortunately neither source nor date is given.

3. Interview with Saito, 15 November 1964.

4. Ibid.

1 *"To Be a Flier"*

1. Interview with Mitsuo Fuchida, 26 February 1953; written replies by Fuchida, 20 June 1968, to a questionnaire submitted to him by Prange (hereafter cited as Fuchida questionnaire).

2. Fuchida questionnaire.

3. Ibid.

4. Interview with Fuchida, 26 February 1953.

5. Reiko Chiba, *The Japanese Fortune Calendar* (Rutland, Vt.: C. E. Tuttle, 1965), p. 10.

6. Fuchida questionnaire.

7. Ibid.

8. Ibid.; interview with Fuchida, 26 February 1953.

9. Fuchida questionnaire.

10. Unfinished manuscript by Mitsuo Fuchida, "From Pearl Harbor to Calvary." (Hereafter cited as Fuchida ms.).

11. Fuchida questionnaire; interview with Fuchida, 26 February 1953.

12. Fuchida questionnaire.

13. Ibid.

14. Interview with Fuchida, 26 February 1953.

15. Ibid.; Fuchida questionnaire.

16. Fuchida questionnaire; interview with Minoru Genda, 21 March 1947.

17. Interview with Fuchida, 26 February 1953.
18. Fuchida questionnaire; Fuchida ms.
19. Fuchida ms.
20. Interview with Genda, 21 March 1947.
21. Interview with Fuchida, 26 February 1953; Fuchida questionnaire.
22. Interview with Fuchida, 26 February 1953.
23. Fuchida questionnaire.
24. San Francisco *Chronicle*, 23 and 29 January 1925.
25. Fuchida questionnaire.
26. Ibid.; interview with Genda, 21 March 1947.
27. Fuchida ms.
28. Interview with Fuchida, 26 February 1953; Fuchida questionnaire.
29. Ibid.
30. Fuchida questionnaire.
31. Ibid.
32. Interview with Fuchida, 26 February 1953; Fuchida's career brief.
33. Fuchida questionnaire; interview with Fuchida, 26 February 1953.
34. Fuchida questionnaire.
35. Fuchida ms.

2   *"Take the Cake"*

1. Interview with Fuchida, 23 August 1967; Fuchida career brief.
2. Interview with Fuchida, 23 August 1967.
3. Ibid.
4. Ibid.
5. Ibid.
6. Fuchida career brief; interviews with Fuchida, 26 February 1953, and Genda, 22 March 1947.
7. Interview with Fuchida, 23 August 1967.
8. Replies to questionnaire Prange submitted to Joe Fuchida on 3 January 1979.
9. Interview with Fuchida, 26 February 1953; Fuchida career brief.
10. Interview with Fuchida, 23 August 1967.
11. Fuchida questionnaire.
12. Ibid.; interview with Fuchida, 26 February 1953; Mitsuo Fuchida, *Shinjuwan Sakusen No Shinso: Watakushi Wa Shinjuwan Jokai Ni Ita* (The true story of the Pearl Harbor operation: I was in the air over there), (Nara, Japan: Yamato Taimusu Sha, 1949), pp. 77–78. Hereafter *Shinjuwan Sakusen No Shinso*.
13. Replies to questionnaire Prange submitted to Miyako Fuchida Overturf, 3 January 1979; interview with Fuchida, 23 August 1967.
14. Interview with Fuchida, 23 August 1967.

3   *"Flying High"*

1. Fuchida questionnaire. The China Incident was the term the Japanese used for the long war with China.
2. Ibid.
3. Interviews with Fuchida, 28 July 1947 and 23 August 1967. Prange knew Fuchida well, and this description represents his own judgment as well as that of a number of Japanese ex-officers who had been long-time associates of Fuchida.
4. See for example John Dean Potter, *Yamamoto: The Man Who Menaced America* (New York: Viking Press, 1965), p. 31 (hereafter *Yamamoto*); Leonard Mosley, *Hirohito: Emperor of Japan* (Englewood Cliffs, N.J.: Prentice-Hall, 1966), pp. 172–76 (hereafter *Hirohito*).

5. Fuchida questionnaire. Prange was acquainted with Hoshina, with whom he had several interviews in June 1951, and thought highly of his intelligence and ability.

6. Interview with Fuchida, 10 December 1963; Fuchida questionnaire; interview with Genda, 28 December 1947.

7. Fuchida questionnaire; Fuchida career brief.

8. Interviews with Fuchida, 26 February 1963 and 23 August 1967.

9. Ibid., 28 August 1967.

10. Ibid., 22 August 1967.

11. Ibid., 23 August 1967.

12. Kusaka career brief.

13. Interviews with Fuchida, 10 December 1963 and 23 August 1967. Prange held many interviews with Kusaka, whom he greatly liked and admired.

14. *Shinjuwan Sakusen No Shinso*, p. 37.

15. Interview with Fuchida, 26 February 1953.

16. Ibid.

17. Ibid., 25 February 1964.

18. Ibid., 16 February and 10 May 1964.

19. Ibid., 26 February 1953.

4 *"To Be Flight Leader"*

1. *Shinjuwan Sakusen No Shinso*, pp. 33–35.

2. Interview with Genda, 28 December 1947.

3. *Yamamoto*, p. 196.

4. *Shinjuwan Sakusen No Shinso*, pp. 37–38; interview with Fuchida, 23 August 1967; Nagumo career brief.

5. Chihaya career brief; interview with Masataka Chihaya, 10 June 1951.

6. Kusumi career brief; interview with Genda, 28 December 1947.

7. Interview with Fuchida, 10 December 1963.

8. Interview with Genda, 28 December 1947.

9. Interview with Fuchida, 10 December 1963.

10. Ibid., 23 August 1967; *Shinjuwan Sakusen No Shinso*, pp. 41–42.

11. Interview with Fuchida, 23 August 1967; *Shinjuwan Sakusen No Shinso*, pp. 43–45.

12. Interviews with Fuchida, 24 and 28 May 1947, and 23 August 1967; *Shinjuwan Sakusen No Shinso*, pp. 44–49; interview with Genda, 7 April 1947.

13. Interview with Fuchida, 23 August 1967.

14. Ibid., 10 December 1963 and 23 August 1967.

15. Ibid., 11 December 1963.

16. Interview with Genda, 28 December 1947.

17. Interviews with Fuchida, 10 December 1963, and Genda, 28 December 1947.

18. Ibid.

19. Interviews with Fuchida, 24 and 27 May 1947; *Shinjuwan Sakusen No Shinso*, p. 64; Shigeru Fukudome, *Shikan: Shinjuwan Kogeki* (Tokyo, 1955), pp. 204–5 (hereafter *Shikan*).

20. Interviews with Kusaka, 23 August and 2 December 1947; Ryunosuke Kusaka, *Rengo Kantai* (Tokyo, 1952), pp. 5–6 (hereafter *Rengo Kantai*).

21. Interview with Fuchida, 28 May 1947.

22. Ibid., 26 and 29 July 1947; interviews with Genda, 10 June and 29 August 1947.

23. Interview with Genda, 20 August 1947; *Shinjuwan Sakusen No Shinso*, pp. 82–83.

24. Interview with Fuchida, 10 December 1963.

25. Ibid., 29 February 1948.

26. *Shinjuwan Sakusen No Shinso*, pp. 116–17.

27. Ibid., pp. 123–25.

28. Ibid., pp. 122–23.

5   *"Tiger! Tiger! Tiger!"*

1. Interviews with Fuchida, 27 February and 28 March 1947; Genda, 25 December 1947; Jinichi Goto, 7 February 1950 (Goto was a torpedo bomber pilot aboard the *Akagi*); *Shinjuwan Sakusen No Shinso*, pp. 128–29.
2. *Shinjuwan Sakusen No Shinso*, pp. 129–30.
3. Interviews with Genda, 26 December 1947; Fuchida, 27 February 1948.
4. Interview with Goto, 7 February 1950.
5. *Shinjuwan Sakusen No Shinso*, pp. 136–37; interviews with Fuchida, 27 February 1948 and 10 December 1963.
6. Interview with Fuchida, 10 December 1963.
7. Ibid.; *Shinjuwan Sakusen No Shinso*, pp. 147–50.
8. *Shinjuwan Sakusen No Shinso*, p. 149; interview with Fuchida, 4 March 1948.
9. *Shinjuwan Sakusen No Shinso*, p. 150; interview with Fuchida, 10 December 1963.
10. Interviews with Fuchida, 28 March 1947 and 10 December 1963; Genda, 27 and 28 December 1947.
11. *Shinjuwan Sakusen No Shinso*, pp. 152, 156–57; interviews with Fuchida, 4 March 1948 and 10 December 1963; Genda, 27 December 1947.
12. *Shinjuwan Sakusen No Shinso*, pp. 160–61, 164; interviews with Fuchida, 4 March 1948 and 11 December 1963.
13. Interviews with Fuchida, 4 March 1948 and 11 December 1963; *Shinjuwan Sakusen No Shinso*, pp. 161, 164, 172.
14. Interviews with Fuchida, 4 March 1948 and 11 December 1963; *Shinjuwan Sakusen No Shinso*, pp. 174–75.
15. Interviews with Fuchida, 4 March 1948 and 11 December 1963; *Shinjuwan Sakusen No Shinso*, pp. 180–81.
16. Interview with Fuchida, 11 December 1963; *Shinjuwan Sakusen No Shinso*, pp. 183–86.
17. Interviews with Fuchida, 6 January 1949 and 11 December 1963; *Shinjuwan Sakusen No Shinso*, pp. 187–89.
18. Interview with Fuchida, 11 December 1963; *Shinjuwan Sakusen No Shinso*, pp. 189–91. It isn't clear whether Fuchida's plane ushered one straggler or two back to the task force.

6   *"Japan Once More!"*

1. Interviews with Fuchida, 4 March 1948 and 11 December 1963.
2. Ibid., 23 April 1948 and 21 April 1949; interview with Genda, 30 December 1947.
3. Interviews with Fuchida, 21 April 1949 and 11 December 1963; interview with Genda, 30 December 1947; *Shinjuwan Sakusen No Shinso*, p. 195.
4. Interviews with Fuchida, 6 January 1949 and 11 December 1963; *Shinjuwan Sakusen No Shinso*, pp. 195–96.
5. Interviews with Fuchida, 4 March 1948, 22 and 23 April 1949, and 11 December 1963; *Shinjuwan Sakusen No Shinso*, pp. 196–97.
6. Interviews with Fuchida, 25 February 1948, 6 January and 23 April 1949, and 11 December 1963; *Shinjuwan Sakusen No Shinso*, pp. 197–99. In his interview of 11 December 1963, Fuchida thought this query came from Oishi, but elsewhere he credited Kusaka, and it seems more likely that the chief of staff posed the question.
7. Interviews with Genda, 28 November 1949, and Fuchida, 25 February 1948.
8. Interviews with Fuchida, 23 May 1948, 6 January 1949, and 11 December 1963; *Shinjuwan Sakusen No Shinso*, p. 199.
9. Interviews with Fuchida, 23 May 1948, 22 and 23 April 1949, and 11 December 1963.
10. William C. Armstrong, "God's Masterpiece," *The Quiet Miracle* (December 1977),

p. 4 (hereafter cited as "God's Masterpiece"). This article was based largely on Armstrong's interview with Joe Fuchida.

11. See for example *Osaka Mainichi and Tokyo Nichi Nichi*, 11 December 1941; *Japan Times and Advertiser*, 19, 20, and 21 December 1941.

12. Interview with Genda, 25 August 1947.

13. *Rengo Kantai*, p. 44.

14. Diary of Fifth Carrier Division, 21 December 1941; interviews with Fuchida, 29 July 1947 and 8 October 1949.

15. Interviews with Fuchida, 29 July 1947 and 26 June 1949.

16. Ibid., 29 July 1947 and 8 October 1949. Many years later, Fuchida gave this historic *kakemono* to Prange.

17. Ibid., 29 July 1947 and 8 October 1949; *Rengo Kantai*, pp. 29–30 and 46.

18. Interviews with Fuchida, 29 July 1947 and 8 October 1949.

19. Ibid., 8 October 1949.

20. Ibid., 29 July 1947 and 8 October 1949.

21. Ibid.

22. Ibid., 8 October 1949.

7   *"We Should Face East"*

1. Interview with Fuchida, 1 March 1964.

2. Ibid., 22 August 1967.

3. Interviews with Captain Tatsukichi Miyo, 30 May 1949, and Rear Admiral Sadatoshi Tomioka, 5 August 1947.

4. Masataka Chihaya, unpublished manuscript on World War II in the Pacific, pp. 62–64 and 68 (hereafter Chihaya ms.).

5. Interview with Fuchida, 1 March 1964.

6. Ibid., 29 July 1947, 8 October 1949, and 1 March 1964; interview with Genda, 16 March 1951.

7. Interview with Fuchida, 8 October 1949; *Japan Times and Advertiser*, 2 January 1942.

8. Prange made notes to this effect on the record of his interview with Fuchida of 23 July 1948 and 6 January 1949.

9. Interview with Fuchida, 16 April 1964.

10. "God's Masterpiece," p. 5.

11. Overturf questionnaire; interview with Miyako Overturf, 3 September 1964.

12. Interview with Fuchida, 16 April 1964.

13. Ibid., 1 March 1964 and 22 August 1967.

14. Ibid., 23 May 1948 and 6 January 1949.

15. Ibid., 25 June 1949.

16. Ibid., 23 May 1948 and 6 January 1949.

17. Ibid., 1 March 1964.

18. Ibid., 1 March 1964 and 22 August 1967.

19. Interviews with Fuchida, 1 March 1964 and 24 August 1967; Mitsuo Fuchida and Masatake Okumiya, *Midway: The Battle that Doomed Japan* (Annapolis, Md: U.S. Naval Institute Press, 1955), pp. 36–37 (hereafter *Midway*).

20. Interview with Genda, 26 May 1948.

21. Interview with Fuchida, 1 March 1964 and 24 August 1967.

22. Interview with Genda, 26 May 1948.

23. Samuel Eliot Morison, *The Rising Sun in the Pacific: 1931–April 1942*, vol. 3 of *History of the United States Naval Operations in World War Two* (Boston: Little, Brown & Co., 1948), pp. 293–96 (hereafter *Rising Sun*).

24. Interviews with Fuchida, 24 August 1967, and Genda, 28 May 1948; *Rising Sun*, pp. 316–20; *Midway*, pp. 39–40.

25. Interview with Fuchida, 24 August 1967.
26. Ibid., 1 March 1964.
27. Ibid., 22 August 1967.
28. Interviews with Genda, 26 May 1948, and Fuchida, 1 March 1964.
29. Interview with Fuchida, 1 March 1964; Fuchida ms.
30. Ibid.
31. Ibid.

8 *"Here Was Our Real Enemy"*

1. Interviews with Genda, 26 May 1948, and Fuchida, 1 March 1964.
2. *Rising Sun,* p. 382.
3. Elizabeth I used this expression before her troops at Tilbury in 1588, as the Spanish Armada approached England.
4. Interviews with Fuchida, 1 March 1964 and 24 August 1967; *Rising Sun,* p. 383; *Yamamoto,* pp. 143–44.
5. Interviews with Fuchida, 1 March 1964 and 24 August 1967; *Yamamoto,* pp. 144–45.
6. Interviews with Fuchida, 1 March 1964 and 24 August 1967.
7. Ibid., 24 August 1967; *Rising Sun,* p. 384; *Midway,* pp. 43–44; *Yamamoto,* pp. 146–47.
8. Interviews with Fuchida, 1 March 1964 and 24 August 1967; *Rising Sun,* pp. 384–85; *Midway,* pp. 44–45; *Yamamoto,* p. 147. Later that day, Fuchida's airmen sank a corvette, a fleet auxiliary, and a merchant ship, but he did not mention these actions to Prange.
9. Interviews with Fuchida, 1 March 1964 and 24 August 1967.
10. Ibid., 23 May 1948 and 24 August 1967.
11. Ibid., 24 August 1967.
12. Ibid.
13. Interview with Genda, 26 May 1948.
14. Interview with Fuchida, 24 and 27 August 1967.
15. Ibid., 23 April 1964; 22, 24, and 27 August 1967.
16. Interview with Genda, 26 May 1948.
17. Interviews with Fuchida, 23 April 1964 and 22 and 24 August 1967.
18. Ibid., 23 April 1964.
19. Ibid., 23 April 1964 and 22 and 24 August 1967; interview with Genda, 10 and 26 March 1948.
20. Undated replies by Genda to a questionnaire from Prange. interviews with Genda, 10 March and 26 May 1948.
21. Interviews with Fuchida, 14 February and 23 April 1964.

9 *"Go to Midway and Fight"*

1. *Rengo Kantai,* pp. 71–72.
2. Genda questionnaire; interviews with Genda, 10 March and 26 May 1948.
3. Interviews with Genda, 10 March and 26 May 1948; *Rengo Kantai,* p. 72; undated replies by Kusaka to a questionnaire by the author.
4. Interview with Fuchida, 24 August 1967.
5. Ibid., 23 May 1948 and 24 August 1967.
6. Ibid., 24 August 1967.
7. *Rengo Kantai,* p. 72; interview with Fuchida, 1 March 1964.
8. Diary of Captain Yoshitake Miwa, 28 April 1942 (Miwa was air officer of the Combined Fleet); interviews with Fuchida, 14 February 1964 and 24 August 1967; *Midway,* pp. 98–99.
9. Interview with Fuchida, 24 August 1967.
10. Ibid., 14 February 1964 and 24 August 1967.
11. Ibid., 14 February 1964.

12. Ibid., 27 August 1967.

13. Genda statement.

14. Teiichi Makajima, "Middoue No Higeki" (The tragic battle of Midway), *Shosetsu Fan*, 1956, (hereafter "Tragic Battle"). This series later appeared in book form.

15. Interviews with Fuchida, 14 February and 27 November 1964.

16. Sei-ichi Hohjo, "The Nine Heroes of the Pearl Harbor Attack," *Contemporary Japan: A Review of Far Eastern Affairs* (April 1942).

17. Interviews with Fuchida, 14 February and 27 November 1964. Ugaki diary for 17 and 19 March 1962 discusses Kusaka's visit to Tokyo on this mission.

18. Interview with Fuchida, 14 February 1964; "Tragic Battle."

19. Interview with Fuchida, 14 February 1964; Genda statement; *Rengo Kantai*, p. 81.

20. Interview with Fuchida, 14 February 1964.

10   *"A Hell of a Time"*

1. Interviews with Fuchida, 14 February 1964 and 27 August and 1 September 1967.

2. Ibid., 14 February 1964 and 1 September 1967.

3. Ibid., 14 February 1964.

4. Ibid., 14 February 1964 and 1 September 1967.

5. "Tragic Battle."

6. Interviews with Fuchida, 14 February 1964 and 1 September 1967. Both Genda and Kusaka later believed that skimping on aerial reconnaissance contributed heavily to the Japanese defeat at Midway (Genda statement; interview with Genda, 26 May 1948; *Rengo Kantai*, pp. 81–83).

7. Interview with Fuchida, 14 February 1964; *Rengo Kantai*, p. 81; *Midway*, pp. 143–44.

8. "Tragic Battle"; interview with Fuchida, 14 February 1964.

9. For a detailed account of the action at Midway, see Gordon W. Prange, *Miracle at Midway* (New York: McGraw-Hill, 1982).

10. "Tragic Battle."

11. Kusaka statement; interview with Fuchida, 14 February 1964.

12. Interviews with Fuchida, 14 February 1964 and 1 September 1967; *Rengo Kantai*, p. 86; Genda statement.

13. Interviews with Fuchida, 14 February 1964 and 1 September 1967; "Tragic Battle."

14. Interviews with Fuchida, 14 February 1964 and 1 September 1967.

15. Ibid., 14 February 1964 and 24 August and 1 September 1967.

16. Ibid., 14 February 1964 and 1 September 1967.

17. *Rengo Kantai*, p. 86; Genda statement; interview with Fuchida, 14 February 1964.

18. *Rengo Kantai*, pp. 86–87; Kusaka statement; interview with Fuchida, 14 February 1964.

19. Interviews with Fuchida, 14 February 1964 and 1 September 1967.

20. Ibid., 14 February 1964; "Tragic Battle."

21. Interview with Fuchida, 14 February 1964.

22. Ibid., 14 February 1964; *Miracle at Midway*, pp. 312–14.

23. Japanese aircraft damaged the carrier *Yorktown*, already in bad shape from the Coral Sea battle, and the Japanese submarine *I-168* sank her. The same submarine sank the destroyer *Hammann*. This was a poor exchange for four carriers.

24. Interview with Fuchida, 14 February 1964.

11   *"It Was Ridiculous!"*

1. Interview with Fuchida, 14 February 1964.

2. *Rengo Kantai*, pp. 90–91; Kusaka statement.

3. Interview with Fuchida, 14 February 1964.

4. Ibid.; *Rengo Kantai,* p. 91; Kusaka statement.
5. "Tragic Battle"; Genda statement.
6. Interviews with Fuchida, 16 February 1964 and 27 August 1967; *Rengo Kantai,* p. 91.
7. Interview with Fuchida, 16 February 1964.
8. Ibid., 16 February 1964 and 25 August 1967.
9. "Tragic Battle."
10. *Rengo Kantai,* pp. 92–98; Genda career brief.
11. Interviews with Fuchida, 16 February 1964 and 25 August 1967.
12. Ibid.
13. Ibid., 25 August 1967; "God's Masterpiece," p. 5; Overturf questionnaire.
14. Murata career brief.
15. Interviews with Fuchida, 16 February 1964 and 25 August 1967.

12   *"Into Dangerous Areas"*

1. Interview with Fuchida, 16 February 1964. In his diary entry for 21 November 1942, Ugaki mentioned a Lieutenant Colonel Tsuji who was concurrently on the Army General Staff and on the staff of the Seventeenth Army. This may well have been the officer Fuchida mentioned.

2. Interview with Fuchida, 16 February 1964; Masatake Okumiya and Jiro Horikoshi, with Martin Caidin, *Zero! The Story of Japan's Air War in the Pacific: 1941–55* (New York: E.P. Dutton, 1956), p. 153 (hereafter *Zero!*); Samuel Eliot Morison, *Breaking the Bismarcks Barrier, 22 July 1942–May 1944,* vol. 6 of *History of the United States Naval Operations in World War Two* (Boston: Little, Brown & Co., 1950), p. 118 (hereafter cited *Bismarcks Barrier*).

3. Interview with Fuchida, 16 February 1964.

4. Ibid., 25 August 1967.

5. Ugaki diary, 18 April 1944. At the time, Ugaki made only the briefest of entries, dictated to an aide. On the first anniversary, 18 April 1944, he wrote the full story, which is the sole Japanese eyewitness account. A number of accounts of the shooting down of Yamamoto exist. For an interesting one stressing the American preparations and execution of the ambush, see Burke Davis, *Get Yamamoto* (New York: Random House, 1969), (hereafter *Get Yamamoto*).

6. Interviews with Fuchida, 16 February 1964 and 25 August 1967.

7. *Yamamoto,* pp. 310–11.

8. Interview with Fuchida, 16 February 1964; *Zero!,* p. 183; Ugaki diary, 18 April 1944.

9. *Get Yamamoto,* p. 153.

10. Interview with Fuchida, 16 February 1964; *Get Yamamoto,* pp. 6–12.

11. Interviews with Fuchida, 16 and 18 February 1964 and 25 August 1967.

12. *Get Yamamoto,* p. 8.

13. *Bismarcks Barrier,* p. 129.

14. Ibid., pp. 23–24.

15. Interview with Fuchida, 18 February 1964.

16. Ibid., 18 February 1964 and 25 August 1967.

17. Ibid., 18 February 1964.

18. A stranger to the subject reading accounts of the Pacific war for the spring and summer of 1943 might conclude that the Japanese navy did not possess a ship larger than a cruiser. It was during this time, however, on 2 August that the destroyer *Amagiri* sliced an American PT boat in two—a routine incident that would interest no one save the principals involved had not the boat's skipper been a young reserve lieutenant named John F. Kennedy. Morison's account of this famous incident, based upon John Hersey, "Survival," *New Yorker* (17 June 1944), is particularly interesting, not only because it is so vivid but because it was written years before Kennedy became president of the United States.

19. Interview with Fuchida, 18 February 1964.

20. Ibid. Fuchida's friend Okumiya stressed this same point in *Zero!*, pp. 148–49.

21. Interview with Fuchida, 18 February 1964.

22. Ibid.

23. Ibid.

24. Ibid. Fuchida's suspicion that U.S. submarines smuggled these pamphlets and perhaps arms and agents into the Philippines might have been correct. From February 1943 to March 1944 American submarines ran many such missions into the Philippines (*Bismarcks Barrier*, p. 85).

25. Interview with Fuchida, 18 February 1944.

13   *"A Little White Monkey"*

1. Interview with Fuchida, 18 February 1964.

2. Ibid., 18 February 1964 and 25 August 1967.

3. Ibid., 18 February 1964.

4. Ibid.

5. Ibid.

6. Ibid.

7. Ibid.

8. Ibid.

9. Ibid.

10. Ibid., 19 February 1964.

11. Ibid.

12. Ibid.

13. Ibid.

14   *"Kakuta Was Crazy!"*

1. Interview with Fuchida, 19 February 1964. If Fuchida's timing was correct, Nagumo's presence on Saipan jumped the gun, for he ended his tour as commander at Kure on 20 October 1943, and from that time until 25 February 1944 commanded the First Fleet based in Japan's home waters. Then he was attached to the General Staff until 4 March 1944, when he took over command of the central Pacific. It is quite possible, however, that with this important position in the mill, he visited the Marianas to familiarize himself with the area and its problems.

2. Interview with Fuchida, 19 February 1964.

3. Ibid.

4. For details of these campaigns, see Samuel Eliot Morison, *Aleutians, Gilberts and Marshalls, June 1942–April 1944*, vol. 7 of *History of the United States Naval Operations in World War Two* (Boston: Little, Brown & Co., 1951), pp. 115–78 and 201–278 (hereafter *Gilberts and Marshalls*).

5. Interview with Fuchida, 20 February 1964; *Gilberts and Marshalls*, pp. 317–19.

6. Headquarters, Far East Command (hereafter FEC), interrogation of Fukudome, 4 May 1949, ATIS document no. 48012.

7. Interview with Fuchida, 20 February 1964; *Gilberts and Marshalls*, pp. 319–31.

8. Interview with Fuchida, 20 February 1964.

9. Ibid.

10. Ibid, 22 February 1964.

11. Ibid.

12. Ibid.; Samuel Eliot Morison, *New Guinea and the Marianas, March 1944–August 1944*,

vol. 8 of *History of the United States Naval Operations in World War Two* (Boston: Little, Brown & Co., 1953), pp. 154–55 (hereafter *The Marianas*).

13. Interview with Fuchida, 22 February 1964.

15 *"God Is Testing the Imperial Navy"*

1. Interview with Fuchida, 22 February 1964.
2. Vice Admiral E. P. Forrestal, USN (Ret.), *Admiral Raymond A. Spruance, USN: A Study in Command* (Washington, D.C.: U.S. Government Printing Office, 1966), pp. 119–21 (hereafter *Spruance*). See also *The Marianas*, pp. 29–34.
3. Interview with Fuchida, 22 February 1964; *Spruance*, p. 121; Ugaki diary, 30 March 1944.
4. Interview with Fuchida, 22 February 1964; *The Marianas*, p. 13; Ugaki diary, 13 April 1944.
5. Interview with Fuchida, 22 February 1964; Ugaki diary, 2 April 1944.
6. Interviews with Fuchida, 22 and 25 February 1964.
7. Ibid., 22 February 1964.
8. Ibid., 25 February 1964.
9. Ibid., 23 February 1964.
10. Ibid.
11. *Hirohito*, p. 273.
12. Overturf questionnaire.
13. Interview with Fuchida, 23 February 1964.
14. Interview with Fukudome, 12 May 1950.
15. Interview with Fuchida, 6 January 1949.
16. Ibid., 23 February 1964.
17. Prange knew Kusaka well, had many interviews with him, and had a deep respect for him.
18. Interview with Fuchida, 23 February 1964.

16 *"God Is Not on Our Side"*

1. Interviews with Fuchida, 23 February 1964 and 25 August 1967; Samuel Eliot Morison, *Leyte, June 1944–January 1945*, vol. 12 of *History of the United States Naval Operations in World War Two* (Boston: Little, Brown & Co., 1958), p. 5 (hereafter *Leyte*).
2. Interview with Fuchida, 23 February 1964; *The Marianas*, pp. 214, 216.
3. Statement by ex-Captain Toshikazu Ohmae, 15 October 1947, to G-2, historical section, FEC, "Statement Concerning the Failure of Aerial Combat in Operation 'A,'" ATIS document no. 51051. Prange knew Ohmae well and had a number of interviews with him.
4. Interview with Fuchida, 23 February 1964.
5. Ibid.
6. Ugaki diary, 27 May 1944.
7. Interviews with Fuchida, 23 and 24 February 1964; Ugaki diary, 30 May 1944.
8. Interview with Fuchida, 23 February 1964; *The Marianas*, pp. 118–33. The latter deals with Operation *Kon*.
9. Interview with Fuchida, 23 February 1964.
10. Interview with Fuchida, 24 February 1964.
11. Ibid.; *The Marianas*, pp. 219–20; Ugaki diary, 9 June 1944. In his interview, Fuchida dated these reconnaissance flights 11 and 20 May. However, as he mentioned that this was "when Biak was just about over," the scout missions must have taken place in June. There can be little doubt that these flights are the ones cited by Morison and Ugaki.

12. Interviews with Fuchida, 23 and 24 February 1964.

13. Ugaki diary, 15 June 1944.

14. Excellent accounts exist of the Battle of the Philippine Sea. See for example *The Marianas*, pp. 257–321.

15. *The Marianas*, pp. 301, 304, 319.

16. Interview with Fuchida, 24 February 1964.

17. Statement by ex-General Shigeru Hasunuma, 31 March 1950, to G-2 historical section, FEC, ATIS document no. 58225.

18. Statement by Marquis Koichi Kido, 17 May 1949, to G-2 historical section, FEC, ATIS documents nos. 61476 and 61541.

19. Statement by ex-General Kuniaki Koiso, 16 December 1949, to G-2 historical section, FEC, ATIS document no. 55906.

20. Yonai was recalled to active duty so that he might join the cabinet as navy minister.

21. Statement by Marquis Yasumasa Matsudaira, 5 August 1949, to G-2 historical section, FEC, ATIS document no. 61636.

22. Koiso statement.

23. Interview with Fuchida, 24 February 1964.

17   *"Kill, Kill, Kill!"*

1. Interview with Fuchida, 25 February 1964. Jo was killed on the bridge of his carrier *Chiyoda* in the Battle of Leyte Gulf.

2. Statement by ex-Rear Admiral Katsuhei Nakamura, 1 October 1947, to G-2 historical section, FEC, ATIS document no. 49257. Nakamura was former chief, Administrative Department, Naval Air Squadron.

3. Interview with Fuchida, 25 February 1964.

4. Ibid.; Nakamura statement; *Zero!*, p. 252.

5. Statement by ex-Captain Mitsuo Fuchida, 24 June 1949, to G-2 historical section, FEC, ATIS document no. 49259; *Leyte*, p. 68.

6. Interview with Rear Admiral Sadatoshi Tomioka, 17 February 1948.

7. *Zero!*, pp. 241–45; *Leyte*, p. 166.

8. Fuchida statement.

9. Samuel E. Morison, *The Liberation of the Philippines: Luzon, Mindanao, the Visayas, 1944–1945*, vol. 13 of *The History of United States Naval Operations in World War Two* (Boston: Little, Brown & Co., 1959), pp. 53, 111 (hereafter *Liberation of the Philippines*).

10. Interviews with Fuchida, 24 and 25 February 1964.

11. Ibid., 25 February 1964.

12. Ugaki diary, 17 and 22 August 1944.

13. Statement by ex-Colonel Takushiro Hattori, 1 June 1948, to G-2 historical section, FEC, ATIS document no. 50735.

14. Statement by Hattori, 1 October 1949, to G-2 historical section, FEC, ATIS document no. 53074.

15. Interview with Fuchida, 25 February 1964.

16. Ibid.

17. Ibid.

18. Statement by ex-Rear Admiral Toshitane Takada, 10 October 1949, to G-2 historical section, FEC, ATIS document no. 50267.

19. Interview with Fuchida, 25 February 1964. Fuchida blamed Ugaki as commander in chief of the Fifth Air Fleet for this action. However, Ugaki was not appointed to that command until 10 February 1945 (Ugaki diary, 10 February 1945). The order seems to have come from headquarters, Combined Fleet, where Toyoda had left Kusaka in charge. According to Ohmae, on 12 October the Combined Fleet ordered the First Mobile Fleet to send all its operational planes to reinforce the Second Air Fleet in the operations off Formosa (statement by ex-Capt.

Toshikazu Ohmae, 10 March 1948, to G-2 historical section, FEC, ATIS document no. 50734).

20. Samuel E. Morison, *The Two-Ocean War: A Short History of United States Navy in the Second World War* (New York: Ballantine Books, 1972), p. 363. (hereafter *Two-Ocean War*); Ohmae statement.

21. Interview with Fuchida, 25 February 1964; Ugaki diary, 19 October 1944; Fuchida and Genda career briefs.

22. Statement by Hattori, 6 October 1948, to G-2 historical section, FEC, ATIS document no. 56425; *Two-Ocean War*, p. 363; Ugaki diary, 19 October 1944.

23. Statement by ex-Vice Admiral Jisaburo Ozawa, 9 January 1950, to G-2 historical section, FEC, ATIS document no. 55130; statement by ex-Vice Admiral Takeo Kurita, 10 December 1949, ATIS document no. 53758.

24. Statement by Fuchida, 31 July 1949, to G-2 historical section, FEC, ATIS document no. 56587.

25. Ugaki diary, 18 October 1944; *Two-Ocean War*, p. 371; *Leyte*, p. 160.

26. Interview with Fuchida, 24 February 1964.

27. Statement by Kurita.

28. *Leyte*, pp. 319, 430–32.

29. Statement by Kurita; *Leyte*, pp. 430–32.

18   "The Situation Was Bad"

1. *Zero!*, pp. 257, 266, 294.

2. Fleet Admiral William F. Halsey, USN, and Lieutenant Commander J. Bryan III, USNR, *Admiral Halsey's Story* (New York: McGraw-Hill, 1947), pp. 238–39.

3. *Washington Post*, 26 May 1975.

4. *Liberation of the Philippines*, p. 59. The full story is covered in pp. 59–87.

5. Shimazaki career brief.

6. *Zero!*, pp. 271–83; Genda career brief.

7. Statement by ex-Colonel Hiroshi Hosoda, 9 September 1949, to G-2 historical section, FEC, ATIS document no. 50573.

8. *Reports of General MacArthur*, vol. 2, *Japanese Operations in the Southwest Pacific Area*, part 2, (Washington, D.C., 1966), pp. 585–86 (hereafter *MacArthur Reports*).

9. Interview with four ex-navy officers, Tomioka, Ohmae, Fuchida, and Commander Yoshimori Terai, 9 September 1949, for G-2 historical section, FEC, ATIS document no. 50572 (hereafter Joint interview). In this instance, Tomioka was the speaker.

10. *MacArthur Reports*, vol. 2, part 2, pp. 580–81; Joint interview (Fuchida); Ugaki diary, 10 February 1945.

11. Ugaki diary, 10 and 21 November 1944; *MacArthur Reports*, vol. 2, part 2, p. 581.

12. Samuel E. Morison, *Victory in the Pacific*, vol. 14 of *History of United States Naval Operations in World War Two* (Boston: Little, Brown & Co., 1960), p. 22. (hereafter *Victory*); Ugaki diary, 16 February 1945.

13. Ugaki diary, 19 February 1945.

14. *Victory*, pp. 53–55.

15. Joint interview (Terai).

16. Ugaki diary, 17 February and 9–12 March 1949. From the midget submarine operation at Pearl Harbor to his own kamikaze action on the last day of the war, Ugaki's diary reveals that he was enamored with the concept of suicide.

17. *MacArthur Reports*, vol. 2, part 2, p. 594.

18. Ugaki diary, 17 March 1945; interview with Fuchida, 25 February 1964.

19. Interview with Fuchida, 25 February 1964.

20. Joint interview (Tomioka)

21. Ugaki diary, 18 March 1945.

22. Ibid., 21 March 1945; *Zero!*, pp. 252–53.

23. Ugaki diary, 21 March 1945; *MacArthur Reports,* vol. 2, part 2, p. 597n.

24. Joint interview (Fuchida and Tomioka)

25. *Victory*, pp. 94–97.

26. Interview with Fuchida, 28 February 1964.

27. Ibid.; statement by ex-Lieutenant Colonel Takashi Kagoshima, 9 September 1949, to G-2 historical section, FEC, ATIS document no. 50571. Kagoshima was on the air staff at imperial headquarters.

28. Interview with Fuchida, 28 February 1964.

29. *Victory*, pp. 181, 198.

30. Statement by Lieutenant General Torashiro Kawabe, 9 September 1949, to G-2 historical section, FEC, ATIS document no. 50569. From August 1944 to April 1945, he was vice chief of the army's aeronautical department, from April to August 1945, deputy chief of the General Staff.

31. *MacArthur Reports,* vol. 2, part 2, p. 600; interview with Fuchida, 28 February 1964.

32. Interview with Fuchida, 28 February 1964; Joint interview (Fuchida and Tomioka).

33. Interview with Fuchida, 28 February 1964.

34. Ibid.; *Victory*, pp. 200–208.

35. Ugaki diary, 8 April 1945.

36. Statement by Kido, 20 December 1949, to G-2 historical section, FEC, ATIS document no. 62131; statement by Matsudaira, 5 August 1949, to G-2 historical section, FEC, ATIS document no. 61636.

37. Statement by Kido, 17 May 1949, to G-2 historical section, ATIS document no. 61541.

38. Statement by ex-Lieutenant General Masao Yoshigumi, 22 December 1949, to G-2 historical section, FEC, ATIS document no. 54484. He was chief of the military affairs bureau in the War Ministry.

39. Statement by ex-Admiral Koshiro Oikawa, 9 May 1950, to G-2 historical section, FEC, ATIS document no. 61341. Oikawa was a former chief of the Naval General Staff.

40. Statement by ex-Colonel Sako Tanemura, 21 August 1950, to G-2 historical section, FEC, ATIS document no. 61977.

41. *Hirohito,* p. 288.

42. Statement by Shigenori Togo, 18 May 1949, to G-2 historical section, FEC, ATIS document no. 50304.

43. Interviews with Fuchida, 28 and 29 February 1964. Fuchida lost another old comrade on Okinawa, Captain Sei Tanamachi, an Eta Jima classmate; Kusaka career brief. On 27 February 1945 Ugaki visited Kushira Air Group, where the commanding officer reported to him "on the progress of extracting fuel oil from pine roots" (Ugaki diary, 27 February 1945).

44. Interview with Fuchida, 29 February 1964.

45. Interview with Overturf, 3 September 1964.

46. Ugaki diary, 11 May 1945.

47. Ibid., 2 June 1945.

48. Interview with Fuchida, 29 February 1964.

49. Statement by ex-Major General Shoichi Amano, 7 September 1949, to G-2 historical section, FEC, ATIS document no. 59617. Amano was chief of the army operations section Imperial General Headquarters from February to August 1945.

50. Statement by Kawabe.

51. Interview with Fuchida, 29 February 1949; statement by ex-Rear Admiral Katsuhei Nakamura, 20 August 1949, to G-2 historical section, FEC, ATIS document no. 50565.

52. Interview with Fuchida, 29 February 1964; statement by Terai, 26 June 1949 to G-2 historical section, FEC, ATIS document no. 50821.

53. Ugaki diary, 24–25 May; *Victory*, pp. 270–71.

54. Interview with Fuchida, 29 February 1964.
55. Terai statement.
56. *Victory*, pp. 266, 332.
57. Interview with Fuchida, 29 February 1964.

19   *"This Must Be the Atomic Bomb"*

1. Interview with Fuchida, 29 February 1964. Kashiwara, located near Osaka, was Fuchida's "home town."
2. Ibid.
3. Ibid.
4. Ibid.
5. Statement by Kawabe, 23 August 1948, to G-2 historical section, FEC, ATIS document no. 61539. See also *Zero!*, p. 288.
6. Statement by Dr. Yoshio Nishina, 29 June 1950, to G-2 historical section, FEC, ATIS document no. 60245.
7. Statement by Sumihisa Ikeda, 23 December 1949, to G-2 historical section, FEC, ATIS document no. 54479.
8. Statement by Lieutenant General Shuichi Miyazaki, 29 December 1949, to G-2 historical section, FEC, ATIS document no. 54478.
9. Statement by Nishina, 12 August 1948, to G-2 historical section, FEC, ATIS document no. 60246.
10. Interview with Fuchida, 25 August 1967.
11. Statement by Kido, 17 May 1949, to G-2 historical section, FEC, ATIS document no. 61541.
12. Ugaki diary, 7 August 1945.
13. Interview with Fuchida, 25 August 1967.
14. Ibid., 29 February 1964.
15. Ibid., 25 August 1967.
16. Statement by Nishina, ATIS document no. 60245.
17. Statement by Arisue, 16 August 1949, to G-2 historical section, FEC, ATIS document no. 61411.
18. *MacArthur Reports*, vol. 2, part 2, p. 441.
19. Interviews with Fuchida, 29 February 1964.
20. Statement by Nishina, ATIS document no. 60245.
21. Interview with Fuchida, 29 February 1964.
22. Diary of Henry L. Stimson, Yale University Library, New Haven, Conn., 5 March 1945.
23. Interviews with Fuchida, 29 February 1964 and 25 August 1967.
24. Ibid.
25. Ibid.
26. *Zero!*, pp. 289–90.
27. Interview with Fuchida, 29 February 1964.

20   *"The Game Is Up"*

1. Interviews with Fuchida, 29 February 1964 and 25 August 1967.
2. *MacArthur Reports*, vol. 2, part 2, pp. 701–2. This book and many others dealing with this period of history contain the full text of the Potsdam declaration.
3. Statement by Shigenori Togo, 17 May 1949, to G-2 historical section, FEC, ATIS document no. 50304.

4. *MacArthur Reports*, vol. 2, part 2, pp. 703–4; Toshikazu Kase, *Journey to the Missouri* (New Haven, Conn.: Yale University Press, 1950), p. 207–10 (hereafter cited as *Journey to the Missouri*).

5. Statement by Toyoda, 1 December 1949, to G-2 historical section, FEC, ATIS document no. 57670.

6. Ugaki diary, 29 July 1945. The "three countries" were the powers signing the Potsdam Declaration: the United States, Great Britain, and the Soviet Union.

7. Statement by Togo, 28 November 1949, to G-2 historical Section, FEC, ATIS document no. 54562; *MacArthur Reports*, vol. 2, part 2, pp. 704–5; *Journey to the Missouri*, p. 211; *Hirohito*, pp. 310–11.

8. Statement by Sumihasa Ikeda, 23 December 1949, to G-2 historical section, FEC, ATIS document no. 54479.

9. Togo statements no. 54562 and 50304.

10. Statement by Toyoda, 29 August 1949 to G-2 historical section, FEC, ATIS document no. 61340.

11. Interview with Fuchida, 29 February 1964.

12. Statement by ex-Vice Admiral Zenshiro Hoshina, 9 November 1948, to G-2 historical section, FEC, ATIS document no. 61978.

13. Togo statement no. 50304.

14. *MacArthur Reports*, vol. 2, part 2, pp. 711–14; *Journey to the Missouri*, pp. 233–35.

15. Ikeda statement.

16. Togo statement no. 50304; *MacArthur Reports*, vol. 2, part 2, pp. 713–14; *Journey to the Missouri*, pp. 233–34.

17. Statement by Ikeda, 27 December 1949, to G-2 historical section, FEC, ATIS document no. 54483. Several versions of Hirohito's words exist. We have chosen this one from Ikeda's statement, which is a full account, apparently verbatim, of the imperial conference of 9–10 August 1945.

18. *MacArthur Reports*, vol. 2, part 2, pp. 714–15.

19. Stimson diary, 24 July and 10 August 1945.

20. Toyoda statement.

21. Statement by ex–Lieutenant Colonel Masahiko Takeshita, 28 February 1950, to G-2 historical section, FEC, ATIS document no. 56367.

22. *MacArthur Report*, vol. 2, part 2, pp. 716–17.

23. Ugaki diary, 11 August 1945.

24. Interviews with Fuchida, 13 and 29 February 1964 and 25 August 1967. There is some question as to the name of this officer. In his interview of 25 August 1967 Fuchida referred to him as Major Miyazaki, but in both 1964 interviews as Lieutenant Colonel Yoshida, so we have assumed that the latter is correct. The fact that a Lieutenant General Shuichi Miyazaki was in the general headquarters at that time might have confused Fuchida.

25. Ibid., 25 August 1967.

26. Hoshina statement.

27. Interview with Fuchida, 25 August 1967.

28. *MacArthur Reports*, vol. 2, part 2, pp. 717–18.

29. Togo statement no. 50304.

30. *MacArthur Report*, vol. 2, part 2, pp. 718–21.

31. Statement by ex-Colonel Saburo Hayashi, 23 December 1949, to G-2 historical section, FEC, ATIS document no. 61436.

32. Statement by Hoshina; *MacArthur Reports*, vol. 2, part 2, p. 718.

33. Interviews with Fuchida, 7 April 1964 and 25 August 1967. According to *MacArthur Reports*, vol. 2, part 2, p. 719, the emperor met with the princes of the blood on the afternoon of 13 August. This helps place Fuchida's story in context.

34. Statement by Hasunuma, 31 March 1950, to G-2 historical section, FEC, ATIS document no. 58225.

35. Interview with Fuchida, 25 August 1967.

36. Togo statement no. 50304.

37. Takeshita statement.

38. *MacArthur Reports*, vol. 2, part 2, pp. 725–26; *Journey to the Missouri*, pp. 252–53. These pages contain the full text of the emperor's speech so far as it is known.

39. Brief, excellent accounts of this coup appear in *Hirohito*, pp. 327–29; *Journey to the Missouri*, pp. 258–60; *MacArthur Reports*, vol. 2, part 2, pp. 731–39. Much valuable source material is contained in statements to G-2 historical section, FEC, by Takeshita, Kido, Major Kiyoshi Tsukamoto, Lieutenant Colonel Masatake Ida, Lieutenant Colonel Masao Inoba, Colonel Hiroshi Fuwa, Colonel Saburo Hayashi and, Chamberlain Yoshiro Tokugawa.

40. Interviews with Fuchida, 13 February 1964 and 25 August 1967. The full text of the imperial rescript ending the war appears in both Japanese and English in *MacArthur Reports*, vol. 2, part 2, opp. p. 728.

41. Interviews with Fuchida, 13 and 29 February 1964. Ugaki did wait for the emperor's broadcast, but it did not change his resolution to kill himself (Ugaki diary, 15 August 1945).

21   *"More Trouble Is Coming!"*

1. Interviews with Fuchida, 7 and 16 April 1964.

2. *Journey to the Missouri*, pp. 261–62.

3. Interview with Fuchida, 13 February 1964.

4. Ibid., 7 April 1964 and 28 August 1967.

5. Ibid., 29 February 1964; *Journey to the Missouri*, p. 261.

6. Statement by Hasunuma, 31 March 1950, to G-2 historical section, FEC, ATIS document no. 58225.

7. *MacArthur Reports*, vol. 2, part 2, pp. 752–53.

8. Interview with Fuchida, 7 April 1964.

9. Ibid.

10. Ibid., 7 April 1964 and 28 August 1967.

11. Ibid., 7 April 1964.

12. Ibid.; *MacArthur Reports*, vol. 2, part 2, p. 752.

13. Interview with Fuchida, 7 April 1964. It is generally accepted that Kozono abandoned his rebellion on 19 August as the result of a telephone call from Prince Takamatsu. (*MacArthur Report*, vol. 2, part 2, p. 751; *Hirohito*, p. 333n.). The story related here is that which Fuchida told Prange.

14. Interview with Fuchida, 28 August 1967.

15. Ibid., 12 April 1964.

16. Ibid., 11 April 1964.

17. Ibid. There is some question as to when this incident took place. Fuchida thought it was 25 August 1945; however, the *MacArthur Reports*, vol. 1, supplement, pp. 31–32, state that "a reinforced company from the Third Fleet Land Force" occupied Tateyama during the afternoon of 1 September. Probably they were ready for trouble, for Halsey's "trust in the Japs was less than wholehearted" (*Admiral Halsey's Story*, p. 272.).

18. Interviews with Fuchida, 11 April 1964 and 28 August 1967.

19. Ibid.

20. Ibid.

21. Ibid., 11 April 1964.

22. Ibid., 28 August 1967.

23. Log of the *Missouri*, 2 September 1945.

24. Interview with Fuchida, 28 August 1967.

25. *Victory*, p. 366.

26. Interview with Fuchida, 28 August 1967.

22 *"Sad and Demoralizing"*

1. Interview with Chihaya, 16 November 1964.
2. Interview with Fuchida, 12 April 1964.
3. Ibid., 16 April 1964.
4. Ibid.
5. Ibid., 29 February 1964 and 25 August 1967.
6. Ibid., 12 April 1964 and 28 August 1967. Prange was acquainted with most of these men. Terai he knew slightly. He knew Tomioka and Ohmae well and had many interviews with both. He often spoke of Chihaya as being like a brother to him.
7. Ibid.
8. Ibid., 12 April 1964.
9. Ibid., 12 April 1964 and 28 August 1967.
10. Interview with "Kimi Matsumoto," 15 November 1964. Prange chose to use a pseudonym for her to spare all concerned unnecessary embarrassment. For this same reason, he preferred not to name the officer to whom she was engaged.
11. Interview with Chihaya, 16 November 1964.
12. Interview with Fuchida, 16 April 1964.
13. Ibid.
14. Ibid.
15. *MacArthur Reports*, vol. 1, supplement, pp. 42, 49.
16. Interview with "Matsumoto," 15 November 1964.
17. Interview with Chihaya, 16 November 1964.
18. Interview with "Matsumoto," 15 November 1964.

23 *"Under the Grace of God"*

1. "God's Masterpiece," p. 5.
2. Interview with "Matsumoto," 15 November 1964.
3. Interviews with Fuchida, 14 April 1964 and 28 August 1967; Overturf questionnaire.
4. Interview with Fuchida, 29 August 1967.
5. Ibid., 14 April 1964 and 28 August 1967. The land reform law passed late in 1946. During 1947 the government purchased over two million acres for redistribution (*MacArthur Reports*, vol. 1, supplement, pp. 212–13).
6. Interview with Fuchida, 14 April 1964.
7. "God's Masterpiece," p. 5.
8. Interview with Fuchida, 16 April 1964.
9. Ibid.
10. "God's Masterpiece," p. 5.
11. Interviews with Fuchida, 14 April 1964 and 28 August 1967.
12. Ibid., 14 April 1964; Overturf questionnaire.
13. Interviews with Fuchida, 14 April 1964 and 28 August 1967.
14. The *White Plains* (New York) *News*, 24 December 1975; "God's Masterpiece," p. 4.
15. Interview with Fuchida, 16 April 1964.
16. Ibid., 14 April 1964.
17. Interview with Overturf, 3 September 1964; Overturf questionnaire.
18. "God's Masterpiece," p. 5.
19. Overturf questionnaire; interview with Overturf, 3 September 1961.
20. "God's Masterpiece," p. 5.
21. Interviews with Fuchida, 14 and 16 April 1964.
22. Ibid., 16 April 1964.
23. Ibid., 14 April 1964.

24. Ibid., 16 April 1964.
25. Ibid., 14 and 16 April 1964.

24 *"In the Name of Justice"*

1. Interview with Fuchida, 14 April 1964. He expressed similar sentiments in an interview of 28 August 1967.
2. "God's Masterpiece," p. 7.
3. Interview with Fuchida, 29 August 1967.
4. Ibid., 18 April 1964 and 29 August 1967.
5. Ibid., 16 and 18 April 1964.
6. Fuchida ms.
7. Interviews with Fuchida, 16 April 1964 and 29 August 1967.
8. Ibid., 16 April 1964.
9. Ibid., 19 April 1964.
10. *MacArthur Reports*, vol. 1, supplement, pp. 187–91.
11. Interview with Fuchida, 19 April 1964.
12. See for example *Hirohito*, pp. 331–32.
13. Interview with Fuchida, 19 April 1964.
14. Ibid., 16 April 1964.
15. Ibid., 14 April 1964.
16. Ibid., 18 April 1964 and 30 August 1967.
17. Ibid., 18 April 1964; *Pacific Stars and Stripes*, 13 April 1949.
18. Interview with Fuchida, 18 April 1964.
19. Ibid.

25 *Where Does This Great Love Come From?*

1. Interview with Fuchida, 19 April 1964.
2. Ibid., 21 April 1964.
3. Ibid., 19 and 21 April 1964; Fuchida ms.
4. Interview with Fuchida, 21 April 1964; "The Japanese Story of the Battle of Midway" (a translation), OPNAV P32-1002, U.S. Office of Naval Intelligence, Washington, D.C., June 1947, pp. 9–11.
5. Interview with Fuchida, 21 April 1964; "Japanese Story"; letter, CinCPAC to CNO, 28 June 1942, Subject: Interrogation of Japanese Prisoners Rescued at Sea off Midway on 19 June 1942.
6. CinCPAC letter.
7. Interview with Fuchida, 21 April 1964.
8. Ibid., 19 and 21 April 1964.
9. Ibid., 21 April 1964; Fuchida ms.
10. Interview with Fuchida, 19 April 1964; Fuchida ms.
11. Interview with Fuchida, 21 April 1964; Fuchida ms.
12. Interviews with Fuchida, 19 and 21 April 1964.
13. Ibid., 21 April 1964; Fuchida ms.
14. Interview with Fuchida, 28 April 1964.
15. Ibid., 21 April 1964; Fuchida ms.

26 *"The Knowledge of Christ"*

1. Interview with "Matsumoto," 15 November 1964.
2. Ibid. Prange saw the daughter, then a teenager, when he interviewed her mother. He was struck by her marked resemblance to Fuchida.

3. Interview with Fuchida, 23 April 1964.

4. Ibid.; Fuchida ms; Charles Hoyt Watson, *DeShazer: The Doolittle Raider Who Turned Missionary* (Winona Lake, Ind.: The Light and Life Press, 1950), pp. 26–30 (hereafter *DeShazer*). This book, highly laudatory of DeShazer, barely mentions Pearl Harbor.

5. Interview with Fuchida, 25 April 1964; Fuchida ms.; *DeShazer*, pp. 30, 40.

6. Interview with Fuchida, 25 April 1964; Fuchida ms; *DeShazer*, pp. 67–72, 109–10, 115. *DeShazer* throughout rather softpedals his initial hatred of the Japanese.

7. Interview with Fuchida, 25 April 1964; Fuchida ms.; *DeShazer*, pp. 83–95.

8. Interview with Fuchida, 25 April 1964; Fuchida ms.; *DeShazer*, pp. 96–144, 160.

9. Interviews with Fuchida, 25 April 1964 and 22 August 1967.

10. Ibid., 25 April 1964; Fuchida ms.

11. Interview with Fuchida, 25 and 28 April 1964.

12. Ibid., 25 and 28 April 1964; Fuchida ms.

13. Interview with Fuchida, 28 April 1964.

27   *"You Must Bear Witness"*

1. Interview with Fuchida, 22 August 1967.

2. Ibid., 2 May 1964.

3. Interview with "Matsumoto," 15 November 1964.

4. Interviews with Fuchida, 2 May 1964 and August 30, 1967.

5. Ibid., 2 May 1964.

6. Ibid.; Fuchida ms.

7. Interview with Fuchida, 2 May 1964.

8. Ibid.; Fuchida ms.

9. Interview with Fuchida, 2 May 1964.

10. Ibid., 23 August 1967.

11. Ibid., 2 May 1964.

12. Ibid., 4 May 1964; *DeShazer*, p. 168.

13. Interview with Fuchida, 29 August 1967.

14. Ibid., 4 May 1964.

15. *DeShazer*, p. 169.

16. Interview with Fuchida, 4 May 1964; Fuchida ms.; *DeShazer*, pp. 168–69.

17. Interview with Fuchida, 4 May 1964; *DeShazer*, p. 162. The Reverend Saito was the son of the pastor who baptized Fuchida in 1952.

18. Interview with Fuchida, 4 May 1964.

19. Ibid.; Fuchida ms.; *DeShazer*, p. 170.

28   *"A Real Soldier of Christ"*

1. Interviews with Fuchida, 4 and 5 May 1964.

2. Ibid., 5 May 1964; Fuchida ms.

3. Interview with Fuchida, 5 May 1964.

4. Ibid.; Fuchida ms.

5. Kazuo Sakamaki, *I Attacked Pearl Harbor* (New York: Association Press, 1949).

6. Interviews with Fuchida, 8 May 1964 and 30 August 1967.

7. Ibid.

8. Ibid., 7 May 1964.

9. Fuchida ms.

10. Interview with Fuchida, 5 May 1964.

11. Ibid.

12. Ibid.; Fuchida ms.

13. Ibid.

14. Interview with Fuchida, 5 May 1964.
15. Ibid., 7 May 1964 and 30 August 1967.
16. Ibid., 7 May 1964.
17. Ibid., 6 and 7 May 1964 and 30 August 1967.
18. Ibid., 6 May 1964 and 30 August 1967.
19. Ibid., 7 May 1964.

29 *"The Fellowship of Christ"*

1. Stimson diary, 22 and 24 July 1945.
2. Interview with Fuchida, 8 May 1964.
3. Ibid.; Fuchida ms.
4. Interview with "Matsumoto," 15 March 1964.
5. Interview with Fuchida, 9 May 1964.
6. Ibid.
7. Ibid., 9 May 1964 and 1 September 1967.
8. Ibid.; Fuchida ms.
9. Interview with Fuchida, 9 May 1964.
10. Ibid.; Fuchida ms.
11. Interview with Fuchida, 9 May 1964; Fuchida ms.
12. Interview with Fuchida, 9 May 1964.
13. Ibid., 9 and 10 May 1964.
14. Ibid., 10 May 1964; Fuchida ms.
15. Ibid.
16. Interview with Fuchida, 10 May 1964.
17. Notes taken by author on a trip he and Fuchida made through Japan in 1964 (hereafter Prange notes).
18. Interview with "Matsumoto," 15 November 1964.
19. Interview with Fuchida, 10 May 1964; Fuchida ms.
20. "God's Masterpiece," p. 7. While his son wrote that after his conversion Fuchida "didn't touch a drop," he always took beer or wine—sometimes both—when dining with Prange.
21. *San Francisco Chronicle,* 7 December 1951.
22. Interview with Fuchida, 23 August 1967.
23. Ibid., 10 and 11 May 1964.
24. Mitsuo Fuchida and Masatake Okumiya, *Midway: The Battle that Doomed Japan* (Annapolis, MD: United States Naval Institute Press, 1955).
25. Ibid., 11 May 1964 and 29 August 1967.
26. Fuchida told a number of newspapers of this offer and his rejection of it (see for example the Oakland *Tribune,* 6 August 1957; Tyler [Texas] *Courier-Times-Telegraph,* 21 January 1962; the Denver *Post,* 18 January 1959).

30 *"My Wonderful Reception"*

1. Interview with Fuchida, 11 May 1964; Fuchida ms.
2. Interview with Fuchida, 11 May 1964.
3. Ibid.; Fuchida ms.
4. Fuchida ms.
5. Ibid.; interviews with Fuchida, 11 May 1964 and 1 September 1967.
6. Interview with Fuchida, 11 May 1964.
7. Ibid.
8. Ibid.
9. Ibid., 12 May 1964.

10. Ibid., 12 May 1964 and 30 August 1967.
11. Ibid.
12. Ibid.
13. Ibid.
14. Ibid.
15. Ibid., 12 May 1964.
16. Ibid., May 12 and 13 1964.
17. Ibid., 13 May 1964.
18. Overturf questionnaire.
19. Interviews with Fuchida, 13 May 1964 and 1 September 1967.
20. Ibid., 13 May 1964.

31   *"The Work of the Lord"*

1. Interview with Fuchida, 13 May 1964. Fuchida kept a log of his travels in the United States during this tour.
2. Ibid., 14 May 1964. *DeShazer,* p. 47, mentions Ms. Andrus's dream.
3. Interview with Fuchida, 14 May 1964.
4. Newspaper clipping in Fuchida's papers for 1952. Unfortunately neither date nor source is given.
5. Interview with Fuchida, 14 May 1964.
6. Ibid.
7. Ibid.
8. Ibid. Fuchida thought this incident occurred in northern Maine, probably at Eagle Lake, but his itinerary for 1952–53 shows no engagements in Maine.
9. Interview with Fuchida, 14 May 1964.
10. Ibid., 15 May 1964.
11. Copies of some of these letters are contained in the material Fuchida gave to Prange.
12. Interview with Fuchida, 14 May 1964.
13. Ibid., 15 May 1964 and 30 August 1967.
14. Ibid.
15. Ibid. It is not clear from Fuchida's interview whether this bell came from a Christian church, a Buddhist temple, or a Shinto shrine.
16. Unidentified clipping in Fuchida's 1953 file.
17. Interview with Fuchida, 15 May 1964.
18. Honolulu *Star-Bulletin,* 17 July 1953.
19. Interview with Fuchida, 15 May 1964.
20. Honolulu *Star-Bulletin,* 8 July 1953.
21. Ibid., 9 July 1953.
22. Interview with Fuchida, 15 May 1964.
23. Ibid., 1 September 1967.

32   *"Be with Me Today"*

1. Interviews with Fuchida, 27 May 1964 and 30 August 1967.
2. Captain Fuchida report, 22 January 1956, p. 1 (hereafter Fuchida report). This was a pamphlet Fuchida had printed as a sort of newsletter for those in the United States interested in his work.
3. Joe Fuchida questionnaire.
4. Interviews with Fuchida, 27 May 1964.
5. Ibid., 26 May 1964. Years later, Fuchida thought this gathering took place in October

1953; however, the schedule published in the Fuchida report, pp. 1–2, shows that he was in Kyoto in June 1954.

6. Interview with Fuchida, 26 May 1964.
7. Ibid.
8. Ibid.
9. Ibid.
10. Ibid., 27 May 1964.
11. Ibid.
12. Ibid.
13. Ibid.

33   "Preparing the Soil"

1. Interview with Fuchida, 27 May 1964.
2. Fuchida report, pp. 1–3.
3. Ibid., pp. 5–8.
4. Overturf questionnaire; Joe Fuchida questionnaire; "God's Masterpiece," p. 7.
5. Interview with Fuchida, 28 April 1964.
6. Fuchida report, pp. 4, 8; interview with Fuchida, 12 May 1964.
7. Interview with Fuchida, 29 May 1964.
8. Ibid.
9. Ibid.
10. Joe Fuchida questionnaire.
11. Ibid., Overturf questionnaire.
12. Pueblo Junior College is now Southern Colorado State University.
13. Joe Fuchida questionnaire. Yoshiya is referred to as Joe hereafter.
14. Ibid.

34   "What a Big Difference!"

1. Interview with Fuchida, 29 May 1964. We have been unable to find independent confirmation of this anecdote; however, Fuchida told it to Prange in obvious sincerity.
2. Interview with Fuchida, 29 May 1964. The restaurant in question might well have been the one from which Japan's spy on Oahu, Takeo Yoshikawa, scouted the U.S. Pacific Fleet in the months before Pearl Harbor.
3. Interview with Fuchida, 30 May 1964.
4. Ibid.
5. Ibid.
6. Ibid.
7. Ibid., 27 May 1964. Fuchida did not remember Mr. Sakuramachi's given name.
8. In his interviews with Prange, Fuchida had very little to say about his work in the United States in 1959. His itinerary is fairly clear from the newspaper clippings and publicity material he gave Prange.
9. *Rocky Mountain News* (Denver), 16 January 1959.
10. Denver *Post*, 18 January 1959.
11. See for example *Arizona Republic* (Phoenix), 8 February 1959; Los Angeles *Examiner*, 9 March 1959; *Star Free Press* (Ventura, Calf.), 31 March 1959.
12. Los Angeles *Examiner*, 9 March 1959; Los Angeles *Herald-Express*, 9 March 1959.
13. *Idaho Free Press* (Nampa), 21 July 1959.
14. Joe Fuchida questionnaire.
15. *Geiger Times* (Spokane, Wash.), 11 September 1959.

16. *Pentecostal Evangel,* 6 March 1960.
17. Joe Fuchida questionnaire; interview with Fuchida, 22 August 1967.

35   *"We Must Have Another Reformation"*

1. Interview with Fuchida, 9 November 1964.
2. This information comes from an article by M. E. Crocker entitled "We Met in Germany," included in a file of clippings Fuchida permitted Prange to use. Unfortunately the source, probably a Pocket Testament League magazine or pamphlet, is not indicated.
3. Interview with Fuchida, 9 November 1964.
4. Ibid.
5. Ibid.
6. Ibid.
7. Ibid.
8. Ibid. Fuchida later found the same film running in Paris under the title *Kamikaze.*
9. Interview with Fuchida, 9 November 1964.
10. Miami *News,* 29 February 1961. Fuchida's file for 1961 contained clippings dated from 16 February to 8 April from a number of Florida newspapers.
11. See for example Lakeland (Fla.) *Ledger,* 22 March 1961; Detroit *News,* 13 April 1961; *Daily Tribune* (Royal Oak, Mich.), 13 April 1961.
12. See for example Miami *News,* 28 February 1961; *Clearwater* (Fla.) *Sun,* 17 March 1961.
13. Lakeland *Ledger,* 22 March 1961.
14. Interview with Fuchida, 9 November 1964; William Green and Joseph Copeland, "Hamburg Report" (as with so many of the clippings in Fuchida's files, this one does not show the source and date).
15. Interview with Fuchida, 9 November 1964.
16. Ibid.
17. London *Daily Herald,* 27 June 1961.
18. London *Daily Mail,* 23 June 1961.
19. Overturf questionnaire; interview with Fuchida, 22 August 1967.
20. Interview with Overturf, 3 September 1964; Overturf questionnaire.
21. Interviews with Fuchida, 22 and 23 August 1967.
22. Letter, Spruance to Fuchida, 29 December 1961.

36   *"A Good Mission Field"*

1. The newspaper clippings and publicity material in Fuchida's 1962 file follow his itinerary, although he said little to Prange about these months.
2. Henderson (Tex.) *Daily News,* 17 January 1962; Tyler (Tex.) *Morning Telegraph,* 18 January 1962; San Francisco *Nichi Bei Times,* 19 January 1962.
3. Ronnie Duggan, *Dark Star: Hiroshima Reconsidered in the Life of Claude Eatherly of Lincoln Park, Texas* (Cleveland: The World Publishing Co., 1967), pp. 98, 170, 239.
4. Joe Fuchida questionnaire; interview with Fuchida, 22 August 1967.
5. Berkeley *Daily Gazette,* 10 March 1962.
6. Interviews with Fuchida, 9 November 1964 and 21 August 1967.
7. Ibid., 9 November 1964.
8. "Mission to Helsinki," undated article in *Vision and Venture,* published by the Pocket Testament League, copy in Fuchida 1962 file (hereafter "Mission to Helsinki").
9. Interviews with Fuchida, 9 November 1964 and 31 August 1967.
10. Ibid., 9 November 1964.
11. Ibid., 31 August 1967.
12. Ibid., 10 November 1964.

13. "Mission to Helsinki."
14. Interviews with Fuchida, 9 November 1964 and 31 August 1967.
15. Ibid.
16. Ibid., 10 November 1964.
17. "Mission to Helsinki."
18. Interview with Fuchida, 10 November 1964.
19. "Mission to Helsinki."
20. Interview with Fuchida, 10 November 1964.
21. Ibid., 10 November 1964 and 31 August 1967.
22. Ibid.
23. Ibid., 10 November 1964; "Mission to Helsinki." Glenn Wagner had a similar experience with a young Russian man.
24. Interview with Fuchida, 31 August 1967.
25. Ibid., 10 November 1964.
26. Ibid.
27. Ibid.

37 *"Return to Japan"*

1. Fuchida's file for 1963 is brief, but as usual newspaper clippings give an idea of his progress.
2. Lancaster (Pa.) *Daily Intelligencer Journal,* 15 November 1963.
3. Ibid.
4. Washington *Evening Star* and Baltimore *Evening Sun,* both 7 December 1963.
5. Interviews with Fuchida, 22 and 23 August 1967; Overturf questionnaire.
6. Interview with Fuchida, 23 August 1967.
7. Fuchida's 1964 file and the dates of his interviews with Prange reveal the course of events in 1964.
8. Except as noted, the balance of this chapter is based on Prange notes.
9. Interview with "Matsumoto," 15 November 1964.

38 *"Remember Pearl Harbor"*

1. Several mentions of Fuchida's plans to become an American citizen appeared in the press. See for example Kamloops (B.C.) *Daily Sentinel,* 16 March 1966; *Province* (Vancouver), 12 March 1966; *Miami Herald,* 17 February 1967.
2. Overturf questionnaire.
3. Ibid.; Joe Fuchida questionnaire; Eugene (Ore.) *Register-Guard,* 19 November 1964.
4. Overturf questionnaire.
5. Joe Fuchida questionnaire.
6. *Philippine Herald* (Manila), 9 November 1966; *Guam Daily News* (Agana), 29 April and 14 November 1966; *Pacific Journal* (Agana), 11, 16, and 17 November 1966.
7. *New York Times,* 8 December 1966. Publicity of 1966 and 1967 in Fuchida's files gives information on Connor.
8. Honolulu *Star-Bulletin,* 7 December 1966.
9. Ibid. Prange interviewed both Fielder and Bicknell for his Pearl Harbor study.
10. Honolulu *Star-Bulletin,* 7 December 1966.
11. In interviews with Fuchida, 3 March 1948 and 28 February 1953, he told Prange the same story.
12. *Hearings Before the Joint Committee on the Investigation of the Pearl Harbor Attack,* Congress of the United States, Seventy-ninth Congress (Washington, D.C., 1946), part 13, p. 630. Shiga answered a detailed questionnaire from Prange, and gave him a most informative interview on 21 December 1964, but he didn't mention this story about intelligence.

13. For a full account of Yoshikawa's intelligence gathering and method of communications, see *At Dawn We Slept.*

14. Honolulu *Star-Bulletin,* 7 December 1966.

15. Ibid.; *New York Times,* 8 December 1966. A picture of Fuchida consulting his watch appears in Honolulu *Star-Bulletin,* 7 December 1966.

16. Honolulu *Advertiser,* 7 December 1966; *New York Times,* 8 December 1966.

17. Honolulu *Star-Bulletin,* 8 December 1966; Honolulu *Advertiser,* 10 December 1966.

18. Honolulu *Star-Bulletin,* 8 December 1966; *Baptist Standard,* 21 December 1966; unidentified clipping in Fuchida's 1966 file.

19. Mention of the fact that Honolulu and Hiroshima were sister cities appears in a letter to Fuchida, 22 December 1966, from A. A. Smyser, editor of the Honolulu *Star-Bulletin.*

20. Overturf questionnaire; Honolulu *Advertiser,* Honolulu *Star-Bulletin,* Washington *Post, New York Times,* all 31 May 1976.

SELECTED

BIBLIOGRAPHY

UNPUBLISHED SOURCES

Allied Translator and Interpreter Section Documents, Military Intelligence Section, Headquarters, Far East Command:

STATEMENT BY	DATE	ATIS DOCUMENT NO.
Amano, Shoichi	9 September 1949	59617
Fuchida, Mitsuo	22 June 1949	49259
	31 July 1949	56587
Fukudome, Shigeru	14 May 1949	48012
Hasunuma, Shigeru	31 March 1950	58225
Hattori, Takeshiro	1 June 1948	50735
	6 October 1948	56425
	1 October 1949	53074
Hayashi, Saburo	23 December 1949	61436
Hoshina, Zenshiro	9 November 1949	61978
Hosoda, Hiroshi	9 September 1949	50573
Ikeda, Sumihasa	23 December 1949	54478
	23 December 1949	54479
	27 December 1949	54483
Kagoshima, Takashi	9 September 1949	50571

Statement by	Date	ATIS Document No.
Kawabe, Torashiro	23 August 1948	61539
	9 September 1949	50569
Kido, Koichi	17 May 1949	61476
	17 May 1949	61541
	20 December 1949	62131
Koiso, Kumiaki	16 December 1949	55906
Kurita, Takeo	10 December 1949	53745
Matsudaira, Yasumasa	5 August 1949	61636
Miyazaki, Shuichi	29 December 1949	54478
Nakamura, Katsuhei	1 October 1947	49257
	20 August 1949	50565
Nishina, Yoshio	12 August 1948	60246
	29 June 1950	60245
Ohmae, Toshikazu	15 October 1947	51051
	10 March 1948	50734
Oikawa, Koshiro	9 May 1950	61341
Ozawa, Jisaburo	9 January 1950	55130
Takada, Toshitane	10 October 1949	50267
Takeshita, Masahiko	28 February 1950	56367
Tanemura, Sako	21 August 1950	61977
Terai, Yoshimori	26 June 1949	50821
Togo, Shigenori	17 and 18 May 1949	50304
	28 November 1949	54562
Toyoda, Soemu	29 August 1949	61340
	1 December 1949	57670
Yoshigumi, Masao	22 December 1949	54484
Joint Interview with Tomioka, Ohmae, Fuchida and Terai	9 September 1949	50572

Career Briefs

Chihaya, Takehiko
Fuchida, Mitsuo
Genda, Minoru
Kusaka, Ryunosuke
Kusumi, Masahi
Murata, Shigeharu

Nagumo, Chuichi
Shimazaki, Shigekazu

Questionnaires

Fuchida, Joe Y.
Fuchida, Mitsuo
Genda, Minoru
Kusaka, Ryunosuke
Overturf, Miyako F.

Miscellaneous

Diary of Yoshitake Miwa
Diary of Henry L. Stimson (Yale University Library)
Diary of Matome Ugaki
Chihaya, Masataka, unpublished manuscript concerning the naval war in the Pacific.
Fuchida, Mitsuo, unpublished incomplete manuscript, "From Pearl Harbor to Calvary."
"The Japanese Story of the Battle of Midway" (a translation), OPNAV P32-1002, U.S. Office of Naval Intelligence, Washington, D.C., June 1947.
Letter, CinCPAC to CNO, 28 June 1942, Subject: Interrogation of Japanese Prisoners Rescued at Sea off Midway on 19 June 1942.
Letter, Eugene Herle to Mitsuo Fuchida, 20 May 1961.
Letter, A. A. Smyser to Mitsuo Fuchida, 22 December 1966.
Letter, Raymond A. Spruance to Mitsuo Fuchida, 29 December 1961.
Log of the U.S.S. *Missouri*
Notes which Gordon W. Prange made of a trip with Mitsuo Fuchida through Japan in 1964.

PUBLISHED SOURCES

Articles

Armstrong, William C. "God's Masterpiece." *The Quiet Miracle* (December 1977).
Hohje, Sei-ichi. "The Nine Heroes of the Pearl Harbor Attack." *Contemporary Japan: A Review of Far Eastern Affairs* (April 1942).
Makajima, Teichi. "Middoue no Higeki" (The Tragic Battle of Midway) *Shosetsu Fan* (1956).

Books

Chiba, Reiko. *The Japanese Fortune Calendar*. Rutland, Vt.: Charles E. Tuttle Co., 1965.

Davis, Burke. *Get Yamamoto*. New York: Random House, 1969.

Duggan, Ronnie. *Dark Star: Hiroshima Reconsidered in the Life of Charles Eatherly of Lincoln Park, Texas*. Cleveland: The World Publishing Co., 1967.

Forrestal, Vice Admiral E. P., USN (Ret.). *Admiral Raymond A. Spruance, USN: A Study in Command*. Washington: U.S. Government Printing Office, 1966.

Fuchida, Mitsuo. *Shinjuwan Sakusen No Shinso: Watakushi Wa Shinjuwan Jokai Ni Ita*. Nara, Japan: Yamato Taimusu Sha, 1949.

Fuchida, Mitsuo and Masatake Okumiya. *Midway: The Battle that Doomed Japan*. Annapolis, Md.: U.S. Naval Institute Press, 1955.

Fukudome, Shigeru *Shikan: Shinjuwan Kogeki*. Tokyo: Jiyu Ajiya-sha, 1955.

Halsey, Fleet Admiral William F., USN, and Lieutenant Commander J. Bryan III, USNR, *Admiral Halsey's Story*. New York: McGraw-Hill Book Co., 1947.

Hearings Before the Joint Committee on the Investigation of the Pearl Harbor Attack, Congress of the United States, Seventy-ninth Congress Washington: U.S. Government Printing Office, 1946.

Kase, Toshikazu. *Journey to the "Missouri."* New Haven, Conn.: Yale University Press, 1950.

Kusaka, Ryunosuke. *Rengo Kantai*. Tokyo: Mainichi Shimbun, 1952.

Samuel Eliot Morison. *History of the United States Naval Operations in World War Two*. 15 vols. Boston: Little, Brown & Co. Of particular interest are the following volumes:

———. *Aleutians, Gilberts and Marshalls, June 1942–April 1944*. Vol. 7, 1951.

———. *Breaking the Bismarcks Barrier, 22 July–May 1944*. Vol. 6, 1950.

———. *Coral Sea, Midway and Submarine Actions, May 1942–August 1942*. Vol. 4, 1949.

———. *Leyte, June 1944–January 1945*. Vol. 12, 1958.

———. *The Liberation of the Philippines: Luzon, Mindanao, the Visayas, 1944–1945*. Vol. 13, 1959.

———. *New Guinea and the Marinas, March 1944–August 1944*. Vol. 8, 1953.

———. *The Rising Sun in the Pacific, 1931–1942*. Vol. 3, 1948.

———. *The Struggle for Guadalcanal, August 1942–February 1943*. Vol. 5, 1949.

———. *Victory in the Pacific, 1945*. Vol. 14, 1960.

———. *The Two-Ocean War: A Short History of United States Navy in Second World War*. New York: Ballantine Books, 1972.

Mosley, Leonard. *Hirohito: Emperor of Japan.* Englewood Cliffs, N.J.: Prentice-Hall, 1966.

Okumiya, Masatake, and Jiro Horikoshi, with Martin Caidin. *Zero! The Story of Japan's Air War in the Pacific.* New York: E. P. Dutton, 1956.

Potter, John Dean. *Yamamoto: The Man Who Menaced America.* New York: Viking Press, 1965.

Prange, Gordon W. *At Dawn We Slept: The Untold Story of Pearl Harbor.* New York: McGraw-Hill Book Co., 1981.

———. *Miracle at Midway.* New York: McGraw-Hill Book Co., 1982.

Reports of General MacArthur. Washington: Government Printing Office, 1966.

Sakamaki, Kazuo. *I Attacked Pearl Harbor.* New York: Association Press, 1949.

Watson, Charles Hoyt. *DeShazer: The Doolittle Raider Who Turned Missionary.* Winona Lake, Ind.: The Light and Life Press, 1950.

Watts, A. J. and B. G. Gordon. *The Imperial Japanese Navy.* Garden City, N.Y.: Doubleday & Co., 1971.

Religious Brochures and Extracts from Fuchida Files

Baptist Standard
Captain Fuchida Report, 22 January 1956
Crocker, M. E., "We Met in Germany"
Green, William, and Joseph Copeland, "Hamburg Report"
"Mission to Helsinki"
Pentecostal Evangel

Newspapers

Arizona Republic (Phoenix)
Baltimore *Evening Sun*
Berkeley (Cal.) *Daily Gazette*
Daily Tribune (Royal Oak, Mich.)
Denver *Post*
Detroit *News*
Eugene (Ore.) *Register-Guard*
Fairchild Times (Spokane, Wash.)
Geiger Times (Spokane, Wash.)
Guam Daily News (Agana)
Henderson (Tex.) *Daily News*
Honolulu *Advertiser*
Honolulu *Star-Bulletin*
Idaho Free Press (Nampa)
Japan Times and Advertiser (Tokyo)

Kamloops (B.C.) *Daily Sentinel*
Lakeland (Fla.) *Ledger*
Lancaster (Pa.) *Daily Intelligence Journal*
London *Daily Herald*
London *Daily Mail*
Los Angeles *Examiner*
Los Angeles *Herald-Express*
Miami *Herald*
New York Times
Oakland (Cal.) *Tribune*
Osaka Mainichi and Tokyo Nichi Nichi
Pacific Journal (Agana, Guam)
Pacific Stars and Stripes
Philippine Herald (Manila)
Province (Vancouver)
Rocky Mountain News (Denver)
San Francisco *Chronicle*
San Francisco *Nichi Bei Times*
Star Free Press (Ventura, Cal.)
Tyler (Tex.) *Courier-Times-Telegraph*
Tyler (Tex.) *Morning Telegraph*
Washington *Evening Star*
Washington *Post*
White Plains (N.Y.) *News*
Yamato Times (Nara, Japan)

INTERVIEWS

With a number of the following, notably Fuchida, Genda, and Tomioka, Prange conducted many more interviews than those listed below. Interviews cited are those containing information used in this study.

Commander Masataka Chihaya
10 June 1951
16 November 1964

Captain Mitsuo Fuchida
27 February 1947
28 March 1947
24 May 1947
27 May 1947

28 May 1947
26 July 1947
28 July 1947
29 July 1947
25 February 1948
27 February 1948
29 February 1948
3 March 1948
4 March 1948
23 April 1948
23 May 1948
23 July 1948
6 January 1949
9 April 1949
21 April 1949
22 April 1949
23 April 1949
24 June 1949
25 June 1949
8 October 1949
26 February 1953
28 February 1953
10 December 1963
11 December 1963
13 February 1964
14 February 1964
16 February 1964
18 February 1964
19 February 1964
20 February 1964
22 February 1964
23 February 1964
24 February 1964
25 February 1964
28 February 1964
29 February 1964
1 March 1964
7 April 1964
11 April 1964
12 April 1964
14 April 1964
16 April 1964
18 April 1964
19 April 1964

21 April 1964
23 April 1964
25 April 1964
28 April 1964
2 May 1964
4 May 1964
5 May 1964
6 May 1964
7 May 1964
8 May 1964
9 May 1964
10 May 1964
11 May 1964
12 May 1964
13 May 1964
14 May 1964
15 May 1964
26 May 1964
27 May 1964
9 November 1964
10 November 1964
27 November 1964
21 August 1967
22 August 1967
23 August 1967
24 August 1967
27 August 1967
28 August 1967
29 August 1967
30 August 1967
31 August 1967
1 September 1967

Vice Admiral Shigeru Fukudome
12 May 1950

Lieutenant General Minoru Genda
21 March 1947
22 March 1947
7 April 1947
6 June 1947
11 June 1947
20 August 1947

25 August 1947
29 August 1947
31 August 1947
25 December 1947
26 December 1947
27 December 1947
28 December 1947
30 December 1947
10 March 1948
26 May 1948
28 May 1948
28 November 1948
16 March 1951

Commander Jinichi Goto
7 Februry 1950

Vice Admiral Ryunosuke Kusaka
23 August 1947
2 December 1947

Ms. "Kimi Matsumoto"
15 November 1964

Commander Tatsukichi Miyo
30 May 1949

Ms. Miyako F. Overturf
3 September 1964

Reverend Ichijiro Saito
15 November 1964

Rear Admiral Sadatoshi Tomioka
5 August 1947
17 February 1948.

INDEX

ABOUT THE AUTHORS

Gordon W. Prange, Ph.D., was born in Pomeroy, Iowa, on 16 July 1910, and educated at the Universities of Iowa and Berlin. He taught history at the University of Maryland from 1937 until his death in May 1980. He served in the Naval Reserve during World War II, and during the occupation of Japan in the Historical Section of MacArthur's headquarters, Far East Command, Tokyo, from October 1946 to July 1951.

Donald M. Goldstein, Ph.D., lieutenant colonel, USAF (Ret.), is associate professor of Public and International Affairs at the University of Pittsburgh.

Katherine V. Dillon is a Chief Warrant Officer, USAF (Ret.).